168 ☞ **W9-ATR-551**

ARNULFO L OLIVEIRA MEMORIAL LIBRARY
1825 MAY STREET
BROWNSVILLE, TEXAS 78520

How to Live With
YOUR CHILDREN

A Guide for Parents Using a
Positive Approach to Child Behavior

Don H. Fontenelle, Ph.D
Co-Author of Purrfect Parenting

ARNULFO L OLIVEIRA MEMORIAL LIBRARY
1825 MAY STREET
BROWNSVILLE, TEXAS 78520

FISHER
BOOKS

Publishers: *Bill Fisher*
              Helen Fisher
              Howard Fisher
              Tom Monroe, P.E.

Editors: *Judith Schuler*
            Bill Fisher
            Joyce Bush

Art Director: Josh Young

Published by Fisher Books
P.O. Box 38040
Tucson, Arizona 85740-8040

(602) 325-5263

All rights reserved. No part of this book may be reproduced or transmitted in any form or by any means, electronic or mechanical, including photocopy, recording or any information storage or retrieval system, without written permission from the publisher, except by a reviewer who may quote brief passages.

Library of Congress
Cataloging-in-Publication Data
Fontenelle, Don, 1946-
    How to live with your children.

    Bibliography: p.
    Includes index.
    1. Parenting—United States. 2. Child psychology. 3. Behavior disorders in children—United States. 4. Parenting and child—United States. I. Title.
HQ755.8.F65 1988 306.8'74 88-30882
ISBN 1-55561-018-8 (pbk.)

©1989 Fisher Books

Printed in U.S.A.
Printing 10 9 8 7 6 5 4 3 2

Notice: The information in this book is true and complete to the best of our knowledge. It is offered with no guarantees on the part of the author or Fisher Books. The author and publisher disclaim all liability in connection with the use of this book.

Fisher Books are available at special quantitiy discounts for educational use. Special books, or book excerpts, can also be created to fit specific needs. For details please write or telephone.

Contents

General Concerns, continued

About the Author

Dr. Don Fontenelle received his Ph.D. in Clinical Psychology from Oklahoma State University. He has served as a consultant for numerous children's programs in the New Orleans area. He is in private practice in Metairie and Chalmette, Lousiana.

Dr. Fontenelle has devoted most of his professional career to working with children and their parents. His efforts are directed to provide parents with a better understanding of their children and how to deal with their behavior. His workshops for teachers and parents on Child/Adolescent Behavior and for parents in the management of child behavior are widely accepted and praised for their positive results.

In addition to *How to Live With Your Children* he has authored or coauthored three other books on child/adolescent behaviour: *Understanding and Managing Overactive Behavior, Changing Student Behavior* and *Purrfect Parenting*.

To my parents, Olga and Irvin.
They taught me the importance of praise.

Acknowledgments

While there are many sources of learning experiences, I am very grateful to the numerous children and parents with whom I have come in contact during my professional career. They have provided many learning experiences reflected in much of the information used in this book.

The first writing of this book was done mostly at night. If it weren't for my wife, Carla, keeping the children entertained or telling them, "Be quiet, Daddy's writing on his book," this undertaking would not have been possible. My wife provided understanding and support during this time and, indirectly, is also responsible for the revision of the book. Our two boys, Jason and Alan, gave me a look at children's behavior from a parent's point of view and served as models for many of the examples used in this book.

Mallary Collins, M.Ed., an educational consultant at our center, provided a great deal of support and assistance that I deeply appreciate.

Dr. Edward Shwery, an expert in sexual abuse in children, basically wrote the chapter on Sexual Curiosity or Abuse? Dr. Annell McGee, a speech and language pathologist, did the same with the chapter on Following Directions & Auditory-Processing Problems. I am extremely thankful to Drs. Shwery and McGee because, without their contribution, these chapters would not have been included.

Drs. Carmela Tardo and Ruth Dowling Bruun reviewed the chapter on Tics, Nervous Habits and Tourette Syndrome and made many useful comments that are included. The Tourette Syndrome Association, Inc., also provided me with a significant amount of information used in this chapter. Dr. William Swanson provided information used in the chapter on Suicide. Sherril Rudd, M.S.W., did the same for the chapter on Drugs & Alcohol.

Final thanks to Diane Armstrong and Maria Landry who typed the manuscript and deciphered my handwriting and dictations. Jeanne Dufour was responsible for copying, collating and proofing parts of the manuscript.

Preface

One often hears that our times have rendered inadequate the simple wisdoms of the past. Consider the fate of Solomon's "Train up a child in the way he should go and when he is old he will not depart from it." Although several thousand years and as many taboos, mores and rules have passed, every age of parents wonders about themselves and correctness of their techniques as used to raise their children. Nowadays, we say that in our generation it is more difficult for parents to raise children because of decreased support from the spread-out family, increased instances of divorce and single parenting, higher frequency of both parents working, and social and economic uncertainties. To this list can be added the continuous avalanche of information being given to parents. It seems that with all of our information, even our solutions are sometimes problems.

So, whatever happened to Solomon's wisdom about children? Clearly he assumed that childrearing is simple as long as it is a natural and intuitive process. But, what if no one knows what is natural, or trusts his/her own intuition or anybody else's ideas? How *should* a child be raised?

Books are a very important help. But consider what a book written for parents must do to be helpful. First, it must be a potentially independent aid, able to provide simple instructions for specific Do's and Don'ts that work for one particular family and for many different families. Often these instructions must work without the help of a professional translator-instructor. Then, the book must also explain and take a stand on the proper parent behavior in a convincing and useful way.

We do not always talk about the approaches to parent training as necessarily moralistic. Nevertheless, the use of *should* cannot be avoided now any more than it could be avoided in the proverbs. Our work in the UCLA Parent Training Clinic has long been based upon rules like "When you see a behavior you approve and want to see more of, you *should* praise your child in a way he/she can accept." Or, "When you must give attention to an intolerable behavior, you *should* set a limit you can back up."

But how is a specific *should* developed? Among other things, it probably depends upon the timing or time period in which we are living, local population mores, individual characteristics of the parents and children, and the therapist or author who prepares the information for your use. Thus, over the decades, theories on childrearing have ranged from permissive lack of control to total parental control. Some professionals advocate involvement of the total family in the treatment of the individual child, while others strongly state that parents need not be involved in their child's therapy. Still others believe that a child behaves and feels as he/she does because of the consequences placed on his behavior.

Our author, Don Fontenelle, takes issue with many of these still-prevalent ideas; but clearly shows that parents and home environments *must* be involved. And, the child may feel the way he does because of the way he evaluates the consequences of his behavior.

The simple proverbs described above are inadequate today; if for no other reason than everybody and their neighbor has a different one, so anxious parents with problems are often in a type of media panic. What is the effect of all these confused *shoulds?* Quite possibly, many parents have singly and together failed to use or outright abandoned their position. Haim Ginott, in one of his books, *Between Parent and Child,* notes that when our grandparents spoke, they spoke with authority; when we speak, we speak with confusion. The child's confused uncertainty is, everyone agrees, what the therapist/author must help reduce.

Fontenelle's efforts in this book are a help to parents. How does it meet the "Helpful Book" requirement? I think very well. First, it can stand alone, but parents will always have questions about a specific application and can profitably use discussion groups or contact with a child counselor. Second, *How to Live with Your Children* is, in a way, unique. It takes a scientifically and personally validated set of *shoulds* called *learning principles.* It teaches parents to think in clear terms about the causes and consequences of their child's actions and feelings. The majority of parents will find themselves and their problems in this book. It is marvelously broad in scope, a virtual handbook of resource ideas about all sorts of children's behavioral aches and pains.

Can we ever look forward to a time when we can return to simple *shoulds* and traditional family values? When books and therapy movements aren't needed? When we don't have to depend on technologists to answer questions about child-rearing? Properly instructed children surely become the best instructors for their own offspring. But how does it get started?

Parents, authors and therapists are likely to continue to need complex technical help for the complex problems of raising children today. Books like this one, providing proven methods and ideas, can help ease our challenge and help increase the joys of childrearing.

W. Hans Miller, Ph.D.
Founder and Former Director
Parent Training Clinic
UCLA Medical Center

1

Helping You Reach Your Goals

In the early 1970s, I was teaching an introductory course in Psychology at a local college. The director of the college asked me to design a course that would be appropriate for individuals interested in taking a non-credit course in child psychology. At that time, several possibilities occurred to me, and I decided to offer a workshop titled "The Management of Problem Behaviors in Children." The workshop was based on techniques, methods and approaches I used daily in my private practice working with children and parents.

Many more people than I expected enrolled for the first workshop; since then it has been offered many times. Thousands of participants, by way of a workshop-evaluation questionnaire, have offered suggestions as to what should be added, deleted, expanded or improved in the workshop. The present workshops have been modified several times based on these suggestions.

At the end of each workshop, participants report the extent of the improvement that has occurred in each child as a result of the techniques learned and applied to specific problem behaviors. To date, the average improvement reported has been 59%. For example, if a child was not listening to his parents and this was one of the behaviors specified for improvement, on the average, the child would have shown a 59% improvement in listening. The response to the workshops has been very positive. Some of the following comments were selected from those made by the participants.

"I never believed there was any other way to correct my children than by punishing. To learn differently and to see such marvelous results was well worth my time."

"The workshop helped me to become less impulsive in my judgment, more tolerant as a mother and more patient as a person. Above everything, I have learned the importance of positive consequences and consistency."

"We derived a great deal of benefit right from the beginning . . . Two things in particular that made such a difference in our home were (1) learning how wrong, how detrimental and how unnecessary it is to yell, threaten and use excessive punishment. We also learned (2) bad behavior does not necessarily have to change immediately—this was extremely helpful. I was overreacting to problem behaviors because I had the feeling undesirable behavior had to change right away by punishment or yelling. I hadn't thought of the children improving themselves permanently by having them work toward rewards. These two ideas made a difference in our home. I didn't like yelling at all, and the kids hated it. But before I took the workshop, I didn't know how to replace it with something positive. Our home is much more pleasant now. When I stopped yelling, our 7-year-old stopped yelling back. One of our biggest problems was it was a struggle to get the 7-year-old to get ready for school in the morning. Now that she is not being browbeaten and is rewarded for her accomplishments, I know she's much happier. She gets herself ready for school independently. The change has really been dramatic."

"I enjoyed this workshop very much, it gave me many new insights in dealing with children—children are people, too. The material was presented in a way that made the listener feel very comfortable. I could really deal with (my child's) problems. The workshop was very educational and informative. I feel your method in raising children is very human. Too many people seem to feel they own their child and must be the big boss. This method lets the child be part of the family."

"I really enjoyed the course and feel I learned a lot of specifics. I had taken another parenting course, but this one was very useful because it dealt with specific ways to deal with my child's behavior. It was very helpful in modifying my behavior as well as daughter's. I have less need to yell as I feel more capable of dealing with her behavior and therefore become angry much less often."

"On the whole, I thoroughly enjoyed the course and feel it ended too quickly. When you attend class, you feel you can ask questions of someone. Unfortunately, you don't learn to be a parent in school. It's just a hit-and-miss proposition."

"The lectures and discussions have made me more aware of myself and much more thoughtful of the way I relate to my daughter and husband. Not always successful, but always trying."

"I think the workshop was excellent. I got a positive feeling that results can be achieved. This is much more than I can say for any avenues we have pursued before attending the workshop. Although I have not yet seen the degree of improvement I would like, I feel it's a matter of us analyzing and applying different programs. We now have the tools at our disposal. I feel the informal nature of the class was good."

"I learned from the workshop what to do about (my children's) problems. Mostly to change *myself*—to praise, compliment and encourage my child."

"I found the workshop very enjoyable. I think everyone, even those whose children are 'perfect,' could benefit from a course like this. I personally saw remarkable improvement in my child and in myself. You made me realize the mistakes I was making in handling problems. When I corrected myself, there was noticeable improvement in how my child reacted to me. I used to feel that my child was the exception—no one could be as bad as him."

"I have discovered my child is not the horrible monster I was beginning to think he was."

"I can say truthfully I enjoyed the whole course. Even though all my problems are far from being solved, at least I have a better understanding as to a correct method of raising my children. The biggest thing parents have to learn is they are part of the problems that show up in the children. Once this is pointed out tactfully and helpfully, as it was in this course, progress can be made. I didn't hear about this (child-management technique) soon enough. That's why I think all young parents should be trained in the proper guidelines for raising children."

The information provided in this book is based primarily on the workshops, the suggestions given by concerned parents and the techniques and methods used in my daily practice.

Role of Parent

The role of parent carries with it complex duties and responsibilities that will hopefully result in happy, well-adjusted children who are able to cope effectively with their environment and adulthood. Most of us receive very little training for this difficult task.

For many years, it has been relatively easy to obtain training to be a welder, lawyer, printer, carpenter or bookkeeper. It has only been in the last 15 to 20 years knowledge has been compiled for being a parent. Techniques are now available to help parents increase the possibility their children will become happy, well-adjusted adults.

This book presents general methods, techniques and patterns of interaction that I feel are very important for parents to know and use to reduce the probability of future emotional problems. And it will help improve family life by developing an ease in living with, relating to and raising children on a daily basis.

This book was written with several goals in mind. One goal is to give you some different techniques and methods to use with children 2 to 16 years old. What makes a child psychologist different from an average parent is that he has a larger bag of tricks and techniques to use with children who exhibit specific behavior. Most parents use disciplinary methods that were employed by their parents. Some work on their children; others do not.

You may also use the same techniques for all of your children and often find they work well with one child but have no effect on another. Children have different personalities, so don't deal with all of them using the same methods. Neither should you assume that a type of discipline that works with one child will work with his brother or sister. The information in this book provides new ideas to use on a daily basis in working with your children. These techniques work!

Although this book is concerned with emotional and behavioral problems, I've primarily focused on normal everyday problems most parents encounter in living with their children. By increasing your skills and providing alternate disciplinary techniques, problem behaviors will decrease. The home environment will improve. The hassles you encounter working with your children will be reduced.

Another goal is to provide methods that allow you to discipline your children without hollering, screaming, getting upset or buying antacids. Consequently, home life will be happier.

The third goal, probably most important to me, is to present information so you can easily understand it. This book is written for parents, not professionals. I've avoided using technical terms, jargon and psychological phrases.

Some mental-health professionals, when communicating with parents, use special terminology or unusual words parents may not understand. As a result, parents leave a conference more confused than when they came in. They may not have any additional information to use in helping their child.

This book is written in everyday language. It will make sense and can be easily understood. I use several examples to explain an idea; hopefully one of them will be similar to something you are experiencing.

In revising the book, I almost doubled its length. Some chapters remain unchanged, while others have been slightly or drastically modified. The major change in the revision is the addition of many chapters. I have written about the most frequent parental concerns I see in my practice.

2

Deciding Which Behavior to Change

Many parents who bring their children to our clinic for counseling or evaluation(s) have various problems.

"He won't listen."

"She's bad as hell."

"His problem is he's always angry."

"He constantly irritates everybody."

"My daughter's depressed and unhappy."

"He doesn't behave in school."

The first thing I do is ask the parent, "What is your child doing that makes you think he's depressed? What behaviors is she showing that make you think she's angry? Give me an example of what you mean when you say he doesn't listen."

I ask the parents to describe or specify the *exact* behavior, not to look at it in *general* terms. As an example, what a parent might mean when she says her child is depressed is he has lost interest in things that were important to him. Or a parent may mean he stays in his room all the time and cries easily.

Behavior Must Be Specified

Behavior to be changed must first be specified by stating it in detail. I may not be able to make a child completely free of depression, but I can help you get your child to spend more time out of her room and to help her cry less frequently.

Most of us find it difficult to be specific in our descriptions because we look at children and behavior in general terms. The first thing we have to do is specify the behavior. "My child is very angry."

OK, what is he doing? "He's sticking a pencil in his sister's ear. That's what makes me think he's angry."

What is *anger?* What does *depressed* mean? What is *immaturity?* Is he 15 years old and still has to be dressed for school? The first step in changing any behavior is being specific in describing it.

ABCs of Change

Once the behavior has been specified, we can move to the next step and analyze the behavior. Let's look at a child who has temper tantrums, whines or pouts frequently.

Parent: "My child has temper tantrums all the time."

Psychologist: "Can you describe or define for me what you mean by a temper tantrum?"

Parent: "He throws himself on the floor or curls up in a chair and whines, screams, hollers, rolls around and sometimes gets violent."

Psychologist: "What usually comes before the temper tantrum? Can you give me an example of what makes him have a temper tantrum?"

Parent: "Well, he walks into the kitchen and says, 'Momma, can I put my bathing suit on, go outside and play with the hose?' It's cold outside, and I know he'll catch pneumonia, so I say, 'No.' That's when it starts. He begins the whining, complaining, telling me I'm mean and finally the full-blown temper tantrum. He rolls on the floor, screams, hollers and won't stop crying."

Psychologist: "What happens next?"

Parent: "Well, he gets me so irritated and upset I finally start hollering. I yell, 'I don't care if you catch pneumonia. Get out of here; you're going to put me in the mental hospital.'"

In this situation, what I have asked the parent to do is to analyze the behavior. We look at the temper tantrum (behavior) and look at what comes before the behavior (antecedents) and what comes after the behavior (consequences). In any behavior, there are three parts—Antecedents, Behavior and Consequences. These are the *ABCs!*

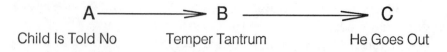

| A ⟶ B ⟶ C |
| Child Is Told No   Temper Tantrum   He Goes Out |

With this information, we have taken the first step in producing a change. We have analyzed the behavior. We have looked at the specific behavior and what comes before and after the action.

In analyzing a behavior, it's also important to see how often it occurs. How many times an hour, day or week does it occur? 10 times a day? Once a week? 3 times an hour? There are reasons for this analysis. I have had many parents tell me, "Once I started looking closely at the behavior and kept a record of how frequently it occurred, I realized it wasn't as bad as I thought it was."

Another reason for analysis is a child doesn't wake up one morning behaving a specific way. His behavior gradually develops over a period of weeks, months or years. To modify behavior, a similar process is necessary. Results are based on a gradual improvement that will occur.

Usually we look at a actions in general terms and cannot see the small changes. Parents may come to me and say, "My child is sassy." We then decide on a treatment plan and ask the parents to try my suggestions.

After 2 weeks, the parents return. If they looked at the overall behavior, they may say, "He's still sassy." But they didn't look at the child's action closely and actually note how frequently the sassiness occurred. Otherwise, they might have observed that before the treatment plan was started, the child was sassy 30 times a day. After the 2-week period, he was sassy only 15 times a day. This is a 50% improvement!

Behavior changes gradually. Look for *small* improvements.

3

Why Children Do
the Things They Do

In analyzing behavior as described in Chapter 2, we look at an important factor in behavior change—consequences. The reason most of us do what we do is because of the consequences of our behavior. The reason we go to work instead of staying home is the consequences are different. We get paid if we work and do not if we stay home. The same is true for children. They behave in certain ways because of the consequences of their actions.

The child described in the previous chapter who was having temper tantrums—why is he misbehaving? The consequence of this behavior is he gets what he wants—he goes outside. His behavior is maintained because it has a purpose. Let's look at another behavior sequence.

Parent: "My child always has to have the last word."

Psychologist: "What do you mean?"

Parent: "He's sassy. He talks back and always has a smart answer."

Psychologist: "Can you give me an example?"

Parent: "I tell him something he doesn't like. 'Go take your bath. Go pick up your toys. Come inside.' He says, 'Wait a minute' or something similar in a sarcastic, harsh voice. If someone saw or heard him do this, they would think he has no respect for me."

Psychologist: "Then what happens?"

Parent: "I usually say, 'You have 10 more minutes' or I remind him several more times. He says 'Stop nagging.' 'Get off my back.' or some other smart answer. After a few more remarks, I'm very angry and we're in a shouting match. Eventually we're in an argument, and I have to drag him to do what he should have done 30 minutes ago." The consequence of this behavior is the child is getting his parent upset. Perhaps that's the reason he continues the behavior.

When I ask most children, "Why are you sassy?" they usually give me a routine answer—a shrug of the shoulders or "I don't know." Or they give me some equally revealing response, such as, "My father won't buy me a motorcycle." "I have to wear black shoes to school." "My brother's stupid."

Many children, especially 10 and younger, honestly do not know why they behave in certain ways. They are usually responding to the environment, events and people in their lives. One question does not lead to the basis of that response. At our center we usually do some psychological testing and interviewing to determine the reasons for and consequences of a child's behavior.

Let's imagine I have a magic wand with which I can tap the child on the head and have him tell me some of the reasons for his behavior. The following are a few examples of what I might learn about a child's actual behavior motivation.

Example 1

The child has to be told many times to do something or the parent must get upset before the son will listen.

Psychologist: "Jason, why does your mother have to tell you 37 times then get upset and holler before you pick up your toys or clean your room?"

Jason: "Well, it takes 37 times because the first 30 times she doesn't really mean it. She's says, 'Jason, pick up your toys or clothes' in a normal voice. She's really talking to hear herself talk, and I let it go in one ear and out the other."

Psychologist: "Then what happens?"

Jason: "About the 31st time, her voice starts getting louder. Around 32 and 33, she starts hollering and saying in an angry voice, 'I really mean it.' Somewhere around the 34th or 35th time, her face starts turning red. She starts pounding on the table."

Psychologist: "What do you do then?"

Jason: "Well, the next thing is the hair on the back of her neck stands up. This usually happens around the 36th or 37th time. When I see this, I know she means business. I'm going to get it if I don't do what she says so I run like crazy and do what she wants me to do."

Psychologist: "It sounds like you wait around for the right signal or cue that tells you a consequence is coming or something is really going to happen. When you see it, you do what your mother wants."

Jason: "That's right."

Example 2

The child is difficult when taken shopping or when he goes to a store with his parent.

Psychologist: "Why can't you take 'No' for an answer when you go to the store with your mother? She tells me you whine, pout, cry, generally give her a hard time and embarrass her. She gets knots in her stomach every time she takes you shopping."

Alan: "We usually go the same store to get groceries. We start off going down the toothpaste aisle. When we get there, I say, 'Mother, can I . . .' and even before I get it out of my mouth she says 'No.' I love barbeque potato chips, so when she says 'No,' what I do is go into routine 23."

Psychologist: "What is that?"

Alan: "I start whining, complaining, telling her she's mean and I talk loud. She then tells me to 'Be quiet' or 'You'll be in trouble.' Then I start talking louder, shaking the cart and saying, 'You don't like me and never get me anything.'"

Psychologist: "Then what happens?"

Alan: "Then I watch my mother to see how she reacts. She starts gritting her teeth and tells me, 'Shut up and behave,' but I keep it up. Then she starts looking over her shoulder to see who is watching us, and her face starts getting red. She grabs the potato chips and throws them at me and says, 'Now behave.'" Now I have the potato chips. I'm happy, and I'll be good until I see something else I want and she doesn't let me have it."

Psychologist: "So the consequence of your behavior is you get what you want."

Alan: "Yeah, when she says or does something I don't like, I can do certain things and she'll change her mind."

Example 3

The child won't get dressed for school. He continually fools around; every morning's preparation for school is a battle.

Psychologist: "Joe, does your mother have a lot of trouble with you before you go to school?"

Joe: "I don't like getting dressed, and I'd rather look at TV. If I fool around long enough, I can look at TV, and after awhile my mother will come in and dress me."

Example 4

The child does not want to take a bath. Every bath time is sure to bring sassiness and conflict.

Psychologist: "Why does your mother have trouble getting you to take a bath?"

Jeff: "I think it's stupid to have to take a bath every day. I'm only going to get dirty the next day. Anyway, she usually makes me take a bath right before I go to bed, and I'd rather stay up. The longer I put it off, the longer I can stay up. Sometimes I get away with it."

Psychologist: "What do you mean?"

Jeff: "Sometimes she forgets about it or says, 'Go to bed dirty. Let the bugs crawl all over you,' and I don't have to take a bath."

I could go on with many more examples, but the point should already be clear that children often behave as they do because of the consequences of their behavior.

Any time two people get together, parents and children included, we teach each other different things about behavior and its consequences. Whenever people relate to one another, they teach each other certain behavior. This is called *social-learning theory.* When we interact with our children, we are teaching them behavior, and they are teaching us to respond to them in certain ways. We often teach our children how to be helpless, dependent, immature, to have temper tantrums, to be sassy and not listen. At the same time, they teach us to holler, nag, scream, get upset, criticize or worry. Social learning, or behavioral interaction, is a two-way street.

If we can teach our children to misbehave, we can also teach them good, acceptable behavior. Unfortunately, most of us go about it the wrong way. We try to change the child directly. How many times have you looked at your children's behavior as their problem and said, "I buy you things, clean your clothes, feed you and you're bad? Why don't you behave?" In other words, "Why don't you change your behavior, and I'll be happy and pleased with you?" It's a very difficult thing to change other people's behavior directly without an intermediate change in your relationship with them. It is much easier if you change the way you relate to your children. In doing this, you encourage them to change their behavior and the way they relate to you.

Suppose I work with someone who continually criticizes what I do. I arrive at work before he does and start on some paperwork. He comes in and says, "Why are you doing that? That's a waste of time. What you are doing is worthless." He goes on and on. Each morning we almost come to blows. We yell at each other and have heated arguments. Each day is a hassle. This disruption has continued for 2 years, and I keep telling this man, "Please leave me alone. Be nice. Quit calling me names." But I have responded to him in this fashion for 2 years, and he has not changed. My techniques have not worked.

All of a sudden I say to myself, "Maybe I'm beating my head against a brick wall trying to change him. It would be much easier if I change the way I respond to him." The next day he comes in and starts his verbal assault, but I stay calm. He criticizes me, but I keep doing my work. He rants and raves for 3 hours, but I don't respond. The next day he comes in and does the same thing, but I keep doing my work. He hollers for about 45 minutes. The next day the criticism lasts for 15 minutes. The following day it lasts about 5 minutes.

After about a week of this, he comes in and says, "Good morning. Do you want a cup of coffee?" Now I have him doing exactly what I want him to do. I accomplished this by changing my responses.

Much of the behavior—good or bad—seen in children, especially under age 10, can be viewed as a response to the environment. Without a change in the environment, it's difficult to change a child's behavior. However, if the surroundings are modified, it's easy to achieve behavioral change in children. A child's most significant environment is his home, so a change in the way you respond to your child often produces a significant behavior change in him or her.

Beginning with Chapter 4, the information focuses on ways you can change you own behavior. By responding to your children differently, you can change their behavior. Just as important as analyzing and looking at your children's behavior is the need to look closely at what you are doing and how you respond to your children.

If you can change how you respond to your children, you'll change *their* behavior. To change your child's behavior, you must look at the total environment. You are a *significant* part of the picture.

4

Being a Consistent Parent

Since the early 1970s, many parents have participated in our parent-training workshops. At the first meeting, all parents are asked to list at least three kinds of behavior they would like to change in their children. The behaviors parents list most frequently include, "Hardheaded, stubborn, not doing what I ask," "I have to really get upset before he'll do what I tell him" or some other phrase that identifies the child's problem as *not listening.*

One of the primary reasons for listing problems is inconsistency in the parents' approach to a child's behavior. They do not mean what they say or do not follow through with what they say. Although this inconsistency seems like a small omission, it's often one of the main reasons why techniques tried by parents do not work.

Consistency can be viewed as the foundation of effective child management. Like the foundation of a house, if it is solid there is a good probability the structure it supports will be fine. However, if the foundation is shaky, problems are certain to arise. By being consistent, parents increase the probability the techniques they use will work. On the other hand, an inconsistent approach to child management almost assures failure.

We don't listen to adults who say one thing and do something else. We can't expect our children to listen to us if we behave the same way. Suppose you have a friend named John who tells you, "I caught 100 pounds of shrimp today and, I'll bring you 25 pounds tonight." You go home and don't bother to cook. You wait, but John never brings the shrimp.

The next week you talk to him and mention your car is broken, but you have to go to the store to get something. He says, "I can take you. I'll be over around 5 pm to pick you up." You get dressed, but he never shows up. The next week John agrees to help you move some furniture but again fails to do what he says.

This interaction occurs for many weeks. Three months later, he calls you and says, "I have two tickets to a new movie. I know you want to see it, so get dressed and call a friend. I'll drop the tickets off at your house at 6 pm." What will you do? Will you hurry home, get dressed and call a friend? Probably not, because John usually says one thing and does something else.

How would you respond to John? You wouldn't listen to him. You'd think he was talking to hear himself talk. More important, he can't control you or get you to do what he wants. He tells you to go home, call a friend, get dressed and wait for him to come. However, you go about your daily business as usual because you've learned John is inconsistent. He says one thing and does something else.

If you are inconsistent in your approach to your child, he feels the same way about you and will respond to you the same way you would respond to John. There are many ways you can be inconsistent and teach children to be confused, to ignore directions and to manipulate.

Making Statements You Don't Mean

You are driving across town and your two children are in the back seat. They're picking on one another, and you keep asking them to be still. However, they continue, and their behavior intensifies. Soon they're arguing and you're telling them to be quiet. Then they start to fight, and you're at the end of your rope. You say something wonderful like, "If you don't stop, I'm going to stop at the next bridge and throw both of you off it." Naturally, they don't stop.

In another instance, you are watching TV with your son and daughter. The boy keeps pulling his sister's hair and aggravating her. You try to get him to stop, but he doesn't respond to your pleas. Eventually you attempt to control him by saying, "If you hit your sister one more time, I'm going to break both of your arms."

Your child is doing poorly in school. To make him study harder you say, "You know, if you don't do better in this school, we'll have to put you in a home or boarding school."

I could give other examples, but the point is we often say things we have no intention of carrying out. We know this and, more important, the child also knows it. Your threats don't stop the behavior, and your child keeps doing whatever you're trying to prevent.

Overstatements

You are sitting down with your son trying to get him to do his homework. He's counting the dots on the ceiling, daydreaming and beating the pencil on the table. Fifteen minutes worth of homework has exhausted 2 hours; all your attempts to get it finished have failed. You are frustrated and finally tell him, "Go to your room; you're punished for the night." He starts crying but goes to his room and pouts.

In a few minutes, he sticks his head out of the door and says, "I'm sorry. I love you. I'll be good; I'll never do it again." You start feeling sorry for him or feeling guilty for what you've done, and 2 minutes later you let him out of his room.

Your daughter leaves her bike outside. The next morning you find it and say, "Your bike is going to be stolen. I've told you many times to put in in the back yard. Now you can't ride it for the rest of the month." However, in 2 days, she is back on her bike.

A child spills soda on the new sofa. You get angry and say, "You can't have soda for the rest of your life." But in a few minutes, after you calm down, you realize there's no possible way to follow through with what you've threatened.

Overstatements like those above are major sources of inconsistency in families. We get angry and make statements we could never follow through. Or we say or do something then start feeling guilty and try to undo it. In both instances, the child interprets your behavior as implying, "Don't believe or listen to what I say because I don't mean anything I'm saying."

ARNULFO L OLIVEIRA MEMORIAL LIBRARY
1825 MAY STREET
BROWNSVILLE, TEXAS 78520

Turning "No" to "Yes" and "Yes" to "No"

Another way to be inconsistent is to say one thing and do something else. It's about 30 minutes before supper, and your 6-year-old son comes up to you and says, "I'm hungry. Can I have a cookie?"

You respond, "No, we're going to eat in a little while. If you eat the cookie you won't eat supper."

However, he doesn't accept this and keeps badgering you. "I want a cookie; I'm hungry." Each time he says this, his voice gets louder and louder. He may also add some other tactics like whining, complaining about how mean you are, hitting his sister or saying how he would rather live with his grandparents.

While all of this is going on, you tell him to calm down, be quiet and stop whining. After about 3 minutes, you're tense, you've burned your finger on the stove and you're fed up with his behavior.

You give him the cookie and tell him to go in the other room to reduce the tension and preserve your sanity. In doing this, you have reversed your original "No" and changed it to a "Yes."

You take your 9-year-old to the department store. He has always given you trouble there, but you are hoping it will be different this time. As soon as you pass the toys, he grabs one and says, "I want this."

You reply with the standard answer, "Put that back. I don't have enough money to buy that car, and you have 10 at home just like it."

But he doesn't put it back and carries it with him. As you shop, he continues to tell you how much he needs the car. You get everything you need and head for the checkout counter but have to wait in line. While in line, your son intensifies his efforts to get the car. He starts complaining. "You never get me anything, and you always buy my brother toys. You're mean." Then he goes into routine No. 13. He starts crying and hitting the counter; he is embarrassing you. To shut him up, you say, "I just found some money I didn't know I had. Now be quiet, and I'll get you the car."

Or how many times have you said something like, "I'll take

ARNULFO L. OLIVEIRA MEMORIAL LIBRARY
1825 MAY STREET
BROWNSVILLE, TEXAS 78520

you to the show this Saturday"? But when Saturday comes, you say, "I'm a little too busy this weekend, so we'll go to the show next week."

The examples are endless, but in this form of inconsistency, a *No* is changed to a *Yes* or a positive statement becomes negative. This teaches your children not to listen to you when you respond in this way. You also show them how to *manipulate* you. You say, "If I tell you something you don't like, do this or this (have a temper tantrum, whine, pout, get me upset), and I'll change my mind." You are showing them how to be con artists. Children are very good at manipulating adults on their own and don't need additional help. Avoid this type of interaction.

See If What You Requested Has Been Done

You can also produce inconsistency by telling your child to do something then not checking to see it has been done. Your child comes home from school, gets undressed, gets his snack and asks, "Can I go outside and play?"

You say, "Sure, as soon as your room is straightened and everything put away." She goes to her room while you are busy in the kitchen.

In about 5 minutes, she comes to the kitchen and says, "Mom, I'm going outside."

You ask, "Did you pick up that mess in your room?" She responds positively and goes outside to play. You continue working in the kitchen. About an hour later, you pass by her room and see that nothing has been changed and she has not picked up a thing. You are furious and go outside to find her but cannot.

You're sitting in the den watching TV and tell your child, "It's time to go to bed. Go brush your teeth and go to bed." He gets up, goes into the bathroom then to his room.

You ask, "Did you brush your teeth?"

He says "Yes." About an hour or so later, you are going to bed. Upon entering the bathroom, you see all the toothbrushes are dry. Your son could not have brushed his teeth. You go to his room to tell him, but he is sleeping.

This form of inconsistency is not important for some children, but for others you have to followup. You must see if the child has done what he or she has been asked or what he is supposed to do. Some children will try to get away with as much as possible if you let them. This is especially true of homework. This form of inconsistency tends to interfere with the development of responsibility and also teaches children to be manipulative and sneaky.

Consistency from Both Parents

Consistency comes from both parents and from the mother and father as a unit. Each parent must mean what he or she says when dealing with the child, but each must also support and back up the other.

A child comes up to his mother and says, "Can I make some popcorn?"

She says, "No."

Then he asks his father and gets a positive answer. He's in the kitchen making the popcorn when his mother comes in and says, "What are you doing? Didn't I tell you not to do that?"

The boy responds with, "Dad said I could do it." The mother storms out of the kitchen and starts a discussion with her husband, but it soon becomes an argument. In the meantime, their son is sitting in the kitchen eating the popcorn.

A child has been sassy all afternoon. At the dinner table he starts talking back to his father and is told, "If you do that one more time, you can't watch TV tonight." The boy continues to be sassy, and his father tells him "Go to your room after dinner. There will be no TV tonight." The child goes to his room, but later the father has to go to a meeting. The mother tells her son, "Come on in and watch TV. We won't tell Daddy."

A child misbehaves in school and comes home with a great deal of homework as punishment from his teacher. He does not start it right away but plays and wastes his time. His mother has told him to do his homework. "I've told you 100 times to finish that work. If you aren't finished by the time you're supposed to go to baseball practice, you're not going."

However, these threats produce no action. Some time later, the child starts getting ready for baseball practice. His mother sees him putting his shoes on and getting his glove. She tells him, "Didn't I tell you you couldn't go if you didn't finish your work?"

The child says, "I'm going; you can't stop me." The mother replies with some further threats, then the child starts hollering. They begin arguing heatedly, and soon they are in a power struggle.

"You're not going."

"Yes, I am."

The father, who is sitting in another room, hears the arguing and comes into the boy's room. He asks, "What's going on?" The mother tells him what has happened, and the boy gives his side of the story. Then the father says, "The team is depending on him, and he needs to go to practice. Now son, you go to practice and do your schoolwork when you come home." The boy goes out to play, leaving his parents arguing.

Parents can produce inconsistency by undermining each other and not presenting a unified approach to the child. There are several results to this inconsistency. First, the child is learning to play one parent against the other and to manipulate them to get his way. When one parent disciplines a child and the other countermands it, the first parent's authority is reduced. Consequently, the child views this parent as the one who holds final authority and will not listen to the other.

By presenting this type of approach, parents tend to differentiate themselves as the bad guy, or the mean one, and the good guy, or the one who steps in and rescues the child from the evil being done to him. This type of inconsistency also produces arguing and fighting between parents. When this happens, some children identify themselves as the cause of the conflict between their parents. This isn't a good situation in which to place a child because the child may then view himself as the root of all the problems and conflicts between his parents.

It's extremely important for parents to be consistent as a unit. If you disagree with your partner or another person who has a significant part in disciplining your child, it's best to support him in front of your child. Later, when your child is not around, discuss the difference of opinion and, more important, resolve it.

Suppose your husband takes your son's bike away for a month because he didn't put it away. Although you feel this is too severe, you should support him in front of the child. Later discuss the problem, and decide how you will handle it the next time it occurs. Maybe the next time it happens the child won't be allowed to ride his bike for 2 days. When the behavior occurs again, a rule and consequence have been established so you and your husband are in agreement and can present a unified front.

Different Parent Responses to the Same Behavior

Depending on how you feel or your mood, people often treat the same behavior in very different ways. When a child knocks over his glass of milk today, you get a dish towel and quietly wipe it up. Tomorrow, when he does the same thing, you go through the ceiling, holler, scream and get upset. The next day, when he does the same thing, you give him a lecture on the cost of milk, rising food prices or how hard you have to work to buy milk. The following day, when he knocks over the milk again, you don't say anything but give him a towel to wipe it up.

Different responses to the same behavior also occur when you discipline your children. One day your son might get a whipping for fighting with his sister. The next day he might be sent to his room. Another time the fighting might be overlooked.

When you respond to your children inconsistently, you establish a situation similar to that in the following example. Let's say that today when I see you, I smile and shake your hand. Tomorrow when I see you, I smile and punch you in the nose. The next time I see you, I smile and take your car away. Another day I smile and give you money. This goes on for several weeks. How are you going to respond to me when you see me? How are you going to feel?

First of all, you can't predict my behavior. Although I am nice to you at times, you never know what to expect. When you see me, you'll probably tighten up, be confused and feel uncertain, tense and insecure. You'll probably try to place some physical distance between us and won't be able to become emotionally close to me or form a friendship. Children who experience inconsistency from their parents feel the same way. This inconsistent, unpredictable, unstructured interaction is difficult for them to handle.

It's best to set up a specific consequence for each behavior, whenever possible. For example, it may be a standard rule at your house that whenever anyone spills anything he gets a towel and cleans it up. If a child hits his sister, he is sent to his room for 5 minutes. If toys are not picked up, your child can't play with them the next day. Children who take their baths without argument can stay up 15 minutes past bedtime.

Setting up rules and consequences reduces inconsistency and makes the environment more structured and predictable. This decreases the probability the problems mentioned above will appear.

Consistency in the Environment

Consistency as discussed above relates to how adults interact with children. Interpersonal consistency is very important in child management. Consistency, structure or routine in the environment can also reduce behavioral difficulties.

A child with a set bedtime gives you less trouble when it's time to go to bed than a child who is allowed to retire at different times every night. Homework is less of a chore if it's done at the same time each day. Other chores, such as bathing, feeding the pets and taking out the garbage, require less reminding and nagging from parents if a routine is established. You don't have to make your home a military operation, but structure it as much as you reasonably can. Establish some routines to make the environment more predictable for the child.

Consistency may seem like a minor concept but it can eliminate about 50% of "not listening" in children. It's a major principle in child management and parent training. Consistency serves as a foundation on which other techniques and methods are built.

Following are two good rules to keep in mind when interacting with your child: Don't say anything you can't or don't want to do. Do everything you say you're going to do. You must follow through for *any* intervention to work.

5

Setting Rules for Behavior

Another major problem common to many child-rearing situations is setting rules or behavioral expectations. Parents usually have thousands of rules and regulations around the house.

Pick up your clothes.

Come home when it gets dark.

Don't be sassy.

Take a bath.

Don't jump on the sofa.

Parents are usually excellent in specifying what they want or in setting a rule. Some other "rules" you have might include some like those below.

When we go to grandmother's house, I want you to listen to me and not run all over the house.

All your homework must be done by the time your favorite TV program comes on.

Random Discipline

Parents frequently do an excellent job of setting expectations but spoil their good work when the child breaks the rule or doesn't live up to behavioral expectations. This is where the mistake is made. If the child at grandmother's does not do what he's told, the parent then decides what is going to happen—the child gets hollered at, goes home or gets a spanking or lecture.

When the child comes home late, the parent then decides if the child goes to his room, can't go out to play the next day or gets his bike taken away for a week.

You state the expectation beautifully but wait till the rule is broken. Only *then* do you decide what the consequence will be.

When you discipline or try to enforce rules and expectations in this way, several things happen that make effective child management difficult.

Random discipline doesn't make child feel responsible

A child doesn't feel responsible for what happens to him when he's not in control of the consequences of his behavior. He doesn't develop responsibility or feel he influences what occurs to him. Many children have told me something similar to, "If I'd known they were going to take TV away for a week, I would have never misbehaved." Children do not develop responsibility and feel others determine what happens to them. They blame others for what has happened to them.

"The teacher didn't tell us we should study that; that's why I failed the test."

"Daddy hollered at me; that's why I broke my toy."

"My sister kept bothering me; that's why I punched her in the nose."

Random discipline creates anger

If you discipline randomly or wait till your child breaks a rule *then* decide the consequences, your child is likely to get angry with you. He feels you are responsible for the bad things that happen to him. When rules are enforced in random fashion, a child is justified in being angry at his or her parents and feels as if he or she is not in control of the consequences of the behavior.

To understand how your child feels under these circumstances, take an example pertaining to the adult world of work and paychecks. Let's say you go to work and your boss tells you exactly what he expects of you. "Come to work every day. Take an hour for lunch. Work from 8 am to 5 pm." He spells out the rules and expectations very clearly.

After you've been working for him for a few weeks, you miss a day of work and receive a paycheck that is $5 less than usual. The next week, you miss a day and your check is $100 short. Another week, you stay home a day and your boss deducts $35 from your check. The next week, the check is $75 short, the next $150, the next $135.

After a couple of months of this, you go to the boss and ask, "What's going on? I miss work, and you take different amounts of money out of my check."

The boss responds, "That's what I think you deserve. I needed you on the day I took out $150, but I didn't need you when I just deducted $5."

How would you feel if you were the employee? You would be angry and think he was mean and unfair. You would also feel he was responsible for what happens to you. You would tend to blame him for your behavior.

Continuing with this example, a friend comes up to you and says, "Why didn't you buy that TV you said you were going to buy?"

You'd probably reply, "My boss took a lot of money from my check, and now I can't buy it." You would make your boss responsible.

This situation occurs many times every day in most families and is a primary reason why some forms of discipline don't work. A child has a difficult time developing a sense of responsibility if disciplined in this manner. He may develop anger and resentment toward you, be confused and have a difficult time knowing where he stands. In addition, he may have trouble becoming emotionally close to you.

Random discipline makes you feel guilty

If you discipline randomly, you may feel guilty for what you have done and try to undo it. This results in an inconsistent approach to the child. For example, you and your children are watching a cartoon special on TV, and the kids are fighting and teasing each other. You tell them repeatedly to stop, calm down and behave, but they continue. You finally reach your breaking point and yell at them, "I've told you 100 times to stop, but you will not listen. Now go to your rooms. You can't watch TV!"

They put their heads down and walk to their rooms. You pick up the newspaper and start reading it. Then you start thinking—you may feel mean, guilty or upset for what you've done—"Maybe I was a little too hard on them. This cartoon special only comes on a few times a year, and I've made them miss it."

After some thinking, you feel like a bad guy, so you go to their rooms and ask them if they can be good. In a few minutes, they're back watching TV, and you've eliminated your guilt feelings. However, nothing constructive has been accomplished.

Rules and Consequences Must Be Clearly Defined

In setting rules, state your expectations and state the consequences *before* a rule is broken. Both the rule and the consequences of the child's behavior must be clearly spelled out.

Let's take the previous example pertaining to work and paychecks to see how clear definition is provided. When you come to work the boss states the rules or expectations. "Come to work every day. You have an hour for lunch. You work from 8 am to 5 pm." But he takes his specifications a step further and states the consequences of failing to meet expectations.

"Each day you come to work and are here a full day, you will be paid $35. If you do not show up, you will not receive the $35." Now you know each day you miss work your weekly check will be $35 short.

At the end of 2 months, you look at your check stubs and note there has been a $35 deduction for each day you missed. By having the expectations and consequences spelled out, you can't make your boss responsible for the deductions. There's only one person to blame—yourself. *You* are responsible for what has happened to you.

If your friend comes up to you and asks, "Why didn't you buy that TV you said you were going to buy?" you should respond, "Because I decided not to go to work, I didn't get a full paycheck. I don't have enough money to buy the TV." In set-

Consequences A   Consequences B

Rules or Expectations

ting up the rules and consequences, your boss has made *you* accountable and responsible for your own behavior.

The diagram on page 27 indicates how to set effective rules. Tell your children, "Here is what I want you to do. This (consequence A) will happen if you do it that way, and this (consequence B) will happen if you do it that way." By defining the consequences of behavior, your child can decide for himself what's going to happen to him.

Taking a bath

"I would like you to go take your bath. If you are in the bath tub by 6:30 pm, washed and out by 7:00 pm, you can stay up 30 minutes past your bedtime. However, if that's not done, you have to go to bed at the same time as you do every night."

Picking up toys

"You can go outside and play as soon as your toys are picked up. If they aren't picked up, you can't go outside."

Sassiness

"I don't like you talking back to me and raising your voice. As long as you talk in a normal tone you can go about your normal business. However, each time you are sassy, you'll have to go into your room for 15 minutes."

Putting things where they belong

"Put your bike in the back yard. Don't leave it in the front of the house. When it's not put where it's supposed to go, you won't be able to ride it the next day. If it's put away, you can continue riding it."

Doing homework

"You mentioned to Dad you want to go to the Jazz basketball game Friday night. That's fine, but you know we've been having a great deal of trouble getting you to do your homework. I'll tell you what we will do. If you come home 3 out of 4 days this week and do your homework without a fight, you can go to the game. But if you give us trouble about the homework more than once this week, you can't go to the game."

Coming home on time

"You've been having trouble getting home on time. You're supposed to be home by 5 pm to have dinner, but you're always late. I know you're aware of the time. On the days you come home on time, you can have a snack at night. When you're late, I'm going to come get you, and you won't be allowed to have a snack that night."

Getting ready for bed

"If you get ready for bed without me having to remind you 20 times or force you to go in your room, I'll read you a story before you go to bed. If you keep putting it off and it becomes a struggle, there won't be a story."

Fighting between siblings

"As soon as you walk in from school, the teasing and fighting starts, and it doesn't seem to end. Starting today, if you can keep the fighting down and get along until after supper, we'll go out and get some ice cream. If you cut up, we won't go."

In the examples given, the parent is in control. The *adult* specifies the expectations and consequences, but the *child* decides what will happen. A map is drawn; all you have to do is sit back and wait for your child to tell you what to do. You don't have to remind him 50 times, nag or cajole. By his behavior, your child will tell you whether he wants to stay up past his bedtime, go to his room, have a story read to him or get ice cream. All you have to do is be consistent and follow through with the consequence the child chooses.

I believe it's extremely important to teach your children they are responsible for their own behavior. Good and bad things happen because of their decisions. Many adults never learn this. They fail to accept the responsibility for the consequences of their behavior.

If a child feels he or she is responsible for the consequences of his or her behavior, then the child will feel a situation can be changed. If things are bad, he can make them better. If he's happy with what's happening, he can maintain it. If he feels a parent is responsible, he is like a puppet on a string who has to wait until others decide to make him feel good.

Expectations and Consequences Must Be Specific

How many times has the following happened in your

home? Your child's room has been messy for 3 weeks, and it seems everything he owns is on the floor. You tell him, "Get into your room and get all that stuff off the floor." About 10 minutes later, he comes out of his room. You ask, "Did you do what I said?"

His response is "Yes." You go in the room and find all the junk that was on the floor is now on the bed! You hit the ceiling, but what has happened? The child has taken you literally and has completely fulfilled your expectations as he understood them.

One morning while I was getting ready to go to work, my wife was trying to get our oldest son up to go to school. He wouldn't budge and continued lying in bed. I passed his room and said, "You'd better be out of the bed by the time I'm finished shaving."

When I finished, I went to check on him and, sure enough, he had done exactly what I told him. He had taken his pillow and blanket off his bed and was now lying on the floor!

Children often do *exactly* what you tell them. When you state rules or behavioral expectations, be as *specific* as possible! "I want you to go into your room and put your toys where they belong and the dirty clothes in the bathroom."

You may also encounter problems with a child's behavior if expectations or consequences are stated in general or cloudy terms. The statements "I want you to behave when we go to the shopping center" or "I want you to be good this afternoon" are too vague. What does "behave" or "good" mean in these contexts? They mean different things to different people. Being good for an 8-year-old might mean hitting his sister only 10 times instead of 25 times. His parent defines being good as not hitting his sister at all. When the child and parent get together to compare notes, they come up with different interpretations of the same expectation. The parent feels the child has misbehaved, but the child feels he has behaved as required and he has been unfairly disciplined.

The same misunderstanding results when you state consequences in general terms. "If you do that again, you're going to get it" or "If you don't pick up your toys, you'll be punished." What does this mean to a child? Probably not much.

In stating expectations, rules and consequences, be specific and spell out *exactly* what you mean. You can't assume the child knows. Both of you must have the same idea of what is expected and what the consequences of failure will be. There should not be a mystery or guessing game for the child. If there is, the child is apt to be confused and resent being disciplined.

How to Set Up
Clear Expectations and Consequences

Expectations and consequences must be spelled out ahead of time to be effective. A map is drawn for the child, and *he* decides what path to take. There are three general ways to accomplish this.

Natural consequences

Some behavior carries with it natural consequences, and these are often sufficient to produce change. If I beat my head on the floor, the natural consequence is that my head will hurt. That result may be enough by itself to prevent me from continuing the behavior. If the only thing a child obtains by having a temper tantrum is a sore throat, upset stomach or hurt head, that behavior will quickly decrease. Natural consequences can be used to manage some problem behavior, and often this is a good place to start.

Many children have eating problems. Meals for some families are a struggle. One way to begin to change picky eating or lack of eating is to use the natural consequences of such behavior. A house rule might be, "Dinner is served between 5 pm and 6 pm. Those who eat can have a snack later tonight. Those who don't will not have anything to eat later." Hunger is a very powerful natural consequence that may be used to change unacceptable behavior.

When I suggest this method to some parents, they look aghast and say, "You want me to starve my child?" But most eating problems seen in children result from the way it is handled by the parents.

Eating is a biological drive; you have to eat to live. Eating is not like doing homework, picking up toys or being polite—you don't have to do these behaviors to survive. It has also been shown a person must fast for a few days before it will significantly affect him.

Usually parents teach faulty eating patterns to their children. The picky eater has a specially prepared dinner. When a child doesn't eat dinner, he may come to you at night and ask, "Can I have some milk and cookies?" Although you want to say no, you think he didn't eat at dinner, so he should have something in his stomach before he goes to bed. The child develops an unusual eating pattern that could have been prevented by using the natural consequence of hunger.

Bed wetting is another behavior that can be corrected by using natural consequences. If a child wets the bed, he must change his clothes, take the sheets off his bed, make the bed, wash his clothes or whatever duties the child is physically capable of performing. If the child wets the bed or his pants and is held accountable for the natural consequences of that behavior, he will soon make every effort to correct the behavior.

Children often get sick to avoid unpleasant situations such as school, tests or other obligations. Later, when the child gets home or when other children are home to play, he recovers very rapidly. Natural consequences can be used to alter this problem behavior.

"If you're sick, you have to go to the doctor"—most kids love that! Or the house rule could be that when a child is sick he must remain in his room, in bed, without play or TV time. The consequences of being well far outweigh the natural consequences of being sick. The child will probably not be tempted to feign sickness.

Parents who have trouble with children failing to put dirty clothes in the proper place may state, "I only wash clothes that are in the dirty-clothes basket. Those articles that are left in other places will not be washed." In this situation, the natural consequence of the child leaving his favorite T-shirt and jeans in his room is they remain dirty and he can't wear them.

In these types of situations, you must respond in a matter-of-fact manner and not get upset. Consistency and following through with what is said are also extremely important.

Grandma's rule

This is a principle many parents use frequently. It can be stated very simply. "First you do what I want you to do, then you can do what you want to do."

Our grandmothers or parents often said, "Eat your meat and potatoes, then you can have your dessert." This method of setting consequences can be used on the spur of the moment. However, it must usually include some type of activity that is of interest to the child. You're having difficulty getting your child ready for school, and you know he enjoys watching TV before school. Using grandma's rule, you would say, "The TV is not turned on until you're dressed and ready for school."

A few other situations illustrate the principle.

"We'll go get ice cream when all these toys are picked up."

"You'll get your snack when you're ready for bed."

"No one watches TV until all of his homework is completed."

"We'll play a game as soon as you take your bath."

"You can't go outside to play until your room is clean."

In these examples, the parent sets expectations and consequences and gives the child a decision to make. As a parent, all you do is carry out the consequence the child decides on.

Arbitrarily setting consequences

When natural consequences or grandma's rule can't be used, you can always identify consequences that are important to the child and set rules or behavioral expectations according to these.

A sassy child might hate being confined in his room. You could tell him, "I don't like you talking back to me and being sassy. Each time this happens, you have to go to your room for 15 minutes."

Another child who's doing poorly in school because he fails to do his homework may love to stay up past his usual bedtime. To improve this child's behavior, you might tell him, "For every homework assignment you bring home and complete, you can stay up 5 minutes past your bedtime."

Maybe your child loves games, such as cards or checkers. But it might be impossible to force him to clean up his room. Use what he loves to change his behavior by telling him, "I'm going to check your room, and if it's clean and your toys are put away, we'll play a game. On the nights it isn't, we won't play any games."

A child who loves to watch TV might have difficulty getting along with his brother. To alter this behavior, you might tell him, "Each time you tease your brother, you lose 10 minutes of TV time."

In these situations, you have identified a consequence that is important to the child and then set the behavioral expectations. It isn't a natural consequence or something that follows an activity but something devised and individualized according to a child's particular interests.

It could be a positive consequence—something the child enjoys and that does not happen everyday at your house. Or, it could be a negative consequence that the child would like to avoid or a loss of privileges.

6

Changing Behavior

Consequences are the most important aspects of modifying a child's behavior. The previous chapter discussed the most effective way to use them. Parents can use three major consequences to discipline their children.

Reward or positive consequences

If you see a behavior you like, reward it. Follow the behavior with positive attention—something that is important or enjoyable to the child.

Punishment or negative consequences

If you see a behavior you don't like, punish it. Follow the behavior with negative attention—something the child views as unenjoyable or withdrawing something positive.

Ignoring or no consequences

If you see a behavior you don't like, ignore it. Maybe the attention you give it is the reason it exists. Don't follow the behavior with negative *or* positive attention.

Rewarding, punishing and ignoring behavior are the three major consequences you can use to discipline your children. These tools are essential to changing behavior as discussed in detail in the following chapters.

7

Reward

There are three major consequences—rewarding, punishing and ignoring—that you can use to discipline or manage child behavior. But most parents usually rely on Punishment. By punishment, I mean negative attention, emphasis on bad behavior, anything from hollering at a child to spanking him. Many times a week, I hear, "I've tried everything on this child, but nothing works!"

The first question I ask is, "What have you tried?" The usual answers I get are varied.

"I've taken him off the baseball team."

"We put her in her room."

"My husband took TV away."

"We wouldn't let him play outside."

"My wife made him write lines."

"I wouldn't let her go out Saturday night."

"We spanked him."

What most parents tell me is they've used every form of punishment they could dream up.

Many problems occur when punishment is used as the main method to control or discipline children. This is discussed in detail in Chapter 8.

Most parents pay more attention to misbehavior than to appropriate behavior. If everything is going well, they don't say anything. But when something goes wrong, they're quick to punish the child. A few examples follow.

A child who is supposed to make his bed does so for 6 days but forgets to make it on the 7th. What day does he get attention for bed-making behavior? The one day he didn't make it!

A child's room has been dirty for a long time. You tell him, "Aunt Mary is coming to visit. Go clean your room." He likes Aunt Mary, so he goes to his room and spends 2 hours cleaning it up. He cleans 99.9% of his room, and it looks beautiful. But he left a book by his bed and a sock by the door.

He calls you and says, "Come see my room."

You walk in; what's the first thing you say? "Look at that book. Pick it up, and put it away. That sock goes in the dirty-clothes basket."

You tell your child you want you home at 5 pm. "If you come home late, you'll take your bath and go to bed." What happens if the child comes home late? You give him attention by yelling or punishing him or giving him a lecture. What happens if he comes home on time? Nothing.

Parents usually stress only bad behavior. Try changing your approach, and you may find your child's behavior changes!

The Positive Approach

Most counselors and child psychologists stress a *positive approach* to discipline. They stress shifting the emphasis from what the child does *wrong* to what he is doing *right*. In doing this, you pay more attention to *good* behavior and less to inappropriate actions or misbehavior. This positive approach is primarily achieved by using the consequence of reward. Parents tell me, "I've tried everything" and go through their list of punishments.

I then usually ask, "Have you tried rewarding him for doing good?"

Parents think I'm speaking another language or I've mentioned something that has never crossed their minds. And many parents have the wrong idea of what I mean by "reward." They usually view it as a bribe, money or something similar.

Reward can be defined as something that will serve as an incentive, an emphasis on anything that is important to the child or anything that will increase the probability good behavior will recur. The primary purpose of reward is to get a child to *want* to do what is asked or expected. Reward often changes the child's motivation. It will change a behavior the child views as undesirable into something he wants to do.

Many parents ask me, "What can I use for a reward?" This is difficult to answer because reward must be individualized for each child. What is important to my son may not be important to yours. What may serve as a reward for one child may be a punishment for another.

When trying to identify possible rewards for children, throw out *your* values and observe closely what the child considers important.

Types of Reward

Possible rewards might be found occur among any of the following categories.

Activity rewards

These could be activities that are important to the child— staying up past his bedtime, having a friend sleep over, playing a game with you, staying out later on Saturday, going to sleep at grandmother's house, playing pitch and catch with you, extra time to ride his bike, extra TV time or going to a dance or football game.

Foolish rewards

These usually involve an activity you might view as foolish or stupid but the child views as a reward—washing the car, cutting the grass, using the vacuum cleaner, taking a shower.

Material rewards

These are usually concrete or material things the child values—an extra dime for school, a toy, candy, a snack at night, a bag of potato chips, football cards, an album, a basketball.

Things you'd usually buy

These rewards usually involve material things that parents would get the child anyway. A child comes home and says, "I want a kite." You would probably buy him one, however, take the opportunity to use the child's desire for the kite as a means to reward good behavior.

Another child might say, "Joey has a pair of new tennis shoes. I wish I had some like his." You look at his shoes, see they're old and he needs a new pair. Instead of going out on Saturday to buy the shoes he needs, use the desire for a particular style of shoe as an incentive to change behavior.

Token rewards

These rewards have little value in themselves. But they represent something important, or they can be traded for a desired object. Money serves as a powerful token reward for adults.

The kindergarten child who behaves or performs in school to get a star on his forehead or a happy-face stamp on his hand is actually working for a token reward. These represent approval, positive attention and acceptance. Points or stars on a chart often serve as tokens that can be traded in for some desired object or activity.

Social rewards

This is the most powerful reward you have, and you have it with you all the time. It doesn't cost a penny. It's praise, recognition and positive attention for good behavior.

Many children will do a great deal to get social rewards. Often social rewards are sufficient to change and maintain behavior. These rewards might be verbal approval, laughter, a smile, a hug or a kiss. They might be recognition for helping you set the table, attention to an everyday behavior (picking up clothes, brushing teeth), telling your child how pleased or proud you are of him and various forms of praise.

Social reward, praise, positive attention, non-verbal approval of good behavior—these are very important and become a major part of the total approach to child behavior described in this book. Use social rewards with all the rewards described above. If your child earns an activity reward (staying up past his bedtime) for not being sassy, praise him for this behavior change.

Intrinsic rewards

This is self-reward or behavior that is performed because it feels good. Patting yourself on the back for a job well done or engaging in a behavior because you enjoy it are types of intrinsic reward.

You have just finished reading a book. Your friend comes

up to you and says, "What did you get out of that book? Did it tell you how to fix your car, build a house or make meatballs and spaghetti?"

You respond, "I read it because I enjoyed it. It was fun to read."

Another person likes to go fishing. He doesn't catch many fish but leaves in the morning with an ice chest full of beer and food. In the afternoon, he comes back home tired. The ice chest is empty, and he has spent $20. You ask him, "Why do you go fishing? You never catch fish, and it costs money."

This fellow might reply, "It gives me a lot of pleasure to be on the water; I enjoy it."

Why do you stop and help somebody whose car is broken down on the interstate? Probably because you enjoy helping someone in trouble. These are all examples of intrinsic rewards—things you do because they make you feel good.

Throughout this book I stress a positive approach to child behavior using reward. Although I emphasize material, social and activity rewards, the purpose of the whole approach is eventually to get your child to function on intrinsic rewards. He does things (making his bed, listening, not being sassy, doing his homework) because he enjoys them or because they make him feel good. The process of how this can be accomplished is discussed in detail in the following section.

The Purpose of Reward

When I start talking about reward at a workshop, school meeting or in my office, several questions are usually asked by parents who do not agree with this notion. They ask two questions: "Isn't that bribery? Are you telling me to bribe my child to be good?"

The answer to both of these questions is *No!* A bribe is paying someone to do something that is illegal or giving a person a reward for an inappropriate behavior. If you get a traffic ticket and pay somebody to fix it, that's a bribe.

I go to work every day. I don't feel my wages are a bribe. You would probably think it was foolish if someone said, "Your boss bribes you to go to work." You and I go to work because of consequences. The positive consequences (rewards) of going to work are greater than staying home. So we show up at work every day.

We do many of the things we do because of positive consequences though we seldomly view them this way. If you are in control and set behavioral expectations and consequences, you are doing the same thing an employer does to get his employee to come to work. By using rewards, you can set up situations so a child will *want* to behave in an appropriate fashion. Positive consequences of being good far outweigh the negative consequences of being bad.

Reward child for something he's supposed to do?

Another question parents commonly ask me is, "Are you telling me to pay or reward my child for something he's supposed to do?"

Children *learn* what is right and wrong and what they're supposed to do. When your child is born, he doesn't know, "I'm supposed to do my homework. I shouldn't talk back to my parents. I'm supposed to pick up my clothes and keep my room clean. I should go to bed when I'm told" or the many other demands you will make on him. If your child isn't doing what you want him to do, you must assume he hasn't learned it. Using positive consequences (rewards) is a very effective way to teach your child what he should and should not do.

Will he misbehave to get rewarded?

"Won't my child learn to misbehave to get rewarded?"

Parents who ask this question are actually saying, "My child will become a con artist and will learn to manipulate me by bad conduct to get paid for being good." This won't happen if you are in control and set expectations and consequences. Manipulation primarily occurs when you are inconsistent, as discussed in Chapter 4.

This behavior will also develop if your child is allowed to manipulate a situation to his advantage. You tell your child 20 times, "Go pick up your toys," but he doesn't respond. Then you say, "If you pick up your toys, I'll give you a dollar." Or the child misbehaves then asks you what you'll give him if he's good.

You must be very consistent and in control to prevent

manipulative behavior from developing. Follow through with what you said when you set the rules and consequences. Although you are in control, your child actually determines what will happen to him.

Rewards for the rest of the child's life?

"Am I going to have to reward my child the rest of his life for being good?"

The answer to this question is both "yes" and "no." Hopefully, you'll continue using social reward (praise) for good behavior throughout your child's life. Use praise in family interactions. But phase out material and activity rewards as soon as possible. The goal of this system is to get the child functioning on intrinsic reward. The child engages in behavior because it feels good and he wants to do it.

Suppose a child views getting dressed for school as an undesirable behavior. You have difficulty every morning getting him up and ready. Some common approaches to the problem include hollering at the child, dressing him, criticism, punishment and emphasis on failure to do what is expected.

A *positive* approach first identifies an incentive or reward for good behavior. Let's say the child loves potato chips. (You can use anything that's important to him.) Tell him, "When I wake you up for school, I'm going to set the timer on the stove for 15 minutes. If you're dressed when the bell rings, we'll stop on the way to school and get a bag of potato chips. If you aren't dressed, we don't get the chips."

The aim of reward in this example is not to continue giving the child a bag of potato chips for getting dressed in the morning until he is a junior in college. The purpose is to change what the child considers undesirable action (getting dressed for school) into behavior the child wants to do. While he is getting dressed for school, praise his getting dressed on time. Give his new behavior a lot of attention. During the first and second week, the child can't wait to get to the store to get the potato chips. By the third or fourth week, the chips will become less important. He may not ask to get them in the morning even though he is still getting dressed for school.

The purpose of the reward or incentive (potato chips) is to make him *want* to do something he previously thought was undesirable. Once you can get him to do it, you are halfway to changing the behavior. When he is doing what you want, all you have to do is associate verbal approval and praise with the new behavior.

Most children will do a great deal to get verbal approval. Often this is sufficient to change and maintain behavior. Eventually, the child will engage in the new behavior because it is more enjoyable and pleasurable (intrinsically rewarding) to get dressed on time than to fool around and get hollered at, punished and be late. Instead he'll want to get dressed for school!

Start with material or activity rewards to motivate the child to engage in the new behavior. Once the child changes his behavior, use social reward. Eventually the material reward can be phased out. Intrinsic rewards will take over.

The following is a silly example, but it stresses the ideas stated above. Let's say I ask you to go into your yard and count the blades of grass. I ask you to separate the different types of grass, the light-green ones from the dark-green ones. I tell you I'll be back the next day to get the results, and I'll give you $5.

What would you think? You'd probably think I was crazy for asking you to do that, and you wouldn't count the grass. The behavior I have requested is undesirable and something you don't want to do (like doing homework, picking up clothes, not being sassy or any other problem behavior you see in your child).

Let me rephrase my request. I ask you to go into your yard and count the blades of grass. I ask you to separate the different types of grass, the light-green ones from the dark-green ones. I tell you I'll be back the next day to get the results, and I'll give you $15,000.

In this case, you'd probably count the grass to get part of the $15,000. What have I done? By using a reward, I have increased your desire to engage in a behavior you thought I was crazy to ask you to do. I've changed an undesirable behavior into something you want to do. Now I have half of the ball game won. Let me stretch a point in this silly example to emphasize the process that occurs when reward is used effectively.

Let's assume I'm an important person to you, such as your

mother or father, and I can get you to count grass every day. When you do what I ask you to do, I use social reward and say, "You're doing a beautiful job. I'm proud of you and never knew you could do this so well. I never saw people count grass so fast." Eventually my praise will gain importance, and the material reward will decrease in importance. Soon you'll be counting grass to receive the social reward. In the next step, intrinsic reward would take over. You'd engage in the behavior because you enjoyed it and derived pleasure from it.

Although this is an extreme example, much of our adult behavior is based on intrinsic reward. People start working to eat and have money. Many who could retire continue working for the pleasure they derive. Some people get involved in coaching Little League baseball for pleasure (intrinsic reward) or engage in other behavior that requires great effort just for enjoyment.

Use material and social rewards as a means to an end. That end hopefully will be children who engage in appropriate or responsible behavior because they enjoy it or want to do it (intrinsic reward).

Reward—Things to Consider

Reward can be used to change behavior, but keep in mind the following points so reward works effectively.

Reward must be individualized

A consequence that is rewarding for one child may not produce the same effect for another. When trying to identify a reward for a particular child, look closely at the child's needs, interests and habits. Throw out your values, what you feel is important and what has worked for another child. Some children will work their hearts out to earn 10¢, while others wouldn't move a finger for $100. If you use extra TV time as a reward for your daughter and it works well, don't automatically assume it will work for your son.

Some parents ask me, "What can I use as a reward?" This is a very difficult question because different children value different things. I tell them to observe their child closely to identify activities that are important.

Another statement I hear frequently is, "Nothing interests

my child. I don't know what I can use as a reward." I haven't met a child for whom *some* reward could not be identified. For some children, a reward is easily found. For others, it's difficult, and a more-detailed investigation is necessary.

I usually tell parents, "Listen to your children very carefully. Observe their play. Ask them what is important to them or what they would like to work toward." All children can be motivated by incentives, but for some children incentives are more difficult to identify.

Always use social reward

Regardless of the type of incentive (material, activity) used, always use social reward (praise). The main purpose of material or activity reward is to motivate the child to behave in a certain way. Eventually intrinsic reward should take over, but praise must be used for this to occur. Whether a child has earned time past his bedtime, a bag of potato chips, a toy or whatever, praise and positive attention should always accompany the behavior.

Don't put the cart before the horse

Parents often use reward but make the mistake of rewarding the child *before* the behavior.

"I'm going to buy you this bike, and I want you to be good at school."

On entering a supermarket, you tell your child, who usually misbehaves in this situation, "I'm going to buy you this candy. Now I want you to listen to me and be good."

"I'm going to let you get your driver's license. Because of this, I want you to pull your grades up."

Consider what can happen if you pay someone to paint your house before the job is complete. It's usually done halfway or not completed to your satisfaction. The same thing happens when you give a child a reward then expect him to behave in a certain fashion.

To be effective, base reward on behavior and always give rewards *after* the expected action. If the reward comes before the desired behavior, you can't expect it to work.

Rewards earned must be received

When a reward is earned, be sure your child receives it!

Parent: I've used that reward system you told me to use. It worked fine for a few days, but now nothing's happening."

Psychologist: "Tell me about it. What did you use for reward? How did you set it up?"

Parent: "Well, we were going to work on his sassiness. We used staying up past his bedtime as the reward. If he wasn't sassy after school until bedtime, he would be able to delay his bedtime by 30 minutes. It worked fine for about 5 days, but now he's just as sassy as before."

Psychologist: "What happened? Did he earn the reward?"

Parent: "He did fine for the first 5 days. No sassiness, and he earned the 30 minutes. But he gave us so much trouble about getting dressed for bed or teasing his sister, we didn't let him stay up."

Often children earn rewards for one behavior but lose them for doing something else. This is a sure way to destroy the effectiveness of a reward system. Rewards earned *must* be received. How would you feel if I told you, "Please clean this chair, and I'll give you $25. Then clean this one, and I'll give you another $25." You clean the first one, and I give you $25.

Then you say, "I don't feel like cleaning the other chair."

I tell you, "Give me back the $25 you earned because you wouldn't clean the second chair." You'd be angry and think I was unjust. If I took money away that you'd already earned, it would be difficult for me to motivate you toward the same behavior again.

The same thing happens if a child earns a reward but you don't bother to see he receives it. A child earns a breakfast at a restaurant for keeping his room clean. But you never take him or keep delaying the reward. Earned rewards must be received as soon as possible. This brings me to another point.

Reward should occur immediately after desired behavior

If a child does something this minute, ideally he should be rewarded right now—not next week or next month. The effectiveness of a reward is, in part, based on how closely it follows the behavior you're trying to control. How well a reward works is *not* based on quantity or cost but *immediacy*. Rewards should be given as soon as possible.

Let's take the example of a 9-year-old who has trouble hanging up his clothes after coming home from school. You know this child loves potato chips and motorcycles. One day you might say, "I'm going to check your room at 3:30 pm. If your clothes are hung up or put away, we'll get a bag of potato chips." The next day you could tell him, "If your clothes are put away by 3:30 pm, we'll go to the dealer and get the motorcycle you've been wanting."

Let's say both rewards work and the child hangs up his clothes or puts them away. But one reward costs 25¢, and the other costs $450. Even so, the motorcycle is *not* going to change the behavior permanently any more than the bag of potato chips. The *immediacy* of a reward is more important than the quantity or price. In regard to school performance or behavior, it's better to reward on a daily or weekly basis than to wait after each report card or grading period.

It's not always immediately possible to reward a child for his behavior, so social and token rewards should be used frequently. Chapter 10 explains how to construct behavioral charts. Social and token rewards are employed to provide immediate reinforcement for desirable behavior.

Reward improvement

Often a reward system doesn't work because parents expect too much change too rapidly, and they don't reward improvement.

Many times parents come to me and say, "My child won't listen." We set up some type of reward system to change that behavior. Two weeks later the parents return and say, "He's still not listening." This may be a fact if we consider the overall behavior. But behavior change must be broken down into steps and evaluated for gradual improvement. A child may not have been listening 30 times a day before we started the reward. After 2 weeks, the not-listening behavior has decreased to 15 times a day. While the child may not be listening to every request made of him, he *has* improved and listens 50% better than he did 2 weeks ago.

In using reward, behavior or goals must be broken down into steps. Reward small goals (gradual improvement). You can't attempt to change behavior 100% or to change the child overnight.

Look at where the child is now and where you want to go. A child who isn't listening 30 times a day should be rewarded if he can decrease that rate to 20 times a day the first week. After that, the amount of improvement necessary to receive the reward can be increased each week. The second week's reward would be received for 15 times a day, the third week 10 times a day and so on. Eventually the child would be rewarded for not listening only 3 or 5 times a week. Allow some room for error. Do not expect 100% improvement to receive the reward.

Reward must be changed

The purpose of using reward is to change behavior. In most cases, interests and attitudes are also modified. A reward that may initially be important to a child might lose its effectiveness with time and use.

Suppose you enjoy steak dinners. I could probably motivate you by saying, "If you help me, I'll take you out to the restaurant of your choice for a steak dinner." However, if you've eaten steak every day for a week, I wouldn't be able to motivate you or change your behavior with the same reward. You'd probably be tired of steak, and the reward wouldn't be seen as important or desirable.

Children respond the same way and become either tired of or disinterested in the same reward. If a reward has worked beautifully in the beginning but is no longer effective, change it because it's probably been used too much or too long.

When you first try a reward, use it consistently for a period of time (usually a week or so) before trying another even though the reward appears ineffective. Often you identify a reward that is important to a child, but because it does not work the first, second or third time it is used, you try another one immediately. Rewards need to be varied but not too quickly.

Reward should be attainable

When a reward system is first started, it shouldn't be too complex or too difficult. The goal should not require a great deal of change, and it should be set up to ensure success and attainment of the reward. You have to lock the child into the system. If you make it too difficult at first and the child isn't able to attain the behavioral goal and incentive, the whole system will probably fail.

Consider a sassy child: You analyze the behavior and find the undesirable action occurs an average of 10 times a day. You set up a positive system to decrease the behavior. You tell the child, "I am going to put a check on this calendar each time you are sassy. If you only have two checks when it's time to go to bed, you can stay up 30 minutes past your bedtime." When it is time for bed, you and the child look at the calendar and find he has 5 checks. The child doesn't receive the reward.

In this case, the total system is likely to fail because the expectations were set too high. The child improved his behavior by 50% and, in a sense, was punished for doing this. Soon the child will become disgusted with this system.

Expectations must be realistic so the child will receive the reward. A good rule to follow is to expect about 30% change at first. In the above example, the child should have received a reward if he eliminated 4 sassy behaviors in a day and received 7 checks.

Another problem that occurs is reward systems are often too complex or difficult. Too much work or change is required for the child to receive the reward. For example, a child may have to:

1. Get out of bed when called in the morning.
2. Eat all his breakfast.
3. Put his clothes away when he comes home from school.
4. Do his homework.
5. Come in on time from playing.
6. Not fight with his brother.
7. Pick up his toys.
8. Take his bath when told.

If he does all this, the reward is having a story read to him at bedtime. The child will probably think, "The heck with this— it's not worth it," and the system fails.

When starting a reward system, the child must be able to achieve the reward easily to accept the system. This increases the probability that future reward will be effective and that change will occur.

Behavior you're trying to change can serve as a reward

The behavior you are trying to eliminate can be the reward. Let's say a child is scared of the dark or going into a room by himself and must be accompanied by a parent. The goal is to eliminate the dependent behavior. This can serve as the reward. The child will not leave the den to go to his room to get a toy without someone with him. What you might initially do is tell him, "Take one step out of the den, then I'll come with you." After the child is successfully doing this, you could tell him, "Take two steps out of the den, then I'll come with you." This would gradually be increased to three steps, four steps and so on before you accompany him the rest of the way.

This procedure is also used to decrease dependent behavior and increase independence. Some parents have to sit with their child to ensure completion of homework. The child becomes very dependent on the parent and can't complete his assignments if required to function alone.

Dependent behavior can often be used as a reward to have the child function without the parent. At first it might be set up so the child has to function independently for 2 minutes or until 5 math problems are completed before you sit with him. The time period or amount of work required is gradually increased before you provide help. Eventually, you spend less and less time helping with the homework, and the child increases his ability to function independently.

This procedure was used with a problem eater who only ate French fries and bread for dinner. Although we were trying to increase the variety of food this child would eat, we used French fries and bread as the reward. At first, the parent placed half a spoon of rice or other food on the plate. The child was required to taste it before he could have the French fries and bread.

As the child increased the variety of foods he ate, he found some he liked, and the portions of these were increased. It was easier to have him eat these before he was rewarded with the French fries and bread. As the portions and variety of foods increased, he ate less of the reward food. This unusual eating pattern soon diminished.

Some small children cannot play independently and require their parent, usually the mother, to play with or amuse them continually. A similar procedure can be used to deal with this behavior. The parent has the child play independently for a few minutes, sometimes in another room. Then she plays a game with him or reads him a story. The time period is gradually increased so he is required to show more independent play before receiving the reward.

This reward system can be very effective in changing some behavior and can be used in a variety of situations. The procedure is to set up two behavior patterns that can't exist at the same time. One behavior is to be increased, and the other is used as the reward. A child cannot be independent and dependent at the same time. By functioning on his own, he is rewarded with assistance. The amount of independent behavior required to achieve the reward (dependence) is increased, and the behavior to be changed (reward) is decreased.

8

Punishment

Most parents are punishers. They pay more attention to their child's mistakes, failures and misbehaviors than to their successes, achievements and adaptive actions.

By "punishment," I mean any negative attention, from hollering to whipping a child. For example, a child is supposed to make his bed or do some other chore every day. He does the chore 10 days but forgets on the 11th day. The day he gets attention for his behavior is the day he doesn't do his chore. On the other days, no one said anything about his behavior.

Another example is the child who spends Saturday morning cutting the grass. He gives it a great deal of effort. He edges, sweeps and cuts the front and back yard. He does an excellent job and 99.9% of the lawn is beautiful. However, he left some grass on the sidewalk and forgot to pull the grass by the side of the house. He calls his father; what are the first words out of his father's mouth? "What about that grass over there? You forgot to pull the grass on the side of the house." We overlook the positive behavior and emphasize the negative.

Report cards or grades is another example. A child brings home 5 A's, 4 B's, 2 C's and 1 F. The grade that usually gets the most emphasis is the failure. The parent asks, "What happened? Why did you get the F? You are going to have to try harder in that subject."

Parents generally pay more attention to mistakes and failures than to accomplishments and successes. By responding to your children this way, you set up a situation in which the only thing the child receives for being good is not being punished or criticized. This type of parental response also results in children who feel it is useless to do nice things because they are never good enough and no one pays attention to them. Like adults, children avoid things that are negative. If sitting down to do homework is a negative situation (there is a lot of punishment or hollering), the child tries to avoid homework and you have trouble getting him to do it. For some personality types, punishment actually makes matters worse. It doesn't work.

I'm not saying you should not use punishment in disciplining children. But punishment should not be used as the main method of behavior management. Many times a parent tells me, "I've tried everything on this child, but nothing works. In fact, his behavior seems to be getting worse."

The first question I ask is, "What have you tried?" Most of the time, the answers I get are fairly similar.

"I've spanked him."

"We sent her to her room."

"My husband took him off the baseball team."

"I wouldn't let her watch TV."

"We decided to take his bike away."

What parents generally are saying is they have tried all types of punishment.

About 95% of parents use punishment as their main form of discipline. When I ask, "Have you tried rewarding him or ignoring his behavior?" parents usually respond as though I am speaking another language. The most effective way to use punishment is to combine it with other consequences. Use *rewarding* and *ignoring* about 60 to 70% of the time. Use punishment only 30 to 40% of the time. Certain problems can occur if parents use punishment as the main method of control.

Problems with Punishment

Children behave because of fear

If I came up to you and said, "I can get your child to do whatever you'd like him to do in one of two ways. First, I can get him to do what you want him to do out of fear of what's going to happen. Or I can get him to do what you want him to out of satisfaction from learning new behaviors or because he feels he's accomplishing something." Which method would you prefer? Most people would pick the latter. But most parents use the fear method (punishment).

A problem with using punishment as the main method of control is most of the time you get the children to behave out of fear of what is going to happen to them.

Most forms of punishment are based on fear. "If you don't bring your grades up, you won't be able to play baseball this summer."

"If you don't stop teasing your little sister, you are going to get a spanking."

"You won't be able to go out and play tomorrow if you don't come home on time."

In these examples, the children behave out of fear of what will happen to them rather than out of a sense of accomplishment. Fear is not an emotion most parents would want to develop excessively in their children. However, when punishment is used as the main method of control, fear may develop.

Anger, aggression and rebellion may develop

Using punishment as the main method of control often produces anger and resentment toward parents. This is especially true if the discipline is decided on and administered *after* the misbehavior. Children who are disciplined this way often feel unjustly treated and develop considerable hostility toward parents. Sometimes these feelings are expressed directly ("I hate you." "My father's mean.").

But more often this anger is expressed through a variety of passive-aggressive behaviors, such as opposition, resistance, stubbornness, defiance and rebellion. For instance, you say it's black, and he says it's white, or she does just the opposite of what you tell her. Anger may also be displaced to other situations and cause fighting with or anger toward siblings, peers and other authority figures. See Anger—Aggressive & Rebellious Behavior, Chapter 32.

Emotional distance is created

Let's say you have a boss who controls you by fear (if you aren't on time, you'll be fired). He pays more attention to your failures and mistakes than to your successes and accomplishments. Whenever he comes around, you know he's going to criticize your work. You often feel he unjustly disciplines and reprimands you.

How would you feel toward this person? Would you feel close to him? Would he become your friend? Would you feel secure and comfortable when he's around? You probably wouldn't want anything to do with him. You certainly wouldn't want to socialize with him or take him on a fishing trip with you.

When punishment is primarily used to discipline, children often feel emotionally remote from their parents. You don't feel close to people you fear or whom you feel give you more negative attention than positive recognition. In this situation, a significant amount of emotional distance is created between the child and parent. This may result in a lack of verbal interaction (only talking to the parent when necessary) or withdrawal (spending more time alone, minimizing contact with the family). A close emotional relationship will fail to develop.

Escape/avoidance behavior may develop

We all tend to avoid situations that produce negative attention. What would you do if every time you made gravy it turned out badly and you received a great deal of criticism and negative attention? Would you run home every day to cook it? No, you would avoid it. Suppose every time you went by a friend's house, he told you everything you were doing wrong and spent 3 hours talking about your failures but devoted only 10 minutes to your accomplishments. How often would you want to go by his house? Probably once every 6 years.

Children often show the same feelings and behavior when punishment is used as the main method of discipline. When fear and negative attention are primarily used in discipline, avoidance and escape behavior develops. If every time a child cuts the grass all his mistakes are pointed out, he'll learn to avoid grass cutting. If a child encounters only hollering, fighting or negative attention every time he sits down to do his homework, he won't want to do homework.

Lying, manipulating and running away from home are avoidance behaviors learned by children who experience these situations. You hear a lamp fall off the table and break.

Your youngest child is in the back room, and this is where the lamp was broken. You go into the back room and say, "Did you break that lamp? What happened?"

The child knows if he admits to the behavior he'll get punished, receive lecture No. 26 or get a great deal of negative attention. So he says, "I was watching TV, and a band of gypsies came through the house and knocked over the lamp. I don't know where they went after that. That's how it was broken." When you see a child not telling the truth, trying to manipulate his parent or using the ultimate escape behavior, which is running away, look at the consequence being used. If punishment/negative attention is the main method of discipline, it may be the cause. See Chapter 46, I'm Running Away!

Punishment doesn't work with some personality types

Reward must be individualized. Some types of reward work with some children but not with others. The same is true for punishment. For some personality types, punishment is sufficient to control behavior. But for others, punishment doesn't work at all, or it only works for short periods of time.

Let us take the example of two children, Alan and Jason, going to rob a bank. I picked robbing a bank because it serves as a good example, but any type of inappropriate behavior could have been used. Alan is getting ready to rob the bank and is thinking, "If I rob the bank, I might get caught and be sent to prison. I won't be able to watch TV, play with my friends or go outside."

On the other hand, Jason is thinking, "I'm going to rob that bank and get some money. Then I'll buy a motorcycle, candy and toys."

Here we have two children getting ready to engage in the same behavior, but the motivations are entirely different. For Alan, whether or not he robs the bank depends on what will happen to him—negative consequences. However, Jason's behavior is motivated only by pleasure and by what he will gain from the behavior. Alan, who is concerned about negative consequences, can be controlled by punishment. But the pleasure-oriented Jason *cannot* be controlled by punishment. Either the money has to be taken out of the bank so the behavior is not pleasurable anymore or not robbing the bank has to become more pleasurable than robbing the bank.

It has been estimated that 30 to 40% of the children in the United States have Jason's personality type. They are more concerned with the pleasure they receive from their behavior than with the negative consequences or punishment they receive. It often appears they act before thinking and don't profit from past punishing experiences. Being caught or punished only temporarily affects their behavior.

These children also show the characteristics of a skilled manipulator or con artist. They often tell you what they think you want to hear but will turn around and do exactly what they please. It is estimated that 3 or 4 children out of 10 will not respond to punishment. Using this type of consequence to prevent certain behavior is ineffective and proves very frustrating to the parents. Other consequences (rewarding and ignoring) must be used to discipline these children. See Chapter 60, Stubborn, Strong-Willed, Pleasure-Oriented Children and Chapter 37, Con Artist—Manipulative Children.

Some develop personality and emotional problems

All children are individuals, and their responses to punishment vary. Some children comply; others become angry and rebel. Others may withdraw, bottle up emotions and become nervous and feel guilty. Some of these behavior types are discussed in subsequent chapters.

One of the primary types of punishment most parents use involves verbal negative attention—hollering, screaming, criticizing and name calling. When used frequently, this type of punishment interferes with healthy personality development. It is usually a very ineffective method of discipline.

Hollering and screaming only create an emotional distance between parent and child and upset both. Criticism ("Your brother can do that better than you. You never can do anything right.") and name calling ("You're stupid.") only make the child feel badly about himself. Controlling children by guilt ("I cook, take care of you, wash your clothes. Why aren't you good in school? I bought you that bike and took you out to eat, but you still won't listen.") or fear ("If you don't straighten up, I'll put you in a home. If you and your sister don't stop fighting, I'm going to leave and let you all take care of yourselves.") only serves to develop unhealthy emotions and feelings in children.

This type of punishment is very ineffective and should not be used because personality and emotional problems are apt to develop.

Model behavior develops until . . .

Many times I hear, "My child didn't give me any problems until recently. He was a model child. But now he won't listen and does just the opposite of what I tell him. Generally I have a hard time controlling him. When he was little, he did exactly what we told him and almost never objected to what we said. It's a different story now, and it seems like he won't listen to anything we say."

When punishment is the main method of discipline, children with certain personalities often develop model behavior when young. It seems these young children are too good. They always listen and never give their parents any trouble. However, between 11 and 14 years of age, they reverse their former behavior. It seems as if the anger that has been developing in them for years suddenly emerges. It is primarily expressed through the passive-aggressive methods described above. This type of personality often fools parents who mainly use punishment because the child behaves so well when young. This model behavior is temporary.

Different behaviors receive same type of punishment

Parents often overuse a certain type of punishment, and it loses its effectiveness as a motivator. A child may have to go to his room for being sassy, hitting his brother, not picking up his toys or coming home late. Another child may receive a spanking for not being good at school, talking back to his mother, fighting, or not cleaning his room. Hollering is probably the most overused punishment because it's used for hundreds of different behavior patterns. When this happens, the punishment becomes a very ineffective form of discipline.

The following example shows how children feel and respond in this situation. Let's say you really like to go out and eat seafood. I tell you, "If you'll help me paint my house, I'll buy a seafood dinner tonight." You'll probably help me because the seafood is a good motivator. However, if you have eaten seafood every day for 2 weeks and I try to motivate you with the same consequence, I'll probably be unsuccessful.

The same thing happens when you use one form of punishment for many different behaviors. The negative consequence is no longer important to the child, and it loses its effectiveness as a motivator. Determine a specific punishment for specific misbehavior. A child will be sent to his room for being sassy or having temper tantrums but for nothing else. Loss of TV time could be reserved for teasing a brother but for no other misbehavior and so forth.

Punishment only temporarily changes behavior

Some people disagree on this point, but many experiments prove punishment does not result in a permanent or long-term change in a behavior pattern. The effects of punishment are only temporary. And after a period of time, the punished behavior reappears. This is the reason some children show good behavior or a period of control after punishment that lasts only for a few days or, with some children, only a couple of minutes. When *punishment* is used as the primary method of control, something like the following situation occurs.

I tell you I'm going to drop by your house in 10 minutes to have a cup of coffee. You look around and see your house is a mess. You want it to look nice when I come over, so you quickly make the house presentable. Things are stuffed in the closet, thrown behind the sofa or put under chairs. Now the house looks OK, but have you really changed anything? No, you've just rearranged things. Eventually, you'll have to go back and put everything in its proper place. This is how punishment often works. It only changes behavior on the surface— like sweeping dirt under the carpet.

When *reward* is used, the behavior may not be changed as quickly, but the improvement will be long-lasting. Reward has the same effect as putting a few things where they belong. Although the house won't look as clean immediately, eventually it would be permanently changed. You won't have to go back and put things away because the situation would have been permanently changed.

With punishment, you can only expect behavior to be

modified for short periods of time. After awhile, it will reappear and have to be dealt with again. The best way to use punishment is to sandwich it between rewards. I discuss this in further detail in another section of this chapter.

Punishment and negative attention may maintain certain behaviors

A phrase often overused in analyzing child behavior is, "He's doing that to get attention." While "getting attention" is frequently used inaccurately to explain certain behavior in children, this statement is sometimes accurate. Some children often misbehave to get negative attention because this is better than no attention at all. Positive attention is very scarce in some families, so children seek whatever type of attention they can provoke.

In other situations, children behave in certain ways to get a reaction from their parents. Whining, complaining, stubbornness and similar behavior is often used by children to get a parent nervous, upset or frustrated so the child can get his or her own way.

Your child asks, "Can I go outside and play?" You tell him no. Then the child starts complaining, whining and hitting his sister. After a few minutes of this disruption, you become agitated and nervous. You eventually say, "Go outside and play. I'll call you when it's time to eat."

Children often behave in certain ways to get attention as a method of expressing their anger and as a way to get back at you. You tell your child, "Go to your room. You're punished."

Now he's angry. He doesn't want to go to his room, and he resents what you've done. What can he do? He can't punch you in the nose so he starts mumbling under his breath. He says things like, "You're mean. You like my brother better than me. I hate you. I'd rather live at Ted's house."

What do you do? You start to get upset and yell, "What are you saying? Speak up. If I hear that again you'll stay in your room longer."

What's happened? You've given the behavior a great deal of attention. This is often sufficient to maintain the child's actions.

In the situation described above, another problem develops. You wind up punishing the child because of his reaction to the punishment. Then you punish him *again* because of his misbehavior. Now he has to stay in his room for 4 hours instead of 15 minutes. Maybe both of you have forgotten what he was sent to his room for in the first place! The punishment snowballs, and the reason for the initial discipline is lost.

Misbehaving or behaving to get attention is usually not consciously planned by the child. One method of dealing with this type of behavior is by ignoring it. This method of discipline is discussed in Chapter 9, Ignoring Specific Behavior.

Punishment may not offset reward or pleasure from misbehavior

Your child comes up to you and says, "I'm hungry. Can I have something to eat?"

You say "No, we're going to eat dinner in 20 minutes. If you eat something now, you'll ruin your appetite."

After you leave the kitchen, the child grabs a bag of cookies and goes into the back room to eat them. About 15 minutes and 20 cookies later, you catch her with the goods and punish her for not listening and being sneaky. However, the behavior for which the child has been punished received a great deal of reward, and the punishment will not offset the pleasure.

Another example is a child who has been told to come home at a certain time. He and his friends spend all afternoon building a bicycle jump. He knows it's time to come home, but he stays another 30 minutes to make some jumps with his bike. He comes home late and is punished, but the punishment hardly offsets the enjoyment he derived from his misbehavior.

One problem with punishment is in some situations the behavior being punished has received a significant reward. If punishment is used as the main method of discipline, it probably won't work or will have to be used extensively to counter the effects of the reward and pleasure received from the misbehavior. This is one reason punishment works more effectively when sandwiched between rewards. In the above example, reward for appropriate behavior would produce better results than punishment for not listening.

Parents and Punishment

You serve as models for your children's behavior

Children learn behavior by observing other people. This is called the *modeling theory of learning* and is the basis for not showing certain programs on TV during prime time or family viewing hours. Children exposed to certain behavior may imitate it and may incorporate it into their patterns of dealing with conflicts, solving problems and interacting with others.

Whether a child models or imitates a certain way of responding depends on two general factors. First, it depends on how similarly the model resembles the child. Secondly, it depends on how significant the child considers the model. As parents, you are the most significant people in your children's early lives. You serve as very powerful models from which behavior is learned. Your children learn many behavior patterns just by observing how you deal with certain situations, conflicts and problems.

Many times I hear a parent say, "My daughter acts just like her mother when she gets mad."

"I get nervous very easily, and so do my children."

"My son's fears are similar to mine."

Then I hear, "He must have inherited that way of acting." For the most part, children are not born with these behavior patterns. They are learned from models.

If a child sees his father throw things when he's angry or deal with conflicts by screaming and hollering, it's highly probable this child will adopt these patterns of responding when faced with similar situations. If a mother is afraid of storms, her child may learn this fear. Psychologists have found a large percentage of parents who physically abuse their children were abused themselves as children.

If you deal with conflicts by hollering, arguing and screaming at one another, your child may be learning to deal with his siblings or peers in a similar way. This brings us to an important point regarding physical punishment (spanking or threats involving control by aggression or force). If I encounter a child in my office whose primary problem involves fighting, hitting other children, losing his temper or trying to control others by physical means, I ask the parents, "How is he disciplined? If he doesn't want to do something, how can you get him to do it?"

The usual answers I get in 9 out of 10 situations include:

"I give him a spanking."

"I tell him if he doesn't behave or do what I want, I'll go get the belt."

"I threaten him with a beating."

The child who is controlled by physical means or threats of aggression learns if people do not do what he wants, he should be aggressive and threaten them with force.

So when another child cuts in front of him in line at school, he shoves or hits him. If a child takes his pencil and won't give it back, a fight will start. The child's primary method of problem-solving involves physical means, force and threats of aggression because he has modeled his behavior on the significant people in his life, his parents.

The mother of a 3-year-old told me, "Every time I slap my child for doing something bad, he hits me back. Lately he's been hitting me whenever he doesn't get his way. He shouldn't hit his mother. What can I do to stop this?"

My answer was very simple. "Stop hitting him!"

If a child lives with hostility, he learns to fight. If he lives with criticism, he learns to condemn. If punishment is used as the main disciplinary tactic, your child may be learning and adopting these methods to control others—peers, authority figures, siblings and eventually his or her own children.

Punishment may make you feel guilty and unfair

Guilt often results if punishment is administered in a random fashion. The type of punishment is decided on *after* the child misbehaves and is not spelled out ahead of time.

A brother and sister are sitting in the room watching TV, and they are fighting. The mother has calmly told them 10 times to quiet down and stop arguing, but it doesn't stop them. Finally, she starts screaming and eventually sends both of them to their rooms for the night. Now they will miss a special program on TV. The mother, sitting in the quiet of the back room, starts thinking, "Maybe I was too hard on them. I should not have done all that screaming. They were so good all day. They've been talking about the TV program all afternoon, and now I've made them miss it."

Guilt starts to develop, and the mother feels responsible for what has happened to the children. To undo the wrong she has done and to feel better, she says, "Come on out of your room. You can watch TV if you're good."

Administering and reacting to punishment in this way results in a very inconsistent approach to child management. Consistency is of major importance to behavior change and management. The approach described above is certain to result in ineffective discipline and continued misbehavior.

Types of Punishment

Most parents tend to be punishers. That is, attention to misbehaviors, mistakes and failures are usually employed as primary disciplinary tactics. The types of punishment used by most parents can be grouped into six general areas. Some are effective, while others should be used sparingly or avoided altogether.

Response-cost is a very effective form of punishment. It is a system in which the child is fined and loses privileges or desired activities for misbehavior. "When you do something bad, it's going to cost you something." This is used frequently in our daily lives. If you get a speeding ticket, you have to pay a fine. When your income tax is late, you are assessed a penalty.

A good example of a response-cost system can be seen when allowance is based on daily chores. Let's say a child has to feed the pet each day and put out the garbage 5 times a week. For these chores, he gets an allowance of $3 each week. He has to perform 12 tasks each week to earn his full allowance (25¢ a task). A record on a calendar or a chart of his performance is kept. Each time he performs the required duty without being told, he earns 25¢ toward his weekly allowance. However, if the task is not performed by a certain time and the child has to be reminded, he loses 25¢. It is totally up to the child whether he earns nothing or his full allowance each week. This is similar to the situation most of us face each day. We can go to work and be paid or stay home and receive nothing.

I have used loss of money as a punishment because a

response-cost system can be described easily this way. However, the fine or loss could really be any privilege or activity. You may have a child who loves to watch TV but is very sassy. You can set up a response-cost system to modify the sassiness by using loss of TV time as the fine for this behavior. A chart can be constructed and put in the kitchen to keep a tally of the number of times a day the sassiness appears. (Setting up behavioral charts is discussed in detail in Chapter 10.)

The child is told, "Each time you are sassy (you will specifically explain what you mean by sassiness), I'm going to put a mark on this chart. At the end of the day, for each mark you have you will lose 10 minutes of TV time. How much TV you watch each night is totally up to you and how well you can control your sassiness."

Another example is a child who has trouble coming home on time. He is always late or never comes inside when he's called. A response-cost system can be employed to change this behavior. The child is told, "For every minute you're late or don't come inside when I call you, you'll lose a minute of play time (TV time, reading time at night or something similar could be used) the next day." If the child is supposed to be home each day at 5 pm but he comes home 30 minutes late today, then tomorrow he will be required to be home at 4:30.

Any type of activity, privilege or event that is important to the child can be used as the fine in a response-cost system of punishment. However, several points must be kept in mind when using this system.

Define behavior—Clearly define the behavior that will be fined and exactly what failure will cost the child.

Use positive consequences and rewards—This type of system works best when positive consequences and rewards are also used.

Don't set up a debit system—Do not set up a system in which the child will owe you, or the loss will be unrealistic. If a child gets $3.00 a week allowance and the parent says, "Each time you're sassy you will lose 25¢ of your allowance," the child may have a *minus* allowance at the end of the week and owe the parent $5.00.

Or a parent may tell a child, "Each time you hit your

brother, you'll have to go to bed 10 minutes early." If the child hits his brother enough, he may wind up going to bed when he comes home from school! This type of response-cost system is sure to fail.

Assess fines—Fines must be consistently assessed whenever the misbehavior occurs.

Time out

This is an effective form of punishment used frequently by parents. A child going to his room or standing in the corner are examples of time out. There are two general ways to use this procedure.

With the first method, a time-out area is designated (a room, a corner, the hall). The child is sent there for a particular misbehavior. Every time a child whines, he is sent to the time-out area. This punishment can be used for temper tantrums, sassiness, fighting between siblings and other behaviors.

The second method involves removing a child from a pleasurable activity. A child may enjoy swimming but keeps going into the deep end of the pool. Using time out, the parent tells the child, "If you go in the deep end again, you'll have to get out of the pool for 5 minutes."

In another situation, two brothers are watching cartoons on Saturday morning. You know they love the cartoons, but they constantly argue and fight with one another. You might tell them, "If I hear any fighting, the TV will be turned off for 5 minutes." The activity from which the child is removed can be anything that is important to him (riding his bike, watching TV, playing with his friends).

Several things must be kept in mind to make the time-out technique successful. It must be very clear what the child must do to be punished. The misbehavior has to be defined and spelled out. You may say, "I don't want to hear or see any more fighting. By that I mean hitting each other, name calling or teasing." Hearing this, the child knows exactly what behavior will be followed by time out.

Some type of warning should also be given.

"The next time I see you do that, you'll have to go to your room."

"I'm going to count to 3, and if the fighting doesn't stop, the TV will be turned off."

The child should know how long he will be in time out or what he must do to get out of the time-out area. "Go to your room for 5 minutes. I'm going to set the timer on the stove, and when the bell rings, you can come out."

Or a child who is having a temper tantrum or being sassy might be told, "Go to your room. When you calm down and can talk to me in a normal tone, you can come out."

The time-out procedure must be used consistently and may have to be employed several times to control the behavior. If your children are watching cartoons and fighting, you may have to turn the TV off for 5 minutes 7 or 8 times during the morning.

Time out should be given in a very matter-of-fact way without displays of emotion. When bringing the child to time out or when he is in the time-out area, don't lecture, fuss, scold, get upset or excited, nag or apologize.

Not receiving reward

When a reward system is used and the child does not receive the positive consequence, it can be viewed as a type of punishment. Often when I am designing a technique using reward to change a behavior, parents ask me, "If he doesn't do what we want him to do, how do we punish him?"

My answer is, "You don't have to punish him. Not receiving the reward can serve as the consequence." Your child teases his sister and eventually makes her whine and cry. He loves to stay up past his bedtime and is told, "If you and your sister get along from dinner to bedtime, you can stay up 30 minutes past your bedtime." When he doesn't comply, he doesn't necessarily have to be punished. Not receiving the reward can be considered as the punishment and is often an effective disciplinary tactic.

Some parents have a hard time accepting this and feel they need to punish the misbehavior in addition to withholding the reward. This is not always necessary. This is similar to the way most of us are disciplined regarding attendance at work. If you go to work, you are paid. If you stay home, you receive less on payday. We are not punished for missing work. We just do not receive the reward, and this is sufficient to keep most of us going to work on a regular basis.

Verbal punishment

Hollering, criticizing, name calling and lecturing, as well as telling the child things to make him feel guilty, embarrassed or fearful, fall into this category. This is a very ineffective form of punishment because some children totally ignore their parent's ranting and raving. The hollering goes in one ear and out the other.

Other children develop emotional difficulties or behavioral problems as a result of verbal punishment. Some children develop resentment and anger toward their parents when this is used, while others become emotionally distant.

Earlier in this chapter, I discussed problems that may occur when punishment is used as the main form of discipline. Most of the potential problems described can occur when verbal punishment is used frequently. I will not restate the behavioral and emotional difficulties that can occur, but negative verbal discipline must be avoided.

Physical punishment

Spanking and hitting children fall into this category. I personally feel there are many other forms of discipline that can be used with children. Use physical punishment very, very sparingly. Parents serve as primary models for child behavior, and children who are physically punished often learn aggressive methods to control others. Other children withdraw, become angry, develop rebellious tendencies or show a variety of emotional and behavioral difficulties.

If and when physical punishment is used, use it infrequently and only for certain specific behavior. A child should not get a spanking for hitting his sister, getting a detention, coming home late, breaking a toy or 40 other different misbehavior types. Reserve spanking for certain behavior.

I also believe physical punishment is more effective when used with younger children (under 4 years). A small child may get a spanking for crossing the street unattended or for fooling with an electrical outlet. But it should not be used for hundreds of different behavior lapses ranging from wetting his pants to hitting his baby sister. Some parents should not use physical punishment because it does not fit their personalities. The spanking upsets them more than it does the child—they feel guilty, mean, unfair and brutal.

Control by force or intimidation

This is similar to physical punishment, but the parent doesn't have to touch the child. "I'm going to get the belt if you don't pick up your toys." The child runs and cleans up. The control or the way we get the child to do what we want is by threats of force.

Another form is by intimidation or the fact you are bigger than the child. Because of this you can control him. People who use this type of discipline forget a child grows; he or she will soon be as big as you. When the child is in adolescence, you need more appropriate control than ever.

If this is the main method used on the child, you'll lose your control when you need it the most. In addition, these techniques teach the child to deal with other children by using force, intimidation and control by overpowering.

Punishment: Things to Consider

Punishment is a consequence that can be used to change behavior. However, keep several things in mind to make punishment work effectively and to minimize the occurrence of problems.

Use other consequences

Three major consequences can be used in disciplining children. Punishment is more effective when *ignoring* and especially *rewarding* are also used. When punishment is used as the main method of control, it is less effective than when it is used in conjunction with reward. Reward and ignoring should be used about 60 to 70% of the time, with punishment being used 30 to 40% of the time. Time-out and response-cost punishment are more effective if the child is earning rewards and privileges for other acceptable behavior.

It is often necessary to point out a child's mistakes or failures, especially when you're teaching him new behaviors. But if only that is done, your correction will fall on a deaf ear.

Criticism is significantly more effective when it is combined with praise and emphasis on good behavior.

You ask your child to make his bed for the first time. After he completes the task, you go in and point out all the mistakes and what he has done wrong. If bed making becomes a negative experience, the child will avoid the behavior. Your attempts to teach this task are minimized. Instead, go in after he makes the bed and point out all his successes and the positive points of making the bed. You can sneak in a little criticism. Your child is more apt to learn and incorporate your correction into his next attempt at bed making. The more reward, praise and positive attention are used, the more effective the punishment system will be.

Define behavior and consequences

Avoid ambiguous statements, such as "be good." State exactly what you mean by being good. "We're going to the store, and I want you to stay by me and not run all over."

Avoid random punishment. Don't decide the punishment *after* the behavior; spell out the negative consequence along with the rule *before* the behavior occurs. "We're going to the store. If you stay by me, you can go outside and play when we get home. If you run all over the store and don't listen to me, you'll have to stay inside when we get home."

Determine length of punishment

Parents often say, "Go to your room" or "You can't ride your bike" or something similar.

The child asks, "For how long?"

The parent responds, "When I decide to let you out" or "When I think you deserve to ride your bike."

This is not a productive situation. When a child is punished, he should know for how long and what he has to do to get out of the punishment. "Go to your room for 5 minutes. If you leave your bike in front of the house, you won't be able to ride it tomorrow."

"Go to your room. When you calm down, you can come out."

"You can start going out to play after school when you bring home all your books."

These statements clearly identify what the child must do to avoid punishment.

Clearly define the behavior to be punished, state the negative consequence ahead of time with the rule and tell the child how long he will be punished and/or what behaviors he must show to get out of the punishment.

Use behavior to set rule

Try to avoid punishing a behavior the first time it appears, but use it to set a rule. You can't always do this, but the principle can be employed in most situations.

Recently, I went into my back yard and found some of my tools rusting in the grass. I became angry and asked my two sons who did it. They both confessed. I felt like setting down some type of punishment for this behavior. However, punishment in this situation would have been ineffective because this was a new behavior whose consequences had not been spelled out ahead of time.

A better way to deal with this situation would be to use it to set the ground rules. "I don't want you going into the garage and playing with my tools or leaving them outside. The next time this happens, you won't be able to watch TV that night."

Use warnings or signals

In an earlier chapter, I used the example of a child who had to be told 37 times to pick up his toys. He was told over and over again. With each request the mother's voice got louder and louder. Eventually her face turned red, then she began hollering and screaming. Only then did the child run to pick up his toys. The child was responding to signals. He sat around and waited for the signal that came immediately before the negative consequences; then he responded. He knew hollering immediately preceded spanking or other punishment. When these signals appeared, he performed the desired behavior to avoid the negative consequence.

Most parents use signals or warnings, but often they involve actions like those above (hollering, getting the belt, getting upset). Using appropriate signals and warnings can make things run more smoothly and eliminate a significant amount of distress at home.

Events in the environment can be made to serve as signals. "I want the garbage put out after we eat dinner."

"The toys have to be picked up before this TV program is over."

"Come home when the street lights come on."

"I want your room clean by 7 pm."

You can let events or clues in the environment warn the child rather than your voice.

Counting to 3, giving 3 warnings, holding up 1 finger at a time, saying, "The next time that happens" or some other verbal statement said in a very matter-of-fact way can also serve as effective signals.

For example, every time the phone rings and the mother starts talking, her young child begins a series of interruptions. "Let me talk. Where's my ball? I'm thirsty." The conversation is interrupted a number of times, and the mother loses patience. The mother could use hand signals to deal with the behavior. The rules, behavioral expectations and consequences would be set up ahead of time and the child told, "When the phone rings, I don't want you to interrupt me. (Explain what this means to the child). Each time you interrupt me, I'm going to hold up a finger. If I get to 3 fingers, you'll have to go to your room for 5 minutes" or some similar punishment.

Reward can also be used. "If I don't get to three warnings, I'll read you a story" or some similar reward.

Pennies, pencils or some other object could be placed on a table to serve as signals. The child is told, "Each time you interrupt me, I'm going to take a penny off the table. When there are no pennies left, you'll have to go to your room for 5 minutes."

You must be consistent when using this type of warning system and give the third or final warning when appropriate. You can't say, "I'm going to count to 3. 1. 2 . . . 2 . . . 2," but 3 never comes. You can't tell the child, "The next time you do that, this is going to happen," but 3 months later you're still saying "The next time . . ." and the consequence of the misbehavior never occurs.

Using signals to create a buffer period may also serve as a way to reduce some behavior problems. Suppose you're watching a good suspense movie on TV. It's almost over. You're about to find out who is guilty of the murder, and your husband asks you to go to the kitchen and get him a drink. What would you tell him? You'd reply, "Wait till this program's over" because you're involved in what's happening or you have waited 2 hours for this moment. You wouldn't like this sort of interruption, but we do this to our children frequently. Your child is outside playing baseball. It's almost his turn to bat when you stick your head out the door and say, "Come in; it's time to eat." You'll probably get a great deal of resistance.

You can avoid this by giving the child a 5-minute warning. A little while before it's time to come in, call him and say, "I'm going to call you in 5 minutes to come in. Start getting ready. The next time I call, you must come in."

Sometimes it isn't wise to demand a child do what you expect at that minute. Giving him a signal as a buffer period may reduce some of the resistance.

"I want those toys picked up by the time this program's over."

"We're going to do this 3 more times, then we'll stop."

Individualize punishment

When deciding on a negative consequence, the interests, values and preferences of each child must be considered. What may be punishment for one child may not be punishment for another child. For some children, going to their room is a major punishment; others couldn't care less. You may tell your child, "If you don't get dressed on time for school, you'll miss the bus and won't be able to go to school." Some children would consider this a negative consequence, while others would see it as a reward. What may work effectively on a child's sister may not work with him. In determining a punishment, consider what is important to the child. The individualization of consequences is discussed in detail in Chapter 7, Reward.

Punish behavior, not the child

When you use punishment, comment on the *behavior* not on the child as an individual. If a child fails a test in school, it doesn't mean he's stupid (a statement concerning a child's self-image). It means he did not adequately study for the test. If a child hits his brother, he isn't necessarily a mean person. However, this type of behavior can't be tolerated.

Stay calm when punishing

When punishment is administered, try to remain calm. Treat the behavior being dealt with in a matter-of-fact fashion. If a child loses a privilege (response-cost) or is put in a time-out area, avoid nagging, scolding and lecturing.

Have specific punishments for specific behaviors. One of the problems with punishment is that overuse diminishes its effectiveness. The main reason is parents use the same negative consequence for many different behaviors. A child may be sent to his room for hitting his sister, getting bad grades, coming home late, being sassy and for many other different things. When this occurs, the punishment (going to your room, in this example) loses its effectiveness as a motivator for behavioral change.

When using negative consequences, use specific punishments for specific behaviors and nothing else. Use loss of TV time only when certain behavior is seen (homework isn't done, sassiness) and not for everything under the sun. Relate physical punishment or confinement only to specific actions. By doing this, you can avoid the problems that occur when negative consequences are overused.

Punishment should occur immediately

The importance or effectiveness of punishment is primarily determined by how closely it follows the behavior you're trying to control and not by its severity, length or harshness. The statement, "Make the punishment fit the crime" isn't always true. Punishment should occur as soon as possible after the misbehavior.

Negative consequences that immediately follow undesirable behavior have the most impact and produce the most change. Avoid delaying punishment. Let's say that right after school a brother and sister get into a terrible fight. You come in and separate the children, saying, "Wait till Dad gets home. You'll both be punished." About 3 hours later, the children are playing together and having a good time. The father comes home and hears about the incident that occurred earlier. He goes in, gives the children a lecture and administers a punishment. What behavior is most affected by the punishment? That which occurred immediately before the negative consequence—playing together cooperatively.

A child's perception of time is different from yours. A 6-year-old may perceive 15 minutes as we perceive 2 hours. If the consequence is too far removed from the behavior, the child may not remember *why* he is being punished. Avoid delays in punishing when possible. This can't always be done but by using behavior charts described in Chapter 10, punishment can be delivered immediately in many situations.

Administering punishment

How much punishment should be given? This is a question I am frequently asked. Parents really mean different things.

"How much should I take away?"

"How severe or harsh should the punishment be?"

"Should I take him off the baseball team or merely not let him ride his bike?"

These are difficult questions to answer mainly because much depends on the individual child. But several points can be made regarding this concept.

One of the main factors that control or change behavior is not large or severe consequences that occur every now and then, but the small consequences that occur and follow a misbehavior *each time* it happens. Why do you avoid touching fire? Probably *not* because you think you'll die, get third-degree burns or have to be hospitalized. The main reason you avoid it because every time you touch fire or something hot, it hurts. It's the little consequence that occurs each time you perform this action that prevents the behavior, *not* the severity or amount of the negative consequence.

Let's say your child isn't doing all his homework because he forgets some of his books at school. You have told him for 3 weeks to bring all his books home, but it isn't working. You finally reach the end of your rope and tell him, "Unless you bring all your books home, I'll have to take you off the football team." This is a pretty significant punishment because this child lives for football. However, the behavior doesn't change, and he is not allowed to play on the team.

Usually in cases of severe punishment, the child feels, "What's the use?" In this example, he probably wouldn't bring home any books at all after being punished this way.

A better way to handle this same situation is to identify something that is important to the child to be withheld each time books are left at school. Suppose you are using a response-cost system. This child loves to watch TV—the cost could be any other privilege that is important to him. He is told, "Every time you don't bring all your books home, you lose your TV privileges for that night. If you want to watch TV, all you have to do is bring your books home."

Each time he fails to do as told, this consequence follows. Using negative consequence in the latter fashion has a greater impact on eliminating undesirable behavior than the former extreme method.

How long should punishment last?

How long do you punish? This frequently asked question involves principles similar to those discussed above. It mainly involves response-cost and time-out types of punishment. The closer the punishment occurs to the inappropriate behavior, the greater the effect.

I'm sure you have experienced something like this. A child misbehaves and is sent to his room for an hour. He goes to his room, and for the first 5 or 10 minutes lies on his bed and pouts, complains, cries or makes statements about how unfair and mean you are. After a short period of time, he gets a toy and starts playing with it, reads a book, counts the dots on the ceiling or occupies himself in some way. After a brief period of time, it appears the punishment doesn't bother him.

Or you take your child's bike away for 2 weeks for some undesirable behavior. During the first day or so, the child is concerned about the punishment. She doesn't like what has happened and asks to ride her bike. After the brief period at the beginning of the punishment, it seems as if she could care less about not being able to ride her bike.

In both of these examples, the probable reason the child developed the I-don't-care attitude about the punishment was because it was too long. Negative consequences do not have to last a long time to work. The most effective part of any form of negative consequence occurs in the *beginning*.

Let's look at the example of sending a child to his room for 1 hour for being sassy. From the above chart, you can see the first 10 minutes have a 90% effect on the sassiness, the second 10-minute period has an 8% effect and the third 10-minute period has a 2% effect. Punishment has *no* impact on behavior during the remaining three 10-minute blocks.

Effect on behavior	90%	8%	2%	0%	0%	0%
Time in Room	10 min.	20 min.	30 min.	40 min.	50 min.	60 min.

The latter part of the punishment is very ineffective. During that time the child occupies himself with other things or develops anger and resentment toward the parent for placing him in this situation.

Rather than sending your child to his room for an hour, it is more effective and behavioral change will occur more rapidly if he is sent to his room for 10 minutes six different times. If he's sassy, he goes to his room for 10 minutes then comes out. When this behavior occurs again, the same consequence occurs. The same principles apply in the example of taking a child's bike away for 2 weeks. Rather than taking the privilege away one time for 14 days, it is better to restrict the child one day 14 times.

All people have different psychological time clocks. They differ in how accurately they estimate time. The same is true for children; that's why it is difficult to answer the question, "How long to punish?" an individual child. A child's estimate of time is *vastly different* from yours. A 6-year-old may perceive the passage of 15 minutes as the same amount of time an adult perceives the passage of 2 hours. Punishing this child for 1 hour is equivalent to punishing an adult for 8 hours. As children get older, their perception of time gradually approximates that of an adult. For some small children, a 30-second time-out punishment is sufficient, while for older children 20 minutes may be necessary.

A good rule of thumb to keep in mind when trying to determine how long to punish your child is to watch him closely to see how he reacts. Observe how long it takes before he occupies himself with something else and appears unconcerned about the punishment. In sending a child to his room for an hour, we observed whining, complaining, crying or similar behavior during the first 10 minutes. But there was hardly any reaction during the remaining 50 minutes.

This gives us some idea of how long to punish the next time—10 minutes. For the child who had his bike taken away for 2 weeks, we see punishment affected him the first day but apparently had little impact on his attitude after that. One day is more appropriate the next time this punishment is used.

Punishment does not have to be severe, harsh or long to work. Its effectiveness is primarily determined by how closely it follows the behavior you are trying to change and how frequently it occurs.

9

Ignoring Specific Behavior

Some behavior in children exists because of the reaction given to it by their parents. Some kids know whining, complaining, pouting, sassiness, temper outbursts or crying get a reaction from their parents. Or it gets them their way. Such behavior is often continued because of the consequences a child receives for his or her behavior.

All behavior exists for a reason. To eliminate some types of behavior, it is necessary to remove the consequence (parents hollering, getting upset, becoming nervous). It's necessary to *ignore* the behavior. Ignoring undesirable actions is a very powerful method of discipline, but it is not often used effectively by most parents.

What to Ignore

Ignoring changes or eliminates only certain behavior. For other kinds of behavior, it has no effect. The obvious question is, "What should be ignored?" Do *not* ignore behavior that is task-oriented, such as actions that perform a duty, disrupt the activities of others or lead to injury of others or damage to property. Do *not* ignore not making the bed, not taking a bath, not doing homework, not picking up the room, hitting a sister, breaking a glass or similar behavior. Use positive or negative consequences to deal with task-oriented behavior.

To determine what behavior to ignore, analyze the action and ask, "What is my child getting out of the behavior?" If your answer includes the following, consider ignoring the behavior all together.

"He's getting me upset."

"He's making me holler."

"I get nervous."

"We get into a power struggle or screaming match."

"I cry or leave him alone."

"I give in to him."

"He gets his way."

Ignoring can be very effective in changing or eliminating behavior that primarily serves the purpose of getting a reaction from you or getting the child what he wants.

Let's say you ask your child to put out the garbage. While he's doing what you requested, he starts mumbling under his breath. You can't understand most of it, but every now and then you hear something like, "They think I'm a slave around here. They always make me do stuff. My brother never has to do anything."

Although your son is putting out the garbage like you asked, you start reacting to the mumbling. "Speak up. What are you saying? You'd better cut that out. Stop mumbling." Each time you speak, your voice gets louder. You may become more upset.

Your child probably continues mumbling because of your reaction to it. Ignore it.

A similar situation occurs when you send your child to her room. She goes to her room and starts making noises, telling you how mean you are, hitting the wall, singing at the top of her voice or doing something else designed to provoke a reaction. If the behavior is ignored and the child doesn't get a response from you, the behavior usually disappears because it serves no purpose.

Ignore behavior that is manipulative and designed to get a child his way (whining, pouting, temper tantrums). Your child asks, "Can I go outside and play?"

It's almost time to eat so you say, "No." This brings a violent reaction from the child. He starts screaming, hollering and throwing himself on the floor. After a little while, you can't take it, so you tell him, "Go outside and play, I'll call you when it is time to eat." Children can wear you down with continuous whining or pleading and finally get their way.

How to Ignore

Ignoring the behavior described above usually produces behavioral change, but this procedure has to be used consistently. There are two ways to provide no consequences to a specific behavior in a child.

Withdraw all attention

Act as though the behavior doesn't exist or the child isn't there. Don't talk to the child. Don't give him any facial or gestural indications of disapproval. Don't mumble to yourself. Withdraw all attention. If you decide to ignore whining and the child exhibits this behavior while you're talking to someone, talk over the behavior. Turning up the TV, putting on the stereo headset, going outside to work in the garden, taking a walk or getting involved with some task are techniques you can use to help withdraw all attention from the misbehavior.

Withdraw emotional attention, but deal with behavior

With this type of ignoring, your verbal reprimands and emotional attention are eliminated. But some disciplinary action, usually time-out or response-cost punishment, is taken. The rule at your house may be, "When someone has a temper tantrum, he goes to his room. When he calms down, he can come out." When your daughter throws a temper tantrum, tell her to go to her room or take her there. Don't get upset. Don't tell her to stop. Don't threaten her with a spanking. Don't react to her misbehavior in any way other than that specified.

Sassiness may be dealt with by stating, "I won't talk to you when you are sassy." (Explain exactly what you mean by sassy.) When the child starts being sassy, ignore it and say, "When you can talk in a normal tone of voice, I'll respond to you."

Your children may like to make various noises or gestures to aggravate you. When this happens, stay calm and carry out the consequence that was previously determined. If your child makes noises that bother you, try setting up a chart in the kitchen. Tell the child, "Every time you make noises, I'm going to put an X on the chart. For every X you have, you lose 5 minutes of TV time tonight." When the child makes the noise, very calmly remind the child he has received an X and record it. You give no emotional attention or consequence to the behavior.

Things to Consider

Be consistent

Be consistent when this disciplinary consequence is chosen to deal with a certain behavior. If you choose to ignore pouting, do it *every* time the behavior occurs. You can't ignore it one time then attend to it the next. If the child gets what he wants from the behavior every now and then, it may be sufficient to sustain the behavior.

By being inconsistent, you may set up a situation for the child similar to that of a gambler. He may lose 7 or 10 times but wins once. One win is enough to keep him trying many more times.

Be sure behavior is ignored

You may think you're ignoring a behavior, but you don't totally eliminate all attention or consequences. When you ignore, be sure *all* verbal (lecturing, hollering, mumbling under your breath) and non-verbal communications (an angry expression on your face, slamming a door) are withdrawn from the child's undesirable behavior.

Behavior may get worse

Sometimes when attention or consequences that are usually given a behavior are withdrawn, the behavior gets worse or intensifies before it diminishes.

Consider a child who has temper tantrums to get his way. It usually takes a 5-minute tantrum to coerce his parents to give in to his desires. Now they have attended one of our workshops and have decided to stick to what they say and ignore the behavior.

The child comes in and asks his mother, "Can I have a soda?"

She says, "No, you've already had two."

The temper tantrum begins, and the child starts his 5-minute routine.

At the end of this period the parent has not attended to his behavior and has not given in. What's going to happen when the child doesn't receive the consequence he usually gets? The behavior intensifies. His voice may get louder. Crying may occur more frequently, and the length of the temper tantrum may increase. It may last 10, 30 or 60 minutes or until the child realizes the behavior is not going to bring him the consequence he normally receives.

The child will eventually realize the behavior is not working and the only thing the temper tantrum gets him is an upset stomach, sore throat and a headache. It serves no purpose and should stop or decrease in frequency and intensity.

Something you are familiar with can serve as an example to illustrate the points made above. Suppose you walk up to a soft-drink machine, deposit your money, make your selection and nothing happens (the machine ignores you). The usual behavior that gets you the desired consequence does not work. What would you do? You would start pressing the coin return and selection buttons. If the machine continues to ignore you, this behavior will increase in frequency. If these attempts are unsuccessful in producing the desired consequence, you may hit or kick the machine. After awhile, you might stop and rest and try it again. But this time, you won't try as hard or as long. This may be done several times, but each time the intensity and frequency of the behavior decreases. If the machine continues to ignore you and you're unsuccessful in getting the drink or your money back, you give up because they are useless. Your behavior changes. You either walk away or tell someone you lost your money.

The same thing happens when this consequence is used to deal with whining, complaining, pouting, noise making and similar behavior. The behavior intensifies and increases in frequency until the child realizes the behavior isn't serving its purpose. Then it will start to disappear.

If a child whines about 5 times a day, 10 minutes each time and is ignored, the periods of whining may increase in an effort to produce the desired result. However, if you ignore the behavior, the length of the whining periods will get shorter. The number of times the behavior occurs will decrease. The child will periodically test you to see if you will stick to your guns until he realizes the behavior is fruitless. Then he'll change his behavior, and the whining will stop.

When the behavior gets worse, continue doing the same thing. Don't give in, and don't go back to your old methods of dealing with the undesirable behavior. The increase in the inappropriate behavior should last 3 to 5 days at the most. However, in most situations, the increase in the undesirable behavior lasts only 1 or 2 days.

If the above procedures are used correctly, the most severe temper tantrums and other similar behavior can be successfully dealt with in a few days.

Other consequences may have to be used

A good rule is to ignore first when trying to change behavior. This produces successful results when the aim of behavior is to get a reaction you and get the child what he wants. In some cases, ignoring the behavior is not sufficient to change it. In these situations, positive or negative consequences must be employed when the ignored behavior does not improve.

Ignore reaction of others

When you are ignoring behavior and other people are around (at a store, company at your house), you may feel embarrassed or pressured into some action to counteract what you are trying to accomplish. Disregard the reactions of others and how you think they perceive you. Deal with your child's behavior—not other people's!

10

Using Charts to Change Behavior

A behavior chart is a formal method of keeping a record of your child's behavior. I find charts work very effectively in dealing with and changing some behaviors. This chapter outlines how and why to construct them, types of charts and things to consider when you use them.

Setting Up a Behavior Chart

Analyze behavior

The first step in developing a chart is to analyze the behavior to be increased or decreased. How frequently does it occur? Under what circumstances is the behavior seen? How long does it last? Chapter 2, Deciding Which Behavior To Change, provides a review of this procedure. It is very important to analyze the behavior because this will determine what type of chart to use.

Identify an important consequence

The next step is to select a consequence that is important to the child. Most charts are based on reward and are set up in positive terms. A behavior chart also easily lends itself to a response-cost system of discipline.

Types of Behavior Charts

The number and style of behavior charts available are limited only by your imagination. Several general types are described below. The type of chart you use is primarily determined from the information obtained when the target behavior is analyzed.

When target behavior occurs
or can occur more than once a day

Sometimes behavior to be changed is seen many times throughout the day (not listening, sassiness, temper tantrums, whining). Two options are available. One chart can be based on time or how often the behavior is seen. The other option is based on frequency or how many times a day the behavior occurs.

Suppose the target behavior is temper tantrums. You have analyzed the behavior and found it occurs on an average of 5 times a day. You decide to construct a chart by breaking the day up into time periods. The chart might look like the one below.

Chart 8
Alan's Be Good Chart

	Mon.	Tues.	Wed.	Thurs.	Fri.
Before school	X	X	★	X	★
3 to 5 o'clock	★	★	★	★	X
5 to 7 o'clock	★	★	★	★	★
7 to bedtime	★	X	★	X	★

Divide the week into days and the days into four time periods (before school, 3 to 5 pm, 5 to 7 pm, 7 pm to bedtime). A reward has been identified; 5 minutes past bedtime. Tell the child, "For each period of time you don't have a temper tantrum (explain 'tantrum' carefully), I'll put a star on your chart. When you have a temper tantrum during a period of time, I'll put an X in that block. At the end of each day, you can trade in each star you have for 5 minutes past your bedtime. Do you understand what I've said? Explain to me what I said to you in your own words." If the child understands the system, begin.

If not, explain it again.

If you have a timer on your stove or a cooking timer, set it for the specified time period. When the bell rings, calmly put an X on the chart if he has had a temper tantrum or put the X when the behavior occurs. If he has not had one, put a star on the chart, and give the child verbal or social reward (praise him for his good behavior). Then reset the timer, and follow the same procedure again.

Depending on the age of your child, the behavior you are trying to change and whether you have previously used charts, the reward can be given several ways.

Reward after each time period—When a child receives a star during a time period, he is rewarded immediately (a piece of candy, a story read to him).

Reward daily—At the end of each day, the child can trade in his stars for a reward (5 minutes past his bedtime for each star. If he has two stars, you will play a game with him).

Reward weekly—At the end of the week he can trade in his stars for a reward (12 stars earns a trip to the park, movie or whatever on Saturday or Sunday).

Reward every other week or once a month—Reward at the appropriate time if this occurs only occasionally.

The most important aspect of reward or punishment is how closely it follows the target behavior. For small children or when you start using charts with children, the time lapse before they receive the reward should be minimal. Reward them as quickly as possible.

Let's say you analyze another behavior (sassiness) and find it occurs very frequently, perhaps an average of 20 times a day. Construct a similar chart with much smaller time periods, possibly every 30 minutes.

With the chart, page 88, the child must earn more stars to receive the same reward as in Chart 1. Under this system, one star may represent 2 minutes past the child's bedtime, or he may have to earn 40 stars to get a trip to the park.

As the child starts receiving more stars each week the time periods are increased, such as every hour. As he improves, the day may be broken into 4 blocks of time as in Chart 1.

Chart 2
Alan's Be Good Chart (1st week)

	Mon.	Tues.	Wed.	Thurs.	Fri.	Sat.	Sun.
7:30 to 8:00	★	X	★				
8:00 to 8:30	X	X	★				
3:30 to 4:00	X	X	X				
4:00 to 4:30	X	★	X				
4:30 to 5:00	★	★	★				
5:00 to 5:30	X	X	★				
5:30 to 6:00	★	X	X				
6:30 to 7:00	★	★	★				
7:00 to 7:30	X	★	★				
7:30 to 8:00	★	X	★				
8:00 to 8:30	★	★	★				
8:30 to 9:00	★	★	★				

As you use the chart and the child improves, the amount of stars he must earn each week to receive the reward is increased. During the second week with Chart 1, the child has to earn 15 stars to go to the park, the third week he needs 17 stars to go to a movie and so forth.

You may analyze a behavior (not listening) and find it occurs more than once a day. You may decide to make a frequency chart based on a selected average of 10 times a day. The chart might look like the one on the next page.

The week is divided into days, and 10 circles are put on each day because not listening occurs an average of 10 times a day. Next identify an important consequence (reward or punishment).

Using a reward system, tell the child, "I'm putting 10 circles on each day of the week. Each time you do not listen (explain

Chart 3
Jeffrey's Listening Chart (1st week)

Mon.		Tues.		Wed.		Thurs.		Fri.		Sat.		Sun.	
●	●	●	●	●	★	●	●	○	○	○	○	○	○
●	●	●	●	●	★	●	●	○	○	○	○	○	○
●	●	★	★	★	★	★	★	○	○	○	○	○	○
★	★	★	★	★	★	★	★	○	○	○	○	○	○
★	★	★	★	★	★	★	★	○	○	○	○	○	○

exactly what you mean), I'm going to go to your chart and color in one of those circles."

If you use a daily reward system, tell him, "At the end of the day, we'll go to your chart and put a star on every circle that isn't colored. You can trade in your stars for the reward (which has already been determined)." If you are using a weekly reward system, tell him the same thing, but stars are traded in at the end of the week instead of daily.

Using a response-cost system of punishment, you can set up the same kind of chart (Chart 3) and do the same thing except put the stars on the chart at the end of the day. Tell the child, "I'm putting 10 circles on each day of the week. Each time you don't listen, I'm going to go to your chart and color in one of those circles."

If you use a daily punishment system, tell him, "At the end of the day, we'll go to your chart and count the colored circles. For each colored circle, you will lose 10 minutes of TV time" or whatever cost has been predetermined.

If you use a weekly punishment system, tell him, "If you have 35 colored circles by the weekend you will lose this privilege (any consequence that was considered important)."

When frequency is used as the basis of constructing a behavior chart, another type could be developed. Suppose your child never picks up her clothes or toys even after she has been told to do so. You analyze the behavior and find it occurs about 7 times a day. You might set up a chart similar to the one below.

Chart 4
Jason's Pick up Chart (1st week)

Mon.	Tues.	Wed.	Thurs.	Fri.	Sat.	Sun.
★	★	★	★			
★	★	★	★			
	★	★	★			
	★	★				
	★					
	★					
	★					

The week is divided into days, but each day is blank. Identify a reward. Next, tell your child, "Each time I ask you to pick up something (explain what you mean by this) and you do it the first time I ask you, I'll put a star on the chart. If I have to remind you more than once, you won't get the star." At the end of the day, week or whatever, she can trade in her stars for the reward.

When working with charts to change behavior that occurs more than once a day, do *not* include more than one kind of behavior on the chart. If you're working on sassiness, that should be the *only* behavior on one chart. If you want to work on another behavior, make another chart. It's best not to use more than two charts at a time.

When target behavior occurs or can occur only once a day

If you're concerned with behavior that is seen infrequently or can occur only once a day (getting dressed for school, taking a bath, bringing books home from school, homework), the chart types described above are not appropriate. In situations similar to these, two different approaches could be used— verbal or written contracts and formal charts.

Verbal agreement—A formal chart is not made, but a verbal agreement is made. This is usually used for only one behavior at a time. The child is told, "On days you get dressed for school on time, you can have an extra dime to take to school. On days you're late, you get only the same amount you usually receive." The child is asked to repeat the verbal agreement to be sure he understands it correctly.

"If you bring all your books home from school, you can stay up past your bedtime. If not, you go to bed at the usual time."

"When you leave your bike in front of the house and don't put it in the back yard, you won't be able to ride it the next day."

Written contract—For some children, a verbal contract isn't sufficient. They forget all or part of the contract or disagree with its terms if they fail to live up to their part of the agreement. In these situations, it's best to formalize the contract by putting it into writing. A couple of examples follow.

```
Date_____
        I agree to put my bike in the back yard. When it is left in
the front yard, I will not be able to ride it the next day.
Signed_____

Signed_____
```

```
Date_____
        I agree to have my room cleaned by 7:00 pm each night.
If it is straight and clean at that time, I will be able to stay up
30 minutes past my bedtime. If it isn't, I go to bed at the usual
time.
Signed_____

Signed_____
```

The agreement is spelled out on paper and both of you sign it. Then it is placed in a conspicuous place, such as on the refrigerator or on the door of the child's room. If the child follows or breaks the contract, the parent administers the appropriate predetermined consequence.

Formal charts—When a behavior occurs only once a day, the chart should include more than one target behavior but no more than three or four. An example follows.

Three target behaviors are specified—getting dressed for school without help, bringing home all the necessary books to do homework and doing homework without a fight. Because the target behavior pertains only to school, the chart is based on 5 days instead of 7. The child is told how he can earn stars and X's, as well as what the stars represent and when they can be traded in (the same procedure as used in Charts 1 to 4).

Three unrelated behaviors are included on this type of chart.

Chart 5
Tony's Chart (1st week)

	Mon.	Tues.	Wed.	Thurs.	Fri.
Getting dressed for school	X	X	★	★	★
Bring all books from school	★	★	★	X	★
Homework without a fight	★	X	X	★	★

Household duties and chores could also be included in this type of chart.

Chart 6
Lori's Chart

	Mon.	Tues.	Wed.	Thurs.	Fri.	Sat.	Sun.
Brushing teeth	☺	X	☺	X	☺	☺	☺
Taking bath	☺	☺	☺	☺	☺	☺	☺
Going to bed when told	X	X	☺	X	X	☺	X

Chart 7
Jason's Duties

	Mon.	Tues.	Wed.	Thurs.	Fri.	Sat.	Sun.
Making bed	☺	☺	☺	☺	☺	☺	☺
Feeding dog	☺	X	X	X	☺	X	☺
Cleaning up after dinner	X	☺	☺	X	☺	☺	☺

In using Charts 6 and 7, you must spell out the conditions, what must be done to earn the reward (allowance could be based on completion of chores) and when the consequence will be given. This is the same procedure I described for Charts 1 to 4.

I have described some general ways to set up charts, but there are many variations. Behavioral charts work better for younger children (10 and under), but they can be used successfully with high-school students. The procedures and principles are the same for any age group; only the consequences are different.

Why Use Behavior Charts?

The advantages of using behavior charts are discussed below.

Immediacy of consequences

The most important thing about reward and punishment is not how large, expensive, harsh or severe it is, but how soon it follows target behavior. Behavior charts help you accomplish this because the behavior can be dealt with almost immediately.

Although the reward may be given at night (staying up past the child's bedtime), it can be meaningfully dealt with almost immediately by placing a star or an X on a chart at 9 am. A consequence that will occur on Saturday (a movie, a fishing trip) can be dealt with on a daily or hourly basis.

Charts also help you break down big consequences. Your child comes to you and says, "Mike got a new pair of tennis shoes, and I want some like his." You look at his old shoes and see he needs a new pair, but you also realize new shoes can be used as a reward. However, the reward is too big to be used for a one-time behavior ("If you clean your room, we'll go get the shoes"). You can make a chart (similar to the one below) that allows your child to earn the shoes with appropriate behavior over a 1- or 2-week period.

Suppose the target behavior is temper tantrums. Explain the chart and how stars can be earned (similar to the procedure described for using Charts 1 to 4). Tell the child, "When Saturday comes, if you have 12 stars we'll go get the tennis shoes.

Chart 8
Alan's Be Good Chart

	Mon.	Tues.	Wed.	Thurs.	Fri.
Before school	X	X	★	X	★
3 to 5 o'clock	★	★	★	★	X
5 to 7 o'clock	★	★	★	★	★
7 to bedtime	★	X	★	X	★

If you don't, we'll start over next week. You can get the tennis shoes this Saturday or any Saturday in the future. It's up to you."

Big punishments or the loss of significant privileges (not being able to go on a camping trip, not being allowed to spend the weekend at a friend's house) can be dealt with similarly.

Although the reward or punishment may be received sometime in the future, behavior charts bridge the gap between occurrence of behavior and consequence. They help you employ an important principle of child management—immediacy of consequences.

**Charts help you look at behavior
differently and objectively**

Parent: "My children never get along. They fight continuously. It's driving me crazy. It seems like I'm always correcting them."

Psychologist: "You probably can set up a behavior chart to deal with their fighting." This procedure is described in detail to the parent.

Two weeks later. Psychologist: "How did that chart work with your children? Did the fighting decrease?"

Parent: "Once we started charting the behavior, I realized it wasn't as bad as I thought. It didn't occur nearly as much as I described last time; now I don't feel it's a problem. Let's focus on something else."

When you analyze and chart a behavior, you may see the behavior in a different light. The problem originally seen as extensive may no longer seem very significant.

Charting behavior also helps you see gradual improvement more easily. Earlier I mentioned parents often look at a child's overall behavior, which causes them to miss gradual improvement. You decide to work on sassy behavior in your child. You tell me, "My child is very sassy. She always has to have the last word and never has anything nice to say."

I outline some techniques for you to try. Two weeks later, you come back and say, "We tried what you said, but she's still sassy." This statement may be accurate if you look at the overall behavior, but it may be a different picture if you look at the behavior more closely. If a chart was used, you can look objectively at the behavior to see if any gradual improvement occurred.

In the first analysis, sassiness occurred an average of 10 times a day. During the first week the chart was used, the target behavior appeared about 7 times a day. The behavior decreased to 5 times a day the second week. Although the child is still sassy, the target behavior improved by 50% in two weeks. That's significant improvement!

Problem behavior doesn't occur overnight. It develops gradually. Any improvement is *also* gradual, and behavior charts help you see this.

Charts help you be consistent

Consistency is the foundation of effective child discipline. Charts help you follow behavior in a very consistent fashion. A chart placed on the refrigerator serves as a good reminder. Children often become involved in getting stars and working toward rewards and are quick to remind you if you forget.

Structure provided by charts is
beneficial for some children

A child can see his chart, put his stars on it and become involved in working toward a reward. This is helpful for some children. Their involvement in charting their good behavior facilitates positive change.

Token rewards can easily be used

Token rewards have little value in themselves, but they represent something important or something to be traded for a desired object. Money serves as a powerful token reward for adults. Some adults work to save money and put it in the bank with no intention of spending it. Some children work just to receive and hoard the tokens with little intention of trading them. This is often true after a chart has been used for 3 or 4 weeks. You might ask your child at the beginning of the week, "What reward do you want to work for this week?" The child may not be able to identify a specific reward but will still work hard all week. At the end of the week, he may have earned enough stars to receive the reward, but he isn't anxious to trade them in. The tokens by themselves serve as a reward.

Many other things can be used as tokens. These include animal shapes, smiley faces, gold stars, stickers or checkmarks. Some parents use more complex systems, such as different-color stars for different behavior (a blue star if a child does not fight with his sister, a red star for not fighting with or teasing his sister). Each color has a specific trade-in value. Others have used numbers (3 = very good, 2 = pretty good, 1 = good, 0 = not good), with a reward based on a specific point total. Just be sure your child understands the system, and the system is appropriate and important to him.

Behavior Charts—Things to Consider

Make it easy to get first rewards

When first using a chart, make it easy for your child to obtain the reward. Once she's locked into the system, expectations can be gradually increased. The best way to lose a child's interest in a chart is to have her fail to achieve the reward at first.

Parent: "You know that chart you told us to use to help Joey control his temper? Well it worked pretty good at first. But now it seems as if he could care less about it. It doesn't seem to make any difference to him whether he gets a star or an X."

Psychologist: "How did you design the chart?"

Parent: "We analyzed the behavior and found he got angry about 10 times a day. We set up the chart with 10 circles on each day (see Chart 3, page 89). Each time he lost his temper, we colored in a circle. At the end of the day, we put stars on the circles that weren't filled in. The first week he didn't get enough stars to get a reward. During the second and third weeks, he lost all interest in the chart. What do we do now?"

Psychologist: "What was the reward, and what did he have to do to earn it?"

Parent: "If he got 40 stars by Saturday (an average of 8 a day), he could go to a movie he wants to see. He only got 20 in 5 days."

Psychologist: "You expected him to change too much. It was probably too difficult for him to do. Because he failed the first week, the chart became negative. This is probably why he lost interest. Remember you told me he was having 10 temper outbursts a day and you required him to get 8 stars a day to go to the movie. That's an 80% improvement in 1 week. That's difficult for anybody. He got 20 stars, an average of 4 a day. By not receiving the reward, you punished him for changing his behavior 40% in a week. This is another reason why he lost interest."

When starting a chart, make the expectations reasonable so the child can achieve the reward. When first beginning a chart, make the reward dependent on 30 to 40% improvement. The child who had 10 temper outbursts a day should receive the reward if he reduces the target behavior to an average of 6 or 7 a day and earns 3 or 4 stars. Each week the chart is used, expectations are gradually increased. During the second week, the child may have to show 45% improvement to get the reward, the third week 55% and so on. Never require 100% improvement for behavior that occurs frequently. Always allow some room for error.

How long should a chart be used?

This depends on the individual child and the type of behavior you are dealing with. Use a chart for a minimum of 4 or 5 weeks after the behavior is no longer consistently present, though it may have to be used longer. One mistake parents make is they discontinue the chart too soon.

Once the chart has been in use for a sufficient period of time and the child is responding adequately, it can be phased out. This can be done in one of several ways. The child can be told he has done well and the target behavior is under control. Then you can use the chart to work on another behavior. Or you can start increasing the number of tokens the child must earn to receive the reward and try to interest him in behaving for the token rewards. Eventually you phase out the entire chart.

Another method is to ask the child if he wants to continue the chart if he is doing well. In many situations, you may notice the child losing interest in the chart. Then it can be discontinued. Try to avoid stopping before the new behavior has had a chance to establish itself.

Keep chart simple

Don't include too many behaviors on the chart or make it too complex.

Once a parent called me to say a chart she was using wasn't working. I asked her what she had included on it. The list below was her response.

1. Get out of bed when called.
2. Get dressed for school on time.
3. Brush teeth.
4. Eat breakfast.
5. Put school clothes in dirty-clothes basket.
6. Homework.
7. Come in from playing when told.
8. Eat dinner.
9. Clean up room.
10. Take a bath without a fuss.
11. Go to bed when told.

There were too many target behaviors on the chart. When this happens, two things could occur. First, the child will give up easily or not attempt the behaviors at all. In the above example, the child may have only gotten 15 minutes past his bedtime for all that work and felt it wasn't worth the effort. A child may also avoid projects that look too big or involve too much work. Secondly, when too many behavioral expectations are included in a chart, the child can easily manipulate the system. He can select certain behavior to perform, ignore the others and still receive the reward. Usually the behaviors the child avoids are the most important ones.

If charts are made too complex, the child may become confused. "A gold star means this, while a blue star represents that. If you have 7 by Tuesday, this will happen. If you have 15 by Friday, this will also happen. However, you could combine the points you get this week with the ones you get next week, or you could add the ones from last week."

After all this, the child is thoroughly confused. He says, "Forget about this chart."

Don't make the conditions of a chart too complex. Don't include too many behaviors on one chart. Three or four target behaviors are enough.

Be sure consequences earned are received

Psychologist: "Mrs. A, tell me about the chart we set up to help Jimmy with his sassiness."

Mrs. A: "Well, it worked beautifully for the first 2 weeks. He showed about a 90% improvement; but the last 2 weeks he's back to the same old stuff."

Psychologist: "Jimmy, what happened? You were doing so well."

Jimmy: "The first week my mother told me I could go to the skating rink Saturday if I earned enough points. I got the points I needed, but she said she was too busy to take me. The next week was the same thing. I earned the points but couldn't go skating. So I figured what's the use."

When a situation like this happens, you can't expect a chart to work for more than a short period of time, no matter how well it is constructed. Be sure to keep *your* part of the contract. If a child earns certain consequences, be sure he receives them.

Make chart positive

Most of the charts we set up involve positive consequences rather than negative. I feel this is a good rule to follow. Verbal or social reward (praise, hugs) should *always* be associated with behavior charts. When the child is placing his token on the chart and when he receives the final consequence, praise him. State descriptions of target behaviors in a positive manner. Don't use negative statements.

"Fighting with your sister . . ."
"Messy room . . ."
"Coming home late . . ."
Descriptions on the charts should be positive.
"Getting along with your sister . . ."
"Clean room . . ."
"Coming home on time . . ."
Charts can also be used to help with school concerns. See Chapter 76, Monitoring School Behavior and Performance: Home-School Communication Systems.

11

"I've Tried Everything— Nothing Works"

Many parents tell me, "I've tried everything I can think of on this child to get him to behave, do good in school, stop being sassy, but nothing works. It seems things are getting worse." There are many possible reasons.

Punishment Is Primarily Used

One of the first questions I ask parents who tell me they've tried everything is, "What have you tried?"

Most answers I get deal with punishment.

"I've spanked him."

"We sent her to her room."

"My husband took his bike away."

"I wouldn't let her watch TV."

"My wife hollers at him."

"I took him off the baseball team."

Usually when I ask, "Have you tried rewarding him or ignoring his behavior?" parents respond as if I am speaking another language. Many people do not consider rewarding or ignoring behavior as disciplinary tactics. This is one reason punishments fail. Many problems are associated with punishment when it is used as the main method of discipline. Punishment may actually make matters worse or not work on some personality types.

Inconsistency Is Present

Another reason some techniques don't work is because

they aren't used consistently. You try something one day, and the next day you do something else. The third day you try the method you used the first day or invent a new one. You don't stick with the same technique long enough.

Inconsistency also occurs when you use the same technique but don't use it every time you should. Suppose you have a child who sucks his thumb. You tell him, "Every time you suck your thumb, you're going to have to go to your room for two minutes." This procedure might be followed in the morning but not in the afternoon. The child might go to his room half of the time, but the other half the behavior is overlooked.

Techniques Aren't Tried Long Enough

Even if you are consistent and use the same techniques, some methods don't work because they aren't tried long enough. Most behavior in children won't change overnight.

A child has been sassy for 10 months, and his parents set up a procedure to deal with this behavior. They use the method very consistently, but after 3 or 4 days the child is still sassy, so they discontinue the procedure. A behavior that has existed for several months won't disappear in a few days. Attempts to change behavior must be tried for at least 1 or 2 weeks before they can be considered ineffective.

Improvements Are Overlooked

Much of the behavior observed in children can be viewed as habits or responses to the environment. They have gradually developed over a long period of time. Children don't wake up one morning behaving in a certain way. Their reactions to situations have appeared gradually and intensify with time. When you look at your children's behavior, you probably look at overall behavior. Look for small improvements.

A mother says, "My child is very sassy." I tell her to try a certain corrective technique. Two weeks later she comes back and tells me, "He still is sassy." This may be accurate, but 2 weeks ago he may have been talking back to her 10 times a day. Today he has reduced it to 4 times a day. Although he is still sassy, his behavior has improved 60% in 2 weeks—a significant improvement. Rather than only look at the overall picture, evaluate the behavior in small steps. Look for gradual improvements.

Children Fool Their Parents

Children are pretty good manipulators and con artists when it comes to escaping discipline. You tell your child, "You can't go outside until you pick up your toys."

She says, "I'm not picking them up, and I didn't want to go outside anyway."

You then think, "What do I do now?"

The child is starting to manipulate you. It may be true she isn't interested in going outside today. But if you know she likes to go outside and make this rule stick *every* day, those toys will eventually get picked up and the procedure will work.

Consequences May Not Be Important

Whether negative or positive consequences are used in discipline, you must be sure they are important to the child. Some children love candy; others do not. For one child, being sent to his room might be the worst thing that could happen, while his sister could care less about going to her room. What is rewarding for one child may be considered a punishment for another and vice versa.

Children also change with time. What may be important to him this week or month may not serve as a motivator the next week or month.

If the consequence used is not important or appropriate, it won't serve as a motivator. The corrective tactic used to change the behavior won't work. In determining a reward or punishment, consider the individual child's interests and values.

Behavior May Get Worse at First

Sometimes when an effective technique is being used, the behavior gets worse before it gets better. This was described in detail in Chapter 9, Ignoring Specific Behavior. Suppose you have a child who is having several temper tantrums a day. An effective technique is set up to change this behavior and you start using it, but the temper tantrums increase in frequency and intensity. When you see the behavior getting worse, you stop using the technique. However, the increase in the temper tantrums means the disciplinary tactic is working; you should have stuck with the method and not given up.

Before feeling that "nothing" will work with your child, analyze what you're doing and how you're going about it. The above conditions are essential to keep in mind and should be reviewed before you say, "I've tried everything; nothing works!"

12

30 Memos From Your Child

As I was going through my files, I discovered some papers reproduced from the *Leaders' Manual for Children: the Challenge* by Driekurs and Soltz (1967). One paper, "A Memorandum From Your Child," included some of the concepts and major points I am trying to convey in this book.

Below, I have reproduced some of Dreikurs' statements, modified others and included some of my own to stress some very important concepts in child management to keep in mind when dealing with your children.

1. Don't spoil me. I know quite well I shouldn't have all I ask for. I'm only testing you.

2. Don't be afraid to be firm with me. I prefer it. It makes me feel more secure.

3. Don't let me form bad habits. I have to rely on you to detect them in the early stages.

4. Don't correct me in front of other people if you can help it. I'll take more notice if you talk quietly with me in private.

5. Don't make me feel smaller than I am. I'll make up for it by behaving stupidly big.

6. Don't make me feel my mistakes are sins. I have to learn to make mistakes without feeling I'm no good.

7. Don't protect me from consequences. I need to learn from experience.

8. Don't be too upset when I say, "I hate you." I don't mean it, but I want you to feel sorry for what you've done to me.

9. Don't take too much notice of all of my small ailments. I may learn to enjoy poor health if it gets me a lot of attention.

10. Don't nag. If you do, I'll have to protect myself by appearing deaf.

11. Don't forget I can't explain myself as well as I would like. This is why I'm not always very accurate.

12. Don't make promises you may not be able to keep. I feel let down when promises are broken, and this discourages my trust in you.

13. Don't tax my honesty too much. I'm easily frightened into telling lies.

14. Don't be inconsistent. That completely confuses me, makes me not listen and teaches me to manipulate you.

15. Don't tell me my fears are silly. They are terribly real. You can do a lot to reassure me if you try to understand and accept my feelings.

16. Don't put me off when I ask honest questions. If you do, you'll find I stop asking and seek my information elsewhere.

17. Don't ever suggest you are perfect or infallible. It gives me too much to live up to, as well as too great a shock when I discover you are neither.

18. Don't think it's beneath your dignity to apologize to me. An honest apology makes me feel surprisingly warm toward you.

19. Don't forget I love experimenting. I can't do without it, so please put up with it.

20. Don't forget how quickly I am growing up. It must be very difficult to keep pace with me, but please try.

21. Don't use force with me. It teaches me to be aggressive and hostile and that power is all that counts.

22. Don't fall for my provocations when I say and do things just to upset you. I'll try for more such victories.

23. Don't do things for me I can do for myself. It makes me dependent, and I feel like a baby. I may continue to put you in my service.

24. Don't let my bad habits get me a lot of attention. It only encourages me to continue them.

25. Don't try to discuss my behavior in the heat of conflict. For some reason my hearing isn't very good at this time. My cooperation is even worse. It's all right to take the action required, but let's not talk about it until later.

26. Don't try to preach to me. You'd be surprised how well I know what's right and wrong.

27. Don't demand explanations for my wrong behavior. I really don't know why I did it.

28. Don't answer silly or meaningless questions. I just want to keep you busy with me.

29. Don't let my fears arouse your anxiety. Then I'll be more afraid. Show me courage.

30. Don't pay more attention to my mistakes, failures and misbehaviors than to my successes, accomplishments and good behaviors. I need lots of understanding, encouragement and positive attention. I can't pat myself on the back; I rely on you to do it.

Treat me the way you treat your friends, then I'll be your friend, too. I learn more from a model than a critic.

13

Allowance

Allowance involves giving your child a fixed amount of money on a periodic basis—weekly, biweekly, monthly. The child can receive the allowance for nothing other than breathing. Or he can receive the allowance for performing household chores or duties. I believe an allowance system should be based on some type of work. It doesn't have to be a lot of work. But some type of behavior or job should be contingent on receiving the allowance.

Many times allowance systems are started to help the child develop responsibility or to teach him the value of money. Several things must be kept in mind when starting an allowance system.

How important is money to the child?

Some professionals feel children should not receive money for certain behaviors; others do. Some people feel children should not be paid for things they are supposed to do. Many of the concepts related to this are discussed in Chapter 7, Reward.

I feel money can be used as a reward, and an allowance system is appropriate *only* if the child values money. Some parents tell me they have started an allowance system, but it isn't working. In many cases, a child doesn't care about money. To him, $1 is the same as $1,000. Does the child need money? This brings us to the next area.

Dry up other sources of income

Suppose you tell your child he will receive a $5-a-week allowance for putting out the garbage and cleaning his room.

He doesn't complete the chores, so he doesn't receive his allowance. However, any time he is with you at the convenience store and wants a soda, you buy it for him. At the shopping mall, when he feels like playing a video game, you give him money to play it. On Saturday he wants to go to a movie, and you give him the money to go to and to buy snacks.

Why does this child need money? He's already getting everything he wants. Whether he does or doesn't do his chores, he is still able to do and get everything he wants. He doesn't need money.

A parent once told me she began an allowance system for her 12-year-old daughter during the summer for performing chores around the home. The first week, the allowance system worked beautifully, but then it didn't work. On questioning the young girl on why she was not doing the chores, she told me any time she needed money, she could go next door and get all the money she needed from her grandparents. If an allowance system is used, dry up other sources of income to produce a need for money.

Another way to make it work is to specify certain activities or things you won't purchase for the child. This brings us to the next point.

Specify what you won't pay for

You may tell a child you will give him $5 every week for doing certain duties. He must use the money for buying candy and soda and playing video games. You won't pay for any of those things or activities. If these are important to the child, he will need money. An older child may receive part of her allowance for gas because you won't pay for it.

How much allowance?

This depends on two factors—your financial situation and the child's needs. You can give a child too *much* allowance. You may create a situation where the child accumulates money. When he has enough money, he doesn't have to work because he doesn't need money. The purpose of the allowance system will be defeated.

Assess the child's needs, and try to base the allowance accordingly. A young child doesn't need as much spending money as an older child or adolescent.

What you expect a child to do with his money should be realistic. It may be very difficult for a 15-year-old who receives $10 a week to use this allowance for his lunch at school and to attend movies on the weekend.

Define what must be done for an allowance

Be very specific about the chores you expect the child to do to receive the allowance. This may also involve setting a time when they must be completed.

If a child earns his allowance for cutting the grass, he receives the allowance if the grass is cut by 5 pm on Saturday. Define exactly what you mean by *cutting the grass*. A complete job might involve sweeping after the job is done, edging and returning the lawn mower to its proper place.

Another child's money might be based on putting the garbage out every night. He receives the allowance if he is not reminded and the chore is completed by 7 pm. The room must be clean by 7 pm on Saturday.

Be consistent

If a child earns his allowance, be certain he receives it. If you're inconsistent with the payment, the child's motivation may decrease and his performance may be affected. If the child performs the chores assigned, pay him his allowance on a regular basis.

Never take away all or part of the allowance when the child has earned it. This decreases the effectiveness of the system. A child has earned his allowance for helping around the house with various chores. On Friday, when he is to receive his allowance, he comes home with a detention. Because he got the detention, you don't give him his allowance. This is ineffective because the next week when it comes to motivate him to do chores, he probably won't comply.

An allowance earned should be received. But don't give the child the allowance if he hasn't earned it.

For additional information, see Chapter 21, Household Duties & Chores, and Chapter 40, Developing Responsible Behavior.

14

Communication Between
Parent & Child

Many parents have problems talking to their children, giving them advice or explaining things to them. Many children have difficulty telling their parents how they feel, expressing opinions or discussing things that bother them. Difficulty in verbally relating to your children is called a *lack of communication*.

Communication problems may be described in various ways. A parent may say, "My son never talks to me."

"Talking to my child is like talking to a brick wall. He doesn't accept anything I say."

"I can't sit down and talk to my child. Every time I try to do this, it seems as if he turns me off."

"Every time I try to explain something to my child or give her advice, she gets all upset or mad and storms out of the room."

"My son is so sensitive. I can't tell him anything."

"My daughter never tells me when something is bothering her."

"I never know how my child is feeling. He keeps everything to himself."

On the other hand, the child often tells me, "My parents don't understand me."

"I can't tell my parents how I feel because every time I do, they tell me how wrong I am or I shouldn't feel that way."

"They never see my side. It's always their way or no way."

"Every time I ask them 'why' they say 'do it because I say so,' so I just quit asking."

"The only time my father talks to me is when I do something wrong."

"They always ask me a million questions. 'Why did you do that? Why did you do this?' Most of the time I don't know the answer, so I don't say anything."

"I never can talk to my parents; they're always busy. I have to talk to my mother when she's cooking or my father when he's reading the newspaper. Don't even think of saying something when the TV is on!"

"Every time I ask my parents something, I get a lecture."

"My mother's always talking, and I can't get a word in. She asks me a question then gives me the answer."

Communication problems are numerous and varied. Below are some ideas to increase the quantity and improve the quality of the communication between you and your child. Using some of the concepts below should make it easier to talk with your child, and verbal interaction should grow more meaningful.

Causes and Cures of Communication Problems

Communication is often negative

Most parents pay more attention to mistakes, misbehaviors and failures than to successes, accomplishments and achievements. A child is supposed to brush his teeth every night. He brushes them 6 nights in a row, but the 7th night he forgets. When does he get attention for this behavior? The night he forgets to brush his teeth! Nobody says anything about the other 6 nights.

A child's room has been a mess for several weeks. She is asked to clean it up. She cleans 99.9% of the room but leaves a sock by the desk and a book by the bed. When the room is inspected, what's the first thing the child hears? "What about that book? Go put that sock where it belongs." We generally overlook the positive behavior and emphasize the negative.

Often the majority of communication you have with your children is negative. Would you frequently communicate with or become fond of a boss who constantly criticizes your performance? You would avoid him and keep your verbal interaction to a minimum. All of us tend to avoid situations that

produce negative attention. If the majority of your verbal interaction with your children is negative, they'll try to avoid it. The
end result is the amount of time they spend talking to you is
reduced.

I once asked a 7-year-old, "What are some things your
daddy does that you don't like or wish he would do less often?"

He responded, "Having discussions."

When I asked him what he meant, he said, "Every time I
do something wrong or get a bad note from school, my father
sits down and has a long talk with me. I hate discussions."

I would bet this father never talked with his son about his
good behavior.

One way to increase the quantity and quality of communication between you and your child is to pay more attention
to his positive behaviors. Communicate with him about his successes, accomplishments and good behavior as much as or
more than you talk with him about his failures, mistakes and
bad behavior. Children who receive a significant amount of
positive verbal attention want to talk with their parents. If this
occurs, the lines of communication will be kept open. You will
become more aware of your child's feelings, opinions and
objections.

Look and listen for things that are important to your children (football, motorcycles, fishing, cars, loud music). Make it
a point to talk with them about these things. Talk to them about
their strong points, skills, successes, appropriate behavior and
things they do well. Then they will feel more comfortable talking to you about their negative feelings, failures, weaknesses
or behavior they see in you that they would like to see changed.

Child's feelings may be explained away

Often a child will come to his parents with sincere feelings
or honest opinions that you explain away, telling him not to
worry and giving reasons why he should not feel as he does.
When this occurs, children will not freely communicate with
you. A few examples emphasize this point.

Your child comes home from school and says, "My teacher
is so mean. She really makes me mad. Look at all the homework she has given us. She must think all we have to do is stay
inside and work."

You respond, "Let's see what she has given you." The child gives you the assignment and you say, "That's not very much. She's only given you this to help you learn. She's concerned about you and wants you to get a good job when you grow up."

Another child tells his father, "I want to play baseball, but I'm afraid to go to practice. I don't know what to do. I've never played baseball before. I might make a mistake." His father may tell him, "There's nothing to worry about. Don't be afraid. You know how to play baseball as well as anybody in the neighborhood."

A third child may say, "I'm bored. There's nothing to do. I feel sad when there's no one to play with."

His parent may reply, "You're always saying that. You went to the movie yesterday, you had Billy over all day Saturday to play and you have a room full of toys."

The children in the above examples are expressing genuine feelings, gut-level reactions. The first child is angry, the second afraid and the third unhappy. But what happens? Their feelings are negated—explained away. In situations like these, you don't have to agree or disagree. But understand and accept your child's emotions and feelings.

If I tell you, "I'm scared to death the building we're in is going to fall down and hurt us. I'm really afraid and nervous." I do *not* want to hear you say, "You shouldn't be afraid. This building is built solidly. It isn't going to fall down. Don't worry about that; buildings don't fall down very often."

Maybe all you need to say is, "I almost was in an automobile accident one time, and I was really scared and nervous. I know exactly how you feel." With this brief statement, you have accepted and understood my feelings. This may be all that is necessary.

There are various ways to communicate with children without explaining away their feelings and showing understanding of emotions expressed.

"One time my boss really gave me so much work to do I felt like I'd never finish it. It really made me angry. I thought he was the meanest person in the world. But once I started it, it didn't seem that bad, and I was able to finish it. I know how you feel about your teacher."

"I had to give a talk at a PTA meeting once. I felt I couldn't do it without making a mistake. I really wanted to stay home and not go to the meeting. I was afraid and didn't know what was going to happen. I felt just the way you feel now. But once I stood in front of the people and started talking, my fears disappeared, and I gave a good talk."

"About a month ago, when you were in school, I had finished all the work around the house and called several of my friends. I wanted to go some place, but no one was home. I know how you feel because I felt unhappy and bored then. But I looked around and found something to do, and in a little while one of my friends called."

By initially responding to your child's communication in ways similar to the above, you increase the probability he will keep talking. He'll feel more comfortable relating to you. You'll be able to increase the quantity and quality of the verbal interaction you have with your child.

True feelings may be overlooked

This problem is a bit more difficult than the others because it involves interpreting the child's communications. Sometimes when children are talking to you, there may be suppressed emotions hidden behind what they say. If you listen only to the words, you may overlook their true feelings. It's sometimes necessary to listen for the feelings behind a child's words to respond effectively and maintain the communication. The examples below deal with this point.

A father and his son have been working on his bike for about a week. They have bought new handle grips, a seat, tires and a variety of other new parts. It's Saturday. All the new parts have been put on the bike, and they have just finished painting it. Now the bike is finished, but they must wait a day for the paint to dry. The son wants to ride his bike *now*. His father explains he must wait for the paint to dry or it will be ruined. However, explanations do not satisfy the boy, and he still asks, "Why can't I ride it now?" Many explanations and a hundred whys later, the father becomes annoyed, hollers and sends the boy to his room. What started out as a nice father-and-son project turns out to be a disaster.

A boy and his father plan to go fishing. The night before, they get everything ready and go to bed early. The next morning, it's raining, and the weatherman does not predict clear weather until tomorrow. The boy becomes upset, complains, whines and pouts. His father explains, "I can't control the weather; sometimes plans don't work out. We'll go fishing tomorrow." But this doesn't satisfy the boy, and he continues to complain. After many fruitless attempts to quiet him, the father becomes frustrated and feels forced to discipline his son.

While there is a great deal of verbal activity in the situations described, it isn't effective communication and it satisfies no one. One way to improve communication and satisfy the child is to listen to what is said and to look behind the verbalization for the feelings being expressed. In both situations, the children are frustrated, dissatisfied and disappointed. Rather than offering various explanations over and over again, the parent must respond to his child's feelings. For example, he might say, "We worked on your bike for a long time, and you really worked hard. Now we've finished, but you still have to wait before riding it. That must make you feel bad. One time something similar happened to me, and I really was disappointed."

"We planned the fishing trip a long time, but now it's raining and we can't go. You must be angry and disappointed. One time I saved money a long time to get a car. When I went to buy it, they didn't have the one I wanted. I had to order it and wait 6 weeks to get it. That made me mad. How do you feel?"

Reflecting the feelings behind what a child says is an effective method of communication and may often prevent negative interaction (getting upset with the child, yelling at him). It may provide the child with the type of interaction he needs to satisfy him.

When your child talks, give him your full attention

You don't talk to people who don't pay attention to you or who appear disinterested when you try to communicate with them. If you seem uncaring about or inattentive to what a child has to say, the child's attempts to volunteer information or communicate with you diminish. A couple of examples will clarify this point.

Your child comes home from school. A great deal has happened, and he has quite a bit to tell you. Because you are preparing dinner, he sits at the kitchen table and starts talking to you. You respond to him and continue cooking. The child must talk to your back. How many people would you continue to communicate with if you had to talk to the backs of their head?

Another child tries to talk with his father who has his head buried in the newspaper. The child makes several attempts to strike up a conversation but gets tired of talking to the newspaper and stops.

One way to minimize verbal interaction between you and your child is to respond to him in ways similar to those in the examples above. To keep children talking and increase the probability they will easily communicate their feelings to you, you must give them your *full* attention. When a child has something to tell you, take a few minutes to stop what you are doing and give him your undivided attention. No one likes to talk if the other party appears disinterested.

Some parents use communication as discipline

Use talk and verbal interaction with your child as a form of communication—*not* as a disciplinary tactic. Most children I work with can't be controlled just by talking to them. Communication between parents and children is extremely important, but don't expect it to be an effective disciplinary measure. In terms of disciplining a child, what you do is more important than what you say. When talk is used to change a child's behavior, it usually doesn't work. It goes in one ear and out the other—and the child will continue misbehaving. Let's look at some examples.

A child continually hits his younger brother. You sit down with him and explain to him how he may hurt his brother; he should love his brother and not hit him. The communication between you and your child is fine, but the child continues to hit his brother.

A young child usually interrupts his mother when the phone rings. She has a business at home, and the phone calls are important. But she can't talk on the phone without her child saying, "Let me talk. I want something to drink. Where's my car? Come play a game with me."

The mother explains the importance of the phone calls she receives and the child shouldn't interrupt when she's on the phone. The verbal interaction the mother has with her child is excellent, feelings are expressed and demands are explained clearly. But the child doesn't stop interrupting when the phone rings.

Talk is just talk, and children learn very rapidly to ignore communication used as a disciplinary measure. Talk and explain things to your children, but don't expect it to control a child or prevent misbehavior from recurring. Consequences must be used for the majority of children to change behavior. In terms of discipline, it isn't what you say, but what you *do*.

Some parents talk too much

A child has a new baby brother. His mother comes home from the hospital with the new baby, and the child asks, "Where did my brother come from?" The mother takes out diagrams, shows the child how fertilization occurs, how the baby grows inside the mother and how the birth process occurs. She spends 45 minutes explaining how children are conceived and born when all the child wanted was the name of the hospital.

Parents may suffer from verbal overkill—they talk too much when explaining things to their children. Most young children have millions of questions, but sometimes our answers are too detailed. This often defeats the child and he learns not to listen to his parents' complex explanations. In answering children's questions, try to be brief and to the point.

Children sometimes tell me, "My mother asks me a question then answers it. I don't have time to say anything." This type of response to a child is a good way to minimize communication between you and your child. Be a good listener, and give your child an opportunity to respond to your questions.

This brings us to another important point—excessive questioning of children. Most children don't know why they misbehave or do what they do. Their behavior is often an unthinking response to the environment. Questioning why they did what they did usually results in the child responding with, "I don't know" or the standard shrug of the shoulders. Repeated questioning only results in more comments, such as, "I don't know" or the child telling the parent what he thinks his parent wants to hear. The whole questioning procedure is fruitless. Instead of putting a child through the third degree or asking him a complex series of questions, discuss the situation with him. Talk with him about what has happened rather than put him on the hot seat.

Most young children don't know why they do certain things. Their behavior is often a response to the environment. In my office, we use many *indirect* methods to identify children's feelings and motivations. We use techniques (testing, interviews, play) that allow a child to project his feelings and experiences and indirectly tell us more about himself. We try to keep direct questioning to a minimum.

We may show a child a picture and tell him, "I'm going to show you this picture. Tell me a story about it. Your story should have a beginning, middle and end. Tell me what the people in the story are thinking and how they are feeling."

After the child tells us the story, we may ask him some questions about it. Hopefully, this indirect method produces a *non-threatening situation* in which the child can project his feelings, experiences and motivations onto the people in the story. By using this procedure, we can learn more about a child.

You can use similar methods to get inside your child. If you can get the child to talk about a situation he does not identify as directly related to his own behavior or motivation, you may get some insight into the reasons for or causes of his behavior.

Let me use an example to show you another procedure designed to get at a child's motivation indirectly. This technique can easily be used at home and is more successfully applied to children under 8. Once I saw a first grader who had been crying every day in class for about a month. His teacher and parents had asked him numerous times for a reason for his crying, but they got only the standard "I don't know" answer. The child was referred to me. When I directly asked him, "Why are you crying?" he couldn't tell me either. So I decided to play a little game with him.

Psychologist (after talking to the child several minutes): "Let's play a little game. I'm going to give you a situation with a little boy, and we'll make up some reasons why he feels a certain way. I'll give a guess, then you can give one. The next time you guess first, and I guess second. Do you understand the game?"

Child: "Yes."

Psychologist: "We are walking down the street, and we see a boy bouncing a basketball. He looks happy. Why do you think he's happy? I'll guess first. His daddy just bought him the basketball. Now, it's your turn."

Child: "Maybe he just finished playing basketball, and his team won."

Psychologist: "That was very good. Let's try another one. Suppose we see a boy in his back yard. He's sitting under a tree, and he looks sad. Why do you think he's sad?"

Child: "Maybe his friends can't come over to play."

Psychologist: "Maybe his dog got out, and he can't find him."

After going through a series of different situations, we finally got to this one.

Psychologist: "Let's say we are walking down the hall of a school, and we look in a classroom. All of the children are listening to the teacher. One little boy is sitting at his desk crying. Why do you think he's crying?"

Child: "He doesn't think his mother will come pick him up. He's afraid something may happen to her."

Usually this game provides many hints or answers about why a child behaves in a certain way. When possible, try to minimize *direct* questioning and provide the child with a situation in which he can project his feelings and motivations. Most children find this easy to do and can relate to situations outside of their own.

Lecturing decreases your effectiveness in communicating with your children. Lectures are interesting the first time you hear them, but they get boring if you hear them over and over again. Some children tell me, "I got a detention in school today. Tonight I'm going to get lecture No. 43 from my father. I know most of his lectures by heart."

Children learn very quickly to become deaf to a lecture and turn off this type of communication. Lecturing and nagging are essentially identical. Avoid saying the same thing over and over.

Communication: Things to Remember

1. Don't try to control or discipline a child with talk. Talk should be a method of communication, not of discipline.

2. Stop what you're doing, look at your child and listen when he speaks with you. Give him the proper attention.

3. Most children don't know why they do what they do. Minimize excessive direct questioning because it usually results in the standard, "I don't know" or shrug of the shoulders. Use other techniques to get inside a child.

4. Children don't always understand everything they hear. Small children are learning a new language, and they may not comprehend a large portion of what you tell them. Avoid complex or abstract communication with small children. After you explain something to a child, ask, "Do you understand?" or "Tell me what I said in your own words."

5. Be sure that most of your communication with your child is not negative—talking to him about his mistakes, failures, misbehaviors or what he forgot to do. Give him positive communication—talk about his successes, accomplishments, interests and good behavior.

6. Avoid talking too much, giving long or too-detailed explanations, repeating lectures, excessive questioning or other forms of communication that result in a child becoming deaf to you.

7. Try to understand a child's feelings. You don't have to agree or disagree with him, but make him aware that you understand how he feels. Do not explain away a child's emotions.

8. Be honest and consistent when communicating with your child.

9. When appropriate, involve children in decision-making and setting consequences for their behavior.

10. Try to create situations in which communication can occur (eating together with the TV off). A young child watching TV in his room establishes a lack of communication between parent and child. Do things together whenever possible rather than separately. The TV is a barrier to family communication.

When you buy a child his own TV to watch in his room, you are creating a monster. This is especially true with adolescents because even without a TV in their room they will spend a lot of time there. If there's a TV in their room, they may only come out to eat or go to the bathroom.

11. Talk with your children about their interests (music, sports, dance-team practice, motorcycles). Talk with them when you're not trying to make a point, teach them something or impress them. Talk with them mainly to talk and have positive verbal interaction—not to accomplish anything but to communicate.

15

Children Have Personalities

Frequently I hear parents say, "I've treated all my children the same. Why is Janey giving us all this trouble?"

"What works with my other child doesn't work with this one. Why?"

"I can't understand it. We do the same for all our children, but Tony isn't responding to us. What's going on?"

"Why does punishment seem to affect my daughter but doesn't affect my son?"

Children have different personalities. All children do *not* feel, think and act the same way. Most parents are aware of this. They may say, "My youngest child is very extroverted and talks to anyone. Nothing disturbs him. My oldest son is shy and sensitive. He seems to worry about everything."

Although parents are usually able to specify different personality characteristics in their children, they often try to manage, discipline or teach their children by using the same methods. But what may work for one child doesn't necessarily work for another.

You and I do not treat all adults the same way. You might walk up to one friend and say, "Boy, did you get fat," and he'll laugh and joke about it. Tell this to another friend and he may punch you in the nose. Depending on an individual's personality, you treat him in certain ways. The same holds true when dealing with children.

Child behavior is a result of the interaction between the child's personality and his or her environment. If I tell a joke, one person may laugh, another get embarrassed, one leaves, the fourth gives me a lecture on my behavior and the fifth punches me. Who's responsible for the behavior? Not the environment (what I said); the same environment produced different behavior in each of the five people. The behavior is a result of the interaction between the environment and the personalities of the people involved.

If your child becomes President of the United States, you can't take all the credit. On the other hand, if he causes trouble in school or shows other unacceptable behavior, you can't assume all the blame. The child's behavior is a result of his personality *and* how he is managed or dealt with.

One purpose of this book is to increase your skills for dealing with your child's behavior. The more techniques you have, the greater the chance that you will be successful. A technique you now use to deal with certain behavior in your child may be a good one in theory, but it doesn't work with your child's personality. If you use the same technique on a child with a different personality, results are great! Or place your child in another environment (deal with him differently), and you'll see different behavior. If a technique you are using is ineffective, it doesn't prove it's a bad method of dealing with children. It may not be a method that works well with your child's personality.

How Does Personality Develop?

This gives rise to the question of heredity versus environment. Is a child born with his behavior? Is it a result of learning that occurs in his environment? Some professionals assign more weight to heredity as a behavioral determinator, while others feel the environment is more important. Most view behavior as a result of heredity and environment. Children may be born with certain personality characteristics, but the environment determines which characteristics become dominant and which play minor roles. Heredity sets the stage, but the environment determines what the players say.

Children may be born possessing an inclination toward many characteristics—sensitivity, stubbornness, affection, shyness, irritability or talkativeness. The child's environment determines what characteristics become dominant aspects of his personality. The child's environment can be a major factor in changing undesirable actions or increasing desirable behaviors.

Parents tell me many things about their children.

"It seems like she has been stubborn all her life."

"Ever since I can remember, he's been that way."

"I think he was born acting like that."

These observations may be accurate, but they do not mean behavior can't be changed or reduced to a minor personality characteristic. A child may have been born shy. As a small child, he never talked to people when spoken to. He hid behind his mother. Wanting to increase his ability to function in social situations, the parent wants to change this behavior gradually. She may tell the child, "When we go to the corner store and the lady talks to you, don't hide behind me. If you stay in front of me, we'll buy your favorite candy. But we won't get the candy if you hide behind me." This could encourage the child to answer "Yes" or "No" to questions or tell people his name when asked until the shyness diminishes. This child may remain shy throughout his life. But this behavior characteristic may assume a minor role and not significantly inhibit his social relationships.

Family Environment
Isn't the Same for All Children

Although you like to feel you treat all your children equally, this is impossible. Children are individuals with different strengths and weaknesses. Some children are more affectionate than others. A child may have trouble with schoolwork, but his brother does not, so he receives more attention in this area. A child who has hyperactive characteristics receives more negative attention than his sister who does not show this behavior. Children have different strengths and weaknesses, and they will require different responses from you.

The home environment is never perceived in the same way by each child. In a family of three, the youngest child has two older siblings who can do things he can't. The oldest child has two younger siblings; the middle child has a younger and older sibling. Bedtimes may differ, the amount of freedom each child may have in the neighborhood may vary and so on.

By looking at a family through the eyes of a child, you can see how his perception of how the treatment of each family member differs. Each child has a different environment that interacts with his personality to produce different behavior.

When dealing with children, keep in mind your children are individuals. Use individual methods to increase the probability of success. A child's behavior is a result of the interaction between his personality and the environment. By modifying the environment, you can produce changes in a child's behavior.

16

Children with High Levels of Intelligence

Most parents would like to have their children exhibit a high level of intelligence, but sometimes high cognitive ability produces problems or concerns. Children I am referring to in this section primarily include those with IQs in the range of 120 and above. I'll discuss some general areas of concerns parents have and the most frequent problems that I see these children encountering.

How Different Are These Children?

Being above average in any skill, ability or characteristic makes a child unique and different. A child's level of intelligence is usually measured by an IQ (intelligence quotient) test. Scores from this test are usually based on a norm of 100. Children who score lower than 90 are considered below average. Those who score above 109 are considered above average. See Chapter 73, Intelligence, for a more-detailed discussion.

Most people who report intelligence scores to parents usually provide a range rather than a specific IQ score. Intelligence is supposed to remain stable and usually does, but there may be some variation in specific scores attained because of motivational factors, how the child was tested and standard error of measurement in tests. Below is a frequency of certain intelligence levels seen in the general population.

IQ Score	Classification	Approximate Incidence in Population
160	Very superior	1 out of 10,000
155	Very superior	3 out of 10,000
150	Very superior	9 out of 10,000
145	Very superior	4 out of 1,000
140	Very superior	7 out of 1,000
135	Superior	2 out of 100
130	Superior	3 out of 100
125	Superior	6 out of 100
120	Superior	11 out of 100
115	Bright	18 out of 100
110	Bright	27 out of 100

Most public-school systems have special-education classes for children with high levels of intelligence. These are usually called *gifted* classes or *gifted and talented* classes. Criteria for program eligibility differs from state to state. Contact your local public-school system for additional information. You may also want to review Chapter 82, Special Education.

Characteristics of Gifted Children

In Chapter 52 on overactive children, I list some characteristics of bright children. Below are characteristics based on research compiled by Dr. J. Renzulli.

Learning characteristics
1. Unusually advanced vocabulary for age or grade level.
2. Quick mastery and recall of factual information.
3. Wants to know what makes things or people "tick."
4. Usually "sees more" or "gets more" out of a story, film or other activity than others.
5. Reads a great deal on his own. Usually prefers adult-level books. Doesn't avoid difficult materials.
6. Reasons things out for himself.

Motivational characteristics
1. Becomes absorbed and involved in certain topics or problems.
2. Easily bored with routine tasks.

3. Needs little external motivation to follow through in work that initially excites him.
4. Strives toward perfection. Self-critical. Not easily satisfied with his own speed or products.
5. Prefers to work independently. Requires little direction from teachers.
6. Interested in many "adult problems," such as religion, politics, sex, race.
7. Stubborn in his beliefs.
8. Concerned with right and wrong, good and bad.

Creativity characteristics
1. Constantly asking questions about anything and everything.
2. Often offers unusual ("way-out"), unique, clever responses.
3. Uninhibited in expressing opinions.
4. High risk taker. Speculative.
5. Often concerned with adapting, improving and modifying institutions, objects and systems.
6. Displays a keen sense of humor.
7. Shows emotional sensitivity.
8. Sensitive to beauty.
9. Nonconforming. Accepts disorder. Isn't interested in details. Individualistic. Doesn't fear being different.
10. Unwilling to accept authoritarian pronouncements without critical examination.

Leadership characteristics
1. Carries responsibility well. Self-disciplined.
2. Self-confident with children his own age, as well as adults.
3. Can express himself well.
4. Adapts readily to new situations.
5. Sociable.
6. Generally directs the activity in which he is involved.

Gifted Personality

There are many characteristics of the bright or gifted child. Most school systems and parents view the concept of "gifted" primarily as it relates to ability. Most school systems evaluate a child in terms of intellectual and achievement skills to determine if he or she is gifted and eligible for special educational services. Most criteria is based on a child having a certain level of intelligence and/or an achievement level (math, reading) above his actual grade placement. Many parents tell me, "He has a high level of intelligence, but he isn't working to his potential."

Some children may be bright or gifted in terms of ability but do not have what I call a "gifted personality." This relates to the school situation and the child's performance. Many children who are classified as *bright* or *gifted* have the intellectual abilities but have an "average personality."

A child with a "gifted personality" can be characterized as self-disciplined, responsible, interested in school and learning and involved in his studies. He usually shows a high interest in school and school-related work.

Some children with the same intellectual skills don't show these personality characteristics. They have more of an average personality. They can take or leave school or could care less about homework, class projects and studying. These children don't like school and would rather be playing than doing schoolwork. School is not fun. It is boring and viewed as an unpleasant activity and something to avoid. They don't spend a lot of time reading or in school-related activities. They usually do just enough to get by.

The child with the "gifted personality" who has 15 minutes of homework will come home and do the 15 minutes of work then go outside and play. The other child may spend 3-1/2 hours figuring out how to get out of the 15 minutes of homework.

When looking at your child's abilities and actual capacity as they relate to his school performance, look at personality characteristics. Just because a child is bright and has a high intellectual capacity does not necessarily mean he will or should perform exceptionally well in school. For children who are bright but do not have a "gifted personality," it may be wise to maintain their motivation, develop responsible behaviors, see that they do what they are supposed to do and accept less-than-perfect work.

If a great deal of negative attention is placed on their inability to perform to their potential, school becomes negative and motivation declines. The child's performance may be below his intellectual capacity and fall below average. Many bright kids with "average personalities" learn to do enough to keep their heads above water. They don't let school interfere with their play, fun or other activities with a higher priority.

Don't place emphasis on grades. Emphasize effort, participation and doing what you are supposed to do. See Chapter 70, Grades, for more information.

Management Problems

Some bright children do not produce any management problems and are generally cooperative and easy to discipline. Others are just the opposite. Dealing with them daily can be quite difficult. It seems you have to always run fast to stay one step ahead of them.

Stubborn, strong-willed personality characteristics

Some gifted children are independent, nonconforming, resistant to authority, stubborn and display other similar personality characteristics that produce some management problems. They buck the system. They want to do what they want to do when they want to do it and for as long as they want to do it. Getting them to cooperate with routine activities (doing homework, taking a bath, coming in from playing, cleaning their room) can be quite difficult if they don't want to do it. Review the chapter relating to these personality characteristics for more information on managing this type of child.

Manipulation

Most children are good con artists and manipulators. Add increased levels of intelligence to this ability, and you may have a very skilled manipulator. Many times bright children are smarter than their parents. They can figure out ways to get what they want and can be more in control of you than you are of them. See Chapter 31, Who's in Control? and Chapter 37, Con Artist—Manipulative Children, for more information.

Avoid power struggles and confrontations

Bright children may find themselves in conflicts with those who place limits on their behaviors or who try to direct them into certain activities.

Stay away from power struggles and confrontations. Deal with the behavior in a calm, matter-of-fact fashion. Set rules and consequences for behavior. Spell them out ahead of time and enforce them consistently.

Because of their intelligence, these children are very skilled in asking questions that you can't answer logically. "Why do I have to make my bed every morning if I'm going to sleep in it at night and mess it up?" If you try to reason why certain things must be done, these children may out-talk and out-reason you. With some requests, there are no logical reasons why they must be done other than you said they must be done.

Suppose you have a child who asks many questions about why he has to take a bath or why he needs to do homework at a certain time. You find yourself talking in circles. For every reason you give the child, he has 37 reasons why he shouldn't do it or why he doesn't need to. Minimize these discussions. Tell him he has to do it because you say he has to. You're the adult, and he's the child. End of discussion!

Review the chapters under the section Methods and Techniques for additional behavior-management techniques.

School Problems

Many gifted children enter school and don't have any problems. They do what they're supposed to do, receive good grades and cooperate with school-related work. These self-disciplined children are interested in school. They have a "gifted personality" to go along with their high intellectual abilities. If you have one of these children, you probably aren't reading this section. It seems like you could lock these kids in a closet, and they would still learn. School placement is not of great concern. These children do well in average or above-average school settings or in a closet.

Other bright children experience problems in school. Parents often wonder why a child has so much trouble in school if he is so intelligent. I'll discuss several situations I have seen and explain how they relate to problems with this type of child.

Average personality

As mentioned above, some children with gifted

intellectual abilities do not have what I call a "gifted personality." They have more of an "average personality" and are not into schoolwork, studying, homework. They receive grades in the C-to-B range. Parents feel if the child would try harder, he or she would maximize his or her potential. If this is the situation, it may be best to accept this performance to help create a positive situation and maintain the child's motivation regarding schoolwork. If a great deal of negative attention, punishment or restrictions are placed on the child because he is not a straight-A student, school may become negative. His motivation to achieve will decline. Even though he has the ability, emphasize effort and doing what he is supposed to do rather than grades. If he has the ability and does what he's supposed to do, grades will automatically follow.

Irresponsibility

These children have stubborn, strong-willed personality characteristics and want to do what *they* want to do. If they're interested in something, they give 1,000% effort, energy, motivation, attention. But if they aren't interested, they'll do it halfway—or not at all. They may not do homework or refuse to study for tests because of a lack of responsibility or self-discipline. They have academic problems. A child in this category often shows irresponsibility in school and in many areas of his life. In dealing with this type of problem in the gifted child, work on developing responsible behavior in school-related activities and in behaviors in the home and neighborhood. See Chapter 40, Developing Responsible Behavior, for more information.

Schoolwork too easy or doesn't challenge the child

When a bright child has problems in school, they generally fall into two types.

The first involves the child who completes his work fast; the work may seem too easy. Although he may have 20 minutes to complete his math problems, he finishes them in 5 minutes. Then he talks, fidgets, gets up and walks around, aggravates others or disrupts the class. This child is doing his work correctly, but it takes him less time than the other children. Behavior problems are apparent when he has free time with nothing to do. The other kids are still working on the assignment. This child may need to be given additional work, advanced work or moved to a higher-level class.

The second situation occurs where the bright child refuses to do work in school and shuts down his performance. Many bright kids having trouble in school say the work is too easy and they're bored. The child knows the work and refuses to do it because it's boring, routine and repetitious. It's like asking you to write your telephone number 100 times so you remember it. Your answer would be, "I already know it, and I'm not going to write it 100 times." This situation usually occurs in a child who has gifted ability, a "gifted personality" and is generally responsible in many other areas of his life. He cooperates with cleaning his room, taking a bath, getting ready for church. However, he shuts down in school and shows irresponsibility and a lack of self-discipline there. If the child is responsible in many areas of his life, but shuts down in school, the work may be too easy or not challenging.

If the child finishes his work quickly then creates problems or refuses to do the work and the school cannot give him higher-level work or move him to an advanced class, it may be best to change schools. If the child shows many other irresponsible-type behaviors, a change in the amount or level of work or a move to a new school will probably *not* alleviate the problems.

The child I am describing is not doing the work because he does not want to do it or is not interested in it. He'd rather be doing anything but schoolwork—like playing or having a good time. This child shows a lack of self-discipline or responsibility in many areas of his life. Change schools *only* if you are very sure work is the problem and difficulties in school are the major difficulties you have with your child.

Study habits not developed

In lower grades, material and information are presented frequently. There is a lot of review. If your child is bright, does some of the work and pays attention some of the time, his grades will be fine. Not studying and partial involvement in schoolwork doesn't work too effectively in the middle grades. Some children's lack of effort catches up with them around the middle grades. They are unable to maintain high grades with this approach to schoolwork.

In the middle grades, more work is presented. There are many teachers and things aren't repeated as frequently. The child who did well in the lower grades starts receiving poor test scores. A's drop to C's, or he begins to fail.

Many times every year I see bright children whose grades have significantly declined when they entered fifth, sixth or seventh grade. In talking to the child and the parents, the only thing that appears to have changed is the decrease in performance. The child still approaches school the way he did in the first four grades. Many of these children tell me, "I'm doing the same thing I did in third grade, but now it's too hard. I can't keep up and maintain the grades the way I used to." These children have not developed any study habits or have *never* done what they were supposed to do. In the lower grades, their level of intelligence was enough to carry them, but this doesn't work in the upper grades.

It is extremely important to help your child develop study skills and habits. If this situation occurs with your child, try to establish some kind of home-school communication system to monitor his effort in his classwork, homework, studying. If you can get your child doing what he is supposed to do in his school-related work, his grades will improve significantly.

Socialization Problems

Although many bright children socialize extremely well and have many friends, some have trouble relating to their age mates. This seems to occur in two general situations.

Lack of age-related social skills

Many bright children are better at solitary play and activities than average children. They can amuse themselves much better, create things, have a good imagination. This child is likely to be very happy in his room playing, reading or building things. He is not apt to aggravate you to have somebody come over to play.

Children with high intelligence levels may get more adult attention or fit into adult conversations more easily than the average child. If you were in a room with a few adults talking and your typical 5-year-old came in the room, you'd say, "Hi. How are you doing? What's happening? See you later. Go ahead outside and play." The bright child may come in and start talking about dinosaurs. Or she sits down and relates to adults much better than another child. She tends to "fit in" with adults better. A bright child may spend more time with adults because she can relate to them more effectively.

An intelligent child may not play and interact with children his own age enough to develop age-appropriate skills. When this happens, socialization skills don't develop. When a bright child is placed with his age mates, he may feel uncomfortable, not know how to relate to them, or relate to them in an adult or inappropriate fashion.

Interaction with peers may be difficult and the child retreats back to solitary play or adult interaction. It's important for gifted children to develop social skills and be with children their own age. Be sure the bright child gets the proper amount of socialization with children his age.

Different interests

Many bright children show different interests than most other children. They may not have a common activity that warrants interaction and the development of friendships. The young gifted child may be interested in dinosaurs, reading, computers or board games. While most other kids his age are into athletic activities or riding bikes, skateboards and cartoons, the bright child may be more concerned about computers, experiments, music and art.

Although it's important to try to develop interests similar to most children, try to get the child involved with other children of similar interests. If the child is interested in computers or art, involve him in a class or summer activity where he can meet other children with similar interests. Some public-school settings have summer-activity programs for gifted students. Many colleges have summer or afterschool programs that may be appropriate.

There's more to life than school and schoolwork. A major part of our lives is dealing with other people. It's extremely important for a gifted child to receive opportunities to develop friendships and age-appropriate socialization skills. See

Chapter 45, Getting Along With Other Children.

Gifted Associations

Most states have associations for gifted children. If you live in a large city, there may be a chapter there. These associations provide valuable information for parents of children with high levels of intelligence. They may be able to provide information on many activities, camps and programs. For more information, write to:

National Association for Gifted Children
4175 Lovell Road, Suite 140
Circle Pines, MN 55014
(612) 784-3475

17

Children with Physical Handicaps or Health-Related Problems

I have been a consultant for the Louisiana Center for Children with Developmental Disabilities since the mid-1970s. This center primarily serves children with cerebral palsy. In my practice, I have seen many children with physical handicaps or significant health-related problems. The information I include here pertains to parent or other relatives' interaction with the child. I discuss certain ways of dealing with handicapped children or those with health-related problems.

Deal with the Child, Not the Handicap

The child is a person with a handicap. Treat him like his brother or sister who does not have a handicap or health-related problem.

When my children are sick with a sore throat, virus or sore leg, my gut-level reaction as a parent is to pamper, spoil, cater to or give in to them. I usually don't let them eat in the den and watch TV, but when they're sick, I allow this. They have a set bedtime, but because they are sick, I let it slide. Most people react like this.

For a child with a physical handicap or serious health problem, your reaction and the reaction of relatives is 100 times greater than for a child with a sore throat. This type of reaction produces problems or intensifies problems that may exist.

Areas of Concern

Self-concept

The child with a physical handicap or serious health problem is automatically different from other children. His problem may make him physically different from other children and/or he may be restricted from activities. He may not be able to play sports, climb a tree, take dancing lessons or participate in physical-education classes. The more people treat him like a child with a handicap, the more obvious this difference becomes. Although you can never eliminate the difference between this child and other children, it can be minimized by your reaction.

Although the child may not be able to participate in some activities, try to find areas where he can excel or have skills that other children do not have. It may be fishing, sports trivia, computers, music. It may benefit a child's self-concept to think, "Although I can't play baseball as well as most kids, I know more about the game and the people who have played it than most kids who play it."

Some children need limits on their behavior to feel secure and develop confidence. If the child is catered to, spoiled and in more control than you are, he may experience confidence problems because of a lack of limits on his behavior.

See Chapter 58, Spoiling, and Chapter 36, Building Confidence, for more information.

Responsibility

One of the major jobs of being a parent is to help children adequately adjust to adulthood and to be happy doing so. For most adults, most of their day involves doing things because they *have* to do them.

A child who is in more control than his parents is not able to be a responsible person. Pampering and spoiling don't result in responsible adult behavior. See Chapter 31, Who's in Control? and Chapter 40, Developing Responsible Behavior, for more suggestions.

Manipulation

Most children are skilled in the act of manipulating you. Children with physical or health problems are probably better at this than most children. This is probably true because adults involved with these children allow them to manipulate.

Some studies of children with physical or health-related problems indicate they show lags in the development of certain skills. This is not because of any physical reason, but because the parents do too much for them. This retards the development of certain abilities in the child.

Children with handicaps have enough going against them that you can't control. The areas I have discussed are things you can influence and prevent. By reacting to your child in some of these ways, you can create other handicapping conditions that will produce additional difficulties for the child. Dealing with them in a different fashion minimizes problems.

18

Dealing with Lack of Cooperation From Others in Child's Life

I often hear parents say, "I'm trying to do what you suggested, but the grandparents have him after school, and they're not following the same procedures."

"My husband thinks this all a bunch of baloney, and he's still spanking the child."

"My ex-husband isn't cooperating."

Significant people involved in the child's life are not cooperating with the treatment plan. Or they ignore the strategies that have been outlined to deal with a particular behavior. This is a difficult situation to deal with and is usually counterproductive to effective treatment. It decreases the probability of change or slows down the whole process. If you use the same techniques to deal with a child 24 hours a day, you'll get faster and better results than if these procedures are implemented only part of the time. This is the reason I like to talk with the child's teacher, ex-spouse, stepparent or any other person who is significantly involved in the child's life.

There are many reasons and situations where lack of cooperation occurs. But the end result is the same—you have different approaches to the child. One person undoes what the other has accomplished. Inconsistency is present. The teacher, baseball coach and 12 other people have suggested the child is experiencing some difficulties. You have accepted it. You work on changing the behavior, but the child's father sees nothing wrong with the child and refuses to cooperate. Grandparents or relatives may care for the child after school and don't follow your methods. Sometimes the other parent refuses to cooperate. This often occurs in separations where anger directed toward the spouse filters down to the child's behavior. Whatever the other person says should be done—the opposite is done. One person sabotages or undermines the other or uses counterproductive techniques.

If this occurs, there is a tremendous amount of inconsistency in the child's life. Attempts must be made to produce more structure, predictability and a uniform method of dealing with the child. Below are several suggestions.

Dealing with a Lack of Cooperation

Have a professional talk with others—Perhaps the child is seeing a counselor, mental-health professional or the teacher is making suggestions as to how to deal with the child. Have the person making the recommendations talk with the individual who is not following the treatment plan. Be sure your husband or wife is involved in all conferences with the teacher or counselor. Have the mental-health professional talk with the grandparent, relative or ex-spouse who is not cooperating. Sometimes it's better if a professional communicates what needs to be done rather than you.

Get some reading materials or books that pertain to what you're trying to accomplish and the most-beneficial methods to obtain the goal. Buy a book for the teacher, relative, ex-spouse. Do everything you can to make sure everyone involved with the child has the same idea of what you are trying to do and what you are trying to accomplish.

Involve someone else—Have someone else talk to the person who is not cooperating. Ask your sister or brother to talk to your parents. Have your in-laws talk to your spouse.

Leave materials for reading—If the other people don't read the material you give them, leave it around the house in a conspicuous place or "forget" the book at the relative's house.

Parental inadequacy—Some people are unwilling to accept or admit problems with their child because it may be a direct reflection on their adequacy as a parent. They think if something is wrong with a child, it might mean something is wrong with themselves as parents or they are doing something wrong.

Childen are often born with characteristics that do not directly relate to a parenting style or a parent's adequacy. Some children are more difficult to deal with than others. Some are overactive or pleasure-oriented. The parent who refuses to accept a problem may understand it more readily if he is told this. Unfortunately, some mental-health professionals believe all children's problems are related to the parents, but this isn't true. Some children will have problems in certain areas because of their personality and characteristics—not the methods used by parents to deal with them.

Model appropriate behavior—Model appropriate techniques of child management for the uncooperative person. One time a mother told me the child's father was screaming and hollering at him because he was jumping on the bed. The father couldn't stop the child from jumping on the bed. The mother walked in the bedroom and told the child if he continued jumping on the bed, one consequence would happen and if he stopped jumping, another consequence would happen. The child got off the bed and went into the kitchen. The mother told me that later that night she saw the father reading the book on child management.

Minimize contact—Minimize contact in child-care activities for those who are uncooperative. This happens many times when an aunt or grandparent cares for the child after school or cares for the child for extended periods of time. The relative's normal role is to cater, pamper and entertain the child. When this person becomes a primary caretaker for the child, the normal style of dealing with the child becomes counterproductive.

If this is the case, it might be wise to minimize contact with the person in child-care activities for extended periods of time. Don't prevent the child from seeing the other person, but have them see the child as a grandparent not a caretaker.

Control what you can control—This occurs in many situations where there is a divorce or separation. You may have the child 80% of the month, and your ex-spouse has her 20%. Perhaps there are problems cooperating with the other person. Asking them to do certain activities or things with the child may result in more problems.

It may be better to try to control and deal with the child

for the 80% of the time you have him and forget about the other 20%. If the majority of the child's life proceeds according to the treatment plan, the probability of change greatly increases. The relative who has the child one weekend out of the month won't significantly impact on the child's behavior if he or she does not cooperate. But *you* must have a structured, consistent environment the remainder of the time.

Keep disagreements private—Don't disagree with the uncooperative person in front of the child. Present a unified front to the child. Minimize conflicts over techniques and discipline in the child's presence. Sometimes this can be done by establishing a rule/consequence system with the child ahead of time. Before entering grandmother's house, you might tell the child, "You don't seem to listen when we're at Grandma's. You bounce off the walls and do things I don't want to you do do. Every time I have to correct you, I'm going to give you a warning. I'll tell you, 'Alan this is number one.' If you don't have 3 warnings when it's time to leave, you can ask Johnny to come over to play when we get home. However, if you have 3 or more warnings, he won't be able to come over and play."

Tie different households together—In a divorce situation, the mother may have the child all week and the father takes him on the weekend. The child is giving the mother trouble doing homework. She sets up a chart on the refrigerator. Every night he cooperates, she puts a check on the chart. The father tells him, "I'll pick you up Friday to come over to my house. If you have 3 or more checks on your chart, we'll rent a movie Friday night. If you don't have 3 checks, we won't rent the movie."

By setting up this type of system, you have actually tied both houses together. What happens at home with the mother during the week is also being dealt with on the weekend when the child is with his father.

A similar situation may also occur when the child goes to a grandparent's or relative's after school. The parent may tell the child, "Grandma will put a check on your notebook for each subject you do the homework for. She won't put a check when you don't cooperate. For every check you have, we'll play 5 minutes of a game you like later on that night."

Use positive consequences—Some relatives or grandparents assume they must use punishment as discipline. This may not be consistent with their personality or the pattern of interaction they have established with the child. When talking to relatives, talk about having the child earn rewards or earn the normal privileges or activities given to her. Sometimes it's easier for relatives to reward the child for being good rather than to punish her for being bad.

19

Effects of Divorce, Separation, Parental Conflict & Other Environmental Changes on Behavior

Children rely very heavily on structure, predictability, consistency and routine in their environment to provide them with security and emotional stability. When significant change occurs, most children become confused and insecure. Some are able to deal adequately with the change while other children become fearful, tense, uncertain, dependent, indecisive, rebellious or stubborn. It's difficult to define significant change because what affects one child may not bother another and vice versa. "Significant change" might include divorce, separation, death of a parent or grandparent, birth of a sibling, move to a new house, starting or changing schools, illness in the family.

The change could also be something that is seen as a minor shift in the environment—loss of a pet, different working hours of the parent, the death of a distant relative, a friend moving out of the neighborhood, a shift in the daily or weekly routine. You may view the change as important, or it may not seem to be an important change in the child's life.

To be significant, it doesn't have to be "bad" or traumatic. It could be seen as a "good" or positive change, such as a mother quitting work or a father having more time to spend with his child, a move to a new house where a child has his own room. Suppose someone offered you a job making 10 times more money than you currently earn. You would see this as a very positive, welcome change. However, because of the change, you'd probably feel insecure and uncertain when you first start the new job.

In this chapter, I frequently refer to divorce and separation as the *change situation.* This is because there often are many shifts in the environment when this occurs. However, you could substitute any change or modification in the environment, and the information discussed in this chapter would probably apply.

Significant change as discussed in this section focuses on the birth of a sibling, a change in schools, a move to another home or neighborhood, the death of a parent, divorce, separation, remarriage, parental conflict or some other shift in the environment.

How Children Respond to Significant Environmental Change

There have been many science-fiction movies and a few TV programs about visitors from other planets or humans venturing to other worlds. When they arrive in the new environment, they are confused and have difficulty predicting and sorting out events. They misinterpret responses from other people, and things do not make sense to them. This is how children often respond to significant shifts in routine living arrangements or situations in which they find themselves with one parent instead of two.

Think of a situation in your life that might involve significant change. Suppose you went to work tomorrow and, without any prior notice, you were fired. Or suppose you woke up one morning and found yourself in another country. How would you feel? You'd be confused or upset and feel insecure or uncertain. You would have a difficult time understanding what had happened and might have trouble making sense of the environment. This is basically how children feel when a divorce, remarriage or significant change in the environment occurs. They cannot predict; they don't know if what exists today will exist tomorrow.

How children react to change

All children react to change. But to what extent they react and whether they will experience problems coping depends basically on two things—what occurs before the change and how the child's behavior is dealt with after the event occurs.

Let's use the separation of parents as an example. Children will react very differently if the separation includes open conflict between the mother and father than they will if the separation is amicable. A child who was close to his father may show different behavior than a child who was not. All children will react to a separation just as they will to *any* significant change.

Divorce or death of a parent is a significant change, as is the death of a grandparent or going to a new school or moving to another state. These changes are traumatic! Children react to them in similar ways but on different levels and with different degrees of intensity. It's almost impossible to prevent an initial reaction, but that isn't important. Consider what you do *after* the change. This will determine the extent of the problem, how severe it will be and how long it will last. If I am treating a child who is very depressed, I'm not overly concerned that he gets depressed. I'm more concerned about what happens after he gets depressed, how it is dealt with and how long it lasts.

Too much information

Sometimes situations occur and a child gets too much information that confuses him. The child hears or the parent tells him too much. This adds to the uncertainty he feels and the unpredictability in the environment. Usually information pertains to adult matters he probably doesn't understand and certainly isn't equipped to handle.

I've had 5-year-old children whose parents have separated talk to me about custody, visitation, child support, court proceedings. They didn't understand what they were talking about, but they had the information. One young child whose parents were losing everything because their business folded knew in detail about what would or could happen. Another parent who was reported for possible child abuse told his young children, "I may be put in jail. You could be taken away from me and put in a home." Some children know more about their grandfather's illness than the doctors treating him.

You should talk to your children, but you can be too honest and give them too much information. If you talk with them about adult matters they have trouble understanding, it confuses them. In addition to the environmental changes, children often have to deal with verbal garbage they overhear or are told. Don't talk to them about adult matters or talk to other adults in front of them. Before telling a child something, ask yourself, "If the child knows this, how is it going to benefit him?" The information may not hurt him, but if you can't see how it'll help him, don't give him the information.

Be brief and to the point when explaining. Many parents use three paragraphs when three words would suffice.

Any child who experiences a significant change is confused. He may have difficulty adapting to the change. Whether any serious problems develop or whether you have trouble after change occurs depends primarily on how the situation is dealt with. When change occurs, you may see dependency, rebellion, opposition, anger, depression, withdrawal, inattentiveness, nervousness or temper tantrums. The child may even try to make you feel guilty for causing the change.

How you deal with responses to change determines whether responses will intensify and expand into other problems or whether they will subside. Below are some typical reactions children have to significant environmental change.

Structuring or gaining control over the environment

Think again about how you'd feel if you experienced a significant environmental change. If you woke up in a foreign country, you'd be confused and uncertain. How would you react? You'd begin planning what to do. You'd seek out people to question and gather information. You'd identify landmarks to help you find your way around. You'd attempt to structure the environment and make sense out of what has happened.

Another such situation might occur when you begin a new job. You show up on the first day, but no one tells you what you have to do or what duties you must perform. You are faced with a cloudy, ambiguous situation. How would you feel? You'd probably feel uncertain, insecure and out of place. You wouldn't know what was expected of you. Faced with this situation, you might quit the job.

But suppose you're like a child who can't escape from the confusing, unpredictable environment and must stay. What would you do? You'd begin structuring the situation by doing the tasks you thought you should or wanted to do. "I'm going to do this. When I'm finished with that, I'll do this. Then I'll take a coffee break." You'd try to make sense out of the situation by doing whatever you thought necessary to make you feel more comfortable in the unpredictable new environment. You would try to gain control over it.

When children experience significant change, they don't know what's going on. Some children become fearful; others cling to their mothers closely. Some rebel. Generally, their behavior reflects insecurity, uncertainty and fearfulness. These are the same kinds of feelings you would experience in the above examples.

What do children do? They *also* try to restructure their environment. They try to make sense out of it by attempting to gain control over it. Put me in a room where I'm confused and don't know what to do, and I'll try to structure the situation. I'll start doing things I think I need to do. I'll probably do some things incorrectly because I don't know what is required of me.

A child responds similarly to change. She thinks, "Things around me are changing, I don't know what's going on. I don't know what I have to do to be right or what I have to do to prevent change." To deal with what's going on in the environment, the child turns more into herself and responds more to her own needs, wishes and rules in an attempt to impose structure.

The child does what she feels is necessary to feel better. Her primary concerns are her needs and wants. She may not listen. She may rebel and develop other problem behavior. Before the change occurred, the child may have shown normal problems all children have, or maybe she was good without any behavioral difficulties.

After a change, she may develop several behavioral problems. She won't take "No" for an answer. She does the opposite of what you tell her and has a smart answer for everything you say. It appears she's never happy. Nothing you do seems to please her. She cries, "I want this, I want that." But when she gets it, she doesn't want it anymore.

The child tries to call the shots in an attempt to get control or be in charge. She often becomes very manipulative. She says, "You're mean. I want to go live with Daddy," to get around you and get what she wants. She's trying to survive just as you would try to survive in the foreign country. The problem is she doesn't know what she has to do to make things right. And what usually happens is she makes it worse.

One little girl I worked with almost totally ran her home and called all the shots—when she would eat, go to bed or take a bath. She had suffered many significant changes that forced her to adopt this behavior. Her parents were divorced, and she and her mother moved in with her grandparents. Her mother went to work. The child changed schools and lost former friends. Behavior problems began in school, and she became more unmanageable at home. The more the child got her way, the worse the situation became.

When a child experiences significant change in the environment, you identify his feelings as the reason for his misbehavior. However, the usual way you deal with the misbehavior only makes him feel worse. When there has been a significant change in a child's environment, such as when parents separate, you realize the child is upset by this and feels insecure. You know he needs love, attention and understanding to make him feel more secure. Your assessment is correct, but you try to accomplish the improvement in the wrong way. You tiptoe around the child and give him his way. You feel sorry for him or feel guilty. To compensate for your guilt, you start giving in, avoiding discipline, relinquishing control to the child.

You make the mistake of removing the kind of structure the child misses. You used to make him take his bath or go to bed at a certain time, but now you let it slide. This type of spoiling approach only intensifies the child's sense of loss and adds to his confusion and uncertainty. See Chapter 58, Spoiling, for more information.

To help the child deal with the change so he'll feel more

comfortable, you must assume *control*. You must be in charge—not the child. Some people correctly identify this need when problem behavior is seen, and give the child more discipline rather than less. However, most of the time the additional disciplining primarily involves punishment.

Excessive negative consequences in these situations usually make matters worse. The control you impose must be very consistent and given in a very supportive, positive way. The type of love the child needs is structure, consistency and predictability. He needs to know that what exists today will exist tomorrow, next week and next month. He needs effective limits placed on his behavior.

This kind of control decreases a child's confusion and makes him feel more secure. To return to the example of an adult waking up in a foreign country, you would feel better if someone helped you map out your new environment by telling you what was acceptable and unacceptable behavior. You would soon feel more at ease. Chapter 31, Who's in Control? gives additional information.

Assume control and administer discipline

When children experience significant change and behavior problems arise, you must assume control and administer discipline in a consistent, warm, supportive and positive fashion. How can you do this? Don't discipline children after the fact. Spell out rules and consequences ahead of time. The child needs to know what is expected, when it is expected and what will be the consequences of misbehavior. See Chapter 5, Setting Rules For Behavior, for a detailed discussion of this process. Use reward for good behavior rather than punishment for bad behavior. See Chapter 7, Reward.

People who are important to the child and deal with him on a daily basis must be consistent and predictable. It also helps the child to adjust if some routine and structure are placed on the environment. Set up a specific bedtime or time to do homework, a certain day to visit his father or sleep with his grandparents, a certain amount of time to play outside or ride a bike.

After a child experiences significant change, he may not be sure if what exists today will exist tomorrow. In the case of a separation or divorce, the child may feel, "Dad's not living here anymore. Maybe Mom will disappear tomorrow, or I'll be sent away." When the family moves or the child changes schools, he may think, "How long will I be here? Should I make friends and risk the chance of losing them again, or should I stay to myself ?"

In situations similar to this, you should use techniques that say or imply that what exists today will exist tomorrow. Some examples are given below.

"Tonight we're going to have meatballs and spaghetti for dinner."

"Saturday we're going shopping."

"Sunday your grandfather is going to take you fishing."

"Next month we're going on a vacation."

"You're staying with me, and you're not going to live with your father."

Statements such as these allow the child to see the same environment will exist in the future. Don't make statements about the future in terms of years or several months. A few hours, days or weeks are sufficient to reassure most children.

Dependency and fearfulness

When significant change occurs, some children become rebellious, contrary or stubborn. They may become discipline problems. However, other children are affected by change differently and do not show bad behaviors. Their responses to environmental shifts are usually characterized by excessive dependency and fear. But these children are of equal concern to parents who must deal with the behavior on a daily basis.

Change seems to affect self-concept and confidence in these children. They feel they can no longer cope with the environment and become insecure, uncertain, fearful and excessively dependent on significant people in their environment, usually their mothers. See Chapter 36, Building Confidence, for a general overview of this type of behavior and techniques for dealing with it.

A problem common to these situations is called *separation anxiety*. The child becomes nervous, tense, fearful or upset when he has to function apart from his parents. It's as if he is no longer sure that what exists this morning will exist this afternoon. He fears his parents will disappear. This is very common when one parent is no longer in the home or when there is parental conflict. The child then becomes afraid to separate from the other parent.

The object of the child's excessive dependency is usually the mother, probably because she has been around more frequently, has been consistently available to him or has been the parent on whom he has depended. Excessive dependency may also be directed toward the father or another significant person in his life (grandparent).

Often the child refuses to go to school or becomes tense, upset or sick in the classroom and wants to go home. He wants to stay home with his mother in a secure environment. He may not let his mother get out of the house without him. Going to the grocery store, on a date or to a meeting may become a chore.

In other cases, the child won't let his mother out of his sight and must be physically in the same room, even the bathroom, most of the time. He may fear sleeping alone and needs to be in the same room with her to fall asleep. He may feel his mother is going to disappear or leave him, just like his father, if he goes to school or allows her out of his sight. See Chapter 79, Refusal to Attend School, for techniques to deal with this behavior.

Dependent behavior is often dealt with indirectly by attempting to strengthen the child's self-image, security and confidence by using the positive techniques discussed in Chapter 36, Building Confidence. Some of the methods discussed pertaining to structuring or gaining control over the environment may also be helpful in dealing with a child who becomes overly dependent.

Much of the excessive dependency seen in some children who experience significant change is based on fear. However, some children show only dependent behavior and do not express direct fears. Others show a combination of fear and dependency, while still others develop a variety of fears and worries. The list of fears and worries children may develop in this situation is endless. Typical fears involve school, the dark, death, being lost and being left alone. I have also seen children who became fearful of riding in a car, walking up stairs, germs, not having air to breathe and sleep.

The basis of the fear is similar to the reason for excessive dependency. Deal with this child in the same way the dependent child is dealt with. The general procedures used with children's fears can also be employed. Read Chapter 44, Fears, and Chapter 39, Dependent Children, for additional information.

Regressive behaviors

Some children regress when faced with significant change. The child starts feeling insecure, upset and uncertain. He tries to go back to an earlier behavior or time when he felt more comfortable or secure. The child shows behavior that is characteristic of a younger child. You move to a new house and your child, who has not wet the bed in 2 years, starts wetting it every night. Or when a new sibling is born, your 6-year-old starts talking baby talk. When a separation occurs, the child who has been toilet-trained begins to have accidents. The regressive behavior may involve temper tantrums, whining, pouting, silliness, immature actions and similar behavior you haven't seen for months or years.

In dealing with regressive behavior, avoid giving the behavior excessive attention. Deal with the child in a calm, matter-of-fact way. Use the consequence of ignoring whenever possible. Natural consequences can also be employed where appropriate.

Reward good behavior. If a child starts wetting the bed, don't punish her. Set up a reward that is earned when the bed is dry.

Don't treat the child like a baby. Although it may appear the child wants to be treated like a younger child, don't give in.

Anger, resentment and hostility

Some children who experience a significant change in their environment develop feelings of anger, resentment and hostility toward whomever they feel is responsible for the change and disruption. As the result of a divorce, the child may blame his father for the breakup of the family. When a sibling is born, the new intruder is held responsible for the loss of parental attention. These feelings are expressed directly (fighting) or passively (rebellion, stubbornness, opposition). The anger is expressed more toward the parent who is around more frequently, usually the mother. See Chapter 32, Anger—Aggressive Behavior, for a more detailed discussion and methods and techniques to use in dealing with this type of behavior.

Unhappiness and withdrawal

Some children show overt signs of depression, dissatisfaction and unhappiness. Or they withdraw from activities with peers and family. This seems more difficult to deal with than the others. In helping the child, encourage him to discuss his feelings, identify the source of his discomfort and express his emotions.

Try to eliminate the child's sources of discomfort. Excess time on their hands and inactivity seem to make matters worse for these children. Keep them busy, and prevent withdrawal from activity with family and peers.

Use a positive approach to the child's non-depressive behavior. Reward him for behavior that counteracts the dissatisfaction. A child who loved parties is now content to stay home and not attend his best friend's birthday party. To use reward for participation, you might say, "If you go to Ted's party, we'll be able to stop and get that toy you wanted. If you don't, we'll have to wait until next week when we pass the shopping center." A child who lived for baseball now wants to quit playing on the Little League team. Use reward for a period of time to see if the child really wants to quit or if this is a temporary feeling stemming from his dissatisfaction. After a period of time, if the child still wants to quit, allow him to. What usually happens is the child no longer expresses this desire after a week or two and is once again happy playing on the team.

What to expect at certain ages

Some children show only characteristics of one of the reactions described above. Others show aspects of two or more of the behavior patterns. Although these reactions occur across all age groups, certain specific behaviors are more typical at certain ages. I have listed some of those below.

Birth to 3 years—Children exhibit regressive behaviors, clinging, separation, dependency and fretfulness.

Between 3 and 6 years—The child may become quiet and look unhappy or become very angry and hostile. Clinging, dependency, regressive behavior, fears and separation anxiety may also appear. The child's fuse may get short, and he may become easily frustrated and upset. Refusal to attend school and conflicts or aggressive behavior with peers may emerge. Temper tantrums, trying to gain control of the environment and sleep and attention problems may also appear.

Between 6 and 9 years—Crying, withdrawal and extreme unhappiness may be seen. Overeating, stealing, lying, possessiveness and an increased demand for material things are possible. Trying to gain control of the environment and aggressive behavior with peers may also be present in this age range.

From 9 to 12 years—In the case of divorce, the 9- to 12-year-old starts identifying a "good guy" and "bad guy." One parent may be blamed or given total responsibility for what has happened. Anger, resentment and hostility may be directed toward this parent. The child aligns with the other parent, the "good guy." Stealing, lying, aggressive behavior and physical complaints may appear.

Adolescence—There may be changes in the parent-child relationship, with an increased investment in home and the custodial parent. Adolescents may gravitate toward childish relationships with younger children or be manipulative and demanding with peers. Worry about sex, marriage, loyalty, morality and financial matters may be seen. Increased experimentation with drugs or alcohol and a decrease in school-related activities may be seen.

Dealing with Change—Things to Remember

1. Try to identify the change and stabilize the environment by being consistent, establishing routines and becoming predictable.

2. Do not pamper, spoil or cater to the child. He needs a great deal of structure. Establish rules and spell out consequences ahead of time. Set limits on his behavior.

3. Do not allow the child to be in control. This creates more confusion because the child doesn't know what needs to be done to make the situation better. You must be in control.

4. Do not foster dependency.

5. The child should be worried about "kid stuff" (What time is Chad coming over to play? Is Wayne going to sleep over? When is my favorite TV program coming on?) not "adult things." Don't discuss adult matters with the child or allow him to hear you talking about matters that do not concern him.

6. Avoid giving the child too much information, talking too much or going into excessive detail when explaining things. This can produce more confusion.

7. Use reward and positive consequences to deal with the child's behavior.

8. Try to minimize other changes (after a separation you may have to move, but try to keep the child in the same school) and disruption of his activities (avoid having the child quit baseball or dancing).

9. If changes must be made, they should produce more stability. If a child has to change schools, don't put him in a school where he will be for the remainder of the year then have to change again. Try to place him in a school he can attend for several years.

10. Get the child involved in children's activities. Have him play with and relate to children more than with adults.

20

Drugs & Alcohol

Let's say we stop the first adolescent who passes by your house. I give him money and tell him to purchase some illegal drugs. At the same time, I give you money and tell you to go get me a six-pack of soda. Both of you would probably get back at the same time with the items I requested.

This is an exaggeration, but not far from the truth. Drugs are available everywhere from the highest socioeconomic levels to the lowest, in the best schools to the poorest schools in your city. Recent surveys by national organizations related to drug abuse and alcoholism show the following.

1. The average age of first drug use is 13. The average age of first alcohol use is 12.

2. Over 50% of all high-school seniors have tried an illicit drug. Over 33% have tried a drug other than marijuana.

3. Nearly 33% of all high-school seniors claim most or all of their friends get drunk at least once a week.

4. Nearly 1 in 16 has tried cocaine or its powerful, addictive derivative, crack.

5. High-school-senior girls ingest more stimulants and tranquilizers than boys. Girls come close to matching boys' levels of use of alcohol, marijuana and other drugs.

6. 33% of fourth graders reported they were already being pressured by peers to try alcohol and marijuana.

Times have changed

Things have changed dramatically since we were children. The drug abuser or addict in our day was seen as a degenerate. Today, drug use cuts across all socioeconomic levels. It is seen on TV and in movies as something done at social gatherings or parties. Negative effects are minimized.

Attitudes and values of the adolescent and preadolescent have also changed. In the late 1950s, adolescents were surveyed regarding the people they most admired and/or who were most influential in their lives. In that survey, parents ranked third on the list. Nine out of the 10 most-admired people were authority-type figures (President of the United States, a teacher, a coach, politician).

In a similar survey in the 1980s, parents ranked ninth and were the only authority-type figure in the top 10. Those most admired were actors and actresses, singers and professional athletes. The movement is away from authority figures toward more pleasure-seeking, big-money, fast-living people. Sex, drugs, money and rock and roll!

In this chapter, I give a general overview of drug abuse in preadolescents and adolescents. I touch on types of situations in which drug abuse is more likely to occur and reasons for this behavior. In addition, I provide signs and symptoms of this behavior. I don't go into a great deal of detail because there are many excellent books on this subject. The substance-abuse agency in your area can provide you with a great deal of literature about drug and alcohol use.

Why Use Drugs?

There are many theories on the causes of substance abuse—they range from a genetic basis to personality characteristics. Drug abuse in children usually seems to be a symptom of confusion, unhappiness or alienation. Let's look at four general areas of characteristics often seen in these children.

Lack of self-discipline

These children often show a lack of internal control and responsibility. They have a self-centered, pleasurable approach to the environment, and feel little personal or social responsibility. These children are often impulsive, act before they think and have difficulty adhering to duties and responsibilities imposed by others.

Trouble with authority figures is frequent, and they show

poor academic performance because of a lack of responsibility. They often set very high goals for themselves but do not have the self-discipline or knowledge of the process necessary to achieve these goals. A child might be sitting in my office telling me he is going to law school and make a lot of money, own a big home and expensive cars. The reason he's in my office talking to me is because he wants to quit high school. They know how to set goals but don't know how to achieve them.

Lack of motivation

Children appear to lack interest in activities, things and events. They show a disinterest in school and do not have any hobbies. They live day to day and moment to moment. They show little or no interest or value in personal achievement or success. They don't plan ahead or show any concern for future events or consequences they may experience.

Unhappiness, dissatisfaction, depression, anxiety, boredom

These are frequent symptoms. Children have a negative picture of themselves and see others as better than they are. They generally lack confidence in their abilities. They are unhappy in their home setting and often feel alienated and not part of their family unit.

Socialization problems

These children usually maintain friendships on a superficial level or do not have many friends. Often they do not have a close friend and feel isolated from their peers. They have trouble with authority, and difficulties at home are usually present. Conflicts with family members exist. They are easily influenced by their peers.

These characteristics are typical but not conclusive. Kids who abuse drugs have many different personality characteristics. There are many different reasons why children use drugs. Below are some of the most frequent reasons for this behavior.

Experimentation—Almost all children try alcohol or drugs. If the child experiments with drugs, this behavior will be seen very infrequently or observed a few times, then discontinued.

Experimentation is the first stage in the four steps toward drug dependency. It is usually followed by occasional use, which is less than once a week, to regular use, where the child is actively involved with the drug. The final stage is dependence.

Peer pressure—All his friends are involved with drugs. He may not be able to go against the influence or pressure of the peer group.

Rebellion—Sometimes drug or alcohol use is based on the child's tendency to rebel against parental or societal values.

Confidence problems—Children who have a negative self-concept are often insecure and lack confidence in themselves. This may be the basis of some drug and alcohol usage.

To promote and enhance social interaction—Some children who have difficulty interacting with their agemates or the opposite sex may feel drugs release inhibitions and make it easier for them to relate with their peers.

To mask depressive feelings—Some children use drugs as an attempt at self-medication. Their emotional difficulties may center around depression, hopelessness and unhappiness. Drugs seem to help alleviate these symptoms.

They like it—Some children are involved with drugs because drugs make them feel good and they enjoy the pleasurable feeling. They are involved with drugs because they like getting high.

Signs and Symptoms of Abuse

There are many symptoms of drug abuse. The list below is not conclusive. If your child shows one or two of the symptoms, it *doesn't* mean he is using drugs. Be concerned when you observe a *cluster* of symptoms. The first symptoms listed are the most obvious. They give direct indications of drug use.

Symptoms you can see

Look first for symptoms you can see. Often appearance is affected by use of drugs or alcohol.

Seeing child loaded—Child is drunk or loaded frequently. Alcohol or medications disappear from the home. You find hidden drugs or alcohol. You discover store-bought drug paraphernalia (packets of rolling paper, various types of pipes, syringes). You frequently find household items that may be used as drug paraphernalia (plastic bags, baggies, lock-type pouches, aluminum-foil strips, small bottles, boxes, razor blades, weighing scales, kitchen spoons and bottle caps burnt black on the bottom).

Loss of interest—Loss of ambition, interest in hobbies, sports or activities. Overall deterioration of morals or values.

Physical changes—Deterioration in health and/or physical appearance. Appetite swings, either a loss or an increase.

Personality changes—Child doesn't seem like himself. Mood swings. Violent or destructive behavior. Severe depression. Threats of or actual suicide attempts. Running away from home or threats of running away.

Loss of interest in school—Grades start to drop. Child misses school.

Secretive behavior—Door to his room is locked. Very private phone calls. Chronic tardiness (late from school, dates, activities).

Avoidance of others—Avoiding family functions, neighbors or old friends. Hanging out with older children. Verbal and/or physical abuse of parents or siblings. Changes in friends or hangouts.

Money problems—Money disappearing around the house. Vague money needs. Sudden school expenses. Child has money but you don't know where it is coming from.

Chronic lying—Frequent alibis, excuses and justification (teachers don't like me, everybody is picking on me, you don't understand me). Inability to keep promises. Uses excuses, such as everyone smokes, drinks, why should you care—it is not hurting you.

Trouble with police—Police involvement of any kind. Driving under the influence citations. Automobile or motorcycle accidents.

Dealing with Drug Abuse

Contact a mental-health professional

If you suspect drug abuse in your child, contact a mental-health professional who specializes in this area. Not all mental-health professionals have this expertise, so be sure you contact one who has training and experience. See Chapter 23, Selecting Psychological Services. Most communities have substance-abuse centers that provide treatment for drug problems or can provide you with additional information.

Identify and alleviate problems

Problems may be related to school, family or peers, as well as to the child himself. If there is marital conflict in the home, discipline problems with the child, school failure or socialization problems, try to resolve these. See the appropriate chapter(s) that relate to your child's areas of difficulty.

Develop new friends

This is more difficult to do with an adolescent than a younger child, but try to help him establish new friendships. Don't put down, criticize or talk negatively about his current friends because when you do that, the child feels you are talking about him. At times it may be appropriate to restrict friendships. Rather than restricting, help him develop new friendships.

Develop interests

Provide opportunities for the child to develop hobbies, interests and activities.

Build confidence

Accentuate positive attributes and look for areas in the child's life that may produce a lack of confidence. Do things to counteract that and enhance a positive self-image. See Chapter 36, Building Confidence, for more information.

Develop overall responsibility and self-discipline

Many children are unmotivated and show problems with responsibility. They don't weigh consequences; this may be part of the problem with drug abuse. Try to develop overall responsibility in areas revolving around the home (chores, keeping the room clean) and with school. See Chapter 40, Developing Responsible Behaviors, for additional information.

Establish communication

Most adolescents tend to withdraw from their families and not communicate as much with their parents at this age. Many times when professionals talk to adolescents about drugs, we try to make a point. Children often see it as a lecture or some type of reprimand. Try to establish an open line of communication with your child. Talk to him about his interests, likes and dislikes. At times, the goal of communicating with your child should not be to teach or communicate information but to interact and exchange information in a positive manner. See Chapter 14, Communication Between Parent & Child.

Don't be manipulated

Many drug abusers are skilled at manipulation. Don't overextend your trust and allow yourself to be manipulated. Establish rules and consequences to follow. Do things to help you build trust in them. Review Chapter 41, Developing Trust, and Chapter 37, Con Artist—Manipulative Children.

Eliminate inappropriate models

If you suspect drug or alcohol abuse in your child, be sure you aren't modeling similar behaviors for him. The old saying, "Do as I say, not as I do" doesn't work too well. The models for this behavior may be occurring in your home, with his peers, on TV or in the movies.

Treat emotional problems

If your child experiences emotional difficulties (depression, unhappiness, anxiety), see an appropriate mental-health professional.

Set rules and consequences for behavior

Avoid protecting the child from consequences or rescuing him. Establish definite rules and consequences. Certain events should follow consistently if the child shows specific behaviors, especially continued drug abuse. Review the chapters under the section on Methods and Techniques.

Some of the information in this chapter was provided by Sherril Rudd, M.S.W., Jefferson Alcohol and Abuse Clinic, Metairie, Louisiana.

21

Household Duties & Chores

Chores are often related to a child's allowance, but they could be contingent on other factors. Establishing chores is beneficial in helping a child develop responsible behaviors. But chores in and of themselves do not promote responsible behavior. Chores can help develop self-discipline, but they can also teach the child to manipulate you if you don't monitor his behavior consistently. A child has to clean his room before he leaves the house on Saturday to go play. If he's able to go play even though he doesn't perform the task, you are developing inappropriate behaviors and a lack of responsibility.

An allowance can be tied to the child's chores. You can also set up a situation in which chores must be completed *before* other privileges are permitted. A child may have to empty the dishwasher after school before he can watch cartoons. Or his room must be cleaned before he leaves the house on Saturday to play.

In assigning duties and chores, be very specific and define *exactly* what you mean by a clean room or a straightened kitchen. Specify the consequences of this behavior ahead of time. Your child's definition of a clean room may be different from yours. If the chore is not completed, deal with this in a calm, matter-of-fact way. Don't nag, remind, aggravate or holler at the child. Just follow through with the specified consequences.

"You have to put the garbage out by 7:00 pm every night. If it's not put out by then, I'll put it out. You won't receive a portion of your allowance that day."

If there are several children in your house and chores must be completed, have the children sit down and assign a weight to each chore or value. This avoids hassles over the fact that one does more than the other, one job is easier and similar complaints. The children may sit down and decide that feeding the dog, emptying the dishwasher and similar activities have a value of 1. Cleaning the table after meals or sweeping the kitchen are each worth 2 points. Vacuuming and putting away the clothes may have a value of 3. Cleaning the bathroom may be worth 4 points.

By assigning different weights to activities, children will feel the system is just and they are receiving fair treatment. If a child cleans a bathroom, which has a value of 4, another child may have to do four activities valued at 1 point that day to equal her brother's work.

Another way to create a fair situation among siblings and chores is to vary the activities. Use a calendar, and place the child's name on the day he is supposed to do a particular chore. If you have two children and one of their chores is to feed the dog, alternate each one's initials on the calendar every other day. When it comes time to feed the dog, all you have to do is look at the calendar to decide whose day it is.

By doing this, one child won't feel like he has fed the dog 10 times for every 1 time his brother completed the chore.

See Chapter 14, Allowance, and Chapter 40, Developing Responsible Behaviors, for more information.

22

How to Deal with Other Children in the Family

In some cases, more than one child in a family has problems. In many situations, the child I am working with is the only one who is having difficulty. The other children in the family are basically doing OK and are not of any significant concern to the parents. The parents focus attention on the problem child, set up reward systems to modify his behavior, take time to visit his school and meet with his teacher. The natural question many parents ask is, "If we are doing all of this with Alan, how do we deal with our other children?"

Treat Children the Same but Different

This statement probably doesn't make much sense. Most people look at me like I'm crazy when I say it.

If you have more than one child, it's very difficult to treat them the *same* because they have *different* personalities. If I ask a parent to describe his or her children, I usually get different personality characteristics.

In some families, the children's personalities are totally opposite. One child is quiet; if he grunts three times in your direction in a day, you're happy. The other child can talk a hungry dog off a meat wagon. When you come home from work, he starts talking and never shuts up. You think, "I hope he gets a sore throat so he'll be quiet." Or one child has 15 minutes of homework. He does it right away and goes outside to play. The other child spends 3-1/2 hours trying to figure out how to get out of the 15 minutes of homework. It's very difficult to treat all your children the same because they have different personality characteristics.

You want to get across to your children that everyone has strengths and weaknesses but are basically the same.

"Your sister gets better grades than you, but you can hit a baseball better."

"Your friend at school can sing very well, but you are better at dancing."

If you focus on a child who gives you problems every night during homework time, but his brother does his homework without any trouble, you want to avoid 2 situations.

No reward system for only one child in the family

First, do *not* set up a reward system for the child who is giving you trouble and ignore the other child. You say to the child you're having trouble with, "Every night you do your homework without a hassle, you can stay up past your bedtime."

The child who is cooperating with homework may think, "I'm doing my homework, not giving them any trouble and getting nothing for it. I'm going to start giving them trouble, and maybe I'll get to stay up late."

Don't use same reward system for both children

Secondly, do *not* say for both children, "Anyone who does their homework without a hassle will get to stay up past their bedtime." The child who cooperates will win all the time, and the other child will not. You can easily create a situation of unfair competition.

Create rewards for both children

If you're trying to improve a behavior in the "problem child," look for areas of weakness to improve in the other child. Ideally, it will not be the same behavior and it may be a behavior of much less importance. Let's assume you're working on improving a child's classroom behavior. You divide the school day up into 6 periods. For each period of time that passes and he behaves, he receives a point. If he receives a certain number of points by the end of the week, his friend can come over on Friday night.

His sister behaves in school and causes no trouble. But she

gets water all over the floor when she takes a bath or she "borrows" things from you without asking. The behaviors of the sister, compared to the brother's misbehavior in school, are unimportant.

But you can set up a system where she earns points and a reward for these behaviors if she improves.

You are indirectly telling both children, "Each of you has strengths and weaknesses. This is what you need to work on, and this is what your sister needs to improve."

For "good" children who don't do anything wrong (you're lucky if you have one of these), you may have to create something. "You'll earn points for helping me empty the dishwasher or by talking to me about what happened in school."

Try to get away from saying or implying your other child has a problem. "We need to give him special attention, because he is having difficulty." Try to minimize anyone has a *problem* and focus on the fact everyone has *strengths* and *weaknesses*. "These are the things your brother needs to improve, and these are the things you need to improve."

Chapter 57, Sibling Conflict, may provide some other ideas for dealing with the other children in the family.

23

Selecting Psychological Services

When trying to locate someone to provide psychological services, be sure he or she has the proper credentials, such as license and certification. Be sure he or she has expertise in the type of counseling or psychotherapy your child needs and primarily works with children. Regardless of the discipline (psychology, psychiatry, social work), select someone who deals primarily with children or adolescents. You don't want your child being helped by someone who also makes his living from marital counseling and seeing adult patients. You want someone who primarily works with children.

You must be involved in counseling or psychotherapy for it to be effective. Any others (teachers, grandparents) who are significantly involved with the child should be made aware of the treatment plan. If I see a child for 1 hour a week, who has him for the other 167 hours of the week? If I can provide information to the people who deal with the child the rest of the week, the probability of success in changing the child's behavior greatly increases. In a sense, the environment (parents, teacher, relatives) also become the child's "therapist." If your child's problem is school-related, the therapist should talk with the teacher, principal or some school person who is familiar with the child.

Become actively involved in your child's treatment. You are with your child more than the therapist.

Counseling and Psychotherapy

If your child becomes involved in counseling or psychotherapy, you should have a general understanding of the process and what will result from it. I will try to give you a general idea of what to ask the therapist to give you a better understanding and increase your involvement.

At the initial meeting

When therapy or counseling is recommended or during your initial meeting with the therapist, ask the following questions.

1. What is my child's problem?
2. How will therapy help him?
3. What are the goals of therapy?
4. How will the goals be accomplished?
5. How much will I be involved?
6. How long do you expect therapy to last?
7. How much will this cost?

When the child is in treatment

Once the child is in treatment, meet *regularly* with the therapist to discuss your child's progress and what you can do to help him at home. Here are questions to discuss during these meetings.

1. How is my child progressing?
2. What areas still need improvement?
3. What can I do at home to help him?
4. How do I deal with his stubbornness, temper tantrums, other problems?
5. His teacher says he is fighting in school, not completing his work. What should I tell her?
6. Is there anything I can read to give me a better understanding of my child and how to deal with him?
7. When will you begin seeing us less frequently?

When therapy ends

When therapy ends, you may ask the therapist many questions, including:

1. What are some things to look for if he starts slipping back?
2. How often should I call to tell you what is happening?
3. How often should I have his teacher(s) report to me or you?

Understand the answers

Be sure questions you ask are answered in terms you can understand. After asking your questions or after your conference, be sure you are not more confused than when you went into the meeting. If you don't understand what's being said, assume it's the therapist's fault, not yours. When I talk to an attorney who uses jargon only he understands, I don't understand what he's saying. I usually stop him and say, "I don't understand a thing you're saying. Please talk to me in every-day language so I can understand."

Do the same with a mental-health professional who uses his terminology or talks over your head. You're not stupid; the professional just isn't smart enough to communicate the information so you can understand. Ask questions. Be sure you leave understanding more than before the conference.

Psychiatric Hospitalization

A few years ago, professionals considered hospitalizing a child or adolescent in a psychiatric hospital when he was a danger to himself or others or when he was severely emotionally disturbed. Today, with the explosion of psychiatric hospitals, the criteria for hospitalization has changed.

Children and adolescents are being hospitalized for many reasons, often before any other form of treatment has been tried. In many cases, the criteria for deciding if a child or adolescent should be placed in a hospital is whether you have "good" hospitalization insurance.

Psychiatric hospitals are a big business and hospital beds must be filled to make money. You can get an idea of the competition by the number and type of ads you hear and see on radio and TV and in the newspaper. Many use "scare advertising" designed to scare or make you feel guilty or to show common behaviors (moodiness in teenagers) as a distress sign or a need for hospitalization.

Ask questions when psychiatric hospitalization is being considered for a child or adolescent. Have other forms of treatment been attempted? Hospitalization is usually seen as the *last step* in the attempt to modify a child's emotional or behavioral difficulties—not the *first step*. In many cases, other forms of treatment (outpatient therapy, family counseling) should be tried before hospitalization is considered.

Even when the child seems out of control, other things

must be considered. Is the child a danger to himself or others? Is he showing signs of severe emotional disturbance? Has he lost contact with reality? If the answer to these questions is yes, then hospitalization may be considered. You might also want to include in this category the child who shows heavy alcohol or drug involvement.

Is the agency or professional spending more time talking about the type of insurance coverage you have than discussing your child's problems? If this is the case, be leery.

Did you get a second opinion? Hospitalization of a child or adolescent is a major decision. Get a second or third opinion. If there is agreement, consider hospitalization.

The psychiatric hospital does not treat the child. A mental-health professional is the one who is primarily responsible for the treatment. When hospitalization is being considered, look for the most competent, reputable person who deals primarily with the difficulties being experienced by your child. Ask your child's teacher, pediatrician or friends for recommendations. Try to gather additional information to make a wise and appropriate decision.

If you still have doubts, contact your child's pediatrician or a mental-health professional who deals primarily with children for additional advice.

Should I Have My Child Evaluated?

If your child is not having any behavioral, emotional or academic trouble, I wouldn't have him evaluated. However, if your child is having trouble at school, at home, in the neighborhood, on the playground or with his friends, and this behavior is not typical for his age group, read Chapter 25, Should I Have My Child Evaluated?

If a teacher, coach, dancing instructor or some other person involved with your child tells you something is unusual, listen.

Read Chapter 30, What Is Normal? for information to help you decide if your child's behavior deviates from the norm and if an evaluation may be appropriate. An evaluation may involve having your child talk to a mental-health professional, or it may involve formal testing.

24

Sexual Curiosity or Abuse?

I frequently see children who may have been sexually abused. Although I identify possible abuse cases, I don't work with these children because it is not consistent with my interests. I do not feel I have the appropriate skills to deal effectively with this problem. When sexual abuse is a possibility or a child has been sexually abused, I refer the child to someone with expertise in this area.

I wanted to include this information in the revised book, so I contacted Dr. Edward Shwery to provide me with assistance. Dr. Shwery is a clinical psychologist with a national reputation for his work in the treatment of sexually abused children. Most of this chapter was prepared by Dr. Shwery. We included information that will be helpful in determining the difference between normal sexual curiosity and the possibility of sexual abuse. In addition, we also give you some suggestions to deal with problems that may be encountered in this area.

What Is Sexuality?

Sexuality is a normal part of healthy psychological and personality development. However, it is often perplexing to pair the concepts of childhood and sexuality together as one idea. Normal sexual development as an adult begins in childhood; it's helpful to understand how this develops. You can learn to recognize and foster normal sexual development in your children, but don't provide too little or too much information to your children.

Children are vulnerable to adults or older children taking

advantage of them and misusing or abusing them sexually. When this occurs, various changes in a child's behaviors may give you clues that there is some interference with normal sexual development.

Sexual abuse covers a wide spectrum—from nudity and fondling to more extensive sexual acts, including intercourse. Introducing a child to pornography can be considered abusive and can interfere with normal sexual development. Growth and change should occur gradually over a span of time with a fairly predictable sequence. Exposure to more extensive sexual experiences too early in life interferes with normal development and creates a variety of problems for a child during his or her adolescence and adulthood.

Normal Sexual Development

Infancy and preschool years

During infancy and the preschool years, it's normal for children to explore their bodies, particularly their genitals. During the preschool years (3 to 6), it's normal for children to become very interested in anatomical differences and to begin understanding (through discovery) the differences between boys and girls. This reflects the first major phase of sexual development—gender identification. Children learn they are boys or girls and the differences between the sexes.

A variety of self-stimulating behaviors occur, including fondling their genitals and putting their hands inside their diapers and pants. Sometimes this extends to exploring another child's anatomy.

The role a child plays is clear and specific. Boys are more aggressive than girls. Girls begin to engage in play and behaviors that are more consistent with being a female. The normal flow of gender development leads children to prefer the company of same-sex children.

Elementary-age children

By the time a child is in elementary school, these behaviors have generally disappeared. Children are gradually taught to respect other children's privacy and through socialization begin to learn to curb certain behaviors. Sexually explicit behaviors can occur, particularly at home.

Girls between 6 and 12 sometimes rub their pelvic area on the couch, a chair or bed in a rocking, self-stimulating manner. This doesn't mean the child is oversexed or is a victim of sexual abuse. Sexual curiosity and interest in self-stimulation are very common in the early childhood and are not by themselves cause for concern.

Adolescence

The next major aspect of sexual development occurs after puberty. During adolescence, the child comes to understand the differences between sexuality and affection. This reaches a peak during middle adolescence (15 to 16), when youngsters work out an understanding of the differences between intimacy and sexuality in preparation for adulthood.

Sexual Abuse

When sexual abuse is present, the normal process is disrupted. Behaviors, attitudes and statements emerge that are not typical in young children. This should arouse suspicion. It usually involves three aspects.

Behavior becomes more specific

Rather than the general curiosity and exploration that is normally seen, sexual behavior becomes more detailed. Young children are not born with knowledge of oral and anal sex or the positions of intercourse. Such behavior is usually not part of normal curiosity.

Children do not have specific sexual knowledge of what to do with certain parts of the body (the young boy should not know where to insert his penis; the young girl should not know about inserting a penis in her vagina). Unless frequently used around the house, a young child should not be aware of slang words for the various sex acts or for sexual parts of the body. When a child is exposed to sexual activity or experience, the child's sexual behavior becomes more "adult-like."

Behaviors are related to situations, locations or people

If you observe a behavior that is not consistent with normal sexual curiosity, ask the child, "Where did you learn that?" The abused or misused child may verbally relate the sexual behaviors to specific situations, locations or persons.

"I do that at John's house."

"I saw that on TV."

"That's in a book at Uncle Joe's house."

"I saw Bobby's daddy do that to his mother."

"That's what Mr. Billy does with me."

"Everybody does that when we're in the clubhouse."

"Mary and I do that."

Behaviors persist and don't change

When a child is being abused, the behavioral clues or changes in the child's behavior do not change or vary, as they do in normal sexual curiosity or exploration.

In a normal situation, the child who attempts to put his mouth on his brother's penis may be asked, "Where did you learn that?"

He might say, "I made that up." You don't observe the behavior again. Sometimes in normal development, you may see one of the behaviors described above, but it is very infrequent, and the child does not continue to exhibit the behavior.

In abused children, the behaviors increase in frequency and continue over a period of time. In the above example, the abused child will continue to engage in the behavior. In addition, he may become preoccupied with parts of the body or become overconcerned or obsessed with sexual matters. Talk or questions about sex may frequent his conversations.

When sexual abuse of a child occurs, it's in the context of secrecy. Pressures are placed on the child to avoid disclosure. There are times when a child's behavior raises suspicions about whether or not sexual abuse has occurred or is occurring. When sexual abuse of a youngster does occur, it's usually with someone known to the child. A relationship with the child usually precedes abuse. The child is more vulnerable to pressures for becoming involved in sexual activities and for additional pressures to maintain secrecy.

It is distressing to realize your child's vulnerability extends to a wide range of people with whom your child has contact. This can include members of the family, professionals in the community, clergy, teachers, scout leaders, coaches, neighbors. The closer the relationship between a child and an adult, the more vulnerable that child is to influence and the greater the potential for misuse of that influence.

Often, sexual abuse in a child is difficult to detect due to many factors.

1. The gradual nature of abuse unfolding in a child's life.
2. The relationship with the abuser.
3. Significant pressures to maintain secrecy.

Signs and Symptoms of Sexual Abuse

Signs and symptoms that may be indicators of sexual abuse are presented below. Sexual abuse of a child occurs under the cover of secrecy in a gradually unfolding manner. Because of this, the signs and symptoms reflecting abuse are usually not dramatic or easily seen.

The list below is not absolute or conclusive but reflects signs and symptoms of concern. When several signs begin to appear with a child, it is not an absolute indicator of abuse but suggests further exploration by a professional is indicated.

Young children (under 5)

1. Preoccupation with sexual issues.
2. Repeated masturbation.
3. Redness or soreness in genital or anal area.
4. Unusual or dramatic changes in general behavior patterns of the child.
5. Withdrawal.
6. Sudden onset of sleeping problems.
7. Sudden onset of eating problems.
8. Chronic medical problems.
9. Chronic diarrhea.
10. Unusual, sexually explicit comments.
11. Mimicking specific sexual behaviors or sexual acts.
12. Unusual changes in the child's mood.

Early childhood (5 to 12)

1. Preoccupation with sexual issues.
2. Repeated masturbation.
3. Redness or soreness in genital or anal area.
4. Unusual or dramatic changes in general behavior patterns of the child.
5. Withdrawal.
6. Sudden onset of sleeping problems.

7. Sudden onset of eating problems.
8. Chronic medical problems.
9. Chronic diarrhea.
10. Unusual, sexually explicit comments.
11. Mimicking specific sexual behaviors or sexual acts.
12. Unusual change in the child's mood.
13. Unusual changes in school performance.
14. Excessive bathing or washing.
15. Becoming secretive.
16. Lying and cheating.
17. Cruelty toward others.
18. Excessive daydreaming.
19. Unusually sensitive or irritable.
20. Unusual changes in body weight.

Early adolescence
1. Preoccupation with sexual issues.
2. Unusual or dramatic changes in general behavior patterns of the child.
3. Withdrawal.
4. Sudden onset of sleeping problems.
5. Sudden onset of eating problems.
6. Chronic medical problems.
7. Chronic diarrhea.
8. Unusual changes in the child's mood.
9. Unusual changes in school performance.
10. Excessive bathing or washing.
11. Becoming secretive.
12. Lying and cheating.
13. Cruelty toward others.
14. Excessive daydreaming.
15. Unusually sensitive or irritable.
16. Unusual changes in body weight.
17. Poor self-esteem.

Late adolescence
1. Preoccupation with sexual issues.
2. Unusual or dramatic changes in general behavior patterns.
3. Withdrawn.
4. Sudden onset of sleeping problems.
5. Sudden onset of eating problems.

6. Chronic medical problems.
7. Chronic diarrhea.
8. Unusual changes in the youngster's mood.
9. Unusual changes in school performance.
10. Excessive bathing or washing.
11. Becoming secretive.
12. Lying and cheating.
13. Cruelty toward others.
14. Excessive daydreaming.
15. Unusually sensitive or irritable.
16. Unusual changes in body weight.
17. Depression.
18. Self-abuse.
19. Avoidance of dating and sexual issues.
20. Drug and/or alcohol abuse.

Dealing with Normal Sexual Curiosity

Your main task is to avoid creating a psychological or emotional problem for the child or to avoid causing the child to be inhibited regarding sexual matters. When children engage in normal sexual behaviors (curiosity), calmly redirect the child away from embarrassing or sexually explicit behaviors.

If you are in a store with your child and he begins putting his hands in his pants, act as you would with other problem behaviors. Try ignoring the behavior. If the behavior persists, redirect the child by giving him something to do with his hands so he can't continue putting his hands in his pants or engaging in sexually explicit behaviors.

If the child is masturbating or rubbing himself on furniture, redirect him to more appropriate affection. Have the child sit next to you and interrupt the behavior. Direct the child to other issues. Express affection for the child to help teach him to be appropriately affectionate. During such discussions, put your arm around the child, touch him on the hand or arm and generally engage in nurturing.

If masturbation continues, there are a couple of things you can do. Direct the child to engage in such behaviors in his own room and with privacy. Usually such behaviors can be dealt with quickly and matter-of-factly, but your anxiety or discomfort often prevents you from dealing directly with your child when he engages in sexually explicit behaviors.

If the frequency of masturbation continues or the inappropriateness of the behavior increases, you might try a reward system to deal with it like you would any other unacceptable behavior (cursing, thumb-sucking). See Chapter 5, Setting Rules For Behavior, Chapter 7, Reward, and Chapter 10, Using Charts to Change Behavior, for more information on techniques to use with this behavior.

Preoccupation with sexual matters or body parts, overconcern for sexual activities and similar behaviors can be dealt with in the same fashion. Keep in mind that these behaviors are part of normal development. Consider attempts to modify behaviors when they frequently occur or are observed in inappropriate situations. It's probably best for you to consult a mental-health professional before you attempt to deal with or modify any sexual behaviors in your child.

Sexual Abuse—What to Do?

If you suspect the possibility of sexual abuse with your child, contact your child's pediatrician for advice. Also contact a mental-health professional who specializes in this area. If your child shows sexual behavior, attitudes or talk that is inconsistent with normal sexual curiosity for his age group, ask him some questions.

"Where or from whom did you learn this?"

"Where did you hear this, see this or were you exposed to this?"

With the help of a mental-health professional, explore these concerns to determine the source of the behavior.

Children may be exposed to a variety of activities or situations that are not appropriate for their age. Is the child sneaking and watching the X-rated channel or movie? Is she playing with older children and being exposed to language or behavior that are not appropriate for her age? Eliminate the source or prevent the child from being exposed to inappropriate material or behaviors. If it seems to be something more serious and there may be a possibility of abuse or misuse, contact the police and the child-protection agency in your state and a mental-health professional, if you have not already done so.

In most communities, there is a limited number of mental-health professionals skilled in dealing with sexual abuse. Most mental-health professionals have little or no experience or training in dealing with sexual abuse of children. It is better to seek a mental-health professional who specializes in this area when treatment is recommended.

Sexual abuse can be successfully treated. New methods are being developed each year and many professionals are receiving specialized training in dealing with these problems. The primary effects of sexual abuse are psychological. We are concerned with the following areas.

1. The presence of significant psychological problems in the child.

2. Psychological problems festering under the surface that have not yet manifested in behavior.

3. Future problems that may develop years from now.

A careful psychological examination is mandatory when you suspect sexual abuse. This will clarify the nature of the problems and help in the development of an appropriate treatment plan. The child is usually treated directly. You are provided with consultation. Often criminal or legal issues also become intertwined with the clinical problems.

It's important to find a professional who has considerable experience in dealing with sexual abuse of children. The goals of treatment are to resolve the current problems, prevent future problems and to help the child back onto a normal track of development.

Sexual Curiosity or Abuse?—Things to Do

Suggestions below are made to prevent the emergence of problems or to deal with difficulties once they arise.

1. Read books about child development so you will be aware of what is normal and unusual sexual behavior for your child. Contact any agencies in your area that could provide you with information.

2. Learn about how to discuss sexual matters with children, and discuss them at the appropriate time.

3. Be sure your child is not exposed to videotapes, movies,

magazines and TV in or around your home that are inappropriate for his age.

4. Minimize play with children who are much older than your child.

5. If sexual behavior occurs, avoid bathing siblings (older than infants or preschool) together, especially if they are different sexes. Don't bathe with an older child, especially a child of the opposite sex. This may overstimulate the child sexually.

6. Avoid children frequently seeing you undress or undressed, especially children of the opposite sex, if sexual behavior occurs. This may overstimulate the child.

7. If normal sexual curiosity or behavior is seen, don't use punishment. Avoid criticism, embarrassment, hollering, guilt-inducing techniques, ridicule or shame to deal with behavior. Remain calm. Treat the behavior in a matter-of-fact manner. Use ignoring, and try to redirect the behavior. If behavior increases in frequency or the above techniques do not effectively reduce the inappropriateness of the behavior, contact a mental-health professional. With his or her advice, you may want to try a reward or incentive system to modify the behavior.

8. If you suspect abuse might be occurring, contact your child's pediatrician and a mental-health professional with expertise in this area. Stay calm. Talk gently and listen, especially if the child begins to talk about sexual matters (remember the significant pressures for secrecy). Do not extensively probe or question the child. Let the conversation flow. Avoid demanding an explanation and confronting or accusing the child. Try to determine the source of the behavior. Where did the child learn, see, experience or hear about this behavior? Children who are sexually abused experience considerable psychological pain and distress. These children are embarrassed, often feel guilty and are conflict-ridden about the abuse. They need gentle support and protection.

Dr. Edward Shwery, a clinical psychologist who specializes in sexual abuse problems, has been practicing for 14 years. During his career, he has practiced pediatric, child and adult clinical psychology. He has worked extensively in the area of child abuse and for the past decade has specialized in sexual abuse cases involving children and adults.

Dr. Shwery has examined and treated over 2,000 children who have been sexually abused. He has also examined and/or treated nearly 1,000 adults who have sexually abused children. He is widely recognized as an authority in the area of sexual abuse. He regularly consults with other professionals, governmental agencies, police departments and courts.

In addition to his busy clinical practice, Dr. Shwery frequently provides expert witness testimony in court and conducts workshops and training programs for professionals. Dr. Shwery practices in Metairie, Louisiana, is married and the father of two children.

25

Should I Have My Child Evaluated?

A saying I use frequently is, "If it's not broken, don't fix it." If a child is not having any behavioral, emotional or academic trouble, I would not have him evaluated. If your child is having trouble at school, at home, in the neighborhood, on the playground or with his friends and his behavior is not typical for his age group, you may want to consider an evaluation.

If your child's teacher, coach, dancing instructor or some other person involved with him tells you something is unusual, listen. Read Chapter 30, What is Normal? to get more information to help you decide if your child's behavior deviates from the norm. An evaluation may be appropriate. This may involve your child talking to a mental-health professional or formal testing.

Some professionals believe if a child experiences behavioral problems, he should be evaluated or tested. Psychological and educational testing is usually more upsetting to you than to your child. Evaluations are designed to provide more information regarding a child's behavior, ability and performance. The more information you have regarding any situation or problem, the better you are able to deal with it. The data provided by evaluations gives you, his teachers and professionals more information by which to understand him, provide help and to alleviate his difficulties.

For many adults, the word "test" produces anxiety, tension and nervousness. We remember the tests we took at school or the ones we took to get a job or promotion. Tests used in evaluations are not used in a pass-fail situation. The child *can-*

not fail. Children often enjoy the testing situation because they receive a great deal of individual attention. Some view the tests as games. Parents have told me their children asked to return to the office for more games.

Psychological tests are designed to compare a child with thousands of other children the same age or in the same grade. Tests may give a personality description or an understanding of the child's behavior. By using this information, a professional should be able to determine why a child is having problems in school, why he acts or behaves in a certain way and what can be done about deficiencies.

Tests and evaluations give us a better understanding of the child. They lead to recommendations that help us deal with the child's problems or eliminate his difficulties.

If your child is evaluated, be sure you understand the results. The purpose of an evaluation is to give you more information to understand your child better. If you leave the conference more confused than when you came in, the evaluation was useless to you. Ask questions. If you don't understand what's said, assume the person giving you the result is not communicating them effectively, *not* that you aren't smart enough to understand them. Ask for the answers to be given in plain everyday language.

If your child is having trouble with schoolwork, fails exams, gets into trouble frequently, gets "held back" a grade or behaves unusually for his age, it's a good idea to have him evaluated. An evaluation will help your child and give you a better understanding of him.

When your child is evaluated, be sure that the individual or agency doing the testing is licensed, certified, approved by the state or has the proper credentials to provide the services you are requesting. See Chapter 23, Selecting Psychological Services, for more information.

26

Single Parenting & Stepparenting

There are many common elements in single parenting and stepparenting. While there are common elements to both parenting situations, there are many unique problems in each. I included these two situations in one chapter because most (75%) single parents remarry, and the stepfamily develops. Many single parents who do not remarry live with someone.

Most of the discussion in this chapter is from the viewpoint of the mother as the custodial parent of the children. I decided to do this because 95% of all single parents who have primary custody of the child are mothers.

Single parenting and stepparenting are usually the result of the death of a parent or divorce. If this is the case, this must be dealt with and discussed with the children. Another significant change in these parenting situations often involves remarriage. This also needs to be discussed with the children.

Discussing separation, divorce, death or remarriage with a child can be difficult. You must give the child some information. But you can probably do more harm than good by providing *too much* information. There is a fine line between giving the child facts that provide him with a better understanding of the situation and overwhelming the child with too many facts so confusion and uncertainty result.

Don't give the child too many details and facts. This information can add to the uncertainty he feels and the unpredictability he experiences in the environment.

Sometimes the information pertains to adult matters a child doesn't understand. Some young children whose parents have separated talk to me about custody, visitation, child support and court proceedings like a Philadelphia lawyer. Other children know too much about their parent's illness or death circumstances. Other young children know the details of their father's love affairs and sexual activities.

After I heard a 4-year-old patient tell me about his father's involvement with other women, I asked his mother why she gave him so much information. She said, "I'm always honest with my child; I had to tell him the truth."

I told her, "There is no such thing as Santa Claus. Do you want me to tell your child that? *That's* being honest with him and giving him the total truth."

Some information should be withheld from a child totally. Other facts can be communicated to him at a later age when he is more mature, can understand what is being said and can emotionally handle it.

Often, when divorce or death occurs, you have a need to discuss and convey your feelings in the situation. Don't do this with your child. Discuss events with a friend, neighbor or another adult. Don't treat the child like an adult. Don't talk to him about adult matters or to other adults in front of him. Although it appears he isn't listening, he probably is.

In deciding if you should tell a child something, ask yourself, "If the child knows this, how is it going to benefit him?" The information you are providing him may not hurt or confuse him, but if you can't see how it will help, don't give him the information. Be brief and to the point when explaining other things. When three words would suffice, many parents use three paragraphs.

When I work with a child who has experienced significant changes, I talk to him about the jobs different people have and about the child's job. The President of the United States has to worry about wars, nuclear weapons and pollution. That's his job. The principal of the child's school must worry about school-related problems and information. His parents need to be concerned about court proceedings, custody payments and settlement of property. His job as a child is to worry about "kid stuff." Who's coming over to sleep Saturday night? What movie am I going to see? When are we going swimming? Let the adults worry about "adult stuff." Kids need to be concerned with their jobs and their worries.

The amount of information you give to a child depends on his age, level of emotional maturing and your feelings as to his ability to cope with the information.

Separation and Divorce

Parents separating

Often I see parents sit down and talk to their children about separating from their spouse, but it doesn't occur. Children may receive this information through a formal sit-down discussion or they may overhear it during parental conflicts.

Tell children about a possible separation *only* when you know for certain it's going to occur. Try to minimize threats or the possibility of separation when the children are present and you are in conflict with your spouse.

Ideally, both of you should sit down with all of the children at the same time to talk to them about a separation. You might explain more to the older than to the younger ones, but tell all the children at the same time.

Tell them the truth but sometimes not the *whole* truth. You can provide too much information. The discussion should revolve around the incompatibility between you and your spouse.

"Your father and I don't love each other any more."

"We can't get along."

Emphasize the fact the children are *not* responsible for the conflict. Although you don't love each another any more or care to be with one another, you do love the children.

Keep communication open

Talking to your children about a separation isn't really a one-time thing because their questions and emotional reactions evolve over time. Reactions to this information are as varied as their personalities. Some children get angry and upset about losing a parent. Others may be totally relieved because this will end the arguing and conflict that has occurred. Other children may be totally shocked because their parents didn't show any indication that they were not getting along.

Let your children express their emotions, and discuss their

feelings with them. Respond to their questions, and provide some opportunity for them to discuss their feelings. But don't give them too much information.

Don't create a "good guy/bad guy" situation. Avoid placing blame on the other parent for the separation. Avoid criticizing your spouse and placing blame in one direction.

It's normal for those involved in this situation to experience emotional upset or distress. You can express some of your feelings to your children, but avoid having the children seeing you frequently distressed or upset. The more the children experience this, the more confusion that will result.

When possible, reassure your children that their environment will remain relatively the same (they will stay in the same school, live in the same house, continue the same activities).

Questions and feelings about a particular parent should be directed to and answered by that parent.

Give your children information so they can digest it and respond. Try to minimize as much change and uncertainty as possible.

Death of a Parent

Whether a death is sudden or related to a lengthy illness determines how you approach and discuss the situation with your child.

Terminal illness

If there is a terminal illness, don't tell the child too far in advance, especially if the parent doesn't show significant signs of physical deterioration. If the parent is in and out of the hospital, talk about the fact that he or she is sick and needs medical attention and medicine. If the parent starts showing significant physical deterioration and/or it is close to the predicted time of death (several weeks), discuss it with the child. Depending on the child's age and his awareness of the situation, older children can be told a little more in advance or given more information than younger children.

Many hospitals have social services and/or counseling for children of a dying parent. Make use of these services or to talk with someone with expertise in this area to determine how and when to relate this information to your children.

If death is sudden

If the death is sudden, tell the children as soon as possible and all at the same time. Reassure the children the environmental structure will stay the same and change will be minimized.

Don't hide your emotions from the children; share *some* of your feelings with them. Try to minimize the frequency that the children see you upset. Let them express their emotions and discuss their feelings with them. But don't treat them like adults. Avoid giving them too much information or discussing the situation in front of them with other adults.

The period following the death

After a death, there is usually a period of denial when a child won't acknowledge the death. The child talks of the parent as if he has not died. This period of denial is usually followed by sad, unhappy feelings. The child may experience some signs of depression and grief because his parent has died. This period usually focuses on the absence of the parent.

"If Daddy were here, we'd be able to do this."

"When Mommy was here, she would help me with this."

After the sad and unhappy emotions are experienced, the next period is a time when the child relives happy memories of the parent and talks about fun things and pleasant times experienced with the parent. When this behavior emerges, the child can begin to get along with his life.

Some experts believe you should let the child experience and participate in the family's grief and attend the appropriate ceremonies (funeral). I believe this is somewhat similar to giving a child too much information. I believe a child can be given too many experiences. Whether the child attends the appropriate ceremonies or not depends on the child's age and his personality. Some children may be able to handle this effectively; others may not.

It may be better for the child to remember his parent the way he was rather than the way the parent appeared at death. This decision should be based on the individual child.

Death is a difficult thing for a family to experience. Often it is wise to seek professional help. If you feel this is necessary, find someone who has expertise in this area.

Remarriage

The child's reaction to a parent's remarriage may be good, bad or indifferent. Discussing the remarriage is easier if you follow the suggestions in the following sections.

Many children of divorce hang on to the hopes their parents will get back together again. Discussion or consideration of remarriage sometimes signifies a step away from parents getting back together. A child also experiences a great deal of uncertainty again.

"Will Mom love him more than she loves me?"

"Who will be in charge at home?"

"Will she like me?"

Discussion of remarriage should allow the child to ask many questions and to express feelings and emotions regarding the change. Adjustment to the possibility of remarriage evolves over time. Tell the child about the event several months before it is to occur.

Involve the stepparent with the child before the marriage. A gradual relationship needs to be established with the new parent.

Change and Confusion

Think of how you felt when your spouse died. Remember your feelings when you were separated? You can probably multiply those feelings and your reaction by a hundred times to imagine how your child probably feels.

A child involved in these situations experiences many changes. She may encounter as many as 10 environmental changes that would be considered very significant (father or mother leaves or dies, a move to a new house or neighborhood, parent starts dating, a change of schools, loss of friends, mother starts working, one or both parents remarry, daily household routines are disrupted). Sometimes just one of these significant changes can produce problems.

Children rely very heavily on structure, predictability, consistency and routine in their environment to provide them with security and emotional stability. When significant change occurs, many children become confused and insecure. Some are able to deal adequately with changes that occur. But other children become fearful, tense, uncertain, dependent, indecisive, rebellious or stubborn.

Science-fiction movies and TV programs depict visitors from other planets or humans venturing to other worlds. When they arrive in the new environment, they are confused and have difficulty predicting and sorting events. They misinterpret responses from other people. The environment doesn't make much sense to them. This is how children often respond to significant shifts in routine, living arrangements or situations in which they find themselves with one parent or a new stepparent.

All children react to change. To what extent they react and whether they experience problems coping with the environment depends on two things—what went on before the change and what goes on after the change.

Let's use the separation of parents as an example. Children will react differently if the separation included a great deal of open conflict between the parents before the separation than they will if the separation was amicable. What happens after the change determines the extent of the problem, how severe it will be and how long it will last.

Any child who experiences a significant change in the environment experiences some confusion and uncertainty. He may have difficulties adapting to the change. Whether any serious problems develop or whether you experience trouble with the child after the change occurs depends primarily on how you deal with the situation. Parents who are cooperative and able to relate to one another in a sane, appropriate way tend to minimize additional confusion and uncertainty in the environment. When parents focus on the children and have the children's best interest in mind, the children tend to have minimal problems. Those who use the children as pawns in a battle against each other or those who react emotionally tend to have children with more serious problems.

Single Parenting

The parent who has custody of the children normally sets the stage. Mothers usually have custody of the children, so most of the discussion focuses around them. Let's look at a few things you can do to minimize problems.

Establish structure and discipline

When your children are sick, your normal parental reaction is to pamper, baby or spoil them. You bend the rules.

When a separation, death, divorce or remarriage occurs, most parents, grandparents, friends and relatives correctly identify the child's feelings and experiences. You may think, "He's experiencing some rough times." or "They no longer have their father." You respond with the reactions described above.

Children need structure

Most children experience change, confusion and uncertainty. They need structure, predictability, consistency and discipline. The above responses give them the opposite of what they need. It removes limits on their behavior, and the environment becomes *more* unpredictable.

Suppose I ask you to come to work for me. When you arrive at my office, I tell you to start working, and I leave the office. I place you in an unstructured situation. You are unsure of what to do. After you've been working for me for several months, you keep asking, "What am I supposed to do here? What's right? What's wrong? What can I do? What is unacceptable?"

I think to myself, "This person has been through some rough times. I do not want to upset her or put any pressure on her." I come back and tell you, "Go ahead and do whatever you want to do."

While I think I'm doing what's best for you, I'm doing just the opposite. I'm taking away limits and structure and producing more confusion and ambiguity. You need me to tell you, "I want you here at 8:00. Between 8:00 and 9:00, perform these duties. You can't do this. These are the only behaviors that are acceptable. Go to lunch at noon, and be back at 12:30. In the afternoon, these are your duties." You may not like anything I tell you, but you're going to feel more secure, at ease and confident because the environment has become predictable and structured.

Children experiencing significant changes need structure,

predictability and consistency to make sense out of their confusing environment.

Role of discipline

Discipline is a very important part of returning stability to your children's changing environment. When everyone cooperates and approaches the children from the same direction, things run more smoothly and problems are minimized. Review the points mentioned in the first section of the book.

Don't pamper or baby your children. Don't feel guilty because of what has happened. Treat the children as you would if your family was together. Place limits on their behavior. Spell out the rules and consequences ahead of time, and enforce them consistently.

Don't foster dependency

Many children who experience change may develop a lack of confidence and/or independent behavior. Try to strengthen confidence and independent behavior; don't have the children rely heavily on you. Your life should not revolve around your child. Develop individual interests and activities for you and your children. Dependency on adults may occur when the children spend a great deal of time with adults. Involve your children with other children and children's activities. See Chapter 39, Dependent Children, for more information.

Treat child like a child, not an adult

Many times after a separation or the death of a parent, the remaining parent needs someone to confide in and talk to. Often the child is the one who is chosen.

If you need a friend to talk to about your problems or adult concerns, find another adult—*not* your child. Children need to be concerned about "kid stuff."

Don't give child too much information

Too much information results in confusion. A young child I recently saw knew all the details of his father's murder by his mother's boyfriend.

When trying to decide what to tell a child, ask yourself, "How is this going to benefit my child?" If you can't see any advantages in your child knowing and receiving the information, don't tell him.

Don't lie to your child. But many times part of the truth is better than the whole truth. It may also be none of the child's business. If a child asks you how much child support his father is paying each month, don't give him details. Answer something like, "That's none of your concern. Let me worry about that, and you worry about kid stuff."

You may talk too much in front of your child. When talking to friends, on the telephone or to a neighbor, you tend to forget your child hears everything. Don't discuss your problems or problems with your spouse in front of your child.

Caretakers should have similar rules

Many times in a single-parent situation, you must rely on others to provide child care for your children. This may involve grandparents, aunts, neighbors or friends. They should have similar rules and expectations. If you have reading material to help you deal with your child, let them read it. Everyone will have a similar idea about how to approach the child. See Chapter 18, Dealing with Lack of Cooperation from Others in Child's Life, for additional information. Consistency in discipline is important, especially immediately after any significant changes have occurred.

Be consistent in contacts with child

If you don't have custody of the child, be consistent in your visits and contacts. More predictability in the environment enables the child to adjust more effectively to the change.

You could call the child every Tuesday and Thursday night or pick him up on Wednesday to have dinner. Establish visitation so the child knows exactly when he will see you and can predict with certainty that this will occur.

Introduce new people gradually

It's difficult for any child to adjust to the many changes that occur in these situations. You'll compound these problems if boyfriends or girlfriends are introduced too soon or too. frequently to the child.

The other day I had a father tell me that 2 weeks after his wife left him and took the children, he moved in with a girlfriend. It's difficult for any child to adjust to the fact his parents aren't together or one parent has died. You compound problems by introducing new mates too soon.

Another child once told me after her parents were separated a month or two, her father brought around a girlfriend and was constantly kissing and hugging the woman in front of the child. The child had a great deal of difficulty accepting and dealing with this.

Introduce any new partners gradually. Minimize sexual overtures in front of the child. After the child becomes more comfortable with the new person, the frequency of the contacts can be increased.

It's not necessary to introduce everyone you go out with to your children. Some children tell me their mother goes out with someone different every week. It's best if your children become involved with those people whom you are becoming serious with.

Spend time with child alone

If you don't have custody, your child probably prefers to be with you—not with other people. Spending time with the child alone may not be a great sacrifice for you to make.

Revolve your weekend visits around the child. Avoid taking the child if she'll have to spend time with the grandparents, an aunt or friends. Your child wants to be with *you*.

Dealing With the Ex-Spouse

When you separated from or divorced your spouse, you assumed the relationship would be terminated. If you have children, the relationship doesn't end—it just changes. Even though you aren't married any longer, you must continue communicating and interacting with him because of the children.

Divorce itself is not psychologically damaging to the child. What determines the impact of the divorce and how it affects the child is what happens before and after the divorce. Fighting, conflict and inconsistencies between parents are significant factors. Keep the child out of your conflict, and minimize the amount of negative behavior he experiences.

When separated and divorced parents cooperate, problems are reduced. But parental cooperation happens to be the exception—not the rule. Many divorced parents still harbor grudges against the ex-spouse. They can't let go of the marriage and experience emotional problems that interfere with their logic and common sense. When making decisions, interacting with your ex, expressing feelings or communicating information, your primary concern should be, "What's in the best interests of the child?" not how you can hurt or get back at your ex-spouse.

Minimize conflict in front of child

This is easier said than done. The major reason most people are no longer with their spouse is because they didn't get along. Try to establish an open line of communication between youself and your ex.

Conflicts can be minimized if you communicate with one another because of and about the children. Avoid other discussions that may produce problems. If you've tried this and haven't been successful, minimize contact or have someone else convey information.

If conflicts occur when parents see one another at visitation, arrange for the child to be picked up at a neutral site. Or have the child wait outside of the house or be looking out the window. When the father pulls up, the child can leave.

Child is not messenger

Don't have your children convey information and messages back and forth between you. This puts the children in the middle.

Adults should deal with adults and be concerned about matters pertaining to them. Children need to be concerned about "kid stuff."

Don't attack, criticize or talk negatively about ex-spouse

This doesn't mean you have to say good things about the other parent. But refrain from saying anything bad.

I had a child once tell me his father continually criticized and said bad things about his mother when he visited him. His father would frequently call his mother an "asshole." The child was telling me he couldn't take it any more. He was having extreme difficulty with his father because of this behavior.

I called the father and conveyed the information the child had told me. He said, "Yes, that's true. But his mother is an asshole." I told him if he felt he must characterize the child's mother this way, he should convey his feelings to his present wife, not to the child. Negative talk about the other parent interferes with the development of a healthy relationship with your child.

You don't have to defend other parent

Although criticism and talking negatively about your ex-spouse should be avoided, it isn't necessary to make excuses or defend him.

A child asks, "Why didn't Dad pick me up or come to see me?"

Your response could be, "I don't know" or "Why don't you call him and ask him?"

It isn't necessary to defend this. Many young children have a difficult time accepting faults in their parent and apparently do not readily see the inconsistent behavior. A father may tell the child he is coming to pick him up Saturday at 10:00. He has kept the promise 5 out of 100 times. However, the young child still gets dressed and impatiently waits for his father at 10:00. Or his dad has promised him a bike for Christmas, a go-cart for his birthday, a trip to the zoo and has done none of these. "I'm going to take you fishing Friday after school." The child comes home from school and gets all his fishing equipment ready only to be disappointed again.

Explanations for parental behaviors in these situations usually fall on deaf ears. It's probably better for the child to confront the inconsistent parent. Try not to answer questions that should be answered by that person.

Around puberty (11 to 16), the child is able to see the behavior in a more realistic light. A 13-year-old told me his father promised him a TV for Christmas, "But he's never followed through with his promises and I probably won't get the TV for Christmas." The older child is able to see the total picture and starts drawing conclusions and inferences about the future based on his parent's past behavior.

Don't ask child to take sides

Don't try to create a "good guy/bad guy" situation.

"Your mother and I are no longer together because she didn't want to be married any more."

"Your father didn't care about us and was never home. That's why I left him."

Your child isn't a judge. Don't tell him it was your ex-spouse's fault the marriage did not stay together. These are adult problems, not the child's problems. There may be a "good guy" and a "bad guy" in terms of the adults involved, but the child should not have to take sides. To him, both of you are "good guys."

Have child develop a relationship with his other parent

Don't force, prevent or interfere with the development of a relationship with your ex-spouse. The child should have ready access to the other parent so a relationship can be established. Flexibility in visitation facilitates this. Using your child to get back at the ex-spouse interferes with this.

I'm not saying you should try to develop something that isn't there. Many times I have mothers tell me the father doesn't want to have anything to do with the child. The mother tries to force him to become more involved. When I question the mother, I hear the father didn't have any involvement with the child when they were living together.

Some people are not cut out to be parents; not living with the children usually enables them to avoid the responsibilities of being a parent. Trying to promote and create something that isn't there often results in more problems than it is worth.

For the father who is involved with his children, make every attempt to develop a relationship. If the father isn't involved and doesn't know the teacher's name or the position the child plays on the Little League baseball team and hasn't seen one of his games—involvement isn't there. You can't develop anything that isn't there or doesn't exist.

Don't act like a family

Separation and divorce ended the family unit. The reason adults continue to interact or communicate is because of the children. But don't try to create a family atmosphere. The family has dissolved.

It is permissible for both parents to attend a teacher's conference to discuss their child. But don't go out to eat as a family or to a movie together. Trying to continue a family atmosphere adds to the children's confusion. The marriage has terminated and the family has been dissolved, but your relationship with the children continues.

Tie households together

This is appropriate if there are some similarities between both parent's houses. This could involve several things. Rules and expectations or behavior, privileges and curfews could be similar in both houses. If reading materials are being used to help deal with the child, both parents should have copies. In this way, everyone involved with the child is aware of similar guidelines and can function in a consistent fashion.

Behaviors at each parent's house can bring similar consequences. A child is giving his mother trouble doing homework. His dad might tell him, "Every night you do your homework without a hassle, your mother will put a check on this chart. On Saturday when you come to my house, if you have 3 checks we'll go skating. If you don't have 3 checks, we won't go skating." Everyone is working together and dealing with the child in a similar fashion.

When both households are tied together, it prevents the child from manipulating his parents. Many children of divorce manipulate and play both ends against the middle to achieve goals they desire. When at his mother's house, a child tells his mother what she wants to hear. At his father's house, the child provides information he thinks his father wants to hear.

If the child tells you something, check it out with the other parent before reacting to it or arriving at a conclusion. This is most easily accomplished when there is communication between households.

Take care of your own business

This primarily applies to the parent who has custody. Often a mother tells me she has tried to get the child's father to cooperate or she has tried to tie the households together and has been unsuccessful. You have the child 80 to 90% of the time and the father has the child the other 10 to 20%. If you take care of your own business and do what you're supposed to do, the negative effects of lack of cooperation from the other parent are minimized.

You can communicate ideas, feelings and techniques to the other parent. But you can only deal with what you can control. If you have the child most of the time, you have more impact on his behavior than the other parent.

Visitation

Visitation time often produces problems for divorced parents and the children. Problems are usually minimized if visitation is flexible. This situation usually exists with cooperative parents who respond to each other in a mature fashion. The parent who has access to his or her children whenever the situation arises and desires to build a relationship usually has children who want to visit and maintain a positive relationship with *both* parents. Rigid, inflexible visitation usually occurs with uncooperative parents. This type of visitation usually involves many difficulties.

Some visits are not positive experiences for child

For some children visits with the non-custodial parent aren't seen as a positive experience. They may be something to avoid. This usually results from three general situations.

1. A visit with the father means the parents come in contact with one another, and a conflict is certain to develop. The child wishes to avoid the visit because he wants to avoid his parents arguing, fighting and not getting along with one another.

Try to avoid fighting, arguing and battling with your ex-spouse in front of the children. If this can't be accomplished, arrange for a neutral site where the children can be picked up. You won't have to come in contact with your ex-spouse.

2. The child infrequently sees his father and must share time with the girlfriend and the girlfriend's children.

3. The father has the child but has him stay with a relative or baby sitter because the father is going out or has to work.

Visits become positive when you spend individual time with your children. They come to see you—not the girlfriend, relative or baby sitter.

Return from visit should be positive

Another reason some children want to avoid visits is the return home results in a negative experience. They may be given the third degree and asked 3,000 questions about what happened, what went on and what they did. Or they are bombarded with adult questions, such as, "Who is your daddy dating? Where is he working? How much did the new television set cost? Did he say when he was going to send the child support?"

Don't question the child about adult matters or things that are none of your business. If you are divorced, it's none of your business whom their father dates. Children are not messengers and shouldn't be in the middle for information.

When your child returns from the visit with your ex-spouse, a question, such as, "Did you have a good time?" might be appropriate. Don't ask specific questions. Let the child's communication flow. If he wants to talk about something that went on at his dad's house, stop and pay attention to him. Discuss it with him when the child brings it up.

Don't place restrictions on the type of information the child can talk to you about. "Don't tell me anything about the girlfriend. I don't want to hear anything about that woman." If a child gets too many questions, he's more likely to tell you what you *want* to hear. He probably does the same thing at his father's house.

Take the pressure off your child. Let him initiate the conversations and determine the extent and degree of the information he gives you.

Visits should be frequent, predictable and consistent

This doesn't mean there has to be a rigid schedule for visitation. If visitation is flexible and the father shows up on time and sees the child frequently, consistency and predictability is accomplished. Unfortunately, some fathers don't want to see their children very often after the divorce.

If the father wants to be involved, allow this to occur as naturally as possible. One purpose of visitation is to have the child maintain and develop a relationship with the non-custodial parent.

If the father doesn't want to become involved with his children, don't try to create something that isn't there. Don't make excuses for him. Have the child direct his questions to the appropriate parent.

Joint custody

Recently there has been a move to award joint custody to parents. How visitation occurs and the extent and method the child spends time with each parent must be determined on an individual basis. Some general statements can be made regarding joint custody.

Structure, predictability and routine are necessary for children experiencing divorce and separation. This is especially true for young children. If the child changes houses frequently in a chaotic way, it can add to the child's confusion. I have seen cases where a young child spends Monday through Wednesday with the father and Thursday through Sunday with the mother. Then he spends Monday through Thursday with the father and Friday through Saturday with the mother. The next week the routine changes. Children in this situation may not know whether they are coming or going. They may have problems adjusting. This adds to problems.

Children need routines and stability. If joint custody is awarded, the child should not make frequent shifts from household to household. The change may occur after a report-card period, a half a year of school or longer. Young children cannot handle numerous, frequent shifts in their environment. Children over 10 handle this much better.

If other parent spoils child

Many times I hear a mother tell me when the children visit the father, it's like they're on a vacation. He continually entertains them, doesn't provide any discipline and lets the children do exactly what they want to do. When the children return home, they're difficult to manage, bored or continually asking to do things.

These are normal feelings for these children because it's like they are going from a concentration camp at their mother's house to an amusement park at their father's home.

The mother must deal with daily routines of homework, bathing, cleaning the room, going to bed at a specific time. When the father has the children on the weekend, all they do is play and have a good time. Any child would be stupid not to want to live or spend more time with his dad than his mom.

This problem may be resolved by increasing the frequency of visits the child has with the father. The situation described above is more likely to occur when the father does not see the child very frequently. This is a normal response on the father's part. If you only see your children twice a month, you might not want to discipline or place limits on their behavior. You'd do as many things as you could to have them enjoy themselves and for you to enjoy their presence.

Increasing visitation tends to minimize this problem. The father could be provided with books to help manage the children. He might not do any less with the children when he has them. But he could create a situation in which they will have to earn privileges by their behavior.

Communicate frequently with other parent

If the child's father lives in another city or out of state, try to communicate frequently. Use letters and phone calls, and send samples of schoolwork, test papers and pictures.

Re-establishing visitation

For the parent who has not seen the child in a long time, establish visitation gradually. In some situations, a father reenters a child's life after many years. He wants the child to spend time with him. Although these two people are blood relatives, this man is a stranger to his young child.

Usually after long periods of time, especially with young children, the person who calls himself "Dad" is unfamiliar to the child. The child doesn't have any emotional relationship with his father. Let the child and parent get to know one another again. This could be started by visits in a secure environment, such as the child's home or the grandparent's house. After repeating this several times, when the child becomes familiar with the parent, the child might go for short trips to the corner store with the parent. Short trips can be gradually increased to include visits to the park to play on the swings or feed the ducks. As the child becomes more familiar with this strange adult, he can eventually work toward spending the night at the other parent's house.

Stepparenting

Being a parent carries with it complex duties and responsibility for which most receive very little training. With stepparents, it's even more complicated.

Stepfamilies must accommodate and adjust more than first families because each individual comes into the new family with another family's customs and expectations. Dealing with "mine, yours and ours" makes the task of the average parent three times more difficult.

Raising children is very difficult when two parents are involved. When three or four parents are involved in discipline, communication, development of values and setting rules, the job becomes much more complicated. Cooperation between adults is necessary to minimize problems the children will experience.

The stepparent who enters an already established family has 2-1/2 strikes against him before he begins. It's easy for him to make a mistake and strike out. The stepparent must enter into and make his presence known in the new family gradually. He must gain acceptance and develop relationships with the children involved. This often requires time; the new parent can't try to institute numerous changes in family routines, values, expectations and demands. Doing this drives the children away and interferes with the development of a healthy relationship with the stepparent.

Set reasonable expectations

Marriage doesn't mean you have an instant, happy family. Although you love the children's father, there's no guarantee the children will love *you*. It takes time to win a new stepchild's trust, especially with older children. They may feel torn between their loyalty to the birth parent and their loyalty to the stepparent.

Don't feel hurt if the stepchild rejects you. The conflicts a stepchild feels are powerful and unavoidable. It can take months or years for a genuine, caring relationship to emerge.

The natural parent should never take a "love me, love my child" position with the stepparent. In a yours-and-mine family, it's unreasonable to expect your partner to feel the way you do toward your own children. Children know their birth parent cares more deeply about them at first than a stepparent does, but the children expect fairness.

Children who are brought together in a stepfamily will not necessarily get along or like one another. Personality clashes and competition may produce conflicts between children.

Get to know children before marriage

You are the outsider and will be met by a certain amount of wariness and emotional distance by the children at first. Don't try to overwhelm them with involvement at first. Don't try to be the super All-American stepparent.

Take it easy. Let things flow and take their course. Be available when the children have needs, and try to provide opportunities for you to develop a relationship with them. A younger child will find it easier to accept a relationship with you than an older child.

An adolescent stepchild may find it hard to accept you and your marriage. In that case, just leave the door open to establishing a relationship later on. Don't force yourself on the children. Try to do things with each child on an individual basis.

Establish new rules and family expectations gradually

All people resist change. If you enter the family and try to establish 400 new rules after the marriage, the children will buck the system. Introduce change gradually.

Get involved in discipline gradually

It may be true the natural mother let the children run all over her and spoiled them considerably. Now they need discipline. If you try to establish a great deal of discipline in a previously undisciplined environment, you're certain to be rejected.

The natural parent should remain boss, with the stepparent gradually becoming involved in the discipline. Eventually, decisions and methods of discipline should be seen as coming from both parents not one or the other.

Try to use reward rather than punishment with your disciplinary measures. Spell out rules and expectations ahead of time. Place the responsibility for what happens on the child's shoulders. If good things happen to the child, it's because of him. If bad things happen, it's also because of the child. Try to take yourself out of the role of "bad guy." Put the responsibility on *his* shoulders.

Avoid yelling, criticism, negative attention and power struggles with the stepchildren. Ease yourself into discipline, and use positive methods whenever possible.

Communicate with children

If most of your verbal interaction with the children involves lectures, criticism and pointing out what they are doing wrong, they'll probably avoid talking to you. Try to keep communication positive. At first, spend more time talking about the child's interests (music, sports, dancing, motorcycles) than giving lectures. Talk to each one just to talk—not to teach something or make a point. Try to avoid asking questions when you already know the answers.

Stepparent and natural parent must function as a unit

This functioning involves two things—consistency in your approach to the children and agreeing with one another in front of the children. Even if you don't agree with your spouse you should back her up in front of the children. Discuss your differences later.

Being inconsistent or functioning as two different people creates a situation where there is a "good guy" and a "bad guy." Although it's OK if you're the "good guy," you're in serious trouble if you're the "bad guy." If you are inconsistent, the children will manipulate one parent against the other.

Let child decide what to call you

Don't force the child to call the stepparent "Mom" or "Dad." Allow the relationship to develop gradually. The child may eventually want to start calling you "Mom" or "Dad," but leave this up to the child. After the relationship develops, this may become spontaneous, especially if there are other children in the family calling the stepparent Mom or Dad.

Make stepchild feel at home

Don't make a stepchild feel like a guest in your home. Establish a room, bed, drawer or part of a locker that is exclusively his. Make him feel like part of the family—not an outsider intruding in your household.

Single Parents and Stepparents—
Things to Remember

1. Try to stabilize the environment by being consistent, establishing routines and becoming predictable.

2. You need to be in control—not the child. Don't pamper, spoil or cater to the child. A child needs a great deal of structure and limits placed on his behavior.

3. Don't talk to a child about adult things. Don't allow him to hear you talking with other adults about matters that do not concern him.

4. Avoid giving the child too much information, talking too much or going into excessive detail when explaining things. This could produce more confusion. Try to minimize other changes and disruptions in the child's life. If changes must be made, they should be made to produce more stability.

5. Get the child involved with other children and children's activities. He should not spend more time with adults than children. He should play with other children and be concerned about "kid stuff," not adult matters.

6. Try to communicate and interact with your ex-spouse in a mature manner. Avoid confrontation, conflict, arguing and yelling in front of the child. Don't put down or criticize your ex-spouse in front of your child.

7. Listen to your child's feelings. Try to understand them. You need to listen to the child's feelings without trying to fix it or make them feel better. Just be there to listen and understand.

8. Stepparents need to be patient. Relationships and friendships develop gradually over time.

9. Stepparents should not immediately establish numerous rules and expectations. Children will resist the change. Establish a few rules, and gradually work into discipline and rule setting in the family. Behaviors do not change overnight, so look for gradual improvement.

10. Use more positive consequences (reward) than punishment with stepchildren. Excessive negative consequences push the children away from you; positive consequences will help develop the relationship.

11. Don't change discipline techniques overnight, and don't try to change too many at one time. Gradual change is best. Do

not undermine or override the other parent's rules or discipline. If you disagree, consult privately, and try to arrive at a rule that is acceptable to you both. If discipline is to be reduced or changed, the parent who set the rule or restriction should be the one to modify it.

12. Don't hide your child's problems or unacceptable behaviors from the other parent. It creates a "good guy/bad guy" situation and teaches the child to manipulate. Keep the other parent informed.

13. Don't believe everything the child tells you about the other household or parent. Children in these situations tend to manipulate. Check it out first.

I could have combined Chapter 19, Effects of Divorce, Separation, Parental Conflict & Other Environmental Change on Behavior, with these two parenting styles to form one chapter. I suggest reviewing the above-mentioned chapter for additional information.

27

Suicide

The incidence of suicide in children and adolescents has nearly tripled since the mid 1960s. Some suicides are based on impulse, but most are planned and given much thought and long consideration.

There is no single answer as to *why* a young person wishes to end his life. Research tends to point to such factors as family problems and pressures, loss of a loved one, loss of an important relationship, identity problems, availability of drugs and alcohol, high academic competition, and needs and goals that are not accessible.

It is difficult to say who will attempt suicide because it is prevalent with many young people. But the child who is isolated, aloof and no trouble to anyone is more likely to attempt suicide. These children often need attention but do not get it at home or at school because their behavior does not demand it. They do not stand out and are easily overlooked. It is difficult to provide personality characteristics of the child who will attempt suicide. But there are many clues and signs to look for. The more symptoms the child shows, the higher the risk.

Danger Signs or Characteristics

Signs or characteristics that help you identify and prevent a possible suicide attempt can be divided into three general areas—verbal, behavioral/feelings and situational.

Verbal

All statements revealing a desire to die.

Direct communications—
"I'm going to kill myself."
"I want to die."
"I want to be with grandpa in heaven."
"I wish I was dead."
"I'm going to shoot myself."

Indirect communications—
"You won't have to worry about me much longer."
"Everyone would be better off without me here."
"I'm causing all the problems in this family."
"I can't take the pressure much longer."
"I'm a burden to my parents."
"My friends don't need me. All I do is cause trouble."

Behavior and feelings

Changes in behavior or personality and the emergence or presence of certain feelings and attitudes may indicate a suicide probability.

1. Withdrawal. The child becomes more of a loner and isolates himself from others or activities. Socialization with his peers and verbal interaction with others decreases. He may appear deep in thought much of the time and unaware of others.

2. Depression, crying, unhappiness and apathy may be present, as well as feelings of hopelessness, helplessness and uselessness.

3. Anxiety, confusion, agitation, moodiness or other signs of disturbance may exist.

4. Academic performance declines.

5. Increase in sleeping or an inability to sleep.

6. Increase or decrease in appetite.

7. Preoccupation with or questions about death, dying, religion, dead relatives, heaven.

8. The child makes final arrangements or tries to "get his affairs in order." This may involve giving away treasured personal possessions (stereo, baseball glove, record collection), paying back debts, doing favors for those he has mistreated, keeping a diary or excessive writing, organizing his belongings.

9. Recent involvement with drugs or alcohol.

10. Lack of optimism or hope about the future.

Situational

Certain situations or environmental conditions are common with children who attempt suicide.

1. Previous suicide attempts or threats.
2. The child has had counseling, therapy or psychiatric hospitalization.
3. Problems or chaos in the family. Disorganized home or breakdown of family structure (death, divorce, separation).
4. Pressure from the family to be successful. The child feels he must be perfect to please his parents.
5. Dissatisfaction with the home situation, rules and restrictions and a feeling things won't change because his parents' rules and behavior are etched in stone.
6. The child feels his family doesn't understand, respect or appreciate him. His feelings of unhappiness, frustration or failure are unacceptable to his or her parents. The child feels rejected by his parents.
7. Physical fights with others and/or family members. Physical and assaultive behavior on family members.
8. Increased tension, pressure, competitiveness and demands from school and/or peers. Failure in school.
9. Loss of a loved one or close important relationship.
10. Adolescent identity problems. Transition from adolescence to adulthood.
11. Suicide plans that involve lethal or quick methods (gunshot, hanging, jumping off a bridge). Suicide plans are specific, with details well worked out.
12. Recent suicide of a friend, relative or admired person.

It is difficult to identify a "suicide personality." The more signs or characteristics the child shows, the higher the risk. Whether the suicide attempt is impulsive or well thought out, lack of optimism, a sense of unhappiness and a lack of hope about the future are usually present.

What to Do?

If your child makes verbal comments indicating a desire to die, it should get your attention. Take it seriously. Identify the situation or circumstances when this feeling is expressed. Does it occur when she doesn't get her way (you don't buy her something she wants or you won't let her go outside to play)? Does it occur after you punished her or when making you feel guilty will be to her advantage? Is she trying to get a reaction out of you or make you upset? Can you predict when you will hear it? Does it occur in an unpredictable situation, such as watching TV, riding in the car, in a conversation about school or her friends? How frequently does it occur and under what circumstances?

Some comments about suicide are manipulative. They can be viewed and reacted to in a similar fashion as many of the things you might hear from a child.

"I hate you."

"You're mean."

"I'm running away."

"I want to go live at grandma's."

This is especially true if the child has a manipulative personality. Have the child express his feelings and discuss them. Stay calm. Don't allow the child to manipulate you.

Whether the expression concerning a desire to die is predictable or not, or whether it is seen as manipulative or not, look for possible danger signs or characteristics. If you can identify several of the above feelings, behavioral changes or situation in your child, take the remark very seriously! The more frequently you hear the comments, the more seriously you should regard them.

Talk to your child about his feelings and suicide. Don't offer simple answers to serious problems or tell your child all the reasons he shouldn't feel the way he does. This may increase his feelings of guilt and make him feel more worthless and hopeless. Try to understand his feelings. Have him generate other solutions to the problem(s). Consult a mental-health professional.

When in doubt or when you have unanswered questions, get in touch with someone who can provide you with more information!

28

Teenage Behavior—HELP!

Most of the information written on teenagers and adolescents places a great deal of emphasis on the change, confusion and uncertainty they experience. Physical, social and emotional changes occur in the adolescent. These changes make this period of time very difficult and confusing. This period in your child's life is very difficult. It's also a very difficult and confusing time for you.

Not much has been written about the changes that occur with you. Some very normal behaviors occur in the adolescent and his parents during this period of time. I often see children who show some of the behaviors and attitudes described, which the parents perceive as a problem. Many times these are normal adolescent behaviors or actions.

Let me use an example to describe some general changes that occur. It is very extreme and ridiculous, but I think it conveys the overall picture of parent-child interaction during adolescence. Imagine you are one of the brightest people in the world. You know just about everything there is to know about everything. Your level of intelligence is equal to Albert Einstein's. Combined with your high intellectual level, you have a tremendous amount of information regarding the world, life, what is important and not important. Your vast intellect makes you aware of everything you should or should not know and allows you to deal with most problem situations in a very effective manner.

Imagine you work for two retarded people. Their level of intelligence is significantly below yours, and their knowledge and understanding of the world is tremendously deficient. These two stupid people tell you what you should do and what you should not do. They are also instructing you on how to do certain things and what's important and unimportant. They tell you to do things that don't make any sense, and you cannot see any logic behind their demands and requests. They talk about things that are unimportant, irrelevant and have nothing to do with your job.

Even after many attempts to get them to realize they don't know what they're talking about, they don't understand the situation. What they have to say has nothing to do with what is happening. They continue to harass you with instructions, requests, demands and information.

How would you feel? You'd probably be angry most of the time because these two retarded people are telling you what you should do. You'd mumble under your breath, shake your head and not talk too much to them. If they told you to do something, you'd probably do the opposite of what they wanted or do what you thought you needed to do. You'd probably stay away from them as much as possible and spend more time with people who were intelligent like you or understood things on your level of comprehension. You'd also probably forget to do some of the unimportant things they requested.

Although the above example is somewhat ridiculous and extreme, the teenager believes he is the one with the high intellect. His peers usually are the only people with intelligence close to his. Your teenager views *you* as the retarded employers.

Adolescence used to occur around 13, 14 or 15. Because of many factors, today we see the emergence of some of the above behaviors at 11 and 12, and sometimes even a little earlier. I discuss some of the changes I see both in parents of adolescents and the children.

Parental Changes

Your intelligence decreases

The energy used to develop breasts in girls and facial hair in boys and other secondary sex characteristics in your children is derived from your intelligence. Although there isn't much scientific research to back this position, the energy required for the child to develop during the adolescence is drained directly from *your* brain. The end result is you lose IQ points and become less intelligent than when the child was 8 or 9 years old. Consequently, you approach life and the world from limited capacity, and your ability to provide information and direction is significantly reduced. As your child gets older, you get stupid and don't know what you're talking about.

You go through physical changes

It is unknown what specific changes occur. It may be dress, your physical appearance or hairstyle. But it seems as if you grow two heads; you are a total embarrassment to your children.

Because of these changes in your physical appearance, your children stop bringing other children over to the house. You embarrass them. If you take the child to a show or basketball game, you have to drop them off a block before the gym or around the corner so no one else (their peers) will see them with you.

They don't like to be seen in public with you. They refuse to go to restaurants with the family or to activities where other people might think you are their parents.

You slept through your adolescence

Either you slept through your adolescence or you have total amnesia about this period in your life. You don't understand what they're going through. You don't have any idea what it's like being 13 years old; there's no way you can relate to their experiences or problems.

You live in the "olden days"

You are old-fashioned and not "with it." You live in the "olden days" when soda was a dime, movies were a quarter and you had to walk 12 miles in the snow to get to school. You listen to old music and don't know anything about what's in style, how people act or what *other* parents allow their children to do. Even some other stupid adults (his friend's parents) know more about what is happening than you do.

You now speak a foreign language

When you talk to your adolescent, he looks at you as if he

doesn't understand anything you say. When you talk to him, he looks at the ceiling or floor, thinks about what he's going to do later in the day or hums his favorite song. Nothing you say is making any sense. Either you have forgotten how to communicate or are speaking a foreign language.

You don't know what he eats

This frequently centers around the child eating what you have prepared. You must have forgotten how to prepare meals because he does not want to eat anything you cook.

You could prepare a delicious 7-course meal, and the typical adolescent would turn his nose up and eat a couple of hot dogs instead.

You also forget how to shop at the grocery store and never have anything to eat in the house. Although you just spent $300 at the store and have the refrigerator and cabinets stocked, his response is always, "There's nothing to eat in this house." If you ask him what to buy at the store or what meals to prepare, you don't get any response.

Perhaps part of not eating what you cook is the child would have to sit at the dinner table with the family. This is unacceptable. If you fix a plate of what you have made and leave it on the stove or put it in the refrigerator, it disappears at a later time.

You become irritating

Sometimes your presence around the adolescent irritates him. Don't even ask him a simple question, such as, "How was your day?" That will aggravate him. You're more likely to get a flip response or a dirty look.

Almost anything you do at times will irritate your adolescent. All you know how to do is ask a bunch of stupid questions, give lectures or tell them things they have heard 4,000 times before.

You lose influence over your child

What you say means very little to your child. You lose influence over his behavior. Other people's opinions, especially his peers, become more important than yours.

Adolescent Changes

Just as you experience many changes when your child hits adolescence, he also experiences a number of changes.

His intelligence increases

He becomes very smart and knows almost everything there is to know. It's difficult to find any subject he isn't familiar with or about which he doesn't know all the correct answers.

His friends' intelligence increases

The neighborhood child you knew for many years suddenly has a dramatic surge in intellectual potential and becomes an authority on many subjects. If your child's friend said it, it has to be true.

A year ago, one of my boys was playing high-school baseball. He was talking about playing softball for the local youth team. I know a little bit about baseball and told him I didn't think it was a good idea to play softball because his timing might be off, he might have some difficulty adjusting from the slow-pitch softball to the fast-pitch hard ball and other reasons.

He looked at me like I was crazy and proceeded to sign up for the team. A couple of weeks later, while we were eating, he mentioned he wasn't going to play softball because Dwayne said, "It would not be a good idea because it might mess up his hitting and timing."

Although I didn't say anything, I thought I'd heard this somewhere before. But when I said it, it didn't mean much. When it came from one of his peers, it was true.

Communication decreases

The young child who used to talk to you quite a bit and tell you everything that happened has little to say as an adolescent. He doesn't communicate often or for very long periods. Questions are usually responded to with minimum verbal output and involve one or two words. You probably wouldn't talk to the stupid people who did not understand much of the world either.

He spends lots of time in his room

Other parts of your house, such as the den and kitchen, are no longer useful to the adolescent. He spends a great deal of time in his room, probably to get away from people who are constantly on his back and don't understand anything.

If he has a television in his room, you'll probably only see him when it's time to eat or when it's time to go to the bathroom. He also spends a lot of time in his room because he sleeps a lot. Getting up early (before noon) is something you did when you were a kid.

He thinks he owns stock in the telephone company, radio station and record company

He must talk on the phone and listen to the radio or his stereo a great deal of time to make his stock more valuable. He spends time on the phone or listening to music you can't understand. Your phone rings all time because the other adolescents also feel they also have stock in the phone company. The more they use the phone, the higher the stock will go.

Another belief adolescents have is the louder he plays the stereo or radio, the more valuable his stock will become in the company.

He seems angry most of the time

Wouldn't you be angry if two retarded people were always telling you want to do? Because of this anger, he mumbles a lot and talks under his breath quite frequently. You ask him to do something, "Please put out the garbage." Even if he does it, he mumbles under his breath, makes faces and shakes his head because these stupid people make him do totally unimportant activities.

Peer groups become very important

Friends know so much and are so intelligent they could become presidential advisers. Your child desires to spend a lot of time with individuals who are similar in ability to him. He tends to withdraw from family activities, doesn't like to go places he used to go (Sunday dinner at Grandmother's), gets highly insulted if you even ask him to do something with you and would rather be with his friends than with you. He might consider coming with you if you ask one of his friends to come, but chances are slim.

Moodiness is common

Your child may become moody, get upset very easily and become quickly frustrated. This is typical of this age. Mood swings often subside quickly and don't last long but occur frequently.

Stubbornness, opposition and resistance develop

The young child who was very compliant and passive may now start talking up and telling you what he thinks and what's on his mind. He may become stubborn and not comply with all your wishes. If this is done in an appropriate manner and not in a flip, sassy tone, this behavior can be seen as fairly typical. If you say it's black, he's likely to say it's white. If you disapprove of a certain type of dress or clothing, she'll probably wear it until it falls off her back.

Dress code changes rapidly

There is an adolescent dress code that changes rapidly. It primarily states you must dress like everyone else in your peer group. If a certain style or brand name of jeans or tennis shoes is on the dress code, you must wear this and nothing else. If you decide to wear a different style, you are out of uniform.

Grades may decline or he is disinterested in school

When a child is 7, 8, 9 or 10, he has a 10-pound bag and must put 5 pounds in it. When the child reaches adolescence, he still has the same 10-pound bag, but now has to put 20 pounds in it. There are football games, the opposite sex, talking on the phone and parties to take up his time. Usually schoolwork is dropped to fit in more pleasurable activities. Because of these additional interests and activities, grades may start to decline.

If your child exhibits some of these characteristics, it shouldn't arouse a great deal of concern.

What should concern you is how *you* deal with your child during this period of his life. Many sections in this book provide techniques to help you deal with your adolescent.

Dealing with Your Adolescent

Being an adolescent is a very difficult time in your child's life. Being the parent of an adolescent may produce more problems. When dealing with your child, try to use techniques that won't produce further rebellion, opposition, anger and defiance. Enough of this is already present.

The most difficult thing for you in dealing with a child this age is to realize you are in transition. You are moving from using methods to deal with young children to using techniques that are more similar to the way you deal with your friends and other adults.

Much confusion occurs during this time on the child's and the parent's part. The child may be asking to be dealt with in an adult fashion but is acting like a child. At the same time, you may be telling the child to act more mature but you treat him like a child.

If I used your car and you asked me to put gas in it and I didn't, what would you do? You wouldn't nag me, holler at me or give me a lecture. You'd probably not let me use your car again. Friends who don't cooperate with you or misuse your friendship aren't the type of people you go out of your way to help. On the other hand, you usually don't force your friends to do certain things. You usually just administer consequences in a very matter-of-fact way.

With children, you may have a tendency to nag, remind and force them to do certain things. By adolescence, this process must change. You have to move more into adult methods of dealing with your child's behavior.

Avoid build up of anger

The adolescent is angry much of the time because he has two retarded people telling him what to do. Try to avoid the build up of additional anger. Reduce the amount of criticism, negative attention and correction you give and try to avoid as much confrontation as possible. See Chapter 7, Reward; Chapter 8, Punishment; Chapter 9, Ignoring; and Chapter 32, Anger—Aggressive and Rebellious Behavior; for more information in this area.

Avoid power struggles

This goes with trying to avoid the build up of anger. Anytime you get into a power struggle, you automatically lose. Avoid forcing her to do certain things. Don't get into power struggles with her. If she refuses to cooperate, try to set some rules and consequences you can enforce and control. See Chapter 5, Setting Rules For Behavior, and Chapter 40, Developing Responsible Behaviors, for ideas on avoiding confrontation.

Try compromise

If you force your child to do what you want him to do, you win and he loses. Or the child flatly refuses to do what you want him to do. He wins, and you lose.

Try to set up situations where both of you win. If your child wants to stay out a little bit later or to use the car more frequently, try to find behavior you'd like improved. Use those as a method of compromise. "You can use the car an additional night provided you put in extra time studying." Try to use compromises to obtain the behaviors you desire. See Chapter 40, Developing Trust, for additional information.

Improve communication

Adolescents don't talk much to adults, so you may not communicate a lot with them. Most of the time when you communicate with adolescents, you try to get a point across, teach him something or correct him. This places emphasis on negative behaviors or faults. Most of your verbal interaction with the adolescent is negative.

Try to improve the communication with him by discussing more-positive behaviors, things he's interested in, hobbies, interests, sports, dancing, music. Try to establish times during the day you can talk with the adolescent and not accomplish or teach him anything. The main purpose of the communication is to have positive interaction with the child. Nothing else is accomplished. See Chapter 14, Communication Between Parent and Child, for more information in this area.

29

Twins

If you think it's difficult dealing with one child, imagine if you had two or more the same age. Everything would be doubled and more than twice as difficult. It's probably more trouble being the parent of twins than it is being a twin. My father is an identical twin, and he's told me many stories about how he and his brother gave my grandparents trouble or confused other adults dealing with them.

Although twins produce similar problems in management as most children, a child's individual identity seems to be an important issue. No matter how hard you try to avoid competition between siblings, there is a certain amount of built-in competition. Some competition can be avoided, but you have to live with other competition. This is especially true of twins.

Try to minimize competition as much as possible. Don't create competitive situations. Try to establish individual identities for each child. Review Chapter 57, Sibling Conflict, and Chapter 22, How to Deal with Other Children in the Family, for additional tips. Below are some suggestions.

The same but different

Don't treat twins as a unit or as one entity. Pursue separate identities and activities for each child. Children have different personality characteristics and can't all be treated the same. Respond to each child based on his personality. Avoid treating both of them exactly the same.

Create individual strengths, and try involve them in different activities. This is more difficult when both children are the same sex. Don't enroll both in baseball, music and karate.

Identify what is important to each child, and develop individual areas of accomplishment.

Don't dress the children exactly the same. Let each have his own toys, games and clothes. As much as possible, avoid shared items.

Encourage the children to develop different playmates and friends. As much as possible, avoid shared friends.

Ask relatives to treat the children individually—not as a unit. Encourage grandparents to do things with only one child.

This section is brief because other chapters deal directly with some of the difficulties experienced with twins. It's best to create an individualized situation so each child is seen and dealt with as a separate person. Try to approach the situation of twins as two children who happen to have the same birthday!

30

What Is Normal?

How aggressive should a child be? How shy, active, talkative? What *is* normal child behavior?

These questions are difficult to answer. *Normal* behavior doesn't interfere with a child's ability to cope with his environment or get along with others.

It's fairly easy to find a child-development book that tells you at what age a child should walk, talk or get his first teeth. Other books tell you what behavior to expect at certain ages (terrible twos). But what is a normal amount of sassiness, fighting or temper tantrums? When trying to decide what is normal or what to expect from a child, several factors must be taken into consideration.

Frequency

All children whine, have temper tantrums, pout or are sassy at some time. To determine if the behavior should produce concern, observe how frequently it occurs. A child who has a temper tantrum once a month isn't revealing excessive behavior. If it occurs 4 times a day, analyze it more closely. Consider how often it occurs. The more frequently the behavior is seen, the more it deviates from normal.

How does behavior interfere with child's ability to function?

Most children don't like to do homework or classwork. But most do it. The child who isn't doing his schoolwork may fail or have to go to summer school. If a child's behavior restricts or prevents functioning like an average child, it may be considered *abnormal*.

How does behavior interfere with others?

Most children fight with their siblings. If this behavior produces a feared or negative reaction from his sister, it may not be considered normal. A child who whines or fights with his brother may cause a continuous disruption in the household. If the behavior significantly interferes with other people's routines, behaviors and activities, it may deviate from the norm (not normal).

Take peer groups into consideration

I'm the last person to say you should keep up with the Jones's. In determining what to expect from your child, consider his peer group. Take into account the behavior and actions of his age mates. You must compare your child with other children his age.

Several years ago, when long hair was fashionable on boys and short skirts were popular with girls, children whose parents refused to let them participate in the fads were considered odd by their peers and subjected to hazing and rejection.

The child's peer group's behavior and values must be taken into consideration before deciding what is normal for your child. It may be necessary to become familiar with other children to determine what to expect from your child or how much his behavior differs from the average.

Individual differences

Children have different personalities. One child may be sensitive, another talkative, a third shy. In determining whether behavior is normal, consider the child's peer group and the individual child. Also consider family differences and expectations. You may expect your child to say, "Yes ma'am" and "No sir," while I don't expect it from my children.

Listen to others who know about child behavior

Teachers, coaches, dance instructors and others who work with children are usually familiar with age-appropriate and normal behavior. Although they may not be able to give reasons for certain behavior or recommendations for dealing with them, they can easily identify unusual actions that differ from those of the child's age group.

Listen to these people if they tell you that your child's

behavior should be investigated. I see many children in fourth or fifth grade whose abnormal behavior was first reported to their parents by teachers in preschool, kindergarten, first and second grade and by other teachers.

If you still think your child's behavior differs from the average after reading this, contact your child's doctor or a mental-health professional who deals primarily with children. He or she will be able to give you information or direction to help answer your questions.

31

Who's In Control?

Many times I see families whose children determine the routines and activities and generally run the household more than the parents. These children have more control than their parents.

Recently I saw a 7-year-old who was having trouble in school. He wasn't doing the required work in class; he was daydreaming and doing whatever he pleased. His parents told me they were having a lot of difficulty with him cooperating at home, especially with routine tasks. They also mentioned he was constantly complaining to them about the fact his 3- and 4-year-old brothers didn't have to go to school. He didn't think it was fair. To solve the situation, the parents put the two brothers in nursery school.

This child was in more control than his parents. Rather than have your child call the shots, it's better to have the child learn there are things he must do, whether he wants to or not.

Parents Need to Be in Control

You must be in control. I'm not talking about control by force or a dictatorship. I mean control that involves setting rules and and being consistent with consequences. I discuss this in great detail in the section on Methods and Techniques. Parents in control develop many positive behaviors and attitudes, and several problem behaviors or situations can be avoided. Let's look at some of these.

Help child deal with reality

I'd rather be fishing most of the time than working, but I

have to go work more than I'm able to fish. For most, the major part of the day involves things you have to do because they have to be done—not because you want to do them. Many times parents tell me they don't want to destroy the child's individuality or his free spirit by placing limits on him.

I answer, "That would be fine if the child lived on a mountain someplace and could wake up every morning and decide what he wanted or didn't want to do. But most of us live in a society with rules, limits, expectations and demands placed on us daily. By placing limits on your child, you help him deal with the real world. Compliance with rules and routines is a common, necessary part of adulthood."

Develop responsibility

One of your major jobs of being as parent is to help your child develop, learn and grow so he'll be a happy, well-adusted adult. Responsibility is a large part of adulthood. A child must have some degree of this to make an adequate adjustment.

A child who is in control usually is not a responsible child. He may have problems in this area. Responsibility is something you don't get with age. It is something you learn. If the child is in control, he is less likely to learn to be responsible.

Add to security and confidence

Suppose I said, "Come to work for me tomorrow morning. Show up at my office at 8 o'clock." The next day, you arrive at my office. I greet you then tell you, "Go ahead and work." I walk out the door and get in my car and leave.

How would you feel? You'd be confused and uncertain. If I continued to expose you to this type of work situation, you might develop some insecurity. You wouldn't have any confidence in your job because you wouldn't know what to do. I placed you in a situation in which there are no limits on your behavior and the environment is unstructured. You are in control because you are left to do whatever you want to do.

This is similar to the way some children feel when there are no limits on their behavior. Children in control set their own limits, and very few external restrictions or rules apply to them.

Suppose I came into the office one day after you have worked for me for 4 months under these conditions. I tell you,

"I want you to come to work at 8 o'clock. I want you to do paperwork, work on this stack from 8 to 9 o'clock. From 9 to 10 o'clock, do this. You can't do this. This is forbidden. Go to lunch at 12 noon and come back at 12:30. Go home at 5."

You might not like anything I tell you, but you're going to feel more secure in the environment. You'll have more confidence in what you are doing because you know exactly what you're supposed to do and not supposed to do. Children in control have no limits on their behavior and may have similar feelings.

Reduce manipulative behavior

Children are born con artists and do not need any additional help in learning these behaviors. Children who are in more control than their parents tend to be very skilled manipulators. They are able to get people to say and do what they want. By establishing parental control, this behavior is greatly reduced.

Minimize hassles, conflicts and power struggles

These behaviors are typical with children who are in control. These children do not readily accept "no" for an answer. They want to do what they want to do, when they want to do it and for as long as they want to do it.

Routine activities (taking a bath, doing homework, cleaning their room) become monumental events if they don't feel like doing it. Hassles with these activities are reduced if you are in control.

Develop emotional closeness and support the child

I usually don't get close to people who argue, fight or get into conflicts. Frequent disagreements and hassles interfere with a positive relationship and emotional closeness with others.

The child in control wants to do what he wants to do. Conflicts are frequent. This may inhibit a strong, close relationship with your child.

Some parents tell me, "I don't want to set limits and discipline my child because he won't like me." However, if you put limits on your child and make sure you are in control, you may start to like each other! Children with fair and consistent limits on their behavior *do* like their parents. You must be in control before you can support and love your child.

Eliminate unnecessary discussions and explanations

My children frequently ask me to tell their friends about how much the movies and soft drinks cost in the old days. Many things have changed since the old days. In the 1940s, '50s and early '60s, you did things as a child because your parents said so. Recently more emphasis has been placed on explaining, reasoning and discussing situations and talking to the child.

If the child is in control, talking, reasoning and explaining are not effective. The only adequate explanation or answer to this child's question is what he wants to hear. If you tell him what he wants to hear, he'll shut up. If not, he continually asks questions. You can explain to him for a year without success.

Suppose I work for you and say, "I think the person who said I have to work 5 days and I only get 2 days off was crazy! I think the rule is stupid. I feel I should come to work 3-1/2 days and be off 3-1/2 days every week. That makes more sense to me."

You could sit down and explain to me that people used to work 7 days a week and you should be lucky you are working only 5. But the answer I want to hear, which will stop further questioning is, "You're right. Take off 3-1/2 days a week and come to work 3-1/2 days."

If you're my employer, you'd probably say, "You're working for me. You can come to work 5 days a week and have 2 off or look for another job."

Let's say you plan a fishing trip for Saturday morning and intend to take your child with you. You wake up Saturday and it's raining. The weather forecast predicts rain all day. You tell your child, "We're not going to be able to go fishing today. We'll go next week or tomorrow."

The child says, "Let's go. We can fish in the rain. It's not going to rain all day. We won't get that wet." After 27 explanations of why you can't go fishing, the child still isn't satisfied. He's still complaining and asking to go. The only answer that will satisfy him is, "OK, let's go fishing. It doesn't matter that much if we catch pneumonia or the boat sinks."

Think of a good answer for this. Your child comes up to you and asks, "Why do I have to make my bed if I mess it up every night when I sleep in it?" There aren't any good explanations for this request other than "because I said so!" Some things you request have to be done simply because you say so. No further explanation is necessary. I'm not saying you shouldn't explain to your child. But in some situations, explanations fall on deaf ears unless it's the response the child wants to hear.

In the example I used at the beginning of the chapter, the child had more control than his parents. Usually school is important in the child's life, and we focus on that. However, in this example, the parents need to get more control of the child's *total* life and develop more cooperation in other, maybe unimportant, areas of his life (cooperation at bath time, homework time, bedtime). It's difficult to gain control of a child's school behavior and performance if you have no control of other areas of his life.

You must be in control to meet your responsibility to the child and to society.

32

Anger—Aggressive & Rebellious Behavior

Anger is a form of disapproval. If you're angry with me, it means I'm doing something you don't like. If your child shows aggressive or rebellious behavior toward you, his peers or authority figures, he disapproves or doesn't agree with what other people are saying or doing. There are a couple of general situations in which anger may be seen. One is a result of a buildup of underlying anger. The other is seen when a child develops inappropriate methods of problem solving or interacting with others.

Underlying Anger

All children become angry and express these emotions in some fashion. Some methods of acknowledging aggressive feelings produce problems while others will not. Think about this situation with the image of an anger balloon. Each time something happens that you don't like, hot air is forced into the balloon. It starts to expand. Air has to be let out of the balloon—anger has to be expressed.

This is done is differently by different people. Some people let the anger build up until their balloon pops. When this happens, there may be an explosive outburst of anger over a minor annoyance. After this display of anger, there is usually a period of control until the balloon blows up again.

Other people release air from the balloon every time it starts to fill. These people appropriately express their feelings at the time they occur. Other people release air though passive-aggressive maneuvers, displacement or psychosomatically.

When dealing with aggressive and rebellious behavior in children, consider three things:

1. How to help the child express and deal with his anger.
2. How to reduce the accumulation of anger.
3. How to deal with aggressive and rebellious behavior when it occurs.

The following sections deal with each topic. I present techniques to help you enable your child to deal with his anger more effectively. I also explain how to reduce inappropriate aggressive and rebellious behavior.

Methods of Expressing Anger

Anger is expressed in many ways. If you block your child's request, send him to his room or do something the child doesn't like, the child can handle his feelings of frustration and anger in five basic ways.

1. Your child can express his feelings appropriately. "I don't like going to my room every time I do something bad. I wish you would stop doing that to me. It gets me angry."
2. He can keep his feelings and emotions to himself and say nothing.
3. He can express his disapproval indirectly through passive-aggressive behaviors, such as stubbornness, sassiness, mumbling under his breath, doing just the opposite of what he is told.
4. He can acknowledge his anger directly through physical actions, such as hitting or attempting to hit the person whom he perceives as the source of his anger.
5. He can displace his feelings to a less-threatening person or to an inanimate object. The child may be angry with you, but he hits his sister, throws something or breaks a toy.

Some ways of dealing with anger get the child in trouble, while others do not. The next sections discuss in more detail the possible ways the child can deal with aggressive feelings, disapproval of others or hostility.

Appropriate communication

The child tells his feelings to the person who made him angry or with whom he disagrees. You may holler at him, and he may say, "I don't like you hollering at me. That makes me feel bad." The child is expressing his feelings. He isn't sassy if it is done in a normal conversational tone.

Strive to have your children communicate their feelings to you. If they can express their anger without hollering, being sassy, flip or smart, reinforce the communication and listen to them.

Some parents view an appropriate expression of feelings as disrespect or sassiness. This is a mistake. The old saying, "A child should be seen and not heard" couldn't be further from the truth when talking about appropriate expressions of anger. Hear what a child disapproves of and what makes him angry. This method of expressing anger produces few, if any, problems for the child.

Bottling up emotions

When a child becomes angry or disapproves of something, he doesn't say anything. He keeps his feelings to himself. Others may not be aware of how he feels.

Feelings of anger emerge in one form or another. If the child keeps his emotions to himself, these feelings are usually expressed by other means, such as headaches or depression. Children who deal with aggressive feelings this way are more of a problem to themselves than to others.

Children may keep their feelings in until some small event occurs, then all the anger is expressed. The seemingly insignificant event is "the straw that broke the camel's back." A tremendous amount of anger is released.

Passive-aggressive behavior

These are indirect or passive ways of expressing anger. Suppose you go to work and your boss gives you a hard time when you arrive. He tells you what a bad job you're doing, and you may be fired. You become extremely angry at him, but you can't punch him in the nose or quit the job. What will you do?

You probably slow down your work and do less. You may take a longer coffee break and may forget to do a few things he told you to do. You have passively acknowledged your anger in an attempt to retaliate.

Children frequently use this indirect method to express

their anger. It usually takes the form of rebellion, doing the opposite of what is desired, negativism, sassiness, mumbling, intentionally doing something annoying, resistance or having the last word.

A child is sent to his room. He is angry, but what can he do? He starts mumbling, "You're unfair. You're always on my back. I want to live at Grandma's." You get upset and start hollering.

The child has effectively and indirectly expressed his anger. This method of dealing with aggressive feelings is likely to produce problems in the child's relationships with others, especially those in a position of supervision or direction over him, such as parents and teachers.

Acting out anger

This usually involves physical violence, fighting or hitting. The child directly and physically retaliates against the source of his anger. A boy won't give another child a football on the school playground. The child threatens to hit him or he starts a fight. This method of dealing with aggressive feelings produces problems in peer interaction and perhaps also in the child's relationships with authority.

Displacing aggressive feelings (displacement)

Sometimes children become angry but don't deal directly with the source of their feelings. Instead they displace these emotions by transferring them to a less-threatening person or to an inanimate object.

You may do something that makes him angry. He doesn't say or do anything to you but goes into the other room and hits his sister. A teacher reprimands a child in the cafeteria. When she leaves, the child starts pushing one of his classmates. A parent sends a child to his room for being sassy. While in his room, he breaks some of his toys.

This method of dealing with anger gives the child problems in his relationships with his peers or siblings.

Reducing the Build Up of Anger

Avoid random discipline

Parents often discipline after the fact. They set a rule and wait till the child breaks it before they decide on a consequence. You tell your child, "You can ride your bike, but stay in front of the house. Don't cross the street." Ten minutes later, you check on the child and find him across the street on his bike. Only then, after the child has broken the rule, is the type and amount of discipline determined. "You can't ride your bike for 2 weeks."

From random disciplining, the child feels others are responsible for what has happened to him. Anger is apt to develop. To avoid the buildup of anger by random discipline, see Chapter 5, Setting Rules for Behavior.

Avoid excessive negative attention

This involves several concepts, but primarily centers on the use of negative consequences or punishment. Don't use punishment as the main method of control. Eliminate verbal punishment, such as yelling, putting a child down, name-calling and excessive criticism.

Use reward as a disciplinary tactic. Emphasize the child's successes, accomplishments, achievements and good behavior. Pay more attention to normal good behavior—when the child brushes his teeth after being told once and so on.

Being on a child's back most of the time may result in a buildup of anger and aggressive behavior.

Avoid power struggles

You tell your child, "Go take a bath," and he refuses. Then you say, "You better. You know what's going to happen."

He says, "You can't make me."

Then you come back with something. He counters, and a full-blown power struggle develops. You then force him to take a bath. The battle is won, but it may result in the development of resentment and anger.

Avoid power struggles when possible. At times, it may be better to have the child experience some consequence of his behavior than to win the battle. Even if you win each battle, you may wind up losing the war. See Chapter 40, Developing Responsible Behaviors, for more information.

Look for change and try to stabilize the environment

Children who experience environmental change,

especially divorce, separation and remarriage, may develop underlying anger. The anger and resentment that results from the changes may be expressed in other ways.

Try to identify the changes and stabilize the environment. Get the child to express his feelings through more appropriate methods. See the chapters related to this for techniques you can use.

Avoid excessive restrictions

Some children are overprotected, excessively restricted and not allowed to be like other children their age. This develops feelings of anger. They want to do things that others do but are prevented from doing so. Sometimes you have to look at your child's peer group and age mates to decide what is too much restriction.

Adolescence is hard on parents

This period in a child's life is difficult for the child, but it's even harder for you. A normal amount of anger, resentment and rebellion exists, especially when people don't understand you, are old-fashioned and are stupid (parents are trying to direct your life and tell you what to do). The only way to avoid anger, opposition, stubbornness and rebellion in a child this age is for you to sleep through his adolescence. See Chapter 28, Teenage Behavior—Help!, for more on dealing with angry, rebellious behavior seen during this period in a child's life.

Ineffective Problem Solving or Interaction

Models

Children learn a great deal from modeling your behavior. The way you handle conflicts and problems is apt to be imitated by your children. If you handle anger by hollering or punching holes in the wall, your children will probably handle their conflicts similarly.

The old saying, "Don't do as I do, do as I say," is ineffective in dealing with behavior. If you see aggressive or rebellious behavior in your child, look at yourself to see if you are modeling these. If you are, you must stop before the child's behavior can be corrected.

If there's a significant amount of yelling in the home or if the adults demonstrate disrespect for one another, it's likely the child will also show these behavior patterns. One time the mother of a young, sassy and rebellious child told me, "Every time I tell my child something, he says, 'I'm not doing that. If you don't like it, pack your clothes and leave.' He's always putting me down. He shows no respect. It's like I'm the child, and he's the parent." After some discussion, I learned this lady was treated the same way by her husband. The child learned his behavior from the model he observed.

Another mother told me, "Every time I hit my daughter, she hits me back. What should I do?"

My answer was simple, "Stop hitting her!" Whenever I see a child whose primary problem is fighting, the first question I ask the parents is, "How is he disciplined?" These children are usually dealt with through physical punishment, such as spanking or threats of physical punishment. When you deal with children through physical means, you teach them to handle conflicts by physical force or aggressive behavior.

It doesn't have to be the actual use of physical force. It could be threats of force. "If you don't go take your bath, I'm going to get the belt."

It could be control by intimidation, "I'm going to get you to do what I want you to do because I'm bigger than you and can overpower you."

If you deal with your children this way, you teach them aggressive, inappropriate methods of problem solving.

When parents use physical punishment as a primary method of dealing with their children, they forget one important thing—children grow and usually get as big or bigger than you. If this is your primary method of control, you'll lose it when you need it most, in adolescence. Then your children may start using this method of problem solving on you!

Aggressive models can also be found in cartoons, movies or TV programs.

Children who are in control

These children are usually in control and have learned to have things their way. They tend to be bossy and self-centered. These behaviors are sometimes seen in their interaction with others. Domination and need to control may develop into aggressive behavior.

Personality characteristics

Some children have dominating, controlling personality characteristics that may result in conflict with others and aggressive behavior. Impulsiveness, acting before thinking and not being concerned about the consequences of behavior may also produce this type of behavior. Examples of this include pleasure-oriented and overactive children.

Play may revolve around aggressive behaviors

Some children whose play centers around fighting, guns, swords and similar activities may have problems with aggressive behavior. These children are usually "obsessed" with a cartoon or movie character. Many of their activities center around a major theme.

Lack of appropriate socialization skills

Some children have not learned to interact with others for a variety of reasons.

Dealing with Aggressive and Rebellious Behavior

Communicating aggressive feelings

Encourage your children to express their negative feelings to you—what makes them angry, what we do they don't like and what do they disapprove of. Encourage them to express their sources of anger and their opinions. If a child expresses these emotions appropriately, don't view this as sassy or disrespectful. Your child asks for permission to visit a friend, but you say no. He tells you, "You never let me go to Jeff's. Every time I make plans with him I can't go."

If these feelings are expressed in a normal tone of voice and the child is actually trying to communicate the way he feels, listen and try to understand his emotions.

This is an appropriate expression of anger and should not be reprimanded or punished. Allow the child to complain, disagree or disapprove, provided he does not do so in a sarcastic, nasty manner. Allowing a child to yell, curse or be sassy isn't teaching him to communicate his emotions effectively. See Chapter 14, Communication Between Parent & Child, for some additional advice.

Ignore passive-aggressive behavior

Children use passive-aggressive maneuvers to acknowledge anger, and they use it to get a reaction from you. Ignoring is often an effective way to reduce opposition, stubbornness, resistance and similar behavior.

In addition, the way you usually deal with passive-aggressive behavior often results in a buildup of anger in the child. Your child asks you, "Can I stay up past my bedtime and finish watching this movie?" You say, "No," and trouble begins. The child starts being sassy, talking back, making faces and becoming defiant. This passive-aggressive behavior is releasing anger and letting air out of his anger balloon.

If you start hollering at the child, get into a shouting match or engage in an exchange of hostility, more anger develops and more air is pumped into his balloon. The anger that was initially released by the sassiness and defiance is offset by a buildup of more aggressive feelings. By using the consequences of ignoring, this buildup of anger can be eliminated. See Chapter 9, Ignoring Specific Behaviors.

Reduce inappropriate models

Look at yourself to be sure you aren't models of the behavior you're trying to eliminate in your child. Serving as an appropriate model is a good way to teach children how to deal with or express their anger. See Chapter 8, Punishment, for additional information on how you serve as models.

If the child's play primarily revolves around aggressive behaviors or he is preoccupied with violent characters, cartoons or movies, you may need to reduce the time he spends in these activities. Substitute different cartoons, TV programs and activities. If your child primarily plays with aggressive-type children, try to vary his playmates.

Develop appropriate socialization skills

See Chapter 45, Getting Along with Other Children, for a variety of techniques to accomplish this.

Help child learn other methods of problem solving

Some children who show this behavior have a small "bag of tricks" to deal with difficult situations. When they have a problem to solve, they reach into their bag for a solution and usually come up with the same one—aggressive behavior.

You might invite a friend over and tell the child, "You know when Julie comes over you usually fight, do not share and argue. When she comes over and you start this, I'll give you a warning. If you stop, that's fine. If not, it'll be counted as a warning. If you don't get 3 warnings by 3 o'clock, she can stay over till 3:30, and we can make cookies. If you get 3 warnings, she'll go home at 3 o'clock."

By doing this, you may be able to get the child to try to learn other methods of problem solving.

Use positive consequences

Avoid using violence to deal with violence. A child who hits his sister gets a spanking as punishment. By using positive consequences, emphasis is placed on not fighting rather than on the aggressive behavior. "If you and your sister don't fight this afternoon, we'll play that game you like."

Behavioral charts can also be used effectively to deal with some methods of expressing anger. Avoid arguing, hollering, excessive punishment and power struggles.

Listen to your child

If the child is complaining about excessive restrictions, punishments or other things he doesn't agree with, listen. If the complaints are realistic, see if something can be worked out and resolved. Talk to other parents and look at his peers' activities to determine the appropriateness of your restrictions.

Don't let behavior get out of control

Once a child is into an aggressive outburst, it's hard to deal with it. Instead of dealing with the behavior when it occurs, it's usually possible and better to try to prevent it from happening.

In some children, aggression development may involve several steps. The child's brother may call him stupid. There are some verbal exchanges. Then a pushing-and-shoving match is followed by a full-blown fight.

Try to catch it early and intervene in the beginning before it gets out of hand. Target the name calling or verbal arguing. Try to stop that rather than zero in on the fighting. A behavior chart or time-out procedure can be used to deal with the target behavior.

33

Bedtime Problems

Many parents dread nightfall because bedtime is approaching, and problems are certain to occur. A variety of behaviors that produce difficulties revolve around bedtime.

Your child may show fears, refuse to go to bed or not want to sleep in her own room or bed. She may not be able to go to sleep unless someone lies with her. She may want to sleep with you. Once in bed, other children call out, forget to tell you something, have to go to the bathroom or get a drink of water.

A child can display other behaviors to get him out of his room or you into his room many times before he actually falls asleep. Several things can be done to make this daily activity a lot easier and reduce problems.

Causes of Bedtime Problems

Habit

The child has not established a habit of sleeping in his own room or by himself. Parents have allowed him to develop other nighttime routines, such as falling asleep while watching television or sleeping with them.

Children who are in control often show this type of behavior. They are more in control of the environment than you. They don't want to sleep in their own beds. Being able to sleep elsewhere or to be able to stay up as late as they want is just one of several behaviors indicating parental lack of control.

Fears

Some children who have nighttime fears have problems going to bed.

Dependency

Children who have not developed overall independent behaviors and who rely heavily on their parents often have trouble at bedtime.

Environmental change

Shifts in the environment may produce feelings of uncertainty, insecurity and dependency in children. Some children who have experienced a divorce, separation, death of a parent, continuous parental conflict or other changes may have difficulty going to bed.

Dealing with Bedtime Problems

Establish a set bedtime

A child who goes to bed at different hours every night is more likely to give you trouble than one who has a set bedtime. Perhaps you have a child who goes to bed at 7:30 some nights, 8:30 other nights, 10:00 on other nights. He is giving you trouble about going to bed. He's apt to give you less trouble if you specify a set time when he must be in bed every night.

What time should a child go to bed?

There is not a set answer to this question because it varies for every child. How much sleep your child requires depends on his activity level during the day, his physical makeup and many other factors. You could consult your pediatrician or a child-development book. Try to get an idea of how many hours of sleep a child requires at certain ages.

It's probably best if a child goes to bed before you so you and your spouse have some time alone. Younger children should go to bed before older children. This can be part of the general seniority system set up in your household. See Chapter 57, Sibling Conflict, for more information. You should be in more control of your child's bedtime than he is.

Have child sleep in his own bed

Many children sleep with their parents, siblings or on the sofa in the den rather than in their own bed. Some mental-health professionals feel serious problems can arise from children sleeping with their parents. I don't think this behavior in and of itself—in most situations—is detrimental. However, I'd bet most children who sleep with their parents are in more control than their parents are.

I often view this behavior like many others a child shows. Refusal to take a bath, not coming home when told or other behaviors indicate the child does what he wants to do rather than what he's supposed to do. For these reasons, I feel the child should *not* sleep with his parents.

A child who sleeps with his brother or sister or is allowed to fall to sleep on the couch may develop habits that will be difficult to change later.

If the child is in more control than you, one method to deal with this bedtime problem is to try to establish control in many areas of the child's life—not just bedtime. See Chapter 31, Who's in Control? If you can get more cooperation from a child at mealtime, homework time, coming in from play and other routine activities, it is easier to get the cooperation required at bedtime.

In trying to change this specific behavior, look for gradual improvement. You're trying to get a child back in his own bed because he's sleeping with you every night. Set up a system so the child can select one night out of the week when he can sleep in his own bed. Let's say this is Friday night. Tell him if he wakes up in his bed Saturday morning and didn't come to your bed during the night, Dad will take him to eat breakfast at a fast-food restaurant.

You don't want to say, "If you sleep in your bed all week, we'll go fishing on Saturday." The odds of the child doing that are slim to none. Look for gradual improvements. If you can get the child sleeping in his own bed one night a week, then move to two nights, to three and so forth.

Keeping the child in his room

When some children are sent to bed, they come in and out of their bedroom several times. They forgot to tell you something, they have to get a drink or they have to go to the bathroom. With all this activity, they have difficulty going to bed. Another situation similar to this is the child who calls out for his parents to come in because he forgot to tell them something or has to be kissed good night.

In dealing with situations similar to these, tell the child he has 2 chances to come out of his room to get a drink of water and go to the bathroom. If he comes out of the room no more than twice, the next night he may be able to stay up a little bit past his bedtime. Or you could use some other reward that is important to him. If he comes out of his room 3 times or calls for you more than twice, he doesn't get the reward. Look for gradual change in this behavior.

Another situation is when your child wakes up during the night and comes to your bed. This may occur once, twice or several times during the night. When this occurs, return him to his bed. Establish a situation similar to the above. If he is coming into your bedroom 5 times at night, try to reduce it to 4, then 3 and 2.

A similar behavior occurs in a child who is put to bed but continues to play and doesn't stay quiet. He has trouble going to sleep. This occurs very frequently in overactive children. Usually—if you can get him to lie quietly—he will fall asleep readily. But the problem is he doesn't remain quiet. Tell the child, "I'm going to set the timer on the stove. If you can lay still and be quiet till the bell rings, I'll come in and read you a story."

Start setting a timer at a very low time interval—say 30 to 45 seconds. After a few times, gradually increase the time interval. As the child lies quietly for longer periods, he is apt to fall asleep.

Deal with fear

If fear or other anxiety is associated with bedtime, you may need to deal with this first. See Chapter 44, Fears, for details on changing this type of behavior.

Be consistent

Say what you mean, mean what you say and follow through with what you tell the child. If the rule at your house is every night you come in our bed we'll put you back in your bed, it should be followed every time the behavior occurs. Be consistent with bedtime and consequences associated with the behavior.

Look for gradual change

Don't try to change the behavior all at once. If a child refuses to go to bed every night, it's ridiculous to say, "If you don't give me any trouble this week, you can have a friend come over to play Saturday."

Try to change the behavior *gradually;* the first 50% of the behavior is the most difficult to change. Once you get a child cooperating 2 or 3 nights of the week, the remainder is fairly easy to accomplish.

Don't foster dependency

This involves two general areas. One is having to lie with the child so he goes to sleep. The other pertains to the child who can only fall asleep in your bed then must be moved to his own bed.

Try to avoid developing rituals or other nighttime routines that foster dependency. Some children who show dependency tend to be overall dependent children. A child may be dependent for many other behaviors, such as dressing and bathing. Bedtime is just one of many behaviors. Try to establish independent behaviors in many areas of the child's life. See Chapter 39, Dependent Children, for more information.

Use positive consequences

Try to stay away from using punishment, yelling, screaming or similar negative behaviors to deal with bedtime problems. Try to stay calm and set up rules and consequences ahead of time. Use positive consequences or incentives to deal with the problem.

Stabilize the environment

Some children who have experienced significant changes in the environment show bedtime problems. More structure, predictability and consistency needs to be established. For detailed information, see Chapter 19, Effects of Divorce, Separation, Parental Conflict & Other Environmental Changes on Behavior.

34

Bedwetting & Soiling

Bedwetting, soiling and daytime accidents are common among young children. These seem to result from two different causes.

Some children wet the bed, soil themselves or have daytime accidents continuously. They have difficulties in toilet training and exhibit the behavior past the acceptable age. Other children become toilet-trained, stop wetting the bed at night or eliminate daytime accidents for a while, then the behavior reappears at a later age.

There are two things to do if this type of behavior is seen after the acceptable age. First, the child must be examined by his physician to rule out physical causes. Secondly, do *not* use punishment, hollering, screaming, getting upset, criticism and embarrassment to deal with this behavior.

Bedwetting (Enuresis)

It's estimated 1 out of every 4 children between the ages of 4 and 16 years has problems at one time or another with bedwetting. Most do not suffer physical or significant emotional problems. It appears many children experience very deep sleep and this causes muscles to relax and bedwetting to occur. Often the bedwetting doesn't awaken the child.

Although some bedwetting may be caused by emotional problems, this is not the case in the majority of children.

Soiling (Encopresis)

Soiling infrequently occurs when a child deliberately defecates or has a full bowel movement on himself. Soiling usually occurs when children retain stools. Bowel movements then become infrequent, and the stools become difficult to pass. Liquid secreted around the large stools is usually the cause of the soiling.

Non-physical Causes

There are numerous non-physical causes of bedwetting, soiling and daytime accidents. Below is a discussion of some of the causes.

Habit not established

Some children fail to develop the habit of being dry or not wetting the bed. They have not been adequately toilet-trained or have not learned appropriate behavior.

Regressive behavior

A child goes back to an earlier form of behavior or level of development. This usually occurs when there are changes in the child's life or significant shifts in his or the family's routines. A child may have not had a daytime accident in a few years. Shortly after the birth of his brother or sister, he begins to wet and/or soil himself frequently. Another child didn't have trouble with bedwetting for 4 years. He moved to a new house and began to wet the bed 3 or 4 times a week.

Unstructured or inconsistent environment

Some children respond to unpredictable, changing environments by wetting the bed or by having daytime accidents. These changes can include spoiling, a lack of discipline, frequent parental arguing or one parent telling the child one thing and the other parent contradicting it. Also included is the child who finds himself in the middle of a divorce, separation or situation that creates a very unstructured, confusing and unpredictable environment. Sometimes the insecurity or uncertainty the child feels is expressed through these wetting and soiling behaviors.

Anger

Some children who have underlying anger or have difficulty expressing hostile and aggressive feelings have problems with soiling.

Dependency

Children who are excessively dependent on their parents, overprotected and babied often fail to develop age-appropriate behavior. This includes bedwetting, soiling or daytime accidents. These children resist growing up in many areas.

Emotional difficulties

Although infrequent, some children who have significant emotional problems sometimes develop trouble in these areas.

Heredity

Bedwetters sometimes have a parent(s) and/or sibling(s) who have had similar problems. Perhaps some of the problems in this area are related to genetic factors.

Treatment

If a child has been examined by a physician who finds no physical reasons for this behavior, use the following methods to correct the problem.

1. Treat the behavior in a matter-of-fact manner. Don't punish, get upset, holler, criticize, belittle or embarrass the child. Deal with this behavior in a calm, matter-of-fact way.

2. Use natural consequences at first. You may tell the child, "I change the bed sheets once a week. If you wet the bed, then you have to change the sheets." The natural consequence of wetting the bed is changing the sheets, bringing them to the laundry and putting new sheets on the bed.

The child who frequently soils himself or has daytime accidents may be required to wash his underwear and clothes. Another child who frequently wets himself while playing outside is told, "Every time you wet yourself when you're playing, you have to come inside, take off your clothes, take a bath and put on clean clothes." The natural consequence of not taking time to go to the bathroom is the child loses some play time. See Chapter 5, Setting Rules for Behavior, for a more detailed discussion of natural consequences.

3. Use positive consequences and behavior charts. Punishment is not a recommended means to deal with this behavior. Use rewards for not wetting the bed. A child could be rewarded for having a bowel movement in the toilet—not in his pants.

Behavior charts can also be made to help the child reduce

his behavior. See the appropriate chapters for a more detailed discussion of these techniques.

Specific methods

If the general methods described above are used and the problem continues, consider the individual child more closely. Then you can choose one of the specific methods described below.

Stabilize environment—Look for areas of upset, and try to stabilize the child's environment. A new home, change of schools or birth of a brother may play a part in the child's bedwetting or soiling. Use the general methods described above, and try to stabilize the child's environment and minimize change. See Chapter 19, Effects of Divorce, Separation, Parental Conflict & Other Environmental Changes on Behavior, for a detailed discussion of techniques to use.

Provide more structure—Provide more structure, consistency and predictability in the environment. Marital conflicts, arguing between parents or different methods of disciplining the child by those who deal with him produce a very ambiguous environment for the child.

The insecurity, uncertainty and confusion the child feels may be expressed through bedwetting, soiling and daytime accidents. Eliminate marital conflict and arguing in front of the child. Those who discipline and direct the child must harmonize their behavioral expectations.

Children who are spoiled, get their way frequently and control their homes reveal a lack of structure or predictability in their environment. Avoid disruptions for these children, especially if they are wetting the bed, having daytime accidents or soiling themselves. See Chapter 4, Being a Consistent Parent, Chapter 5, Setting Rules for Behavior, and Chapter 58, Spoiling, for ideas on how to provide more structure and predictability in the child's daily environment.

Child must grow up—Let the child grow up. Treat him according to his age. Don't baby the child or allow him to be excessively dependent on you. Don't do things for him you know he is physically capable of doing for himself. Avoid overprotection. Promote independent and age-appropriate behavior. If you treat a child like an infant, he's apt to remain one.

Limit fluids—Limiting the amount of fluid a child drinks before bedtime or restricting all drinking after a certain hour has been helpful with some bedwetters.

Sleep patterns—Most individuals go through predictable stages of sleep during the night. The pattern goes from light sleep to deep sleep, back to light sleep then to deep sleep. This cycle occurs 4 to 6 times each night.

It has been found that bedwetting occurs during the deep phase of sleep, so your child may show a pattern (he usually wets the bed 30 to 50 minutes after going to bed).

If a pattern exists, wake him and take him to the bathroom *before* he wets the bed.

Treatment with medication—Some medications, Tofranil® (imipramine), have been somewhat successful in treating bedwetting. Consult your child's pediatrician.

Medication is often used with older children when they start sleeping at friends' houses, going on camping trips and being involved with other activities where bedwetting may cause embarrassment or problems.

The dose for nighttime bedwetting is usually 25mg/day (age 6 and over) 1 hour before bedtime. If relief of bedwetting doesn't occur within 1 week, the dose is usually increased.

If the medication reduces the bedwetting, it is continued for a couple of months. When the medication is discontinued, some children return to wetting the bed. Others will have developed a habit and stay dry at night.

Conditioning method—A conditioning technique using a pad and bell has also been used to treat bedwetting. This involves a device that turns on a light and rings a bell when the child urinates. This is supposed to condition the child to become more aware of the fullness of his bladder and to awake before the bedwetting. Consult your child's pediatrician or a mental-health professional for more information.

Many companies sell these devices. Some companies are out to make money; others help the child with bedwetting. Work with a physician or mental-health professional when using this technique to minimize the chance of being manipulated by someone trying to sell a product.

Counseling and psychotherapy—Counseling or psychotherapy with a child who is a bedwetter is not an effective method of treatment. Counseling may be more appropriate for the child who soils and has full bowel movements or purposefully defecates on himself. Parents of children who wet the bed or soil themselves may benefit from some counseling in effective techniques of child management. The professional may be able to provide them with behavior-modification techniques to help manage the behaviors.

Rewards—Use positive consequences and reward with the above techniques.

Not taking time—Some children have daytime accidents because they are playing or involved with something and don't take the time to go to the bathroom. Or they wait till the last minute and do not make it to the toilet. This often happens with overactive children.

Some of the techniques described above can be used, but use a time-out procedure or one that involves natural consequences. "If you have an accident while you're playing, you'll have to come inside for 5 minutes." "If you wet or soil yourself, you have to come inside or stop watching TV and wash your clothes." Under these conditions, it may be more to the child's advantage and take up less of his fun time to take the time to go to the bathroom.

Problems with soiling—If soiling is a problem, consult your pediatrician, or seek professional help as soon as you notice your child is constipated or beginning to pass large, infrequent stools. This is probably the best way to prevent soiling or to avoid the behavior from getting very difficult to treat.

Try treating soiling with a diet that softens the stools or with suppository laxatives. This allows the child to become regular and usually eliminates the difficulty or pain he experiences when he goes to the bathroom. This is a complex behavioral-medical problem, so when seeking help, be sure the person has expertise in the area.

Note the pattern of the child's bowel movements. Make him sit on the toilet during the time he usually soils himself. Ask him during certain periods of the day if he has to go to the bathroom.

35

Biting

Biting usually occurs in children under 4 or 5. Whether it's a concern and how it should be dealt with depends on the age it occurs and under what conditions. It is very common for 1- to 2-1/2-year-olds to bite because they are teething. After 2-1/2, conditions under which biting occurs should be explored.

Method of problem solving

If the young child gets along fairly well with others and seems happy but bites someone when he gets into a conflict or fight, it may not be of any concern. If the behavior occurs infrequently and it seems to be one method the child uses to solve problems, don't put a great deal of emphasis on this behavior.

If the child seems unhappy and/or bites others for no apparent reason, this may be of more concern.

Excessive negative attention

Some children bite if there is a significant amount of punishment, negative attention, correction, hollering and similar kinds of interaction in the home. There is too much negative discipline.

Lack of socialization

Some children who haven't had much opportunity to interact with other children may show this behavior when interacting with others.

Environmental change

This behavior may occur when there has been some environmental change. It may involve significant change, such as a divorce, separation or a move to a new house. Or it may involve confusion, change and ambiguity resulting from less-significant changes, such as parental conflict, different working hours of the parent, changes in routine.

Lack of emotional closeness to parent

Biting is sometimes seen when the child doesn't have enough quality time with you. This usually happens with the mother. The child doesn't spend enough time with you in fun activities, such as reading stories and playing together. Some conditions exist that prevent emotional closeness to the parent.

Dealing with Biting in Young Children

Don't model the behavior

If a child bites you, don't bite him back. This is an inappropriate way of trying to reduce the behavior. Don't model the behavior you are trying to eliminate in the child.

Avoid being bitten

In very young children, the best way to deal with the behavior is to avoid being bitten. Don't allow her to bite you or place yourself in situations where biting can occur.

Develop socialization experiences

Have the child interact with other children. Place her in situations where she is not alone or primarily involved with adults. Get her with children her own age.

Increase quality time with child

Try to set aside some time in the day that result in quality interaction between your and your child. Play with him, read stories or go outside and get involved in some type of activity with him.

Be consistent

Say what you mean, mean what you say. Don't tell him anything you can't or don't want to do. Follow through with everything you say you're going to do. Deal with the biting in the same way every time. You may remove him for a short period of time, place him in the corner, say, "No," or something similar, depending on the age of the child. Do the same thing each time.

Use positive consequences

Depending on the child's age, rewards for *not* biting could be used. Give praise and positive attention for interaction with agemates or adults when biting is not observed.

36

Building Confidence

I often see children who are described by parents as lacking confidence, having a negative attitude, always feeling guilty, having their feelings hurt easily, tending to give up easily or feeling other children are better than they are. These statements are reflective of a negative self-concept or a lack of confidence.

Development of a Poor Self-Concept

Self-image and self-concept refer to how you feel about yourself, what you think about yourself and how you see yourself when compared to others. When a negative self-image exists, the child sees himself as possessing more negative qualities than positive traits. Many other problems may also emerge as a result. This type of situation usually develops when more emphasis is placed on a child's faults, failures and misbehaviors than on his successes and accomplishments.

Suppose the above circle represents your personality when you are born. Half is comprised of positive qualities—things you can do as well or better than other people. The other half is comprised of negative qualities or skills—things you can't do as well or things other people do better than you.

Let's say you can cook—that falls on the plus side. I can't cook very well, so in my circle this skill would fall on the minus side. However, I know something about refinishing furniture; that falls on the plus side of my circle. You don't know anything about furniture refinishing, so for you this skill is a minus. You could go on listing skills and abilities and placing them on the plus or minus sides of the circle.

Although you have many skills that are superior to mine, I have an equal number of abilities superior to yours. When we look at the overall comparison, we find you and I are basically the same in terms of our value, worth and competence. What makes us different is that we have different skills in different areas. The same situation exists for children.

When a situation exists where more emphasis is placed on negative traits than on positive ones (diagram below), a negative self-image develops. This can happen under several conditions.

Attention to misbehavior

A negative self-image may develop if more attention is paid to a child's misbehavior than to his appropriate actions. Suppose a child does 50 things in a day; 25 are good (+) and 25 are bad (-). The child gets positive attention for 2 of the 25 good behaviors and negative emphasis on 24 of the 25 bad ones.

Good behavior is overlooked because it is expected. If the child is doing what he's supposed to, no one says anything. But if he does something wrong, you're quick to condemn. A child is supposed to make his bed. He does the job for 6 days but forgets to make it on day 7. When is attention given for bedmaking behavior? The day the child fails to make the bed.

Excessive punishment

Excessive negative attention can also occur when a great deal of punishment is used on a child. Negative consequences tend to place emphasis on bad behavior and overlook good behavior. You tell a child you want him home by 5 o'clock. "If you're late, you won't be able to look at TV tonight." The child comes home late, gets a lecture, is punished and receives a great deal of attention for this misbehavior. If he had come home on time, he wouldn't have gotten punished. And he would not have received any attention for good behavior!

Personality characteristics

Children who have academic difficulties or certain personality characteristics receive more negative attention than others. Students who have trouble with schoolwork experience frustration, failure and emphasis on their negative traits more than children who have few academic problems. A child who is "hyperactive" must be corrected (don't touch that, keep still, be quiet, sit down) more frequently than a child without these behavioral traits. The strong-willed child doesn't listen as well as other children and has to be corrected more frequently.

Expectations exceed capacities

If expectations exceed capabilities, your child will fail more frequently than succeed. Some parents expect a 6-year-old to act like a 12-year-old. The child has average intelligence, and his best is represented by C work in school. But his parents expect A's and B's. When this happens, the child will fail to meet the expectations. If behavioral or performance expectations are set above the child's capabilities, he will fail and receive unnecessary negative attention.

The negative emphasis is due to direct attention to minus personality characteristics. Parents, teachers and peers don't have to accentuate the negative behavior for a poor self-concept or a lack of confidence to develop. It can be an indirect result of situations similar to those described below.

Overprotection

Suppose I have someone who works with me. Every time I'm asked a question, I turn to him for the answer. He tells me what to say, then I tell the person who asked the question what to do. This continues for several months. One day, the person on whom I have depended doesn't come to work. The phone rings, I answer it and I'm asked a question. What do I do now?

I would probably tell the person to call back because I'd feel I couldn't handle the problem by myself.

Children who are dependent, overprotected, spoiled or rely heavily on others to do things for them are often faced with this same situation. They feel as if they can't handle problems. The *I can't* is accentuated, and the negative side of the personality is emphasized. A poor self-image and a lack of confidence may be apparent when this child is required to function apart from those on whom he has depended.

Significant change

Situations that involve significant change (separation, move, change of school) and inconsistent, fluid environments put the child in a position where he doesn't know where he stands. These may indirectly produce an emphasis on negative personality characteristics. The child may feel insecure. He doesn't know if what exists today will exist tomorrow. He has no assurance things will remain the same. And he can't predict his environment. He feels as if he can't handle certain situations. A lack of confidence is apparent.

Regardless of the origin of the negative emphasis, when it happens, certain personality changes occur. The most dramatic is represented in the following diagrams.

There is a gradual change in how the child sees himself. The positive side of his personality decreases, with a corresponding increase on the negative side. He tends to view himself as made up of more faults, failures and mistakes than of successes, accomplishments and achievements. He sees his peers as more capable, effective and competent than he is. He generally lacks pride in himself and his accomplishments.

If you view this process as the action of a scale (diagram, page 264), what you see happening is the child sees the negative side as a very large pile of rocks, while the positive side of the scale has very few. Once the scale tips off-balance

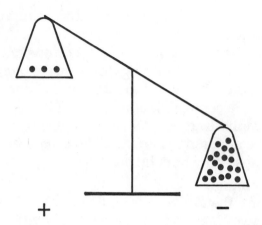

(a negative image develops), something must be done to swing it back to where it should be—balanced (equal number of weak and strong points).

The Child's Attempt to Deal with a Poor Self-Concept

Everyone tries to keep their scales balanced. One way a child with a poor self-image attempts to get his scales balanced is to avoid getting any more rocks on the negative side. He tries to avoid situations that may produce failure, frustration, criticism or mistakes—or any situation that accentuates his weak points.

The child may avoid competition or any win-lose situation. If he does compete, he is usually a poor loser because he can't bear to come in second. If the child with a poor self-image starts something that becomes difficult, he may give up easily. He would rather not try something than to try it and fail. He doesn't like new situations and avoids going places or doing things where he isn't sure of himself.

He won't try things where success is doubtful. This avoidance may involve lying. But the behavior is usually geared toward staying away from anything that may accentuate his inadequacies. You usually interpret this behavior as a lack of confidence.

If you punish, criticize, reprimand or do *anything* to stress a weak point, a child with a poor self-concept often reacts significantly. You may not mean anything serious by your comments, but it provokes a major reaction. A child is putting a model together but is going about it the wrong way. You very calmly say, "Don't do it that way. Why not do it this way—it'll be easier." The child violently reacts to the suggestion.

Although you didn't mean any criticism by what you said, the child reads it as, "You're wrong again." When this happens, he feels as if another rock has been placed on his negative side. Depending on the child's personality, you'll see sensitivity, easily hurt feelings, pouting, outbursts of anger or temper tantrums. We all look for things in the environment that support the way we feel about ourselves. A child with a negative self-image looks for things that support his feelings. He may be hypersensitive to things he views as negative.

A child raises his hand in class to answer a question, but the teacher calls on someone else. A child with a negative image may feel the teacher doesn't like him. Or you may bring home something today for the child with the poor self-concept and nothing for his brother. The next day, you bring home the same thing for his brother. On the second day, the child with the negative image complains, "You always get something for him and nothing for me. You like him better." The child looks for things in his environment that confirm the way he feels about himself.

Another way the child can get his scales balanced is to seek out situations that produce positive attention. He tries to pile rocks on the plus side of the scale. The child gravitates toward things where he experiences success, gets pats on the back or feels a sense of accomplishment.

Let's say the child helps you bake a cake. Some neighbors come over, and they tell the child how good it is; they never tasted anything better. For the next several days, he may ask to help you bake another cake.

Another example is a child who writes a note telling you how much he loves you. You get the note and extravagantly praise it. You hug and kiss the child, and tell him how much you love him. For the next 6 days, you receive many similar notes. Children want to engage in behavior that gets them positive attention. This may involve things or activities where the child experiences success.

To get positive attention, a child may develop inappropriate or bad behavior, such as being the class clown, talking excessively or constantly demanding attention and approval from the teacher. Or he may get involved with an unacceptable peer group because he feels comfortable with this negative group of children.

How a Poor Self-Concept May Be Expressed

Behaviors described above result from a child trying to balance his scales or to overcome negative emphasis in his personality. The child may also adopt one or a combination of the behavioral styles described below. It's his way of dealing with a negative self-concept.

Accepting what he feels environment is saying

If the child feels he's trying his best, but it isn't good enough, the environment is unpredictable or he doesn't know how to perform properly. He may accept what he feels the environment seems to be telling him, "I'm trying my best, but I still don't know what's happening. I'm getting more negative attention. There must be something wrong with *me*. Maybe I'm useless, bad, worthless and inferior to others."

The same effect occurs if you are called *stupid*. You start thinking you are stupid and begin acting that way. If your faults are pointed out frequently enough, you begin thinking you have an excessive number of them.

Children who have accepted a negative environment are often shy, somewhat withdrawn, timid and show an obvious lack of confidence. They tend to belittle themselves and may appear unhappy and dissatisfied.

Masking inadequacies

Another way children deal with a negative self-image is by trying to mask their inadequacies and faults. They try to present a front showing only positive qualities. If I had a negative image and used this method to deal with it, I would communicate to others I am the greatest. I would say, "I have the best house. My children are never bad. I send them to the best school money can buy. I never make mistakes. I'm never wrong."

I wouldn't admit to any inadequacies. I'd present a front of total competence. What I'm actually telling you is I feel as if I have numerous faults. But I am not going to let you see any of them because if you see one, you'll know what a bad person I am and won't like me.

Children often respond like this when they have a negative self-image. They must have the best bike, electric train, shoes or bigger, more-expensive things than others. They don't admit to mistakes and don't accept responsibility for their own behavior.

Someone else is always at fault. They quickly blame others for their mistakes and always have a string of excuses to justify their behavior.

Pleasure-oriented

A third way children deal with a poor self-image is to tune out the environment. They become more concerned with their needs and wishes than the wants, desires and rules of others.

If a child encounters a changing or unpredictable environment, he may feel he doesn't know what he has to do to be good or to get positive attention. If he is in an environment that places great attention on his mistakes, he may feel his best isn't good enough.

In both these situations, some children act as if they think, "I don't know what I have to do to get positive attention or to please other people, so the heck with them. But I know what pleases me and makes me happy. So I'm going to do that."

The pleasure-oriented child is primarily concerned with satisfying his own needs and wishes. He responds to the environment accordingly. He is more concerned with the pleasure he derives from his behavior than the punishment that may result. He may know he isn't supposed to do something and will be punished if he does. But if it's fun, he'll do it and worry about the punishment later.

If you ask him to do something and he wants to do it, it will be done. If you ask him to do something and he doesn't want to do it, it is ignored. It may seem as if this child acts before he thinks, but this isn't true. He behaves this way because he is more concerned with what *he* wants to do than with what will happen to him.

These children are quick to manipulate people and events to satisfy their own needs and wishes or to avoid unpleasant duties and responsibilities. The manipulation is pleasure-oriented because the child wants something that someone or something prevents him from getting. He knows what he has to do to get around what is blocking him so his needs will be fulfilled.

Although he can be polite, charming and affable when it's to his advantage, he usually has problems with authority or those in a position of supervision or direction. Children who are pleasure-oriented are often rebellious, stubborn, contrary and resistant.

In school, a variety of problems are often characterized by an inability to follow classroom procedure. This child does only what he wants to do in the classroom. The teacher may say, "Take out your reading book, and turn to page 35." The child doesn't feel like doing it, so he takes out some paper and starts drawing. He may also daydream, be inattentive or over-active. It seems this child has not developed any internal control, self-discipline or responsibility because he doesn't follow classroom procedure. He does what he pleases when he pleases. This behavior pattern produces significant problems in school.

Because of his pleasure orientation, punishment doesn't work well—often not at all. Negative consequences, when they work, affect this type of child only temporarily—a few minutes or a few days.

Suppose we have two children planning to rob a bank. We want to stop this behavior. The first child thinks, "If I rob a bank, I might get caught and sent to jail. I won't be able to watch TV, play with my friends or see my parents."

The pleasure-oriented child thinks, "I'm going to get some money and buy some candy, toys and a motorcycle."

You can tell the first child, "People who rob banks are punished by being sent to jail." This will stop the behavior.

This consequence is meaningless to the pleasure-oriented child because he is not concerned about what will happen to him. He's more concerned about what's in it for him—what he will get out of the behavior.

This is the major reason punishment does not effectively work with this personality type. In the above example, you would have to take the money out of the bank (take the pleasure away from the behavior) or make not robbing the bank more pleasurable than robbing the bank to deter the pleasure-oriented child. Reward must be primarily used when dealing with these children.

Changing a Poor Self-Image and Building Confidence

To eliminate a negative self-concept, to build confidence and to make the child feel better about himself, you must reverse the process that produced it. More attention must be given to the child's successes, accomplishments and positive personality characteristics than to his failures, mistakes and misbehaviors.

The plus side of the personality increases, with a corresponding decrease on the negative. The child's self-confidence improves. There are several ways to accomplish this process.

Using reward

When I tell parents to take the emphasis off of what a child is doing wrong and place it on what he's doing right, they often misinterpret my recommendation as reluctance to discipline the child. To the contrary, this child needs a great deal of structure and discipline. But minimize negative consequences. Use reward as the primary means of providing structure. See Chapter 7, Reward, for a detailed discussion of how this can be accomplished.

Attending to everyday positive behaviors

Sometimes when I tell parents we want to strengthen the child's self-image and build his confidence by attending to his successes, I hear, "We already do that. When he brings home a good grade, hits a home run or wins the science fair, we praise him."

These parents are saying anytime something *major* happens, the child gets positive attention. How often do these things happen—once a week, twice a month, 3 times a year?

Major accomplishments happen *infrequently*. How many interactions do you have with your child daily? It could be 50, 100, 200 or 400. If most of these are negative, the positive events that happen once a week or twice a month aren't going to offset the negative buildup.

Although you want to attend to your child's major successes, you can accomplish more by paying attention to his daily good behavior because it occurs more frequently.

A major way to increase confidence and positive image is to acknowledge normal everyday behavior. Look for daily good behavior and praise the child when it occurs. It may be making his bed, helping you set the table, going to bed when told, picking up his toys, doing his homework or saying thank you. By looking at such behavior, you can increase the amount of positive attention the child receives each day. This will produce change.

Have realistic expectations

Behavioral and performance expectations should be in line with the child's capabilities so he can experience success, approval and other forms of positive attention. If you expect him to get A's and B's when he is capable only of C's or expect him to act like a 14-year-old when he's only 8, the child is certain to fail. He'll experience unnecessary negative attention.

Provide structure and consistency

Lack of confidence, uncertainty or poor self-image seen in some children may result from an inconsistent living situation or an environment in which significant change has occurred (separation, divorce, birth of a sibling). In these situations, try to provide a predictable, structured environment to make the child feel more secure and confident.

If the lack of confidence and poor self-image primarily results from the family's inconsistent, overprotective or spoiling approach to the child, see Chapters 4 and 5, Being a Consistent Parent and Setting Rules for Behavior. These chapters provide suggestions on how to structure the environment to alleviate these problems.

37

Con Artist—Manipulative Children

In the 1960s you could buy tapes to listen to while you were sleeping. You could learn a foreign language or develop self-confidence while you slept. There's also a tape they play in the nursery at the hospital before they let you take your child home. It's called "Manipulating Your Parents—How to Become a Con Artist."

This is why most children are good at these skills. They can lie with a straight face, know exactly what to say and are great at reading people. They can tell you *exactly* what you want to hear. They explain what happened in school and why they got a detention. You think, "That doesn't sound fair. I'm going to talk to the teacher." When you speak with the teacher, you get an entirely different story.

You talk to your child and tell him what the teacher said. He gives you a different account of what happened. The new version sounds exactly like the teacher's story.

To deal with a manipulative child, you must become aware of the behavior. Listen when others tell you the child is manipulating or has put one over on you. With a child like this, you can't be too trusting. You have to doubt much of what he says. You must check what he says happens before you believe it. Call your neighbor, talk to the teacher, ask his friend's mother.

The best way to deal with the behavior is to stop it from working. Don't allow the child to get away with the con job. If he says, "I don't have any homework," check it out. Have his teacher sign his assignment, call a parent who has a child in his class or check with the teacher at the end of the week to see if all the homework has been completed.

Some parents spend 10 minutes explaining how manipulative their child can be. Then a few minutes later, they tell me their child said, "The teacher won't help me. That's why I don't understand the work. I ask her a question, and she tells me to sit down and be quiet."

It's part of being a parent to trust your children. But after the parent tells me this, I usually say, "You just told me how much your child manipulates you. If you believe what he told you about the teacher, I have some land in Florida for sale. I'll sell it to you cheap. Do you want to buy it?"

The type and number of con jobs a child is capable of are many. He will probably make a good used-car salesman or politician when he's older. But you have to deal with him now. Question, inquire and check out his stories and activities. Don't be too trusting. Assume he is *not* telling the truth or only giving you *part* of the story. Don't blindly believe him or give him the benefit of the doubt.

See Chapter 40, Developing Responsible Behavior; Chapter 59, Stealing; Chapter 60, Stubborn, Strong-Willed, Pleasure-Oriented Children; Chapter 50, Lying; and Chapter 41, Developing Trust. All provide more information about dealing with this type of behavior.

38

Cursing

Although cursing or saying "dirty" words isn't an extremely common problem, it does occur frequently with some children. This behavior usually upsets and shocks the adults interacting with the child and draws concern and attention. There are several causes. Methods for modifying cursing aren't very difficult.

Causes

Models

Modeling is an important type of learning. Children learn behavior by observing other people. This is the basis for not showing certain programs on TV during family viewing hours. Children exposed to certain behavior may imitate it and may incorporate it into their patterns of dealing with conflicts, solving problems and interacting with others. Whether a child needs models or imitates a certain way of responding depends on several factors.

1. How significant the child considers the model.
2. How similarly the model resembles the child.
3. How frequently the behavior is observed.

You are the most-significant people in your children's early life. You serve as very powerful models from which behavior is learned. The child may learn to curse by hearing other people demonstrate the behavior.

If you, his grandparents, close relatives or friends are in the habit of cursing and using "dirty" adjectives to describe people, situations or feelings, your child is likely to curse. I saw a child whose first word was "shit." This was his mother's favorite word when something went wrong. An 8-year-old used "dirty" adjectives to describe his mother. They were the same ones his father used!

Peer groups can also serve as powerful models for learning. If a child plays with children who curse, the probability he will show this behavior greatly increases.

Attentional

Sometimes when small children curse adults laugh or think this behavior is cute. When this happens, the behavior is reinforced. The probability of it recurring greatly increases.

Some children curse because it gets the parent or adult upset.

Neurological

Some children have Tourette Syndrome; it sometimes includes involuntary cursing. See Chapter 63, Tics, Nervous Habits & Tourette Syndrome, for a more-detailed discussion.

Treatment

The best way to deal with cursing is to remove the model or have the model show more appropriate behaviors.

The old saying, "Do as I say, not as I do," doesn't work. If your child curses and you curse, stop cursing around the child.

Try to prevent the child from interacting with children who curse. Don't let him watch TV programs that use bad language.

Remove all attention—both positive and negative—from the behavior. A chart or other procedure described in the Methods and Techniques section could be used.

"Cursing is an unacceptable behavior. Every time I hear you curse, I'll put a check on the chart. At the end of the day, you lose 10 minutes of TV time for every check you have."

"You have been asking to have Glen sleep over. I've been asking you to stop cursing. If you reduce your cursing (be specific and explain exactly what you mean by this), Glen can come over Friday night."

Cursing related to Tourette Syndrome is very rare. But if your child exhibits features of this syndrome, contact your physician or a pediatric neurologist.

39

Dependent Children

Dependent children tend to show two different patterns of behavior when they are required to act independently.

Inability to function independently

Some children may look lost and act as if they don't know what to do. They lack independent skills and must have people near them to make them perform. If left alone doing homework, they daydream and/or are unable to complete tasks.

In school, attention problems may be evident. The child is unable to do independent seatwork. If the teacher stands next to him or works with him on a one-on-one basis, performance is fine. At home, the only way the homework can be done is to sit next to the child or tie him in the chair and make him do the homework.

If independent behaviors are required, the child appears not to know where to start and seems confused about what to do. These children may seem passive, effeminate, confused or lack age-appropriate behaviors. They may be unable to dress themselves, bathe themselves or do things on their own. They rely heavily on other people to do things they should be doing (tying shoes, getting a drink from the refrigerator).

This type of dependent child usually doesn't show an emotional reaction when dependency is not available or they are required to function independently. They don't perform or complete the task. They are often described as "space cadets."

Anxiety, worry and fear

When required to function independently or apart from the person they depend on, some children show significant nervousness, anxiety, worry and sometimes fear. They may show excessive crying and/or panic attacks if you leave and they must remain alone at a birthday party or with a baby sitter. Often this child has trouble attending school and shows similar behaviors when it's time to separate from the parent.

Certain environmental conditions and patterns of interacting with the dependent child make matters worse. Other conditions improve the situation. Here are some to consider.

Causes and Treatment

Genetic and heredity

Some very-young children want to bathe and dress themselves. They resist you if you want to do things for them. Other children would let you dress them until they are 35 if you wanted to do it.

Some children seem to be born with the ability to get others to do things for them. They have a passive approach to the environment and allow others to do for them rather than do it themselves. They think, "Cutting my meat at dinner, wiping myself after I go to the toilet and dressing myself all require energy, effort and work. If I don't do it, someone else will do it for me—so why put forth the effort?"

If your child is like this, don't foster the dependency. Don't do things for him that he can do himself.

Overprotection

Overprotection may involve several different reactions to the child, such as pampering, spoiling, babying, excessive attention and restrictions. Overprotection occurs in three general situations.

Doing things for him that he can do for himself—Doing his homework, dressing him, giving him a bath, talking for him when others ask him a question, feeding him. I've even seen situations where a parent of a 7-year-old wiped his behind every time he went to the bathroom. If this occurs, imagine in how many other situations this parent did things for the child.

Get a book on child development to see at what ages your child is capable of performing certain tasks, such as tying his shoes or caring for himself at the toilet.

Children of parents who react like this are usually seen by the other kids at school as "mama's baby, a sissy, a weinie, a nerd."

Dealing with your child this way doesn't allow him to develop independent behaviors. It will also interfere with his peer relationships. Many times children in this category also sleep with their parents and are treated as if they are much younger than their actual age.

Protecting the child from consequences—Some parents run interference for their children and don't allow them to experience the consequences of their behavior. This occurs in several different situations.

The child who forgets his lunch money at school or his books at home has a parent who brings the book or money to school. The child who waits until the last minute to do a book report has a parent who will do it for him.

I have seen children who have been in six schools by third grade. The reason they have changed schools is because they had a poor teacher, an ineffective teacher, a teacher who screamed and hollered, a crazy principal, etc. This parent makes excuses for the child; the child is *never* wrong. It's always someone else's fault.

If another child hit this child, it could never be their child's fault because their child does not do anything wrong. It was the other kid's behavior that caused the problem. These parents have difficulty accepting problems or deviations in their child's behaviors and continually find excuses to project blame elsewhere.

Your child needs to experience the consequences of his behavior to develop independent behavior, responsibility and adapt and adjust to adulthood. It could be natural consequences, such as not eating if he forgets his lunch money or not being able to do homework if he forgets a book in school. Or it could be other types of consequences.

"If you're able to get in and take a bath by yourself, I'll be able to play a game later with you tonight. If I have to come in and bathe you, we won't play the game."

"The mornings you are dressed and ready for school without my help, we'll stop and get you a donut on the way to school. If I have to help you, we won't stop and get a donut."

Doing things for a child who should be doing for himself, not finding fault in your child and projecting blame to others, and protecting him from experiencing the consequences of his behavior result in problems.

Restrictions from normal activities—Some parents won't buy their child a bike because he may fall down and hurt himself. They won't let the child play in front of the house or go to a neighbor's house without the parent being there because he may be kidnapped. This may also include a restriction from activities, clubs or sports other children are involved in.

These children spend a lot of time in their home away from other children. Independent skills are not developed. There is a high probability they will become excessively dependent on the parents, and age-appropriate social skills will not develop.

Get an idea of what children in your neighborhood are doing. What is acceptable behavior and restrictions for children your child's age? Allow your child to do the normal things most children do. Get him involved with other children. Let him be a child.

Mother is too close to child

This usually occurs when the mother shows an excessive or abnormal attachment to the child. Her life revolves around the child. This usually occurs in three general situations.

Parental conflict or absent father—In some situations where there is parental conflict and the mother and father do not get along, the mother may center her life around the child. Everything is done with the child. In some situations, the mother becomes the child's playmate. This also happens in first-born children when the mother doesn't work and a great deal of time is spent with the child.

In most separations and divorces or in single-parent households, the child spends more time with the mother than the father. In other situations, the father isn't home because of work or involvement in other activities. In these situations, the mother is the one who tends to do things with and for the child. Dependency may develop in these areas. In addition, the child may lack male models.

Get the child involved in activities with other children.

Suggest the father spend more time with the child. If the father isn't present, another male role model should become involved. Try to promote more independent behavior. Don't become the child's playmate. Emotional closeness to your child is something that is very positive, but you can go overboard. Don't promote dependency by having your child's life primarily revolve around interaction with you.

Symbiotic relationship with mother—The mother bonds with the child in a very close relationship. She gets a tremendous amount of satisfaction from the child being dependent on her. The mother becomes the child; anything that happens to the child indirectly affects the parent. It's almost as if the child and parent are one person and cannot be separated. This abnormal relationship usually results from some emotional problems on the parent's part. If this is the case, counseling for the parent is certainly recommended.

Parent(s) believes child has a problem—This could be a physical, social or other related problem. A dependency develops because the parent must help the child or run interference for him.

Emotional closeness to your child is a positive part of parenting. But if it goes overboard, problems are certain to occur.

Lack of confidence

Children who have a negative self-image tend to see others as more capable and competent. Sometimes a lack of confidence makes the child withdraw. The child may have trouble functioning independently. Dependency on others becomes a safer situation.

To alleviate dependency, try to strengthen your child's confidence and help him to develop a positive self-image. See Chapter 36, Building Confidence, for more information.

Environmental change

Sometimes shifts or changes in the environment shake a child's confidence or security. This can create dependent behavior.

Try to stabilize the environment and develop more consistency and structure. Minimize ambiguity and change. Chapter 19, Effects of Divorce, Separation, Parental Conflict & Other

Environmental Changes on Behavior, discusses this in detail.

Lack of socialization skills

Children who spend a great deal of time with adults often fail to develop skills to relate to and interact with their peers. They may avoid interaction with age mates and gravitate toward parents. This also occurs when children are not allowed to participate in clubs and activities that help develop these abilities.

Chapter 45, Getting Along with Other Children, gives some ideas on developing age-appropriate skills. These decrease the child's dependency and increase his independent behavior.

Punishment or negative attention are primary discipline methods

The major method of control of the child is through fear. Some children are hesitant to function independently for fear mistakes may be made and discipline will follow: The less I do, the less chance I take.

The probabilities of failure and negative attention are minimized. See Chapter 7, Reward, and Chapter 8, Punishment, for additional information.

Separation anxiety

The child develops a dependency on the parent, usually the mother. He experiences a great deal of anxiety, worry or fear when separated from her.

In extreme cases, the child follows the mother around the house and must be in the same room, even the bathroom. In a situation when the parent chooses for the child to be separated, there is usually a great deal of resistance on the child's part.

If the *child* makes a decision to separate, difficulty is not experienced. A friend knocks on the door and asks this child to go outside to play. He may go readily and show no difficulty separating.

This child often experiences trouble attending school. He doesn't want to leave the parent and is a lot of trouble at home when it's time to leave for school. Or he cries excessively when it's time for the parent to leave after bringing the child to school.

Separation anxiety often occurs when there has been a significant change in the environment. It also happens when the child has become excessively dependent on the parent. This usually revolves around two situations. The child lacks confidence in himself and feels he can't handle situations if required to function independently. The other occurs because the child feels if he lets his parent out of his sight, the parent may disappear and the child will be left alone. Although the mother has never been late picking the child up, every morning she gets 400 questions.

"What if you're not here when I get out of school?"

"Are you sure you'll be on time?"

"What if you get in a wreck on the way to pick me up?"

Chapter 19, Effects of Divorce, Separation, Parental Conflict & Other Environmental Changes on Behavior, and Chapter 79, Refusal to Attend School, provide information and methods and techniques to deal with dependency.

40

Developing Responsible Behavior

Many children I see are described by their parents as irresponsible, lacking self-discipline or internal control, not doing what they are supposed to do. Parents' comments are varied.

"He's 12, but I still have to tell him to brush his teeth. I often have to bring him to the bathroom to be sure he does it."

"I never know when my child has homework because he never tells me. He sometimes brings home an assignment, but then he doesn't bring home the books he needs to do his homework."

"I can't trust her. She tells me one thing and does something else."

"The teacher says she doesn't do her work in school. She daydreams or does whatever she wants."

"He never cleans up his room. I have to force him to do routine duties, like take a bath. How many times do I have to tell him to do these things before he just does them without being told?"

"She's so irresponsible. I've told her when she says she's going to play at Paula's house, she must stay there. If she leaves, she's supposed to call me and tell me where she's going. However, she never calls. She just leaves. I usually don't know where she is."

"He's always losing things—books, pencils, sweaters."

The basic complaint about children who show a lack of responsibility or self-discipline is they don't do what they're supposed to do. You can't believe what these children say. You may have difficulty depending on them to do things. They can't be trusted. They are often forgetful and frequently lose their belongings.

These children have a pleasure orientation because they do their own thing and take the easiest way. They do just enough to get by. Pleasure-oriented children see no reason to do things that are unpleasant to them. If you ask them to do something and they want to do it, they'll give you 100% of their effort.

If you ask them to do something—no matter how easy or small—and they don't want to do, it'll never get done. These children only do what they're supposed to when they want to. If it doesn't fit their needs, they don't do it. They often have difficulty following daily household routines (picking up toys, cleaning their rooms, taking a bath) or the daily classroom procedures (doing class work, turning in homework, completing other tasks). You must constantly remind them or force them to do what is expected.

How Responsibility Develops

There are three ways children acquire responsible behavior or self-discipline.

Born with "good" behavior

Some children seem to come to us with this behavior. They inherit it, and show it from a very early age. They're generally cooperative, do what they are supposed to do and even do things before they are told to do them. If you had this type of child, you wouldn't be reading this chapter.

Attitude kids

The attitude develops first, then the behavior follows. You may tell a child, "If you put your toys away, they'll be easier to find. By keeping track of the pieces of your game, you'll be able to keep it and enjoy it for a long time." Or you may tell a child, "If you hang up your new jacket, it'll last longer and look nicer."

After hearing these reasons a few times, some children pick up their toys, hang up their clothes and keep their rooms clean. It seems as if they develop an attitude first, and the behavior follows. I call these children *attitude kids*.

With these children, you can develop responsible behaviors by talking to them and establishing or changing an attitude. By giving them information, explaining things to them, being logical or getting them to see the situation from a different angle, an attitude develops. Their behavior follows. It's almost as if a light bulb comes on. You might say, "You have to brush your teeth to prevent cavities. If you don't, you'll have rotten, ugly teeth." The child brushes his teeth every night without you telling him again.

You might explain the importance of homework, why he shouldn't ride his bike on the highway, and the child behaves accordingly. "Don't touch the pot on the stove. It's hot. You will get burned, and that hurts." Or he could see his sister get injured by touching the pot, so he doesn't touch the pot. You probably wouldn't be reading this chapter if you had one of these children.

Behavior kids

Behavior must be established first, then the attitude follows. Some children can be told many times to clean their rooms, but they still leave them messy. You could explain the cost of living, inflation and how many hours you had to work to buy their clothes to some children, but their jackets would still wind up on the floor. These children don't develop responsible attitudes from discussions with you. You must first establish the behavior and get them into the habit of doing something. Then the attitude follows.

Talking, reasoning, excessive explaining, lectures, yelling and screaming don't work with these children. This approach to developing responsible behavior in a child is as effective as asking a door to open by itself. They develop attitudes and responsible behavior by experiencing consequences.

What you do is more important than what you say. You can explain to this child all the reasons why he has to do his homework, get a good education, clean his room. He will probably understand and agree with 99% of what you say. However, the information or lecture goes in one ear and out the other. He will do what *he* wants to do.

With the "attitude kid," a light bulb comes on (the attitude is established), and behavior follows. With the "behavior kid," the light bulb comes on, but it's very dim. It increases with intensity each time you are able to get him to perform the behavior. The attitude develops gradually over time as he repeats the behavior.

The more you can get him to behave a certain way and something happens that he likes or doesn't like, the faster the attitude develops.

He must experience the consequences of his behavior. He must touch the pot to learn hot pots cause pain. It may be all right to explain why a child needs to do his homework, but the most important thing to this child is what will happen if he does it and what will happen if he doesn't. You might say, "You've been giving me a hassle every night with the homework. You whine and complain. Every night the homework is done and you cooperate and are pleasant, you can stay up 30 minutes past your bedtime. If you give me trouble, you'll go to bed at your regular time."

This child doesn't have a lot of self-discipline, internal control or responsibility. He must develop it. He needs external controls and structure to develop the internal control. The more this child is on his own, in an unstructured setting where he must rely on his internal control, the more irresponsible behaviors will be seen. You'll also see irresponsible behavior in situations where the consequences are the same or where there is a lack of limits on his behavior.

Developing Responsibility and Self-Discipline

To develop self-discipline or the attitude of responsibility, you must first develop a habit in the child. Focus on the behavior. After developing a habit, hopefully an attitude will be established. The child will continue behaving in this manner. The techniques discussed below help a child develop self-discipline, independent behavior and responsibility.

Spell out rules and consequences

Tell the child what you expect or want him to do. Tell him what will happen if he complies with your request and what will happen if he doesn't. Spell out the rule and consequence at the same time. This can be accomplished in three basic ways.

Natural consequences—"I won't buy any more toys until you show me you can keep yours organized and put them where they belong." The natural consequences of not caring for toys is you won't be able to get any more.

Grandma's rule—"You can't go outside and play until your room is clean and everything is put where it's supposed to go." You do what I want you to do, then you can do what you want to do.

Arbitrary consequences—"I'm going to check your room after dinner. On the days it's clean, you can stay up past your bedtime. When it's not clean, you go to bed at the regular time." You pick a consequence that is important to the child and set up the rule.

These three methods of setting rules and consequences are discussed in detail in Chapter 5, Setting Rules for Behavior. These rules are the primary techniques used to develop responsible behaviors in children.

When trying to develop responsibility in children, most people focus on giving the child chores (making the bed, putting out the garbage, feeding the dog). This is fine, but it is *not* the main way children develop responsible behavior.

Chores usually involve consequences. If the child doesn't put out the garbage, he doesn't get his allowance. The reason chores are often used to develop responsibility is that predictable consequences follow the child's behavior.

When trying to develop responsibility or self-discipline in children, spell out the rule and the consequence ahead of time. Whatever happens to the child is a result of the child's behavior, no one else's. Responsible behavior can be developed frequently throughout the day by stating the rules and consequences *before* the rule is broken. By doing this, you put the responsibility for the child's behaviors on his shoulders.

By spelling out consequences ahead of time, you avoid random discipline. You avoid giving the child the impression others are responsible for what happens to him. Most parents are beautiful rule setters. They spell out rules very carefully and specifically. You may tell a child, "You haven't been bringing all your books home from school. I want you to bring home the books you need for homework. Don't leave any at school."

This is a good rule. It is very clearly and specifically stated. What happens when the child breaks the rule? Then you decide what to do to him.

You decide the consequences *after* the rule is broken. When the child doesn't bring his books home from school, you tell him, "I've told you to bring all your books home from school. Because you didn't, you can't watch the TV special tonight."

You decide the consequence after the child breaks the rule. At 7:00 pm, the TV special is on, the child is in his room, angry at you and pouting, and feeling it's *your* fault he's missing the special. In a sense, he's right!

You could choose any consequence as a punishment. You could take his bike away, make him stay inside, miss baseball practice or anything else you decided. He feels *you* are responsible for what has happened to him.

If children are dealt with primarily in this way, it's difficult for them to develop responsibility. They feel what happens to them is *your* fault.

When trying to develop responsible behavior in children, spell out the rule and consequence ahead of time. You encourage the child to feel that whatever happens to him is because of his choices. He will feel responsible for his own behavior. In the above example, you could have told the child, "When you bring home all your books, you can watch TV. When you don't, you won't be able to watch TV."

When stated ahead of time, the consequence is within the child's control. He must be responsible for it. If he gets to watch TV, it is the result of his own choice. If he misses the special, it's his fault not yours.

Tie consequences to child's behavior

When trying to develop responsibility in some children, it's best to tie everything to their behavior in the beginning. Set up a situation where the children earn rewards and pleasures, as well as punishments and disappointments. Spell out disciplinary measures ahead of time and tie all consequences to behavior. An example will make this point.

Suppose a family is watching TV when the mother suddenly says, "Let's go get an ice cream." They get an ice cream and the child enjoys it. Who is responsible for the pleasure he experiences? His mother because she decided to take him.

When trying to establish responsible behaviors in a child, try to relate everything to his behavior. In a case like the one above, you may designate some duty for the child before he earns the ice cream. It could be something important. "If you clean your room, we'll get an ice cream. If your room isn't clean, we'll stay home." Or it could be something relatively un-important you ask the child to do. "If you get the papers on the bed and bring them to me, we'll go get an ice cream. If you don't, we won't go get the ice cream." Regardless of how it is set up, the child earns the ice cream. He is responsible for the pleasure, happiness and enjoyment he experiences.

Don't assume responsibility for the child

Make your child responsible. If you force or make a child do his homework or you do it for him, you're more responsi-ble for the work being completed than he is. The next night, you'll have to do the same thing again. The child isn't develop-ing any responsibility or independent behavior.

Suppose every morning you came to my house, woke me up, helped me dress and eat breakfast then brought me to work. I would be doing what I'm supposed to do—going to work every day. But what would happen to me if you weren't there one day? I probably wouldn't go to work because past habits have made you responsible for my behavior. The same thing happens when you stand over a child and force him to do what he's told. He doesn't feel responsible for that behavior.

A parent has been telling a child to clean his room, but it never gets done. Eventually, the mother gets fed up, drags the child to his room, stands over him and says, "Clean this room. Hang up your clothes. Put the toys in the toy box. Make your bed." After 15 minutes, the room is finally clean.

A better way for this parent to get the room cleaned and encourage responsibility in her child is to spell out ex-pectations and consequences ahead of time.

"You can't go outside and play until the room is clean."

"If your room is clean by the time we leave to go to Grandma's, we'll stop at the store and get some gum."

Put the responsibility on the child's shoulders. Avoid forcing a child to do what he's supposed to.

The same situation occurs when you allow your child to become dependent on you. You help the child to do things he can do by himself, or you do them for him. With younger children, this often involves self-help skills (getting dressed, taking a bath, feeding, cutting meat). With older children, it may involve picking up after them, keeping their rooms clean, waking them up for school, locating their baseball uniforms and equipment before a game. When this occurs, a child finds it difficult to learn independent, responsible behavior. It's easier to let Mom do it.

Children who are spoiled, who have their needs met for them by others or who often get their way have a difficult time developing responsible behavior. Avoid this type of parent-child interaction when trying to establish internal discipline or responsibility. Chapter 31, Who's In Control, and Chapter 58, Spoiling, have more detailed discussions.

Make consequences different

Some children don't develop responsible behaviors because the same thing happens to them if they do the required task or if they don't do it.

"I'll be able to go to the movie Friday night whether I do my work in school or not."

"I'll be able to watch TV if I clean my room, but I can watch TV if I don't clean it."

If someone told me, "You can go to work and I'll pay you, or you can stay home and I'll pay you," I'd be fishing. I'd have to be stupid to go to work.

The same situation exists for a child who feels if he gets in a jam, he'll be able to manipulate his way out of the situation. Consequences will be the same if he cooperates or not.

Make consequences different if you expect to change behavior or develop an attitude of responsibility. If I go to work, I get paid. If I stay home, I don't. Be sure the child experiences different consequences for his behavior.

Lose a battle but win the war

It may be more important for the child to experience the

consequences of his behavior than it is for you to get the task accomplished. You know a child loves to play outside. Tell him, "You can't go outside to play until your room is cleaned."

He says, "I don't care. I didn't want to go outside and play. I'm going to watch TV."

You think, "What am I going to do now?" The answer is nothing. The rule sticks. With this example, getting the room clean is actually the fourth thing you're trying to accomplish. The first is to make him realize there are different consequences to this behavior. Something will happen if he cleans the room. Something entirely different will happen if he doesn't.

The second thing you're trying to achieve is to teach the child he is responsible for his behavior. "If you go outside to play in 2 minutes, 2 hours or 2 days, there's only one person in the entire world who's going to determine that. That's you. You're responsible for what happens to you."

The third thing you're trying to accomplish is to teach him you're going to do what he tells you to do. You're going to consistently follow through with consequences. The consequences depend on his actions. If he doesn't clean his room, he's telling you he doesn't want to play outside. You're going to follow through with what he wants. If he cleans his room, he's telling you he wants to play outside. You'll follow through with that. Getting the room cleaned is the fourth thing you're trying to accomplish.

Sometimes you battle with your child all day—homework, bath time, picking up. You try to win each battle by forcing the child to do what you want. If this is the case, you may be fighting the same battles until the child leaves the home to go to college. Although you win each battle, the child doesn't develop independent or responsible behavior. Sometimes it is better to lose a few battles but win the war.

A child refuses to take his bath. You tell him, "If you're in and out of the bathtub by 7 o'clock, you can watch TV. If you don't bathe, you go straight to bed at 7." The child may refuse to bathe and go straight to bed. You may look at this as "I lost. He won." But it may be more important for him to experience the consequences of not taking the bath than for you to win the bath battle. After this happens a few times, he may be more responsive when you say, "It's time to take your bath."

For some behaviors, it may not be that important if the child does what you ask. You don't die if you don't take a bath, do homework or clean your room. Experiencing the consequences today may get you more cooperation tomorrow. For some behaviors (those that are dangerous or may produce injury), you may have to control the child or get him to do what you request it. However, most of the time you can forget about the battles and focus on the war.

Avoid power struggles

Don't get into battles or power struggles with the child if he refuses to cooperate. You tell the child, "Go take a bath."

He says, "I took one Thursday. I don't have to take one tonight." Then you begin arguing, and a power struggle begins.

Avoid this when possible. Deal with him in a calm manner. Suppose I work for you, and you come in one morning and tell me, "I want you to stay at work. Don't go home until you finish this paperwork."

I respond by saying, "I'm not going to do that. You can't make me. I refuse to do that."

You wouldn't yell, scream or nag. You wouldn't tie me in a chair and make me do it or stand over me with a baseball bat and force me to work. You'd say, "If you do the work, you're still working for me. If not, you're fired." You'd imply you don't care if I do the work or not, but you're going to be sure one thing will happen if I do the work and something totally different will happen if I don't.

This same approach helps the child realize *he* is responsible. It helps avoid some problems described in this section.

Maintain a business-like approach

Some people will do things for you because of a relationship that has been formed or you have been nice to them. Other people would see this as a weakness that can be exploited.

Suppose you do 10 favors for me. Then you ask me to drive you to pick up your car. I'm busy, or I don't want to take you, but 10 flags pop up in my head. I remember the favors and how nice you have been to me. So I say, "Come on, I'll take you."

Another person may think he has put one over on the person 10 times and say, "No, I can't take you. I'm busy."

You can pay some people to paint your house before the job is done, and you know the job will be completed. For others, you wouldn't pay them to paint the house until the job was finished. If you pay them before the job is complete, it would never get done.

Never say, "I'm going to buy you this candy. Because I did, I want you to be good the rest of the time we're shopping." The good behavior will last until the candy is eaten! Instead say, "We're going shopping. I usually have to correct you many times. Each time I have to correct you, I'll give you a warning. If you don't have 3 warnings when we're finished, we'll get some candy. If you have 3 or more warnings, no candy." The child needs the rules or expectations and consequences spelled out *ahead of time.* Consequences should occur *after* he fulfills the expectations. "Even though you promise to cut the grass this afternoon, you'll receive your allowance *after* the grass is cut. Not before."

Avoid severe, harsh, long or big consequences

Some children learn responsibility by repetition of consequences. It's better if 20 small consequences are experienced. Suppose you have a child who loves Saturday-morning cartoons. It is 7:30 am, and he's jumping on the couch and chair in the den. You go in the room and say, "If you jump on the couch again, you'll have to go to your room for the rest of the morning. You'll miss all the cartoons."

At 7:35, he jumps on the couch again, and you send him to his room for 3 or 4 hours.

This is *not* the best way to discipline some children. It works best with the "attitude kid"—the one you can talk to and reason with to produce behavioral change. The "attitude kid" will go to his room and start thinking, "I missed my favorite cartoons. It's boring in my room. What I did was stupid. It wasn't worth it." He develops or changes his attitude. The correct or expected behavior follows.

If you send another type of child to his room for 3 or 4 hours, he'll holler, cry or pout for about 5 or 10 minutes. Then he'll play with his toys, find dust balls and make houses, count

293

the dots on the ceiling, read or go to sleep. Big, long or harsh consequences don't make an impact.

For some children, it's better to say, "If you jump on the couch or chair, you have to go to your room for 5 minutes." He jumps, and you send him to his room for 5 minutes. After the time passes, he comes back into the den and jumps again. Send him back to his room for 5 more minutes. This procedure is repeated if he jumps again. For this child, it's better to send him to his room 50 times for 5 minutes than 1 time for 3 or 4 hours.

Big consequences don't significantly affect behavior. The more you can get a child to do something and something happens he likes or doesn't like, the faster the behavior will change and an attitude develop.

Another example is telling a child to do something. "Go clean your room." You repeatedly tell him to do it, but nothing happens after telling him 87 times. The 88th time you tell him, he still doesn't do it. You're really angry and give him a severe, long or harsh consequence. Rather than let something slide 88 times then come down with one big consequence, it's more effective to give some children 88 small consequences. You have to establish a cause-and-effect relationship.

Big incentives or rewards that occur after a long period of time don't work well with this type of child. In January you say, "If you pass all your classes this year, we'll go to Disney World this summer." Or "If you don't get suspended again for the rest of the school year, I'll buy you a motorcycle."

If you set up this type of long-term incentive for some children, the child will work like crazy for 3 days but rapidly slides back into his old behavior. Or he won't show any behavioral change until 3 days before the report card. Then he'll study 24 hours a day. For this particular child, it's better to get a weekly report from the school and base his privileges for each weekend on his performance at school. If there is a long-term goal, he can earn points toward the goal on a weekly basis.

Avoid giving sentences

"Go to your room. You're punished until you're 18."

"You can't use the phone for a week."

"You won't be able to play for the whole week."

These punishments work with some children but not

others. Some children will go in their room and serve the sentence and come out and do the same thing again. Sentences are primarily given to change an attitude and to get a child to think differently.

Sentences work with the "attitude kid." Some children work better when there are goals or incentives. If you give these children a sentence, put a light at the end of the tunnel. They need a way to can work *toward* something. Example: "Because you have been doing poorly in school, you can't talk on the phone this week. However, each evening you do your homework and don't give me any trouble, you can talk on the phone that night."

If all you give this child is a sentence, the only thing you are positive will happen is he won't talk on the phone for a week. Give him a sentence with a light at the end of the tunnel (a way to work out of the sentence), and you may get some homework completed.

Avoid excessive explaining, lectures and reasoning

Many parents talk, explain, reason or lecture too much. For some children, this approach doesn't help them develop better understanding of the situation or help them acquire responsible behaviors. A child may not accept explanations or reasons why he has to do something (homework, washing his face). One, 10, 100 or 1,000 explanations won't satisfy him or make him understand. The only thing that will please him is hearing what he wants to hear.

A child may come up to you and ask, "Why do I have to study history? I'll never use it. It's stupid." After many logical reasons and explanations, he still gives you a hassle. The only thing that will satisfy him is for you to say, "Yes, you're right. History is stupid. Don't study for the test."

Sometimes the only reason that is necessary is, "Because I said so!"

Sometimes kids ask questions that don't have logical answers. Give me a good reason for, "Why do I have to make my bed every morning if I am going to mess it up every night?" There is none. The only answer is, "I have the job. I pay the rent, electricity and phone, and I bought your furniture. You have to do it because I said so. You won't be able to watch TV when you come home from school until your bed is made."

Model responsible behaviors

You are a very powerful role model for your children. They learn much, both good and bad behaviors, from watching you and seeing how you solve problems and deal with situations. If your child sees you acting in an irresponsible fashion or showing a lack of internal control, there's a strong probability he will learn this behavior. Show him responsible actions.

Chores

Many parents feel chores and duties around the house are a big part of developing responsibility. Chores are a way to develop responsible behavior. Giving a child duties around the house doesn't, by itself, develop responsibility. But it helps. When giving a child tasks to perform around the house, state what you expect and what the consequences of failure will be. There are several ways to do this.

Allowances and rewards—Allowance may be based on duties. A child gets an allowance of $1 a week. His job is to put out the garbage 4 times a week. Each time he does it without being told, he earns 25 cents toward his allowance. Whether he gets the full $1 or not is his responsibility.

Logical and natural consequences—The use of logical or natural consequences can be used by telling a child, "This is our house. We are all responsible for what has to be done. Your father has certain responsibilities, your sister has duties and there are many things I have to do to keep the house running. If you do not hold up your end and do what you're supposed to do, someone else has to do it. When that happens, they use their time to complete your responsibilities. That means they will have less time to do things for you."

Another child might like to stay up late to watch a TV program on Friday night. He's supposed to put his dirty clothes in the hamper by Friday night so you can wash them on Saturday morning. If this is done by 8:00 pm Friday night, he can stay up. If not, he goes to bed at his usual bedtime.

Your child's job is to cut the grass. If the grass is cut before 5:00 pm Saturday, he can use the car on the weekend. If it isn't cut, he has to find another means of transportation.

A child's duty is to feed the dog, but he never does it without being told. You may say, "You don't get your supper until the dog is fed." The natural consequence of not being responsible is the child's supper is delayed, and he may get hungry.

Another child's responsibility is to clean the bathroom on Saturday. He may be told, "If the bathroom is clean by noon, I'll drive you to your friend's house. If it's not clean by then, I'll have to clean it. Because that will give me more work and involve more of my time I will not be able to drive you. You'll have to walk to your friend's."

"Your job is to put the dishes away. If you don't, I have to do it. I have less time to do my duties. So I'll have to stop doing something that I do for you. If I don't have the time because I'm doing what you're supposed to do, I won't be able to wash your clothes. You'll have to do that."

If the child can't perform duties and tasks around the house to help other family members and make things easier for all involved, then the other people in the family won't do things for the child. See Allowance, Chapter 13, and Household Duties & Chores, Chapter 21, for more information.

Developing Responsibility—Things to Remember

1. Many children do not develop responsible attitudes as a result of conversation or discussion. Communication is fine, but some children must first establish the behavior (get them into the habit of doing something), then the attitude follows. It isn't so much what you say, but what you do.

2. When trying to develop responsibility or self-discipline in a child, spell out the rule and consequences of his behavior ahead of time. This makes the child responsible for what happens to him.

3. After the expectations and consequences are clearly stated, the child might decide for the bad thing to happen. When this occurs he may try to blame others for what has happened. "You're mean. You won't let me play. It's your fault I missed the cartoon."

Tell him in words he can understand, "It was *your* decision. It's *your* responsibility. I only did what *you* told me to do. *You* knew what was going to happen, and *you* decided to miss the cartoon."

4. At first, the important thing in developing responsibility is not completion of a task. It's important for the child to experience the consequences of his behavior and feel he is responsible for what has happened.

You may tell a child, "You can't watch TV until your room is clean." The child doesn't clean his room, so you don't let him watch TV. At first, getting the room clean isn't as important as the child experiencing the consequences of his behavior (missing TV). Don't feel as if you *lost* because the room wasn't cleaned. You *won* because you made the child responsible for what happened to him. If you're consistent, responsible behavior will begin to emerge, and the room will be cleaned.

5. Avoid random discipline. Don't determine consequences after a rule is broken. Tie the consequences of the child's behavior to him. Make him responsible for his rewards and pleasures, as well as his punishments and disappointments. Pleasure or punishment must be tied directly to the child's behavior so he is responsible for the consequences of his actions.

6. Avoid power struggles and forcing children to perform duties and tasks. This doesn't lead to development of self-discipline and responsible behavior.

7. Avoid long, severe, harsh and big consequences. Rather than have one big thing happen, it is better if 20 small consequences are experienced.

8. Don't let a child become excessively dependent on you to perform tasks you know he can do. This type of parent-child interaction makes it difficult for children to learn independent, responsible behavior.

9. Meeting a child's every need, giving her everything she wants, letting her have her way and spoiling her often interfere with the development of responsible actions.

10. Giving a child duties or chores around the house doesn't by itself develop responsibility—but it helps.

41

Developing Trust

Most parents develop a lack of trust in a child because the child says one thing and does another. You can't believe what he says.

"Do you have any homework?"

He tells you no, but on Friday you get a note from the teacher saying he hasn't turned in half the homework for the week.

"I'm going by Clark's house." You call Clark's house. His mother says your child has not been there all day.

"I'm going to a movie," but he goes some place else.

A lack of trust usually develops in several situations—when a child lies or steals, lacks responsibility or is manipulative. See the chapters that relate to these behaviors for more information. If you can deal with or reduce these behaviors, you may be able to develop more trust in your child.

Here's an example I use frequently with children. "Suppose you and I see each other every day. We go to school together or see each other every day because we live in the same neighborhood. Once a day I ask you to lend me a nickel or a quarter. I tell you, 'I'll pay you back tomorrow.' But tomorrow comes, and I don't pay you back. This goes on for 6 months, and I have not repaid you. Then I come to you and ask, 'Lend me $100. I'll pay you back tomorrow.'"

I then ask the child, "What are you going to tell me?"

Most of the time, he tells me, "I'm not going to lend you the money."

I ask, "Why?"

The child usually says, "Because you're not going to pay me back."

Then I ask, "Why?" again.

The usual answer I get is because he doesn't trust me. I say one thing and do something else.

I then explain this is the same reason his parents don't trust him or question what he says.

Re-establishing Trust

Three things must happen for trust to be re-established.

Ask for small things

They can't go to their parents and ask for big privileges. They can't ask to borrow $100 because they probably won't get what they request. They have to request small things. "Could you lend me a penny." What is a penny? The child has to start out asking for small privileges or requests.

Grant the request

The second step is the parent must lend the money. You have to grant the child the request for the small privilege. If you never lend me the money or give the a chance, you'll never be able to develop trust.

Do what you say

The third step in this process is for the child to do what he says he will do. The child might say, "I'm going to Robbie's house. I won't go anyplace else." To develop trust, you have to check to see the child has done what he said he would.

I usually tell the children, "I know you manipulate your parents and lie sometimes. But when you're trying to build trust, you have to do *exactly* what you say you're going to do. By doing this, trust will develop, and they will allow you more privileges."

Children who frequently ask or tell their parents, "You don't trust me. You never believe me. Why do you have to check up on me? Why do you have to call Robbie's mother to see I am going to be at his house? Why do you have to check with the teacher to see if I have homework when I said I don't have any?"

I tell the parents to respond, "If I don't check to see that you've done what you said, there's no way I can trust you."

You must put the responsibility on the child's shoulders. If his behavior indicates he can be trusted, you can allow him more freedom or privileges. If his behavior does nothing to reduce your lack of trust, he can't have more freedom or privileges.

42

Eating Problems

Eating is a biological drive—you have to eat to live. You don't have to pick up your clothes, take a bath, come home on time or make your bed to live. But you do have to consume food. If you give a child the choice whether to eat or not, eventually he must decide to eat. Only in extremely rare cases will a child refuse to eat *anything*. Usually, children are selective about what they eat, or they don't eat enough of the proper foods. Most finicky, picky and faulty patterns of eating in children are learned. Consequently, they can be dealt with and changed by the techniques and methods described in the first part of this book.

How Eating Problems Develop

Several situations are certain to produce eating problems in children.

When force or punishment is used to get child to eat

If hollering, guilt, fear or physical means are used, problems are certain to develop.

You run a cafeteria

You cook different meals for each family member. The whole family may be eating a certain dish except for one child. He gets a special meal. When this happens, you usually wind up cooking the same thing for your child. After a period of time, the selection of food that your child will eat narrows, and an eating problem develops.

Child can avoid a balanced meal

A child doesn't eat anything or eats very little at dinner. He is told, "If you don't eat anything now, you won't be able to have anything to eat later tonight." He doesn't eat, but at bedtime he complains he's hungry and asks for some milk and cookies. You know you shouldn't give him anything, but you think, "He didn't have anything to eat earlier. He's going to go to bed hungry. The milk and cookies are better than nothing." The child gets the milk and cookies.

Suppose I go home tonight and find beans and rice for dinner. I refuse to eat it. Later tonight I ask my wife to cook me a T-bone steak, and she agrees. If this pattern continues, I soon learn not to eat the prepared dinner and wait for the goodies that come later. Children who are treated this way usually avoid balanced meals because they're able to fill up on junk food at a later time.

When child is in control

This pattern develops picky eaters and overeaters. The child manipulates you and eats what he wants. For most children, this means more junk food than real food. Parents who are unable to set limits on their children may also have been overeaters.

If you cannot set limits on the child, he is left to his own self-discipline or control. If a child lacks this, he may overeat or eat what he wants.

Models

If you are a picky eater, if you don't eat nutritional meals or if you eat junk food, your child is apt to develop similar patterns.

Other foods are readily available

If the picky eater who didn't eat supper can later find cereal, cookies or other preferred foods to eat, he will avoid supper. If ice cream, candy and other snacks high in calories are readily available, the overweight child may have trouble losing weight or eating the proper foods to reduce his caloric intake.

Dealing with Eating Problems

Do *not* use verbal or physical punishment to change this behavior. The best way to deal with this type of problem is to stay calm, treat the situation in a matter-of-fact manner and use natural consequences.

Hunger is very powerful

Hunger is a very powerful force that can easily be used to deal with a child who is a picky eater or doesn't eat much at mealtime. Establish the rule, "Anyone who doesn't eat his dinner (define exactly what you mean by this) cannot have anything else to eat tonight. Those who eat can have a snack later tonight."

When the child who hasn't eaten later complains, "I'm starving. I'm hungry. I think I'm going to die if I don't have something to eat," ignore him. Hunger serves as the natural consequence of his behavior.

It has been proved that a child must be starved for about 3 days before he will suffer any physical harm. Sending him to bed hungry a night or 2 will not damage him. It is a powerful natural consequence to help him develop more normal eating habits.

Anorexia nervosa, characterized by loss of appetite or inability to relish food, is a condition in which the individual does not consume much food. It is almost nonexistent in young children. Children are not apt to stop eating. Many of their eating problems can be successfully dealt with by using natural consequences.

For the child who eats only certain foods and won't even try others, a similar technique can be used. However, try several other procedures. Close down the cafeteria—serve the same meal for everyone. If the child does not want to eat, use natural consequences as described above.

Get him to taste food

Sometimes the first step is to get him to taste a very small portion. Let's say you are serving pork chops, peas and French fries. Of these foods, the French fries are the only thing your child eats. Your goal is to get him to eat a small amount of the pork chops and peas. This can done in two ways.

First, put a very small amount (maybe a spoonful) of peas and pork chop on the child's plate. Use the same procedure as described above. "If you eat this small amount of peas and meat, you can have a snack later tonight. If not, you can't have a snack."

Or make eating the French fries contingent on eating the other foods. The child must taste the other foods before he gets the French fries.

Sometimes eating problems can be solved by gaining more control over other areas of the child's life. The overeater or the child who only wants to eat what he wants may give you trouble in other areas (taking a bath, coming home on time, doing homework). He may buck a lot of routines when he doesn't want to do them. By getting some of these other behaviors under control, the eating problem may be more easily controlled.

Reserve behavior charts and other methods of using consequences (you can't go outside and play until you eat) for extreme or severe eating problems. Don't get upset, and don't overemphasize the behavior. Stay calm, deal with it matter-of-factly and use natural consequences. Keep a few other points in mind when working with a child who has eating problems.

1. Don't make her eat everything placed in front of her. Some days she may not be as hungry as others.

2. Don't expect your child to like everything. There may be some foods he won't eat (cauliflower), but don't allow him to ignore a whole food group. Let him refuse *some* foods.

3. Use small portions. Get the biggest dinner plate you have to serve the child. The amount required to eat *seems* smaller.

4. Use positive consequences and reward to deal with eating problems. Avoid punishment, yelling, guilt, fear or other negative techniques. Having a child sit at the kitchen table for 2 or 3 hours until she finishes the meal doesn't work well either. Forcing a child to eat can cause problems.

5. Don't model inappropriate eating habits. If you overeat or pick all the "green things" out of your food, don't do it in front of your child.

6. Close down the cafeteria. Cook one meal and have something the child eats. Don't cook a special dinner for him.

7. Get rid of junk food. Don't keep goodies (candy, cereals, ice cream, potato chips, cookies) in the house. This also helps the child trying to lose weight.

Overeating

There is no excuse for young children to be overweight. This results from a lack of parental control, poor parental modeling and the constant availability of fattening foods. Children who don't have self-discipline and don't have external controls imposed by their parents may overeat. If you gain control over other areas of your child's life, it may be easier to restrict and control his eating habits. Control what your young child eats because it is harder to restrict his diet when he gets older.

Overweight parents model inappropriate eating habits to their children. Do not overeat in front of your child. If your child is trying to lose weight, eat non-fattening snacks with him. Get rid of the candy, cake, ice cream and other fattening foods. Keep salad, carrots, raw vegetables and other appropriate foods around.

If you have an overweight child, consult your child's doctor to obtain a proper diet. Stick to it! Be consistent. Control his eating habits *and* your own. Help him get exercise to burn calories. The number of people who are overweight because of glandular difficulty ranges from 1 to 10%. This is a poor excuse for being overweight. There is a greater probability your child's weight problem is related to some of the factors discussed above.

43

Excitability & Moodiness

Some children can be described as excitable, having poor emotional control, moody, unpredictable or having a dual personality (calm one minute, excited the next; sweet then mean). I'll discuss several methods of dealing with these behaviors.

Some children become more excited or active in fluid, unpredictable and changing environments. Everything is relatively calm at home. Everybody is sitting down watching TV when a neighbor drops over unexpectedly. The child becomes active, excited, restless and bounces off the walls. He is less likely to show these behavioral problems in a consistent, predictable and structured situation.

One way to reduce the appearance of these characteristics is to reduce change, uncertainty and ambiguity in the child's surroundings. The sections on Methods and Techniques will give you some tips on how this can be accomplished. Chapter 19, Effects of Divorce, Separation, Parental Conflict & Other Environmental Changes on Behavior, discusses this.

Avoid inconsistency. Say what you mean, and mean what you say. Don't say anything you can't or don't want to do. Follow through with everything you say. Establish routines in the environment (set bedtime, bath time). Avoid "maybe" and "if."

"If I can get off of work early tomorrow, I'll come home and we'll play baseball."

"Maybe we'll go to Grandma's tomorrow if she's home."

"Mr. Jobe said he may get off of work Saturday. If he does, he's going fishing. We might be able to go with him."

Deal in *certainties*. Don't tell the child about something unless you *know* it's going to happen.

This brings us to another important point. When do you tell a child with these characteristics about an event? You want to make the environment predictable and not do things on the spur of the moment. However, if you tell an excitable child about an event too far in advance, he's apt to drive you crazy with questions. You have to reach a happy medium.

Let's say a child is to go to a birthday party Saturday at 3 pm. If you tell him this at 9 am, the child may continue asking or saying, "What time is it now? How long till we leave? When is it going to be 3 o'clock? I want to leave now."

It's better to tell the child at 2:30 pm, "Start getting dressed. You're going to Preston's birthday party."

Another child's father tells him on Monday, "We're going to the football game Sunday." The child is excited and wound up all week. The excitability could have been reduced if the father waited until Saturday to tell the child about the football game.

There is no standard answer about when to tell a child about an upcoming event. It has to be done on an individual basis. Each child is different. Observe your child to determine when to tell him about a future event.

When excitable children are faced with a new situation, it's often helpful to try to make the situation as predictable as possible. This can be accomplished by telling the child what will happen step by step. This could be the first day of baseball practice, a doctor's appointment, the child's first school fair or whatever. By telling the child what to expect and what may happen, you provide some structure. It makes the situation more predictable and less ambiguous. It's often helpful to prepare these children for new situations.

If you have children with these characteristics, you probably can almost predict the situations in which the child will become excited or moody. If this is the case, try to avoid these situations. This may involve playing with more than one child, long shopping trips or some of the situations described above.

Avoid winding a child up then saying, "It's time to quit." A father and his son may be wrestling. They roll around on the floor, tickling each other. Then the father says, "Let's stop." The child is excited or wound up for the next hour. Try to avoid this, or engage in these interactions when it's all right for the child to remain excited (when he can go outside to play) not when it's time to get ready to go to bed or when it's necessary to calm down.

The above suggestions are preventive measures. Once a child becomes excited or gets in a "bad mood," other steps must be taken. Again, some parents have learned methods to "calm down" the excited child or to get the child in a better mood. These techniques may involve removing the child from the situation, talking to him, using reward or employing some of the suggestions discussed in the sections on Methods and Techniques.

Pleasure-oriented children often show dual personalities. When everything is going their way, they act fine. If you tell him no or try to make him do something he doesn't want to do, his mood changes dramatically. Chapter 60, Stubborn, Strong-Willed, Pleasure-Oriented Children, provides ways to deal with these behaviors.

44

Fears

At some time during childhood, all children express some type of fear. Like many other behaviors, the appearance of a fear is not as important as how it is dealt with once it appears. Some fears may be the result of an event (a bad experience when swimming may result in a fear of water, getting trapped in an elevator may produce a fear of riding in one). Others may originate from being frightened by TV or by peers. Some arise because of insecurity. Others result from changes in the environment.

While some fears seen in children are based in reality (what is feared could actually happen), the vast majority of children's fears are unrealistic (a child may fear going into a dark room because a monster may get him). They are not apt to occur and can't be confirmed (monsters do not exist). Because fears increase and strengthen when they are confirmed by actual events, it's fairly easy to eliminate those fears in children that do not have a basis in the real world.

Although the majority of children's fears usually can't be confirmed in reality, they may be strengthened by the way you deal with the behavior. A child cries out at night, "I'm frightened. I'm afraid Godzilla is going to come in the window and get me." Parents know this *isn't* going to happen, but to comfort the child you let him come into bed with you. By doing this, you confirm the fear in a sense. You communicate to the child, "Come and lie by me. I'll protect you because there *is* something to fear."

A child may fear separation from you. Every time you leave

him with a baby sitter or with grandmother, the child cries and whimpers. To comfort him, you stay home. Another child is afraid someone will break into his house at night. Before he goes to sleep, he and his mother go around the house checking that all the windows and doors are locked. In situations like these, your reaction to the child's fears may strengthen them. How you deal with a child's fear usually determines if it will increase or decrease.

Let me use an example to show how most fears in children can be increased and maintained. Suppose we are sitting in a room, and you tell me, "I'm afraid to go out that door because I think there's a monster out there. If I open the door, he'll get me. I'm scared to death."

I could talk to you all day saying, "There are no such things as monsters. You don't have anything to be afraid of. A monster isn't waiting outside the door. There's nothing to worry about."

All this talk probably won't reduce your fear. You decide to leave the room. As you get up and start walking toward the door, your fear increases. The closer you get to the door, the stronger your fear becomes.

When you put your hand on the door knob, your fear is at its height. At that moment, I notice you are very frightened and tell you, "Come on and sit back down. Don't go out the door." You sit down, and I comfort you. You feel comfortable, less afraid and more at ease. However, I have just confirmed your fear. In a sense, it has been strengthened.

Each time I repeat this procedure, the fear increases. In a short time, it will be intense. Children's fears often develop the same way. Although there is nothing to fear, the way you deal with the child's reaction to the situation actually tells him, "There's something to fear."

In the above example, how could we decrease or eliminate your fear? Not by talking about it. You'd have to be encouraged to open the door. By doing this, your fear would not be confirmed (the monster would not get you), and it would decrease. The first few times you do this, you'll probably be scared to death. But each time you open the door, the fear will decrease. If you do this often enough, the concern about the monster outside the door is eliminated.

To reduce a child's fear, encourage him to confront it. The fear is not confirmed and usually decreases. When first confronting the fear, the child experiences a significant amount of discomfort. It can't be removed all at once. It has to be done gradually.

In the case of the monster behind the door, you would first have to open the door only a 1/16 of an inch, then close it. After doing this several times without the fear being confirmed, you would open it 1/8 of an inch, then 1/2 inch, next an inch until you are able to open the door without much fear. This gradual process becomes clearer as we discuss several different types of fear and how to deal with them.

You can also use positive consequences.

Don't use fear to eliminate a fear ("If you don't stay in your bed all night, you'll get a spanking)."

Fears that can't be confirmed in reality

Most fears in children are fear of the dark, sleeping alone, monsters or others that have no basis in reality. This type of fear commonly occurs in children at 4 or 5. Fears can develop from the child being scared by peers or older siblings or as a result of seeing a movie or TV program.

The common element is the fears cannot be confirmed. There are several ways to deal with this type of fear. One method is to use a behavior associated with the fear as a consequence to eliminate the undesired behavior. By doing this, the fear is not confirmed and starts to decrease. A few examples help clarify this point.

A child is afraid of the dark. You are sitting in the back room, and the child wants to go in the kitchen to get something to eat. The light is out. He asks you, "Come with me to the kitchen to get something to eat."

You might say, "Go one step into the kitchen and call me. Then I'll go the rest of the way with you. If you don't take one step into the kitchen, I'm not going to go with you."

The behavior you are trying to eliminate (accompanying the child into dark rooms) is actually used as the consequence to help the child reduce the fear. After doing this several times, make the child take 2 steps into the kitchen before you go with him. After he has successfully done this, require 3 steps, then 4, 5 and more.

The child may not want to go into the room because he fears the dark, monsters or separation from you. Regardless of the reason for the fear, when this procedure is used gradually, the fear is not confirmed and it is reduced.

Another child may fear sleeping alone. You must lie down with him before he will go to sleep. Using the same procedure, tell the child, "I'm going to set the timer on the stove when you go to bed. When the bell rings, I'll come lie down with you." At first, set the timer for a very short time, like 30 seconds. Each night the time is increased. Eventually, the child will lie for longer periods of time by himself without the fear being confirmed. Eventually he will fall asleep without you.

Another method to deal with unrealistic fear is to use positive consequences to provide an incentive. The child will want to place himself in the feared situation. The fear will not be confirmed and will decrease.

For the child who fears the dark, a chart can be set up. See Chapter 10, Using Charts to Change Behavior. Each time the child engages in the feared behavior, he receives a star on his chart. The stars can be traded for a reward. By using a reward, the child has an incentive to confront and overcome his fear. The procedure can be used with the fear of sleeping alone, of staying in bed all night or other fears that have no basis in reality.

Some forms of shyness, not participating in competitive activities and not talking in class are often based on unrealistic fears. Positive consequences can be used to deal with these fears. When provided with an incentive, a shy child may be encouraged to talk to the cashier at the corner store, in class or at a family gathering. When this happens and the child realizes he can do it, the fear is reduced.

A child who talks about playing baseball, joining the band or getting involved in scouts may take no action when it's time to sign up. There may be several reasons for this reluctance, but it is often based on unrealistic fear. The child may not want to play baseball because he believes everyone will play better and he'll look foolish. By using an incentive to get the child to play baseball, you may show him he's no different from other kids. When using this procedure, leave your child a graceful way out. By doing this, you avoid forcing him to remain in an activity in which he doesn't want to participate.

A child has been talking about joining the school band. When it's time to sign up, he refuses to join. You might say, "If you sign up for the band and go to practice for 2 weeks, we'll go visit your grandmother in the country. At the end of 2 weeks, if you still don't want to participate in the band, you can quit." By setting up a situation similar to this, you avoid two things— reinforcing the child's fears by allowing him to avoid a situation and forcing him to continue participating in something he wishes to quit. See Chapter 36, Building Confidence.

Separation fears

These fears usually result from significant changes in a child's environment or sudden shifts in the child's living situation and daily routines. Fears are often expressed by a child refusing to go to school, by anxiety or fear when in school or when away from the parent, by refusal to be left with a baby sitter or by wanting to be in close proximity to his parents. These fears and how to deal with them were discussed in detail in Chapter 19, Effects of Divorce, Separation, Parental Conflict & Other Environmental Changes on Behavior, and Chapter 79, Refusal to Attend School.

The source of the fear is not what it seems to be. Anxiety and fearfulness result from separation. A child refuses to go to school. He experiences a great deal of anxiety, tension and fear when in school. You have a hard time getting him to go to school and keeping him there. Look at the school situation to see what has happened there to make him fearful. On closer examination, you may discover the child's fear is not of school but of separation from you.

He may get dressed without objection and not give you any trouble getting ready for school. When you drive him to school, you notice the closer you get, the stronger the fear becomes. The fear is most intense when the child has to get out of the car and leave you.

These fears can usually be dealt with indirectly by producing more consistency and stability in the environment and by minimizing change and unpredictability. Use procedures mentioned above to decrease this type of fear.

Fears resulting from real experiences

Sometimes fears develop as a result of something that actually happens to a child. A child who has a bad experience swimming may develop a fear of water. Another child who is in an automobile accident is afraid to ride in a car. Fears based in reality are more difficult to deal with. These may be fears of death, someone breaking into the child's house, storms, automobile accidents, large dogs and so forth.

Don't use punishment, threats or fear to deal with these fears. Use positive consequences to reduce them gradually. A child who is in an automobile accident is afraid to ride in a car. You might set up a reward system for the child entering the car and sitting in it in the driveway or in front of the house. After he becomes comfortable, start the car and move it back and forth a few feet. As the child becomes used to this, provide a reward for driving to the corner, then to the neighborhood grocery store and farther.

Fears resulting from lack of independent behaviors

Some dependent children are insecure when faced with new situations or when they have to function independently. Fears they develop tend to draw people to them (fear of the dark, fear of monsters) to help them cope with the situation. They seldom fear insects, riding over a bridge or other concerns that don't rely on people coming to their aid. To deal with this type of fear, try to establish more independence. See Chapter 39, Dependent Children, for suggestions on modifying these characteristics.

Fears resulting from changes in the environment

For some children, change produces problems, and the emergence of fears may be seen. Chapter 19, Effects of Divorce, Separation, Parental Conflict & Other Environmental Changes on Behavior, will give you some ideas on stabilizing the environment to reduce this type of fear.

School phobia or fear

Some children show extreme anxiety or fear centering around going to school. This behavior usually doesn't result from events at school but is related to other factors. See Chapter 79, Refusal to Attend School, for additional information.

Modeling fears

Some fears based in reality may not be as easy to deal with. If you fear storms or someone breaking into the house, it's probable your child will learn similar fears. To reduce fear, stop serving as a model. Although you may fear a certain situation, don't show this to the child. Engage in behavior contrary to the fear to be a more appropriate model.

Dealing with Fears: Things to Remember

1. Treat the behavior in a calm, matter-of-fact manner.
2. Don't use punishment to deal with the fear. Avoid criticism, embarrassment, hollering, guilt-inducing techniques or similar techniques.
3. Don't use fear techniques to control other behaviors ("If you go outside, the monster is going to get you.")
4. Reduce the modeling influence. If you have fears or excessive concerns, don't show them in front of your children.
5. Use techniques to build confidence and reduce uncertainty and insecurity.
6. Don't reinforce the fear. Avoid doing things that will confirm the fear and make it stronger. If your child is afraid to sleep by himself and you let him sleep with you, you are telling him, "There is something to be afraid of. Come sleep with me."
7. Look for gradual change. The fear won't change overnight. If a child shows a fear of the dark every night and you can do something to reduce this to 1 night out of 7, this is a significant improvement.

The first 50% of the behavior is the hardest to change. Concentrate your effort on this percentage. If a child refuses to stay in school all day, every day, work on him staying for one period. Then have him stay two and so forth. Getting him to stay for half the day will be hardest. Once this is accomplished, the second half is easy. Concentrate on small improvements and change to the positive rather than totally eliminating the fear.

45

Getting Along with Other Children

There is a saying, "The only things in life you *have* to do are to pay taxes and die." For most, you could add "getting along with people" to that list.

Dealing with others is a significant part of your life. The same is true for children. Problems in this area are related to two general situations. This first results from development of ineffective or inappropriate methods of problem solving or interacting with others. The second relates to a lack of socialization or lack of the development of the age-appropriate skills necessary to interact with peers. I'll discuss some of the causes and ways to deal with socialization difficulties.

Aggressiveness, Fighting, Name-Calling and Similar Behavior

Aggressiveness with other children may be seen in two general ways. The first is physical, such as hitting, pinching, pushing, shoving, biting. The second is verbal, such as name-calling, sarcasm, flip attitude, putting down others, cursing. When I see children showing these behaviors, I look in two areas.

Models

Developing a behavior from seeing someone else acting that way is a powerful form of learning for children. If you use physical punishment (spankings) or threats ("I'll get my belt if you don't pick up your clothes"), you're teaching your child to become aggressive when people don't do what you want them to do. If you control your child because you are bigger and can intimidate and overpower him, the child is learning similar behaviors to deal with his peers. A sarcastic, hollering, screaming parent may develop similar behaviors in his child.

I've seen many children who call their mother names, have fits, punch holes in walls and become violent like their father. They didn't inherit these characteristics—they learned them!

If you want to eliminate certain behaviors in your child, be sure you don't model the same behaviors at home. The old saying, "Do as I say, not as I do" doesn't work. Children *do* as you *do,* not as you *say*.

If you tell your child to fight, to not let others pick on him and convey this method of problem solving, he is highly likely to show this behavior.

Other models children imitate may be found in their peer group, on television or in the movies. If your child belongs to a peer group where violence and a flip attitude are condoned, this may be the reason for the behavior.

If your child's play involves fighting, guns and aggressive behaviors, he may use this in other situations as a method of problem solving. Children who watch a lot of violent cartoons or movies and are somewhat obsessed with the characters may also develop this pattern.

Underlying anger

Children with a significant amount of underlying anger may release this anger through aggressive behaviors with other children. This underlying anger may result from many factors. These may include parental conflict, school failure or frustration, changes in the environment, conflict at home. Anger— Aggressive & Rebellious Behavior, Chapter 32, contains more information.

Spoiling

Spoiled children often develop problems because they are more in control than you. They may develop a very self-centered approach with their peers and want to control them. The bossy, domineering attitude that characterizes their play is often the primary reason for the difficulties they experience in relationships with other children. They need to be the leader, take control and tell everybody else what to do.

This behavior/attitude may be an attempt for the child to structure the environment. He wants to be in control and call the shots. "I'll pitch. Jeff, play first base. Jason, you catch. Preston, play outfield." This child is bossy; this usually upsets the other children. Friction, conflict, fighting and arguing usually occur. This is often followed by rejection from the other children.

Lack of Age-Appropriate Social Skills

Some children have difficulty with others because they have not had the opportunity to develop appropriate skills. This occurs in several different situations.

Lack of experience

Some children don't know how to play with others because they haven't had the opportunity to learn. Although children are in school 6 to 7 hours a day, they only have about 30 to 40 minutes to socialize (before school, recess, lunch, after school). If the child goes to school, comes home and stays inside or there are no other children in the neighborhood, your child may not develop appropriate skills.

Playing with younger and/or older children

Children who don't play with children their own age may develop inappropriate skills. If the majority of their play involves children significantly different in age, problems may arise. If a 9-year-old primarily plays with 5- and 6-year-olds, he is probably dominating the play and learning these social skills and/or immature methods of interacting with others.

If a child plays with older children, he may develop passive patterns of interaction because he is being dominated. Or he may become aggressive because he needs these skills to compete with older children. A younger child interacting with older children may also be exposed to attitudes, conversations and behaviors he shouldn't be seeing or hearing. When he gets with children his own age, he may feel uncomfortable and out of place. Or the skills he learns may cause him to be rejected by his peers.

It's important for your child to play with children his own age. He'll be able to learn age-appropriate skills. A child with socialization difficulties may need more contact with children his age than he gets in school.

Adult interaction

Children who spend a lot of time with adults or interact with them more than their age mates may not develop age-appropriate socialization. These children are often 7 going on 25. They talk like adults, are concerned about adult things and worry about adult things. Because of the skills they develop, they often have trouble playing or interacting with children their age.

Overprotection

If you restrict, overprotect, pamper or baby your child, he may have trouble interacting with others. If a child stays in the house and isn't allowed to play with others, he won't develop interpersonal skills. If he isn't allowed to sleep at his friend's house, go to the movies or play, he may show lags in development of social skills. He can be described as immature.

If every time a friend asks you to do something, you have to make up an excuse because you know you can't do it, the friend stops asking. Look at your child's peer group, ask other mothers of similar-age children to get an idea of what is appropriate and inappropriate protection and restriction.

Dependency, insecurity, lack of confidence

Children who are highly dependent on their parents sometimes have difficulty separating from them. These children would often rather stay close to their parents at home than to play with other children. Some children also develop dependency on their siblings.

Dependent behavior, as well as other situations, leads to insecurity, a lack of independent behavior and a lack of confidence. This makes it difficult for the child to assert himself, socialize, deal with unfamiliar situations and meet new friends. More dependency develops and the child's negative view of himself strengthens. The dependent child's patterns of interaction are often described as immature. Dependent Children, Chapter 39, and Building Confidence, Chapter 36, have more information.

Personality types

Some personality characteristics by themselves may result in socialization difficulties. This is especially true with the shy, introverted, withdrawn child. The "man of few words" is usually in the background in most social situations, doesn't meet new people easily, has difficulty maintaining verbal interaction, doesn't initiate conversation and usually responds to questions with 1- or 2-word answers. These children have trouble establishing and maintaining relationships.

Often I get a referral of a child like this. The mother or father says their son or daughter is exactly like they were as a child. Or their child's personality is very similar to their own present behavior (no friends, a loner, introverted).

The manipulative child—The manipulative child may have some difficulty maintaining close relationships because he often has a self-centered approach to his environment. He is more concerned about his needs, wishes and wants than the feelings of others.

Others have difficulty depending on or trusting a manipulative child. These children are extroverted, talkative and often very popular. But most of their relationships are very superficial. On first meeting this person, he is likable, and initial friendships are formed easily. However, once you become more familiar with him, you realize he is not dependable or trustworthy and is mainly concerned about himself. It's hard for others to maintain close, long-lasting relationships with an individual with these personality characteristics.

Genetic factors—The environment affects and shapes some personality characteristics, but genetic factors are heavy contributors to behavior. Sometimes you have to work around the basic characteristics and look for improvement but not change. The shy child may always be shy but not to the extent it interferes with his life or socialization.

See Chapter 15, Children Have Personalities; Chapter 39, Dependent Children; Chapter 36, Building Confidence; Chapter 37, Con Artist—Manipulative Children; and Chapter 60, Stubborn, Strong-Willed, Pleasure-Oriented Children.

Emotional difficulties

Some children with significant emotional problems have

difficulty relating to people. They maintain emotional distance from others and have difficulty establishing and maintaining relationships. Their behavior or attitude is often seen as unusual or weird, and other children tend to stay away from them.

Chapter 52, Overactivity, Attention-Deficit Disorder & Hyperactivity, contains a section on overactivity resulting from emotional problems. This section provides additional information on this type of child.

Sibling conflict

Most siblings argue, disagree and fight. To what extent it becomes a problem depends on how frequently it occurs and how it disrupts the family or household activities. For more information on this subject, read Chapter 57, Sibling Conflict.

High intelligence

Sometimes children with levels of intelligence very significantly above average have difficulties in socialization. See Chapter 16, Children with High Levels of Intelligence, for information on this and techniques to deal with interpersonal difficulties with this type of child.

Dealing with Socialization Problems

Increase socialization

The way you learn to deal with and relate to people is by being with them. The major way to deal with socialization problems is to have your child interact with other children who are his age and preferably the same sex. Minimize playing with siblings, younger or older children and time spent with adults or in solitary activities (in front of the TV or computer). You don't want to eliminate time with siblings, younger or older children and adults. Just be sure the majority—at least 51%—of time in social interaction outside school is spent with children his age and the same sex.

Some children's interests are not the same as children their age, and this minimizes interaction. A 9-year-old boy may not like sports but is more interested in art, music or computers. Get the child involved in clubs, camps and activities that place him with children of similar interests. This way friendships may easily be formed because of common concerns and goals.

Have your child get the phone numbers of the children in his class, on his baseball team or in school clubs. Invite children to the house to play. Invite another child to come with you if you go to the zoo, to eat pizza or go fishing. Meet other parents in the class, karate class or scout troop. Have other children sleep at your house. Get your child more involved with children his age.

There are many types of socialization experiences:

1. Piano lessons, karate and classroom environment are situations in which other children are involved. But there is very little interaction between the children.

2. Baseball, soccer, gymnastics and dancing are activities where there is adult supervision and a directed activity. But this allows for more interaction between the children.

3. Scouts, youth activities at church and 4-H are activities with adult supervision and direction. These enable more opportunity to interact.

4. Inviting children to the house for a few hours, taking a child and his friend to play miniature golf and having your child visit with other children are situations that allow for the most socialization experiences.

The socialization experiences toward the bottom of the list afford more opportunities for social interaction. Focus your energy on these activities.

Decrease inappropriate models

The other day the mother of a preschool child called me. He was hitting, punching and pushing in school. Her child had been doing fine since we'd started working with him. I asked her if anything had changed. She said no but mentioned he wouldn't listen that morning. His father pulled his hair, shook him and slapped him.

It drives me crazy when a parent tells me every time their child gets in fight at school they get a spanking. If I handle my anger by punching holes in the wall and my children start doing the same, they didn't *inherit* those qualities. They *learned* the behavior as a method of problem solving.

If you have an aggressive child, minimize control by force and intimidation. If your child hollers and screams at others or is flip, negative and sarcastic, don't use these methods to deal

323

with him.

If you are shy, introverted and lack confidence, don't model these behaviors in front of your child. Try to increase appropriate methods of problem solving. Model effective behavior.

Create social situations

If you have a child who is aggressive, shy, doesn't share or fights, create situations to decrease behavior and promote more appropriate behaviors. When faced with a problem, most people reach into their bag of tricks and come out with a solution.

When the aggressive or withdrawn child reaches in his bag of tricks, he keeps coming out with the same solution or an inappropriate method of problem solving. Try to increase his bag of tricks and give him alternate techniques to deal with situations.

Suppose you have an aggressive child who fights, doesn't share and argues. Invite one of his classmates over to the house for a couple of hours to play. Before his friend comes over, tell the child, "You know how you and Clark fight and argue. Each time I see that kind of behavior starting, I'll give you a warning. If it stops, fine. If it doesn't, it'll be counted as a warning. If you don't have 3 warnings when it's time for Clark to go home, we can stop at the park and feed the ducks. If you have 3 or more warnings, we won't stop."

A child who cries as a method of problem solving has a child over after school on Friday. Tell him, "Wayne is coming over after school and staying until 6 o'clock. I'll break the afternoon into 6 parts—3:00 to 3:30, 3:30 to 4:00, 4:00 to 4:30, etc. and put it on a piece of paper. I'll put the paper on the refrigerator. Each period of time that passes that you don't cry or whine, I'll put a check. If you cry, I'll put an X. For every check you get, tonight we'll play 5 minutes of that game you like."

By using these techniques, you attempt to get the child to try other methods of problem solving and increase his bag of tricks. See Chapter 10, Using Charts to Change Behavior, for more information.

Start with one child

When trying to create social situations and getting your child to effectively interact with other children, start with one child. Sometimes problems occur or are more intense when the child plays with more than one playmate. Some children play fine with one child. When you add one, two or three, problems occur.

Reduce peer problems by restricting the number of children he plays with at one time. Allow him to play with only one child. Introduce other children gradually.

Limit time he plays

When you're trying to increase a child's socialization, limit the amount of time he plays with others. Rather than have a child initially come to the house for 4 to 6 hours, let the child come over for 1 hour after school. Or have the child come over 30 minutes to play before going to the movie or out for pizza.

Sometimes having your child play with another child for long periods of time may defeat the purpose. The interaction may start out positive and end up negative. He may be able to play fine with another child for 30 to 45 minutes, but after that, he has difficulties. If your child shows this pattern, or you try to establish friendships, limit play periods to the length of time he can handle. Two 45-minute play periods with a 30-minute break may produce significantly fewer problems than 90 minutes of play.

To determine how long a play period should be, look at the individual child and analyze his play. See if there's a pattern to the conflicts. As the child becomes successful in his interactions, increase the time spent with other children.

Import children; export your child

Some neighborhoods don't have children of the same age, or you may not want your child to play with the children who are his age. Bring children to your neighborhood, or export your child to other areas. In the past, the neighborhood school allowed the child to meet many children around his neighborhood. Today, schools may draw children from all areas of the city. Or the students attend the school because it's close to the parent's place of employment.

Get phone numbers of the children in your child's class. Involve him in clubs, sports and activities at playgrounds or schools in the neighborhood. Although the children who become involved in the activity may not be within walking distance from your house, they may live in the neighborhood. Make friends with the parents of children in your child's class and other children your child interacts with, such as the ball team or his karate class.

Reduce interaction with "undesirable" children

You may not want your child to play or interact with some children. The best way to do this is not to restrict his play with a certain child, but try to increase his socialization with other children. If there is only one other child your son can play with and you tell him he can't play with that child, that's difficult to handle. However, if there are 10 children to play with, restricting play with one child is easier. Your child may be able to see more clearly the negative characteristics in the "undesirable" child as his socialization increases with other children.

Sometimes you have to restrict interaction, but generally try to build new relationships. Your child only has so much time to socialize. The more children involved, the less interaction he will have with one child.

Provide child with techniques
to deal with teasing and bullying

Some children have difficulty with other children because they are the victims of teasing, ridicule, name-calling and other verbal or physical assaults. Try to get the child to go through a three-step procedure to deal with this type of situation.

Try to Change Yourself—What is the child doing that contributes to the teasing? What can the child change in himself that might stop the name-calling? How is he responding to those who make him the target?

If he cries every time he's called a name, he might want to stop crying and make a joke of the teasing or come up with something funny. I saw a young girl who was teased because she was overweight. When called names, she got upset and ran after the child who called her a name.

One day she decided to respond to another child who

called her elephant by saying, "Yes, I might get a job in a circus." After using this and several other lines, the kids stopped bugging her and went on to tease someone else. She stopped giving them what they wanted.

It's easier for me to change me than for me to change you. Sometimes by changing me, you will change. It is easier for your child to change himself than other children.

Look closely at how the child responds to other children. Give him alternate ways of responding that may produce the opposite reaction of what he is currently doing. He may have to ignore if he reacts, or he may have to react if he is ignoring. If the child makes several changes in himself and nothing has significantly changed, it is time to move to the next step.

Try to Change Others—The child could communicate his feelings to the other children.

"I wish you would stop calling me names."

"It hurts my feelings when you do that. I wish you'd stop."

If this doesn't work, try to get the child to go tell someone in authority—his teacher, principal, the teacher on yard duty, counselor, baseball coach or some other appropriate person. By communicating the problem, the adult may be able to intervene and correct the situation.

If these techniques don't work, try this.

"If you call me another name, I'll knock your head off!" I'm no proponent of aggression, control by violence or fighting. But there comes a time when you may have to stand up for yourself, and this may involve a fight. However, this is the second-to-last thing I suggest—not the first.

Usually the child who is teased is basically a good kid in school and almost never gets in conflicts or fights. I usually suggest the child tell the principal, teacher or someone else, "I tried this, this and that. I've even asked you to help me with this, but nothing has helped. I told Chad this morning if he calls me another name, I'm going to punch him." The child may not win the fight, but the one doing the teasing may choose someone else to tease who'll give him less trouble. If this is tried without significant improvement, the last step is suggested.

Avoid the Situation—If every time a child goes to a particular part of the playground or neighborhood he gets teased, maybe he should stay away from that area. Escape or avoidance of the situation is a method of dealing with the problem if any of the other techniques have been tried. Sometimes a child develops such a reputation at school that he can't shake it. In these situations, a change of school might be warranted if all other methods fail.

Strengthen self-confidence

If the child's difficulty with other children seems to be related to a negative self-concept or a lack of confidence, take steps to build a more positive self-image and confidence. See Chapter 36, Building Confidence, for a detailed discussion.

Avoid pampering and spoiling

Children who fail to develop independent skills or who do not develop age-appropriate patterns of interaction may experience problems with other children.

For additional information, see Spoiling, Chapter 58 and Dependent Children, Chapter 39.

Work around personality characteristics

Some children seem to be born shy or with personality characteristics that may interfere with their ability to maintain and/or establish effective relationships with others. You may not be able to change the characteristics significantly, but they can be modified so they won't produce significant problems. Read Chapter 56, Shy Children, and Chapter 60, Stubborn, Strong-Willed, Pleasure-Oriented Children.

Treat emotional problems

If the child's peer problems are resulting from significant emotional problems, counseling may be the best way to deal with it. Chapter 52, Overactivity, Attention-Deficit Disorder, Hyperactivity, addresses the types of therapy and characteristics of the emotionally disturbed child. Review this, as well as Chapter 23, Selecting Psychological Services.

Psychotherapy and counseling

This treatment may be helpful for any children experiencing socialization problems. If you try the above methods and the child still has trouble, consider counseling. There are various types of therapy. Look for certain things when selecting a therapist or counselor.

Ask around. If you start hearing a name frequently and people say good things about the person, you may want to consider him or her. Ask the child's teacher or pediatrician. Call your local mental-health center and ask for a referral.

46

"I'm Running Away!"

"**I** hate it here!"

"I'm running away."

"I want to go live at Grandmother's house."

"Chad's parents are nicer than you. I want to go live there."

"I can't take this house any more."

"I'm never coming home."

"I can't wait until I'm old enough to get my own apartment."

These and similar statements are frequently made by some children. Others say nothing; they just don't come home from school one day.

There are several reasons children make these statements or attempt to run away from home. Some are discussed below.

Punishment is Major Method of Discipline

Everyone avoids situations that produce negative attention or fear. Children often show the same feelings and behavior when punishment or excessive restrictions are used for disciplining. When fear and negative attention are primarily used, avoidance and escape behaviors may develop. If every time a child cuts the grass, all his mistakes are pointed out, he'll learn to avoid cutting the grass.

If a child encounters only hollering, fighting or negative attention every time he sits down to do his homework, he won't want to do homework. Lying and manipulating are avoidance behaviors learned by some children who experience these situations.

The ultimate escape or avoidance behavior is running away. If I get a bad report card on Friday and know if I bring it home from school I'll be punished or restricted for a month, I may not come home from school.

If you send me to my room for doing something, and I know I'll "get it" when Dad comes home, I may sneak out of the window in an attempt to run away.

If you have a child who makes statements about running away or has attempted to run away, look at your methods of discipline. If you use a lot of negative consequences and/or excessive restrictions, it might be the reason. Perhaps you need to change your control methods and use more reward, incentives and positive consequences.

Dissatisfaction with Policies, Rules and Treatment at Home

Many children feel your rules are etched in stone and can't change. Running away or suggestions about running away are attempts to avoid an intolerable situation they feel can't be changed. The child may or may not voice complaints about rules on what he is allowed or not allowed to do. After I speak to a child about a runaway attempt, he usually gives a list of things he wants changed at home.

Sometimes the attempt to run away may have nothing to do with the child. A child may want to leave home because of a tremendous parental conflict or arguing. He may want to leave because his oldest sister separated from her husband and has moved back home with her three kids. They've taken over his bedroom, and he's sleeping on the couch.

In this situation, have the child talk about areas of dissatisfaction in the home environment. If the child will verbalize his concerns and something can be done to change them, you minimize the dissatisfaction and his desire to run. Some things possibly can be changed—others can't be modified. But it's helpful to have the child feel he can discuss and express his feelings. This may allow him to realize some things are not etched in stone and can be changed. See Communication Between Parent & Child, Chapter 14, and Anger—Aggressive & Rebellious Behavior, Chapter 32.

At Your Request

It drives me crazy when something like the following happens. It's 2 am on Sunday, and I get a phone call from a mother who's upset and crying. Her 12-year-old left at 3 pm on Saturday afternoon and isn't home.

She tells me the child and his father were arguing over cleaning his room. The child didn't feel like he should clean his room, and the father was telling him why he had to clean it. An argument developed. Finally the father said, "If you don't like the rules in this house, you can leave." Guess what happened? The kid left.

I usually tell the parent, "What do you expect the kid to do? You told him to leave if he didn't like the situation. He didn't like it, so he left. He did exactly what he was told."

If you don't want your child to run away from home, don't make statements you'll regret later.

As Manipulation

Some children know making statements about running away from home elicits the same reaction in their parents as saying, "You're mean. You love my brother more than you do me. I hate you." It makes the parents feel guilty and question their interaction with their child and their disciplinary tactics. Statements may elicit reactions ranging from extreme concern to violent outbursts on the parent's part. The statements and behavior are primarily designed to manipulate or get a reaction out of the parent.

If you have a child who makes statements like these when he's disciplined or doesn't get his way, he is being manipulative. By being aware of this, you can prevent the manipulation. If it seems like this is designed to evoke a reaction from you, don't react. Deal with the statement in a calm, matter-of-fact way.

In all running-away situations, it's best not to punish the behavior. Get the child back home. Later you can discuss with him areas of dissatisfaction and the reason he ran away. By doing this, perhaps some modifications in the environment can be made. Often your reaction to the behavior or statements will determine whether it will continue.

47

Immaturity

Maybe you've noticed I seldom use the word *immaturity*. I avoid this word as much as possible because it means many things. There are several general areas of immaturity. According to the dictionary, "immature" is defined as lacking complete growth or development. This can occur in a variety of different areas.

A parent may tell me, "My child is immature." Or "The teacher suggested he repeat a grade because he's immature."

The first questions I ask are, "What did the teacher mean by immaturity? What exactly is the child doing that makes her feel he's immature?"

To change or deal with any behavior, it must be specified by stating it in detail not in general terms. To modify any behavior, it must be defined in *exact* terms not in *vague generalizations*. There are some general areas where lags in development may occur. Let's look at some of these.

General Areas of Immaturity

Physical immaturity

This is a lag in the development of a physical skill. The child may be 7 but shows physical development in one area or several like a 5-year-old. This may occur in coordination (fine or gross) or in specific skills necessary for learning (ability to follow directions, processing information a child hears, processing information a child sees).

Some delays in physical areas may not significantly impact on a child's life. If a child is deficient in gross motor skills, he may not be able to hit a baseball or ride a 2-wheel bike very well. Other areas of physical immaturity, such as an inability to remember the sounds of words or follow verbal directions, may significantly affect the child's life. These deficits affect school performance.

Review Chapter 77, Perceptual Motor Deficits; Chapter 75, Learning Disabilities; and Chapter 69, Following Directions, for more information.

Academic immaturity

This relates to lags in the development of academic skills. Physical immaturity may have an impact in this area, and some of the above deficits may affect academic skills. A lag in fine-motor coordination may interfere with the child's ability to copy from the board or complete required seatwork in the specified time.

Although the child is 8 years old, his hand-eye coordination may be like a 5-year-old's. It is like taking a kindergarten student and having him do the written work required of a second or third grader.

Another academic lag results from a poor foundation. You may have a child in fifth grade with reading skills only developed to a third-grade level. He has difficulty in school. This poor foundation could be a result of many factors, such as a lag in physical development of skills necessary for learning, absences from school, not doing required homework or classwork or ineffective teaching. Regardless of the cause, the end result is the same—the child is below his grade placement in academic skills.

Deficits in intellectual function may also result in academic lags in development. If a child's level of intelligence is in the low average, slow learner or lower range, he may be behind in school, even though he's working to his capacity. A child may be in fifth grade and working up to his intellectual potential but is only achieving at a mid-third-grade level. See Intelligence, Chapter 73 for more information.

Social immaturity

Lags in this area result in an inability to get along with or interact with children in the same age group. The child may be able to relate very well with adults, older children or younger children, but has difficulty relating to his age mates. He does not know how to relate to his peers, or he uses inappropriate methods to interact.

A child who primarily plays with much younger children may develop immature methods of relating to and dealing with his age mates. Children who are overprotected, restricted or dependent may relate to others in an immature manner. An eighth-grader may show the social skills of a fifth grader.

There are many causes of social immaturity. Review Chapter 45, Getting Along with Other Children, for more detailed information and methods to improve the child's social interaction.

Emotional immaturity

Lags involve emotional reaction to situations, frustrations and problem solving. A 10-year-old may become upset and cry whenever he is frustrated. The 5-year-old continues talking baby talk. A 12-year-old whines when she doesn't get her way. The child does not show the emotional development of his age mates.

Emotional immaturity results in similar situations that produce social immaturity. A child who is babied, pampered, overprotected or dependent may show these behaviors. Review Chapters 58, Spoiling, and Chapter 39, Dependent Children, for more information. Significant changes in the environment may also result in these behaviors.

Behavioral immaturity

The child shows behaviors that are not appropriate for his age. This may occur in several different areas.

Some children don't show the level of responsibility most of their age mates demonstrate. They may lose their belongings, not complete classwork and have trouble cleaning their room. In general, they don't show as much self-discipline or internal control as they should. Review Chapter 40, Developing Responsible Behavior.

Other children don't show an appropriate attention span or activity level for their age. They may be easily distracted, can't keep their mind on what they're doing, fidget in their chair, not be able to sit still or show other lags in the areas of attention and ability to stay still. See Chapter 52, Overactivity, Attention-Deficit Disorder & Hyperactivity, for further discussion.

Behavioral immaturity is also seen in children who lack independent behavior. They may need a significant amount of one-on-one attention to perform in school or to complete tasks. As long as the teacher is standing over them, they do the work. If independent work is required, the child usually doesn't complete the task. This behavior may also be seen when children have extreme attachments to their parents or have difficulties in making decisions or functioning independently. See Chapter 39, Dependent Children, for methods and techniques to improve this type of immaturity.

Children who are overprotected, pampered or babied may also show some behavioral immaturity. This may involve thumb-sucking, soiling, bed-wetting, daytime accidents or similar behaviors. See the chapters that discuss these areas for more information.

Many areas overlap. When someone describes your child as *immature*, have her specify exactly the behaviors the child exhibits that indicate a lack of development of age-appropriate skills. Before making any other decisions, you must know exactly what you are working with.

Some behaviors improve with time; others get worse. Others do not change. If immaturity is seen in the academic setting and there are concerns about having a child repeat a grade, then it's important to identify the type of immaturity he is showing. In some situations, repeating a grade will help; in others, it won't. See Chapter 81, Should My Child Repeat the Grade? for more information.

48

Impulsiveness & Acting Before Thinking

Many children are described as impulsive, not thinking before they act or having poor judgment. Parents often state they show daredevil behavior, a lack of concern for what will happen to them and poor planning. They show little concern for the consequences of their behavior and a reckless, careless approach to the environment. Although they may have been told many times not to do something and "know" they'll be punished, they do it anyway.

A child who shows these characteristics acts before he thinks, does things on the spur of the moment and is very impulsive. These behaviors often result in accidents, inappropriate actions and repeated disciplining.

Reducing Impulsive Behavior

Reducing impulsive behaviors and getting a child to think before he acts isn't an easy task. You usually have to help the child think about what will happen before he does something. Or you must teach the child to weigh the consequences of his behavior before he acts.

Thinking about the behavior

There seem to be two ways you can try to reduce this type of behavior. Let's take an example of a child who jumps off a very high porch onto cement. It's dangerous. The child may get hurt. It appears he doesn't care or isn't thinking about what will happen to him.

One way to deal with this is to talk to the child. Explain to him what could happen to him and how he could get hurt. Unfortunately, this method doesn't work well with all children. I'm not saying that you should avoid talking and explaining things to your children. But don't expect talk to control and reduce this behavior in some children. Change is related more to what you do than what you say.

Spell out rules and consequences

The second, more-effective method of reducing this behavior is to spell out the rule (don't jump off the porch). Specify a consequence (if you jump off the porch again, you have to go sit inside for 10 minutes). Draw a map for the child, with rules and consequences spelled out.

Whatever happens to the child is a result of the child's behavior; he knows about it ahead of time. If "good" or "bad" things happen to him, it is because of the child and no one else. If this is done consistently, the child's impulsivity should start decreasing. He should begin to think before he acts. This method of stating the rules and consequences is discussed in great detail in Chapter 5, Setting Rules. Review this to get some additional ideas on how to deal with these behaviors.

While this relates to discipline, you can also use this method on other behaviors to get a child to think before he acts. If "good" things happen, it's because of what the child did. If "bad" things happen, it's also because of what the child did. In a sense, you set up a situation in which the child earns his rewards and pleasures, as well as his punishments and disappointments.

Spell out disciplinary measures ahead of time. For some children, tie *all* consequences to their behavior at first. An example will make this point. Suppose your family is watching TV. All of a sudden you say, "Let's go get an ice cream."

You get an ice cream. The child enjoys it. Who's responsible for the pleasure he experiences? You—because you decided to take him for ice cream.

When trying to get a child to think of the consequences of his behavior before he acts, try to relate everything to *his* behavior. In the above example, you may pick something for the child to do before getting the ice cream. It could be something important. "If you clean your room, we'll go get an ice cream. If your room isn't clean, we'll stay home."

Or it could be something relatively unimportant you ask the child to do. "If you go get the papers on the bed and bring them to me, we'll go get an ice cream. If you don't, we won't get the ice cream." Regardless of how it's set up, the child *earns* the ice cream. He is responsible for the pleasure, happiness or enjoyment he experiences. Hopefully, this will enable him to start weighing consequences before he acts.

Don't use random discipline

When trying to establish responsible behaviors in children, prevent things from "falling out of the sky." The punishment or reward doesn't appear because of someone else. Tie the pleasure or punishment directly to the child's behavior. He is responsible for the consequences of his actions. Rules and consequences are spelled out ahead of time.

Playing games that require planning, foresight, and thinking before you act may also help.

For more information, see Chapter 52, Overactivity, Attention-Deficit Disorder & Hyperactivity; Chapter 40, Developing Responsible Behavior; and Chapter 60, Stubborn, Strong-Willed, Pleasure-Oriented Children.

49

Immediate-Need Satisfaction

Many children are impatient. They want things *now* —not in 5 minutes or 1 hour. They have a difficult time with delays and find it hard to wait. Several things can be done to help a child develop patience and/or reduce the hassle that centers around these behaviors.

Try to minimize waiting time. If you tell a child at 9 o'clock Saturday morning, "We're going to go to Grandma's house at 2 o'clock," you're likely to hear every 5 minutes, "Is it 2 o'clock yet? When are we going to leave? I want to go now. How much longer till we leave?"

Instead of telling the child at 9 o'clock, at 1:30 tell him, "Start getting ready. We're going to Grandma's in a few minutes."

Avoid giving the child long waiting periods. Tell him about events relatively close to when they're going to happen. Avoid telling him about things in the distant future.

"Next Saturday we're going fishing."

"Tomorrow you're going to Steven's birthday party."

Use cues in the environment to signify the end of the waiting period.

"When this TV program is over, we're going to get an ice cream."

"When Mom comes home, we'll go to the show."

"As soon as the bell rings on the timer, you can go outside and play."

By doing this, your voice is not the cue. This can often significantly reduce the child asking you hundreds of questions

("When are we going to leave?").

If you know a child will have to wait (at the doctor's office, when his brother is playing a baseball game), give him something to do. Bring some toys, paper and pencil, a book or anything else that may help him stay amused.

Positive consequences and rewards can be used to help a child learn patience. Suppose you have a child who can't wait 10 minutes. At first, you tell him 2 minutes before you are scheduled to leave the house. "We're leaving to go swimming in a few minutes. I'm going to set the timer on the stove. If you don't ask me when we're going to leave (explain exactly what you mean), we'll stop and get a bag of potato chips on the way to the pool. If you ask me questions about when we'll leave before the bell rings, we won't stop and get the chips."

At first the time periods should be short. As the child is able to successfully handle the delays, increase the time he has to wait before he receives the reward.

This procedure can be applied to many different situations. The sections under Methods and Techniques give you some additional information on how to use this method to help the child learn to delay his need satisfaction.

50

Lying

Somewhere between 4 and 6 years, most children learn about lying and start experimenting with it. Almost all children *stretch* the truth. Whether or not lying becomes a problem depends on why and how frequently it occurs, under what circumstances and how you deal with it:

When lying is first seen—at whatever age—the best approach is to catch the child in the lie as much as possible. Prevent the child from getting away with not telling the truth. At first it isn't necessary to punish the lying. But try to stop the behavior from gaining anything for the child. All behavior exists for a purpose. If lying doesn't serve a purpose, it won't be reinforced and should decrease in frequency.

Things You Can Do to Help Prevent Lying

Another general principle in dealing with this behavior is not to give the child an opportunity to lie. A child knows he's not supposed to ride his bike in the street. We look outside and see him in the street. A few minutes later, he comes inside and you ask, "Were you riding your bike in the street?" What would you say?

If you see a child do something, don't give him a chance to lie by asking him if he did it. Simply make a statement, "I saw you riding your bike in the street" or "Because you rode your bike in the street . . . "

Reactions that help the lie

Some reactions a child gives when questioned about a situation or when caught in a lie make his story more believable.

His reaction may also evoke feelings that will get you off his back.

Becomes emotional—Gets big tears in his eyes. Cries long and hard. Looks hurt. "How could you think I would do such a thing?"

Looks innocent—Sprouts wings, and looks like an angel. He can get you to think, "He could never think of doing a thing like that." Or "How stupid of me to think he could do that."

Makes parents feel guilty—"You never trust me. You always think I'm lying. You believe everything my brother tells you."

Loses memory—"I forgot what happened." "That happened a long time ago; I don't remember." "There were a lot of people there, and I couldn't see what happened."

Blames someone else—"The window got broken, but Joey threw the rocks. I was just there." "I wasn't doing anything. The teacher gave the whole class punishwork."

Accepts blame but in a flip manner—"Sure I did it. I'll confess to anything just to make you happy. Do you want me to confess to the bank robbery that happened last Thursday?"

Denial—Lies with a straight face. "No, I didn't go in the yard today. I promise. Where's a Bible, I'll swear on it." "I'll bet you $1,000 I did not do that."

Tells the truth but not the whole story—"Mr. Ray wouldn't let us play ball in front of his house." But he failed to say he and his friends were pulling up flowers in the garden. "The teacher erased the assignment off the board before I had a chance to copy it." He didn't tell you the assignment was on the board for 4 hours and he was supposed to copy it 3 hours before it was erased.

Causes of Lying

There are six reasons why children don't tell the truth. I briefly discuss these and some ways to deal with them.

For positive attention or approval

Some children stretch the truth to gain positive attention, approval and acceptance from others to strengthen their self-concept. This is usually an attempt to compensate for a negative self-image. These children exaggerate situations and tell stories.

Mother: "How was school today?"

Child: "I got the highest grade in the science test. During gym class, I hit 5 home runs, and we won the game." (None of this actually happened.)

Although this type of stretching the truth isn't as much of a concern as other types of lying, excessive storytelling may indicate a poor self-image or a lack of confidence. This type of lying is not directly dealt with but indirectly by working on building the child's confidence, pride in himself and positive self-image.

This is accomplished by providing consistency and structure, using reward as the major disciplinary tactic, and emphasizing the child's successes, accomplishments and good behavior. See Chapter 36, Building Confidence, for a more-detailed account of this process. Withdraw attention from the stories. Don't act as if the behavior is cute. Catching the child in the lie and preventing the behavior from working is also helpful in decreasing this type of lying.

Behavior is modeled

The child learns to lie by seeing other people significant in his environment demonstrate the behavior. Perhaps you or his grandparents tell little lies, and the family situation is inconsistent. If the child can't believe what you say, he is likely to lie and say one thing and do something else.

The old saying "Do as I say, not as I do" doesn't work. Model emulation is not a major reason for lying. Lying can easily be changed by providing significant models who tell the truth.

Need for satisfaction

Some children lie because they get away with it.

Parent: "Do you have homework tonight?"

Child: "No, I did it in school."

The lie is manipulative because it is geared toward satisfying the child's needs, wishes and desires or avoiding unpleasant duties and responsibilities.

Child: "Can I go outside and play?"

Parent: "Sure, as soon as your room is clean."

Child 10 minutes later: "Mom, can I go outside now?"

Parent cooking: "Did you clean your room?"

Child: "Yes."

Twenty minutes later the mother goes to look at his room and finds nothing has been touched.

These children lie because it works. To deal with this situation, stay one step ahead of the child. Check out what he says. If he says he doesn't have homework, call a parent of a child in his class or have his teacher sign his assignment pad. When he insists he did the homework in school, make him bring it home. If he says he cleaned his room, check it before you let him go outside. Once this type of lying stops working and the child's needs are not being satisfied, he should start relaying more truthful information.

To avoid punishment

The many problems can occur when punishment is used as the main method of discipline. This was discussed in Chapter 8, Punishment. Avoidance behavior can develop; lying is a major form of avoidance behavior.

Some children lie to avoid being punished or out of fear of what's going to happen to them.

Parent: "John, did you break that lamp in the back room?"

John knows if he admits to breaking the lamp, he'll be punished. If he lies, there is a chance he may avoid the punishment: "No, Mom. I don't know what happened. Maybe the wind blew it over."

This is a difficult situation to deal with because you need to minimize the use of negative consequences as methods of discipline. Rather than punishing the child for the lying, it's preferable to remove punishment from telling the truth. The child is told, "If you tell the truth, nothing will happen. But if you lie, you'll be punished." The consequences are different. It's more to the child's advantage to tell the truth than to lie.

Charts can also be used to increase telling the truth. Give rewards for telling the truth, or a response-cost type of punishment could be given for lying. See Chapter 10, Using Charts to Change Behavior, for a more-detailed discussion.

Not accepting responsibility for behavior

This seems to be a combination of the two types discussed

above. It is primarily seen in children who have difficulty accepting responsibility for their actions. They tend to blame others or events rather than themselves for things that happen to them.

"It's the teacher's fault I failed the test. She told us to study the wrong material."

"If you hadn't bought me the baseball, I wouldn't have broken the window. It's your fault the window's broken."

"He made me hit him because he was teasing me."

Lies occur when the child has been caught, or almost caught, doing something. But he won't admit to doing it. Everyone in the world may know he did it and the child may be confronted with the facts, but he'll strongly deny his participation or guilt in the matter. Six children may be playing ball in the back yard when a window is broken. Five of the children say Jeff broke the window and all of their stories are the same. However, Jeff won't admit to the act even when confronted with the evidence.

This type of lying usually occurs in children who project blame for their behavior onto other people. In dealing with this type of lie, don't directly attack the behavior. Indirectly treat it by trying to make the child more responsible or accountable for his overall behavior. This is accomplished by setting rules and consequences in the fashion described in Chapter 5, Setting Rules for Behavior. Review the chapter and Chapter 40, Developing Responsible Behavior, and Chapter 41, Developing Trust.

Personality characteristic

Children who are strong-willed, manipulative or pleasure-oriented are more apt to show these behaviors than children with other personality characteristics. See the chapters that discuss these children for additional information.

51

Not Listening

Not listening seems to be a very common problem for parents. Most parents who have participated in our workshops over the last several years have listed behavior that can be classified as "not listening" as one of the three major problems they would like solved. They list "hardheaded, brickhead, not doing what he is supposed to do, not following rules, telling him several times to do something."

One main reason this behavior exists is inconsistency in your methods of dealing with your child's behavior. Consistency is the foundation of any effective behavior-management system. Review Chapter 4, Being a Consistent Parent.

Another major cause of not listening in children is you often use talk or verbal interaction as a method of discipline.

When punishment is used to manage children, they often don't listen. They become deaf to you quite rapidly when disciplined this way. A child sticks a pencil in his sister's ear, and you say, "You know you shouldn't do that. You really make me upset when you and your sister fight. You may hurt her, or she'll be deaf for the rest of her life. She's your sister. You should love her. You know how much she likes you."

This type of communication is fine and necessary, but do *not* expect talk to control behavior. If talk is the only thing used to prevent the child from sticking the pencil in his sister's ear again, it probably won't work. It will seem the child is not listening.

A large percentage of the children I deal with can't be disciplined effectively with reason, talk and verbal interchange.

But they behave when consequences are employed. Although there should be a great deal of communication between you and your child, restrict talk to conversation. Do *not* use it as a disciplinary tactic. Talk to children when problem behavior occurs, but do *not* stop there. Employ consequences to change behavior.

Talking, reasoning, explaining and lecturing works with the "attitude kid." If you have this type of child, you probably aren't reading this chapter. Read Chapter 40, Developing Responsible Behavior, for more information.

Overactive, stubborn and strong-willed children also have problems listening to their parents. See chapters that discuss these children for additional techniques to deal with this behavior.

52

Overactivity, Attention-Deficit Disorder & Hyperactivity

Overactivity is a very common problem. For many families, this is a major concern. An overactive child is difficult to manage at home or has trouble in school because of his inability to sit still, his short attention span and his distractibility. Not much information is available for parents. Almost all the information on overactivity/hyperactivity is written for professionals. It is not easily understood by the average person.

Many parents who come to me with children who have been diagnosed as *overactive* or *hyperactive* usually don't know what this means. Or they have a very vague understanding of their child's behavior.

Usually when I ask them, "Has anybody ever explained to you what *hyperactive* means?" most don't know. Or their explanation may be inaccurate or superficial (he's nervous, he has a lot of energy). The information provided in this chapter gives you a better understanding of the possible causes of your child's behavior and how to deal with your child.

I have presented most of the methods used today to manage and deal with overactive children—to decrease a child's overactive behavior and make him more manageable. Some methods are not consistent with my own philosophy.

Characteristics of Overactivity

How active should a child be? How restless, distractible, talkative, stubborn? What is normal overactive behavior? Generally, *normal* behavior is behavior that doesn't interfere with a child's ability to cope with his environment or get along with others.

Normal or overactive behavior?

It's relatively easy to find a child-development book that tells you at what age a child should walk, talk, get his first tooth. Other books tell you what behaviors to expect at certain ages ("terrible twos"). But what *is* a *normal* amount of sassiness, activity, distractibility and ability to concentrate? When *is* an attention span *short?* How *much* should a child fidget or be restless? What *is* the difference between being "all boy" and being overactive?

Answers to these questions are difficult to find. Almost all children—at some time or other—show overactive behaviors. When trying to decide what is normal or what is an average amount of behavior to expect from a child, several things should be taken into consideration.

Evaluate frequency

All children whine, have temper tantrums, show periods of stubbornness, squirm, cannot keep still. To determine if the behavior should produce concern, look at how frequently the behavior occurs. For a child who has a temper tantrum once a month or who can't sit still through some TV programs, these behaviors may not be of concern. But if the temper tantrum occurs 4 times a day or the child can't be still for almost all TV shows, even cartoons, you need to look at it more closely.

To determine if your child's activity level is normal, look at how *often* it occurs. The more frequently the overactive behavior is seen and the more it deviates from the average, the more of a concern it should be.

Compare with peer groups

In determining what is a normal amount of activity or what to expect from your child, look at his peer group. Take into consideration his agemates' behavior, activity level and ability to concentrate. Compare your child to other children his age. The child's peer group's activity and span of attention must be taken into consideration before deciding what to expect or what is normal for your child.

It's necessary to become familiar with or observe other

children to determine what to expect from your child or how much his activity level and related behaviors differ from the average.

Consider individual differences

Children have different personalities and show a variety of behaviors. One child may be sensitive, another talkative. In determining if a behavior is "normal," consider the child's peer group and the individual child. There are also family differences and expectations. You may expect your child to "sit still" while watching TV, but I may not expect this from my children.

Listen to those who are aware of child behavior

Teachers, coaches, nursery-school teachers, dancing instructors and others work with children of similar ages. They are usually familiar with "age-appropriate" or "normal" levels of activity, ability to concentrate, distractibility and stubbornness. Although they may not be able to give reasons for certain behaviors or recommendations to deal with them, these people are often capable of identifying unusual behaviors or actions that differ from the child's age group. Listen to them. If several people tell you about your child's activity level, investigate it. It's easy to ignore what you don't want to hear or believe about your own child.

Symptoms of Overactivity

While there seem to be several different reasons why children are overactive, the behaviors of concern fall into two general areas:

Motor activity

The overactive child fidgets or squirms when he sits. He's unable to remain seated for long, runs when he should walk, goes from one thing to another, can't remain still when watching an interesting movie or cartoon, continually gets out of his chair during mealtimes, never stops talking. Or he shows other characteristics that imply physical activity or being in constant motion.

Cognitive activity

When compared to other children his age, he appears to

be impulsive and distractible, has a short attention span and acts before he thinks. He has difficulty following a series of directions, forgets easily, becomes easily upset or irritated and does not profit from past experiences. He daydreams, is moody, has difficulty concentrating, has a low tolerance for frustration. Or he shows other characteristics that indicate deficits in attention span or concentration and/or the ability to control feelings.

Characteristics of overactivity

Below is a list of characteristics of overactive children. The majority of statements were obtained from parents and teachers of overactive children. I divided the characteristics into six areas. Only a few or many of the characteristics may appear in a given child.

Motor behavior—Symptoms include:

1. High activity level
2. Unusual amount of energy
3. Excessive activity
4. Restless
5. In constant motion
6. Fidgeting
7. Inability to keep still
8. Goes from one thing to another
9. Never stops moving
10. Inability to sit still during meals, TV
11. Inability to keep his hands to himself
12. Over-talkativeness
13. Nervousness
14. Unable to sit still for any length of time
15. Clumsiness
16. Poor gross motor coordination
17. Poor fine motor coordination
18. Accident-prone

Attention and concentration—Symptoms include:

1. Short attention span
2. Poor concentration
3. Daydreams
4. Easily distracted
5. Inattentiveness
6. Easily bored
7. Short interest span
8. Rushes from one activity to another
9. Inability to maintain attention
10. Frequently changes activities
11. Inability to listen to a story or take part in a table game for any length of time.

Impulse control—Symptoms include:

1. Acts before he thinks
2. Daredevil behavior
3. Low frustration tolerance
4. Poor planning and judgment
5. Flies off the handle easily
6. Inability to control himself
7. Temper outbursts
8. Acts without thinking
9. Gets upset easily
10. Poor foresight
11. Low boiling point
12. Poor organization

Emotions—Symptoms include:

1. Unpredictable
2. Moody
3. Poor emotional control
4. Feelings easily hurt
5. Impulsive, then remorseful
6. Cries easily
7. Fearless
8. Becomes overexcited and more active in stimulating situations
9. Has good and bad days
10. Difficulty in coping with environmental changes
11. Reckless
12. Uninhibited
13. Dr. Jekyll-Mr. Hyde personality
14. Can tell when he wakes up what kind of mood he's in and what kind of day he'll have
15. Poor self-concept

Relationships with others—Symptoms include:

1. Stubborn
2. Disobedient
3. Inability to accept correction
4. Hard to discipline
5. Defiant
6. Refusal to take "No" for an answer
7. Inability to listen
8. Resists controls by adult
9. Negative attitude
10. Sassy
11. Independent
12. Extroverted
13. Poor peer relationships
14. Often gets into fights
15. Bossy with children
16. Difficulty when playing with more than 1 or 2 children
17. Attempts to control peers
18. Overexcitable in normal play
19. Socially bold and aggressive
20. Easily led by peers

School—Symptoms include:

1. Gets out of seat
2. Speaks out of turn
3. Daydreams
4. Disturbs others
5. Makes disruptive noises
6. Sloppy
7. Disorganized
8. Messy
9. Forgetful
10. Inability to work well alone or in groups
11. Works best in 1-on-1 situation or when you stay on top of him
12. Can't stay in seat
13. Poor conduct
14. Failure to follow or confusion of directions
15. Academic trouble
16. Poor grades
17. Inability to keep mind on work
18. Doesn't complete task
19. Can't finish work in a reasonable amount of time
20. Can't stay on one task
21. Poor penmanship
22. Wastes time
23. Difficulty retaining information

Difficulties in these areas—Most overactive children show some difficulty in all six areas. It's important to realize a child doesn't have to have characteristics in all or even many of the above areas to be called *overactive*. It is not uncommon for a child to have more problems in one area than another.

All overactive children do not have coordination problems. One overactive child may be able to sit and remain in his desk all day but can't concentrate for more than 30 seconds at a time. Another child may have good concentration but constantly fidgets, squirms and can't remain in one place long enough to attend to the task. A child may be overactive and get along well with his peers. Each overactive child is an individual who presents his own distinct picture.

Hypoactive Children

This is a somewhat unusual situation and does not occur frequently. I have seen about 10 to 15 hypoactive children in the last 15 years. These children show all of the attention problems described above. Although they may be somewhat fidgety, their activity level is the *opposite* of the hyperactive child. They are very *slow moving*.

Some parents describe this child as being in "slow motion," even when he's riding his bike. He has trouble completing work, daydreams and is distracted easily, but the activity level is below average. Methods of treating this child are the same as for the overactive child.

If you still have doubts or feel your child's activity level differs from the average, contact your child's doctor or a mental-health professional who primarily deals with children. They will be able to help and give you some information and answer your questions.

Causes of Overactivity

Overactivity can be grouped into five general categories based on the reason(s) for increased levels of activity. Overactivity can be related to:

1. Management techniques used by parents and/or personality characteristics of the child.
2. Attention-deficit disorder, with or without hyperactivity.
3. Significant emotional problems.
4. Intelligence.
5. Combinations of the above.

In 90% of the children I see for overactivity, the first and second reasons account for increased levels of activity. Most overactivity can be attributed to the child's personality characteristics or management techniques used by parents and/or hyperactivity/hyperkinetic reaction of childhood or an attention-deficit disorder with hyperactivity. A few cases—probably about 10%—can be attributed to other causes.

This chapter focuses on what I feel are the dominant factors. I'll briefly discuss overactivity due to the other factors mentioned.

Ineffective Behavior Management or Personality Characteristics

When ineffective or inconsistent management techniques are used by parents or there is inadequate discipline in the home, some children may develop overactive behaviors. Some children can avoid unpleasant duties and responsibilities or manipulate others to have most of their needs met.

Because of faulty management, other children "call the shots" at home. They have more control than their parents. These children usually determine when they go to bed, if they take a bath, what time they come in from play, when and if they will do their homework.

Other children are "spoiled" because they get what they want. At home, they do not listen, appear moody, get upset easily, do not settle down when warned and show a number of the overactive behaviors.

Some children are stubborn, strong-willed and want to do what *they* want to do, when *they* want to do it. These children are likely to show overactive behaviors.

Some overactive behaviors are the result of the way the child is managed, an attitude he develops, patterns of behavior he has learned and/or personality characteristics. Below is a discussion of several situations in which overactive behaviors are likely to be seen:

Ineffective management techniques

When screaming and yelling are used to discipline children, they often do not listen and show other overactive characteristics. If your approach to the child is inconsistent, unpredictable and unstructured, the probability of overactive behaviors greatly increases. Section I, Methods and Techniques, describes in more detail what is meant by ineffective management techniques and gives you tips on how to avoid this situation or deal with it when it occurs.

Spoiling

This could have easily been called *pampering, catering to children, giving in to children.* Spoiled children often get their way. These children easily manipulate you to get what they want (staying up late, going outside to play after they've been told no). The child has more control than the parents.

Control may involve material things (toys, candy), but more often it includes a variety of things (getting his own way). There usually is a lack of effective discipline or parental control. These children are allowed to do their "own thing" and get what they want. They control their environment.

This type of overactivity is seen when limits are placed on

the child or he must do things he doesn't want to do. If the child can "call the shots" and do what he wants, what happens when he enters a classroom setting? He'll try to do what he pleases rather than what he is supposed to do. (This often occurs in first or second grade rather than in kindergarten because there is more structure and more demands are placed on the child in the later grades.)

The child looks out the window and daydreams. He doesn't stay in his desk. He doesn't complete his work. He shows many overactive behaviors.

You need to be in control. Children need structure, predictability, discipline and external controls. When spoiling occurs, it produces an unpredictable environment for the child. The child may become confused, try to gain more control over the environment or become rebellious, self-centered, demanding and selfish. These behaviors may often be seen as overactive.

Spoiled children often develop a self-centered approach to their environment, have problems in peer relationships because of being "bossy," fail to develop responsibility, have difficulties at school, become rebellious, do only what they want to and show other overactive characteristics.

Lack of discipline or supervision

The child in this category does his own thing because of a lack of management or limits placed on his behavior. The child is frequently unsupervised. He may be left to discipline himself. While you may think this child "runs the streets," this isn't always the case. I've seen situations in which parents are present, but the child is allowed to do his own thing and is basically undisciplined.

Overactive behaviors are primarily related to a lack of behavioral limits. If the child is allowed to control his behavior in one situation (at home), others will have difficulty controlling him in another situation (at school).

Pleasure-oriented

Some children develop a pleasure-oriented personality. Some children show these characteristics at a very young age. Frequently, a child with this personality exhibits characteristics of overactivity and must be managed differently to get him to listen, conform, do what is told, calm down.

The pleasure-oriented, sometimes called *strong-willed,* child is primarily concerned with satisfying his own needs and wishes. He responds to the environment in this way. He is more concerned with the pleasure he derives from his behavior than the punishment. He may know he isn't supposed to do something and will be punished. But if it's fun, he'll do it. He worries about the punishment later. He starts doing what he pleases and disregards rules and responsibilities imposed by others.

If you ask him to do something, no matter how difficult, and he wants to do it, it'll be done. If you ask him to do something, no matter how small, and he doesn't want to do it, look out—it's like trying to run through a brick wall.

It may look as if this child acts before he thinks, but this isn't totally true. He behaves this way because he is more concerned with what he wants to do than what will happen to him. He doesn't listen, appears impulsive, does what he wants and shows many overactive characteristics.

Pleasure-oriented children also become very skilled con artists. They may become very much aware of inconsistencies in the environment. They are quick to manipulate people and events to satisfy their own needs and wishes and/or to avoid unpleasant duties and responsibilities.

Manipulation is pleasure-oriented, in the sense the child wants something, but someone or something prevents him from getting it. He knows what he has to do to get around what is blocking him so his needs will be fulfilled. Although he can be polite, charming and affable when it is to his advantage, this child generally has problems with authority or those in a position of supervision or direction over him. The child often is rebellious, stubborn, oppositional and resistant.

In school, a variety of problems are characterized by an inability to follow classroom procedure. It seems as if the child has not developed any internal control, self-discipline or responsibility because he does not follow classroom procedure.

Because of his pleasure orientation, punishment doesn't work well—often not at all—with this child. Punishment or negative consequences only affect him temporarily. Other forms of child management must be employed.

Overactivity in these situations results from an attitude the child has developed and/or certain personality characteristics, The child in this category daydreams and looks out of the window at school because he does not feel like listening or would rather look outside. He gets out of his desk and talks out of turn. Most of his overactive behaviors are within his control.

Dealing with overactivity

Overactivity resulting from the above situations can usually be effectively dealt with by employing effective techniques of child management. If not dealt with adequately, the overactive characteristics usually increase with age. Section I, Methods and Techniques, gives you some tips on how to deal with overactive behaviors resulting from the above causes.

Unlike other types of overactive children, those who fall into this category usually do not show any significant deviations in their developmental history. They usually develop within normal limits. The identifying characteristics are primarily found in the patterns of parent-child interactions and in personality factors.

Some children have personality characteristics that make them difficult to manage, and their behavior often reflects overactivity. This type of overactive child is able to concentrate and sit still when he chooses or is interested in something. He may be able to sit very still and quiet for 2 hours watching cartoons but can't keep still for 2 minutes during your favorite TV program. This child appears to have some control over his level of activity. If you look closely at the patterns of family interaction, the child is in more control than his parents. Consistent and effective limits are not placed on his behavior. If action isn't taken, the overactive behaviors seem to increase with age.

Attention-deficit Disorder, with or without Hyperactivity

Not all overactive children are hyperactive. I reserve the term *hyperactivity* to describe the behavior of children who are overactive as a result of an Attention-deficit Disorder of Childhood.

In recent years, the term used to describe children with this type of overactivity has been changed from *Hyperkinetic Reaction of Childhood* to *Attention-deficit Disorder with or without Hyperactivity*. This change stresses two types of activity (motor and cognitive). The term was changed to eliminate the idea a child has to be fidgety, extremely active or bouncing off the walls to be considered hyperactive. Most hyperactive children have problems concentrating and keeping still.

A child who can sit relatively still and quiet but is distractible and has a short attention span can also fit into the category. This type of overactivity results because the child has not physically developed adequate controls. He does not complete his work in school because he can't concentrate long enough to finish it. He daydreams because of a short attention span. He can't follow directions because he is easily distracted.

He doesn't have enough control, so he can't force himself to stay still for long periods of time. He fidgets, squirms, taps his pencil and keeps moving. Most of this child's overactive behavior is beyond his control. Even if he tries hard to prevent them, he cannot.

Causes of overactive behavior

Overactive behavior results from a developmental lag or deviation. If you look at two children, they do not physically develop the same—one child may walk at 10 months, another at 12 months. Another child may get his first tooth at 5 months, while his brother gets his first tooth at 8 months. If you look at one child, he has hundreds of skills and abilities that are developing within him. Some skills may develop more slowly. In a hyperactive child, his center of control is not developing as fast as the rest of his body.

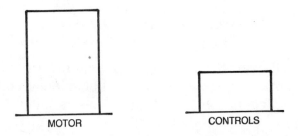

MOTOR   CONTROLS

The diagram shows the hyperactive child's controls do not develop as fast as his "motor." Some of his behaviors may be beyond his control. No matter how much the child is disciplined, he can't stop his actions. Because this child's overactive behavior is a result of a developmental lag, the level of activity usually decreases with age. As the child grows, the gap between his motor and his controls decreases. If you look at this child at 5, he is less active than he was at 3. At 7, he shows less activity than when he was 5.

Around puberty—11 to 16—his controls catch up with his motor. His activity level seems to decrease dramatically. His concentration and attention span improve. This child outgrows his overactivity.

Children in this category have an intellectual potential in the average or above-average range. See Chapter 73, Intelligence. Most have trouble in school because of behavior (inability to concentrate, attention span, inability to sit still). Some have academic problems resulting from other factors—learning disabilities and/or perceptual-motor difficulties.

Learning disabilities

Some hyperactive children (not all) may have a learning disability that interferes with their ability to perform in an academic setting. Most parents I see don't know what a learning disability is. They see the learning-disabled child as lazy, bad, dumb, a slow learner. This is incorrect. For a child to be classified as having a learning disability, he has to have average or above-average intelligence or have the potential for this level of functioning. See Chapter 75, Learning Disabilities, Dyslexia & Other Learning Problems, for further information.

Some children classified as hyperactive show perceptual-motor deficits that may interfere with schoolwork. "Visual-motor deficits" and "fine-motor coordination" are terms also used to describe this problem. These relate to hand-eye coordination. Can a child reproduce with a pencil what he sees with his eyes?

Perceptual-motor skills improve with age. A 3-year-old can be expected to draw a circle but usually has trouble with a square. A 5-year-old can usually reproduce a square, but has difficulty with a diamond. When a child shows perceptual-motor problems, it means his hand-eye coordination is below his chronological age. A 7-year-old may show the hand-eye coordination skills of a 5-year-old. Developmental lags are believed to be primary factors contributing to these problems.

As with the developmental problems that result in hyperactivity and learning disabilities, deviations in a child's development may result in poor hand-eye coordination. The child's perceptual-motor skills may not develop as fast as they should. Problems in this area usually affect the child's handwriting skills. In some instances, they interfere with the child's ability to read or perform in the math area. The child usually "outgrows" perceptual-motor deficits around puberty.

Children experiencing these problems usually do not have problems with their eyes or hands. They can see well and usually have adequate vision. Their motor development is appropriate for their age. The problem usually lies in the brain processing the information from the eyes. The eyes receive the information and the child's hands are fine, but there is some problem transmitting the information from the eyes to telling the hands what to do.

Most children who have perceptual-motor deficits have difficulty with handwriting tasks. Writing is hard because it requires a great deal of effort and energy. Paper-and-pencil activities do not come easily to these children. Penmanship is usually poor. They have trouble copying from the board because they leave out letters and words. Their work usually looks sloppy or careless. It requires a great deal of effort for these children to perform these tasks. They are "slow" when it comes to writing and may not complete seatwork. They take a long time to do a few minutes of written homework. Their writing may start off neat but progressively gets worse. They often reverse letters and numbers.

Some children with perceptual-motor deficits also show gross-motor coordination problems. They tend to be poorly coordinated and clumsy. But this isn't always the case. Some children with significant visual-motor deficits are excellent ballplayers or very well coordinated. In some hyperactive children, overactive behaviors may decrease. But the child may still have school problems related to perceptual-motor deficits.

Chapter 75, Learning Disabilities, Dyslexia & Other Learning Problems, and Chapter 77, Perceptual-Motor Deficits, discuss techniques used to help a child with a learning disability and/or perceptual-motor deficit.

Other developmental patterns

Children whose behavior results from an Attention-deficit Disorder often show other developmental patterns and traits. Some characteristics and developmental patterns of certain types of overactivity overlap. If your child shows a few of the signs, it doesn't necessarily mean he is hyperactive. Look for patterns. Children in this category usually show many of the characteristics described below.

Often these children are identified as overactive very early. As a young infant, a child is described as having an activity level greater than the average infant. During the first year, many of these children have trouble sleeping or eating (he may not sleep all night, have colic). He climbs out of his crib. It seems you have little peace once he starts crawling.

Once the child starts walking, additional problems occur. He is more mobile and seems to be constantly into things. Some children unlock doors, cabinets and gates. They must be constantly watched or they will be outside roaming the neighborhood. Others get up during the night and rearrange the kitchen cabinets or refrigerator.

As the child grows older, it may be difficult to get him settled at night. He constantly gets out of bed, talks to himself, gets a toy and plays with it, calls you 40 times. If and when you can get him to lie quietly and still, he will go to sleep quickly and usually sleeps soundly. As he gets older, he sleeps all night, but he may be a restless sleeper.

They may have problems in impulse control. They act before they think and show poor judgment. Attentional problems may be present and they have difficulty concentrating.

Most children establish their dominant hand at an early age (around 2). This type of overactive child often establishes his hand preference at a later age. Some continue to use both right and left hands to perform tasks (eating, writing) even after they start school. Although they are over 2 years old, parents can't determine whether the child is right- or left-handed.

These children sometimes show opposite reactions to some medications. The child's doctor may give him some medication for a cold or sore throat and tell you, "This medication may make him sleepy and drowsy." You give the child the medication, and it keeps him up all night or makes him more overactive. Medications that may calm other children or make them sleepy often produce the opposite results in an overactive child.

Peer problems are often present. The child can play well with one child, but there may be conflict and arguing if there are other children. Problems are more evident in group play because this child is "bossy" and tries to control others. The child also may show immature behavior in peer interaction.

Although this child has average or above-average intelligence, he often has problems in school. These problems are more behavioral than academic, but in later grades behavior may interfere with school performance. Some may have learning disabilities, and many have perceptual-motor difficulties.

This child tends to be impulsive and moody. He often has problems following a series of directions.

Overactive behaviors and attention difficulties in this child seem to decrease with age. The child is more active at 3 than at 5 and shows more overactive behaviors at 7 than at 9. His ability to concentrate also improves with age.

Intelligence

Level of intelligence appears to be related to increased levels of activity in some children. As children approach the extremes (both high and low) of the range of intelligence, the probability of overactive behavior increases. Some gifted children with high intelligence and some children with relatively low intelligence show increased activity levels, short attention span, impulsivity and distractibility. Review Chapter 16, Intelligence.

Some children on the extremes show overactive behaviors. Some children whose ability falls in the upper limits of the superior range of intelligence and above, or in the lower limits of the slow learner/educationally handicapped range of intelligence and below show characteristics of overactivity. *Some,* not all, children in these ranges show increased levels of activity, distractibility, impulsivity, stubbornness and short attention span. Both types of overactive children are discussed below.

High intelligence

Some children whose level of intelligence falls within the middle limits of the superior range of intelligence and above (IQ of approximately 125 and higher) show overactive characteristics. About 7 to 8% of the total population falls within this intellectual range. While the environment or culture affords children learning opportunities, high levels of intelligence are inherited.

Some children falling in this range of ability are difficult to manage. You have to run faster than you would with the average child to stay one step ahead of the brighter child. The child is often curious, overtalkative, asks a lot of questions, requires logical reasons for "No" or "You can't do that." He shows some overactive characteristics in the home situation, but the biggest problem he presents is discipline (doesn't listen, is stubborn, wants to do his own thing).

Although bright, this child sometimes has problems in school. He talks out of turn, doesn't pay attention, doesn't complete seatwork, refuses to do repetitive activities and may have poor grades because of incomplete work. He may be bored with schoolwork or the material isn't challenging.

Some overactive behaviors come with the high level of intelligence and have to be accepted. Behavior patterns can be changed by using some of the techniques and methods described in Section I, Methods and Techniques. Some suggestions as to how to help these children in the classroom are discussed in Chapter 65, Academic & Behavior Problems.

Children with intelligence significantly above average show other developmental patterns and traits. It doesn't mean a child is very intelligent if he shows a few of the signs. We look for patterns; most gifted children show a majority of the characteristics listed in the following paragraphs.

While some gifted children have slight delays in speech development, more reach developmental milestones early. Their accelerated development in the areas of language and understanding relationships are usually the first things you notice.

These children show an early use of a large and accurately employed vocabulary. At an early age, they use entire sentences and have an ability to tell or reproduce a story. They are keen observers and retain a significant amount of information about things observed. There is an early interest in books, calendars, telling time and clocks.

These children ask many questions and show an avid interest in exploration and discovery of cause-and-effect relationships. They are curious and generate many ideas or solutions to problems and questions. They see many aspects of one thing (fantasize, imagine, manipulate) and are adventurous and speculative.

These children communicate easily with others and relate well to adults. They get along better with older children than those their own age. While these children often exhibit leadership qualities, they are sometimes aggressive, domineering and "bossy" with age mates.

They can often amuse themselves. Their solitary play often involves complicated projects or elaborate stories with many characters. They may also have imaginary playmates.

These children learn rapidly and easily but often prefer to learn by creative ways rather than being told by an authority. It may seem as if they want to "do their own thing" in the classroom. They are easily bored with routine tasks and may refuse to complete seatwork or tasks that are already known (writing spelling words 5 times, doing a page of addition problems). They may also cause problems in the class because they finish work faster than other students.

These children often read independently for information and pleasure and usually perform academically at least two years above grade level. They get involved and absorbed in a particular task and strive to complete it. They have unusual abilities in structuring, organizing, integrating and evaluating ideas.

In the classroom, they are alert, keenly observant, quick to respond and display common sense and practical knowledge. They reason things out, see relationships and understand things other children find difficult. They ask many questions and are interested in a wide range of things. They seem to know about many things other children are unaware of.

Although with some children the activity level increases with age, the majority maintain the same level of activity. See Children with High Levels of Intelligence, Chapter 16, for more information.

Depressed intelligence

Some children whose intelligence level falls within the middle limits of the slow learner/educationally handicapped range and below (IQ of approximately 75 and lower) show overactive characteristics. About 7 to 8% of the total population falls within this intellectual range. Some of these children show overactive behaviors.

A depressed level of intelligence can be inherited, but it can also result from several other factors. When a fetus is developing, improper nutrition, mother's illness (German measles) and other factors may interfere with adequate fetal development. This may cause a depressed level of intelligence and/or brain damage. After a child is born, he may experience a sickness, disease (high fever) or injury that produces brain damage and results in a lowered level of intelligence.

Some children in this category are easily distracted, impulsive, stubborn. At home, they are generally difficult to manage and may be a discipline problem. At school, they can't sit still, talk out of turn and have peer problems. They also are "slow" in their schoolwork. They tend to have difficulty with academic studies. They may not understand the work or are "behind." Some of what may be happening in the classroom doesn't make sense to them. They may daydream, talk, not complete work and show other school-related overactive behaviors.

Usually overactive behaviors in these children stay the same or increase with age. However, other behaviors can be modified by using some of the techniques and methods described in Section I, Methods and Techniques.

In the school environment, special-education services may be necessary and/or some form of communication system may have to be established between you and the school. A more detailed discussion of intervention in the school situation is discussed in Chapter 65, Academic & Behavior Problems.

Children whose increased activity is related to depressed intelligence often show other characteristics and certain developmental patterns. Some characteristics and developmental patterns of certain types of overactivity overlap. If your child shows a few of the traits, it doesn't necessarily mean he has a low level of intellectual functioning. Look for patterns. Children with depressed intelligence usually show many of these characteristics.

Children who fall in this category often show mild to moderate delays in developmental milestones (walking, speech, habit training). They are often unable to combine words into sentences, and they lack imagination. Their play is often simplistic. Social immaturity is present, and they tend to choose younger playmates.

If children who fall in this category are not identified earlier, they are identified when they start school. The main characteristic of this group is difficulty with schoolwork. They may have trouble learning the alphabet and numbers. In kindergarten, and especially first grade, the teacher tells you the child isn't ready for the next grade, and it is better to retain him.

These children have difficulty abstracting and dealing with complexities in the environment. School failure and difficulties are always present. If steps are not taken to remediate and alleviate problems, other behavioral problems may arise (withdrawal, negativism, aggression).

The activity level in these children usually stays the same as the child grows. In some instances, it may increase.

Emotional Problems

Although many overactive children are described as "nervous," only a very small portion of overactive behavior in children results from emotional difficulties. About 2 or 3% of the total child population experience significant emotional problems. Some children show significant problems at an early age, regardless of the home environment. Their behavior seems to result from genetic factors. Some children seem to be born with certain behavior patterns that differ significantly from the average. Other children who experience an unpredictable, ambiguous, chaotic or inconsistent environment sometimes become confused, uncertain, insecure or start losing contact with reality. Children in either situation often show increased levels of activity.

If you or I say we are "nervous" or we experience some emotional discomfort, what does it mean? It usually means we are fidgety, can't stay still, have a hard time concentrating, can't keep our mind on what we are doing, have a short attention span. Some overactivity seen in children is similar to this. It results from emotional difficulties children experience. This is an infrequent cause of overactivity, but it does occur.

Children with serious behavior problems don't necessarily have emotional problems. But the behavior of a seriously emotionally disturbed child almost always deviates from other children his age.

Behavioral problems? Emotional difficulties?

Before I go any further let me explain the difference between behavioral problems and emotional difficulties. You are sitting with me in a room and a man comes in and puts a gun to my head, but you don't see it. All you can see is my behavior. I'm shaking. My voice trembles. I start to sweat. I have difficulty paying attention to what you are saying.

You'd look at me and say to yourself, "He has a problem." You are right, but I have more of a behavioral problem than an emotional one. My behavior is related more to the environment than to underlying or internal emotional difficulties.

A *behavior problem* is a response to the environment and is more superficial than emotional difficulties. Change the environment (take the gun away from my head), and my behavior will change.

An *emotional difficulty* can be viewed as a "deeper" or more internally based problem. This man keeps putting the gun to my head every hour for a few months. Soon the gunman would not even have to be present. I'd be a "nervous wreck" and show many problem behaviors. I would have emotional problems because they would be internal and more a part of me than a response to the environment.

There are three theories about how serious emotional problems develop in children. One views genetic factors and heredity as a major factor—the child is born this way. The second stresses environmental influences—the child's behavior is a result of what he has experienced. The third combines heredity and environment. Heredity sets the stage, and environment determines what players are used. A child may inherit a predisposition for emotional difficulties but must experience certain environmental conditions for emotional problems to appear.

While the third explanation makes the most sense to me, I have seen children whose history and behavior are consistent with the other two theories. A child from an apparently "normal" and "emotionally healthy" family shows emotional problems. Some children experience horrible environments (neglect, abuse, locked in closets for weeks, seriously disturbed parents) and emerge free from significant emotional problems. Others are apparently free from serious emotional disturbances until they experience a chaotic, unpredictable, changing environment.

Emotional difficulties do occur. Only a few children show these type of difficulties; some of these children show overactive characteristics. The psychological terms often used to describe the children who fall in this category are *pre-autism, autism, childhood psychosis, childhood schizophrenia, borderline personality* or *severely neurotic* (excessive fears, anxieties, worries, compulsive behaviors). Most children who fall in this category are identified early, usually before they enter kindergarten.

A child whose increased activity has an emotional base often shows other characteristics and certain developmental patterns. Information presented below is based on my experience and research data. Some characteristics and developmental patterns of certain types of overactivity overlap. If your child shows a few of the traits below, it doesn't mean he has emotional problems. Look for patterns. A child with emotionally based overactivity usually shows most of the characteristics.

Infancy

In infancy, these children show two different patterns. Some are described as "too good" and never give any trouble. They are placid, passive and undemanding. They may seem content lying quietly in bed all day. They don't cry often, and the mother often has to base the feeding schedule on the clock because these children do not cry when they're hungry. They don't raise their arms to be held. They don't seem to like being comforted. They may show some rocking behaviors when falling to sleep, but these may also occur at other times.

The other type of infant also shows little active interest in the environment but is often described as a problem or a difficult baby. They often have sleep problems, cry a great deal and fight daily routines (bathing, dressing, changing diapers). These children may also have feeding problems and difficulties sucking or may be unable to perform this function. They also are difficult to comfort. Unlike the passive infant, they may become stiff when held or actively resist physical contact. Although holding them won't reduce crying and distress, some calm down when held in an unusual manner (in a stiff position on their mother's hip).

In infancy, as well as throughout their early life, these children often show some general characteristics. They appear socially aloof, withdrawn and act as if other people are not present or do not exist. They resist changes in routines and in the environment. A change in schedule or daily routine may result in a violent reaction. They also show an inability to play and may show specific fear.

Children age 2 to 5

Between 2 and 5, problems these children show become more noticeable. While some children show lags in developmental milestones (crawling, walking, toilet training), most show difficulties in speech development. This is probably the reason most of these children are identified early.

Lags in speech are often significant. These children may not speak at the appropriate time. If they do speak, they show definite problems. Their speech may be delayed or immature. Poor pronunciation (leaving out letters, missing parts of words) may be present, as well as baby talk. They may speak in meaningless or scrambled sentences, and most of their attempts at communication may be unintelligible. They may confuse words (shoe for sock) or develop their own language (uncommon names for familiar objects—BINT might mean gum).

Echolalia or "parrot talk" may be present. They repeat what others say. They may say things over and over again.

Often parents or teachers feel there may be hearing problems. The child often ignores sounds and doesn't listen or respond when spoken to. Difficulties in voice control may be evident (they talk loudly at one time, softly the next). While they may ignore certain sounds (dropping a pot right behind them), they may be highly sensitive to others. They may show violent reactions to some sounds (vacuum cleaner, fire-engine siren).

Some children reach the developmental milestones at the appropriate ages but show a regression in behavior when they experience a change in the environment and/or a traumatic situation. A child may start talking at the normal age but is in an auto accident or experiences a significant conflict between his parents. He stops talking. Another child may have been toilet-trained for months, but a new sibling is born or he moves to another house and starts having accidents. For some children, environmental changes and traumatic experiences may result in regressive behaviors and emotional difficulties.

Children with emotionally based overactivity may also have problems seeing things. They may not respond to or understand gestures. Their eyes usually do not fix on one object, especially people, but constantly scan the room looking for movement. When an object or person moves, they may focus on that. They may become fixed on or fascinated with moving or whirling objects (blender, fan).

These children may show other unusual behaviors. They may be hypersensitive to or show little reaction to pain. They like to feel or rub textured materials, furs or smooth objects. They may like to put everything in their mouths, taste things or smell their food before eating it.

Some overactive children with emotional problems show unusual body movements, such as rocking, head bumping, unusual walking patterns and preoccupation with movements of their own bodies (fingers). They also may show difficulties in fine-motor coordination or clumsiness.

School-age children
Although 75% of these children are identified by age 5,

many of these characteristics are also seen in the school-age child. Some children have academic problems; many do not. Most have difficulty in peer interaction and are described by teachers as "a loner, in a world of his own, not following classroom procedures or routines."

Most overactivity in these children is seen from an early age and intensifies with time. At 5, these children are more active than at 3, and at 7, they show more overactive characteristics than at 5.

Some children show overactive characteristics related to severe neurotic problems (anxiety, depression) or situational events (parental conflict, school stress, moving). These children do not show the early characteristics or developmental patterns described above. But they usually respond to the treatment methods used to deal with children with significant emotional problems.

Combinations

As with most behavior, there is seldom a clear-cut cause. Behavior is complex and usually results from the interaction of several factors. The same is true for overactivity. Overactive behaviors seen in children often result from a combination or interaction of the factors discussed above.

Overactivity resulting from level of intelligence and emotional difficulties are very infrequent causes (probably less than 10%) of increased levels of activity in children. Management difficulties/personality characteristics and attention-deficit disorder, with or without hyperactivity, are factors that account for most overactive behavior in children.

A child may show signs of attention-deficit disorder and/or hyperactive behaviors and is somewhat difficult to manage. His parents may overlook some of his behaviors and/or "give in" to him to avoid a hassle. The result is an increase in his overactivity behaviors.

Management Techniques

At our center, I frequently see children who are overactive. But test data, developmental history, teacher reports and behavioral observations only give marginal indications of a hyperkinetic reaction of childhood or an attention-deficit disorder. There are only slight-to-marginal signs to indicate the child's overactive behaviors or attentional problems are beyond his control and due to developmental factors. In this situation, there are usually problems in management or discipline. Some of the child's overactive behaviors result from a lack of effective, consistent and predictable behavior management techniques by parents.

Before using any specific technique for managing overactivity behaviors discussed below, you must determine what overactive behaviors the child can and cannot control. This is done by using techniques of behavior management discussed in this book. I try to have the parents establish a consistent, structured and predictable home environment and to use reward/positive consequences as the main method of discipline.

A child has trouble "keeping still" during mealtime. He fidgets, gets up from his chair, talks. Rather than punish him to control the behavior, identify a reward to try to modify behavior. Suppose he loves ice cream. You might tell him, "I don't want you getting up from the table and moving all around while we eat. I'm going to give you a warning each time you get up. If you don't get more than 3 warnings, you can have some ice cream after dinner. If you get more than 3 warnings, no ice cream."

If the child can control the behavior, he will receive the reward. No matter how much he wants the ice cream, if he can't control the overactivity, he won't get the reward.

By using this method, you are able to determine what overactive behaviors a child can and cannot control. See Section I, Methods and Techniques, for a more-detailed discussion. When overactivity is due to a combination of factors, determine what can and cannot be brought under control before using more specific management techniques.

Providing a Structured, Predictable Environment

All overactive children respond well to predictable, structured environments. In a fluid, changing, inconsistent and/or unpredictable environment, overactive behaviors seem to increase. Most parents of overactive children see this often.

A family is sitting down watching TV. Everything is calm. Preston is quietly playing with his cars. The father says, "Let's go get an ice cream." It seems like Preston has suddenly been activated. He jumps up and down, talks and displays many overactive behaviors. Or someone drops over unexpectedly. Everything is calm, but as soon as the bell rings or the person comes in the house, the child is "bouncing off the walls."

Children in these examples react to a change or something new in the environment—and the fact the environment lost some of its structure and predictability.

The more structure, predictability and consistency that exist in the environment, the more overactive children will "slow down" and listen. A predictable, structured environment involves many things but primarily centers around how consistent parents are in dealing with the child and the manner in which rules are set and enforced. Section I, Methods and Techniques, provides some general principles to help produce a more consistent, structured, predictable environment.

By using these techniques, overactive behaviors should decrease. These methods can be applied to all types of overactive children.

Counseling and Psychotherapy

This specific management technique involves consultation with a mental-health professional (psychologist, psychiatrist, social worker). When trying to locate someone to provide these services, be sure he or she has the proper credentials (license, certification) and has the expertise in the counseling or psychotherapy your child needs. Select someone who primarily deals with children and is familiar with overactive children.

Counseling

Counseling is often viewed as a more superficial form of treatment that provides information and advice. Counseling is also seen as educative because the individual is given certain information or taught new things to apply to his life.

Psychotherapy

Psychotherapy is usually seen as a more "in-depth" form of treatment dealing with inner conflicts, feelings and emotions. Regardless of the type of treatment, research has shown this is a very ineffective method of treating overactivity if *only* the child is involved.

Parent involvement

Parents must be involved in the counseling or psychotherapy. If I see a child 1 hour a week, his parents have him the other 167 hours. If I can provide the parents with effective methods to deal with the child the rest of the week, the probability of success in changing the child's behavior greatly increases. In a sense, the parent becomes the child's "therapist." Be actively involved in your child's treatment.

Counseling and psychotherapy should be geared toward the parents when dealing with overactivity because the parents are with the child more. If they have some specific techniques to deal with the child's behavior, change occurs faster. If the child's problem involves school, the teacher should become involved. Other significant caretakers (nursery school, aftercare program, grandparent, relatives) should become involved in the treatment plan. Several forms of counseling/psychotherapy are beneficial to overactive children. I discuss a few of these below.

Parental counseling

This counseling provides parents with suggestions, methods and techniques to deal with their child's behavior. The therapist usually gives the parents general suggestions and works with the parents on specific behavioral concerns. This type of treatment is beneficial for all types of overactive children.

Parental workshops or meetings

These are very similar to parent counseling, but it is not on an individual basis. Workshops are usually conducted in groups. The workshops/meetings are fixed (2 hours a week for 10 weeks), or they are open (meetings every week for 2 hours without a set ending date).

This treatment gives parents an opportunity to see that

they are not the only ones having problems with their children. It also gives parents a chance to discuss their feelings and frustrations with other parents who experience similar difficulties. Parental workshops and meetings are beneficial to all parents of overactive children.

Counseling or psychotherapy for child

If your child becomes involved in therapy, you should be actively involved in the treatment. There are two general types of counseling or psychotherapy—group and individual therapy.

Group therapy—Group therapy involves the child meeting with one or two therapists and several other children (usually 3 to 7) of similar ages who are experiencing similar difficulties. Treatment may include discussions, play, activities or a combination of these. The goals may be socialization (helping the child deal more effectively with his peers), educational information (how to express anger, what to do if someone teases you), dealing with underlying feelings or building confidence.

Family therapy is another form of group therapy. The "group" involves the child, his family members and the therapist.

Individual counseling—With individual counseling or psychotherapy, the child meets with a therapist. This may involve discussion, play and activities. Goals may be similar to those above and are usually based on the child's individual needs and problems.

Parent involvement—Therapy or counseling for an overactive child without parent involvement may not be productive. Parents must be involved to facilitate change and increase the probability of success. If your child becomes involved in counseling or psychotherapy, understand the process and what will result from it. See Chapter 43, Selecting Psychological Services, for more information.

All parents of overactive children, regardless of the cause, will benefit from parental counseling in effective techniques of child management. Use individual counseling when the child has emotional difficulties. Group therapy may be beneficial for all types of overactive children. But group therapy is only effective if it is geared toward the child's specific problems (peer problems, socialization difficulties, building self-confidence).

Medication

Medication is one way to deal with overactive behavior. Most parents and professionals don't like to give medication before other things are tried. I agree. I usually set up a management system with parents to deal with behavior before considering using medication. If techniques are implemented and overactive behaviors continue, some of the specific techniques outlined above can be tried. If all the non-drug methods are used correctly and are unsuccessful, then it is appropriate to consider medication.

Use medication with one of the methods of treatment described above, specifically counseling for parents in effective techniques of child management. Different drugs are used to treat different types of overactivity.

Attention-deficit disorder

This type of overactivity results from a developmental lag or deviation. The child does not have sufficient control to prevent his behavior or enable him to sit still or concentrate for long periods of time. Central-nervous-system stimulants, such as Ritalin,® Ritalin-SR, ® Dexedrine® or Cylert® are the drugs used most often to manage this type of overactivity.

Some medication works the opposite in hyperactive children. The above medications are stimulants. If you took them, they would make you overactive. But it "slows down" a hyperactive child. If you give a hyperactive child a tranquilizer or drug that would slow you down, it usually increases his activity level.

Medications used with these children are not tranquilizers. The drugs used are central-nervous-system stimulants that activate certain parts of the body. The central nervous system is the basis for a child's control. The medication stimulates this area and gives the child *more* control. By having more controls, he can sit, attend and concentrate for longer periods of time.

The child is easier to manage and shows fewer school-related problems. The medication (shaded area in the diagram below) indirectly benefits the child by giving him more control. He is not sedated or "doped up." His controls catch up with his motor, and he can control some of his actions.

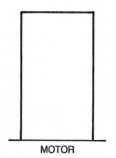
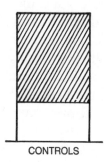

MOTOR   CONTROLS

Hyperactive children usually experience a great deal of difficulty in the classroom. They can't sit still for long periods of time, they fidget and generally do not stay still. The cognitive overactivity (short attention span, inability to concentrate, distractibility) interferes with school performance.

Let me use an example to show how the medication helps this area. Suppose I'm sitting down with you to give you directions on how to get to my house. However, seven people are standing behind me. One is telling funny stories. One is giving the weather. One is telling dirty jokes. Another is reporting the news. I start giving directions, "You go down Judge Perez Drive until you get to the second red light." You hear a good joke and start paying attention to the "joke man."

While you're listening to him, you catch some interesting bit of news and start concentrating on the "news man." As I continue talking, you are repeatedly distracted by one of the people standing behind me.

You focus your attention back to me and hear, "It's the third house from the corner." When I ask, "Do you know how to get to my house?" your answer would be, "No." You answer negatively because you didn't receive the information. You were distracted or you didn't concentrate on what I was saying.

This often happens to a hyperactive child in the classroom. His performance is poor because he is easily distracted or cannot pay attention to the teacher for long. He never receives the information. When he is tested or has to perform, he fails.

Medication doesn't make a child smarter or able to learn faster but eliminates interfering symptoms of hyperactivity.

In the above example, medication would eliminate the seven people standing behind me. You'd be able to pay attention to my directions and find my house. The medication helps the child concentrate on what is going on in the classroom and prevents him from being easily distracted by the other children, activities outside the classroom window and other things.

If you take any child and give him one of the medications mentioned above, one of four things will happen.

Medication will "calm him down"—He will be less active and able to concentrate and attend to things for longer periods of time. He will be able to control himself better. Most "hyperactive" symptoms will decrease, and he will show a positive improvement. If this occurs, you know he is hyperactive and the dose is adequate.

Nothing happens—The child doesn't show any significant change. The child is probably hyperactive but is not receiving enough medication. The dose needs to be increased.

Child appears drowsy—The child acts as if he's tired and may fall asleep when watching TV or when he sits still. When this occurs, he probably is hyperactive but receiving too much medication.

Child may become more active—If this occurs, the child is not hyperactive. Discontinue the medication.

Child's dosage

Do *not* increase or decrease the dosage of your child's medication without consulting his doctor. If the second, third or fourth reaction occurs, contact your child's doctor.

You can usually see one of the above results in 1 to 7 days after the child starts taking the medication.

Most physicians give the child the minimal amount of medication. The effects are observed. If there are no positive results, the amount of medication is increased. When you first give the child medication, keep in touch with his doctor. Most medication is given for school problems and is primarily given during the school hours (before breakfast and before lunch). It is necessary to get reports from the child's teacher(s). Tell the teacher(s) when the child starts the medication. Ask them to report any behavioral changes immediately.

Parents' Questions About Medications

Most parents who give children medication for hyperactivity have many questions regarding the drugs and their effects. Some of the questions have been answered, but below are some typical questions asked by parents, along with brief answers.

Is there a risk of drug dependency in later years?
No. Years of clinical experience and research have failed to reveal an association between medical use of stimulants in the young child and later drug abuse.

How long will the child have to take the medication?
This is difficult to answer because it's different for every child. Most children take medication until they reach puberty (11 to 16). The gap between his "motor" and controls changes constantly. There is some possibility, although minimal, the child will "outgrow" his hyperactivity before puberty.

Some pediatricians take the child off the medication at the start of school and right after Christmas holidays. This is done to see if the child has developed additional controls and if the medication is still necessary.

What if the medication does not work and appears to have little or no effect on the child's behavior?
Consult your child's doctor. There is a possibility he's hyperactive but needs a stronger dose of the same medication. Or your child may require a different type of medication.

What do I do if the medication makes him more active?
Consult your child's doctor. There is a possibility your child's overactivity does *not* result from a developmental lag or a lack of controls.

What if the child is drowsy or sleepy?
Consult your child's doctor. The child may be receiving too much medication.

What should I do if he has to take other medication for a sore throat, cold, allergy?
Consult your child's doctor. Some medications can be taken with other drugs; some cannot.

Will the child be "doped up"?

The child will *not* be "doped up." The medication seems to activate a part of the child's body and give him more control so he can sit longer. His concentration and span of attention increase.

If I give him medication to improve his school behavior and performance, do I have to give it to him on weekends, holidays and during the summer?

Ask his doctor. Some physicians require the child to take the medication all the time. Others suggest that the child be on the medication only when in school.

How long do the effects of the medication last?

For Ritalin® and Dexedrine® the effects usually "wear off" in 3 to 4 hours. For this reason, a child taking these drugs usually takes a dose in the morning and a dose at lunch. The entire school day is covered. If the child's overactive behavior is a concern at home, the child may also take another dose when he comes home from school.

The effects of Cylert® are longer lasting, about 6 hours. A child on this medication usually receives one dose in the morning. Ritalin-SR® (sustained release) is effective for about 8 hours.

What is a minimal dose of medication?

This is different for different children and usually depends on the child's physical size.

Are there any side effects with these medications?

Loss of appetite and inability to fall asleep are the most common side effects. Most children become tolerant of these side effects within the first week or 2 of treatment.

Other side effects, which occur less frequently, include mild stomachaches and headaches, and increased "tension" behaviors including nail-biting, eye-blinking, sensitivity or moodiness. Tourette Syndrome has occurred in rare instances, see Chapter 63. When these occur, medication may have to be changed. If side effects continue, contact your child's doctor.

These are short-term effects of the drugs. There is little research evidence of long-term risks of stimulant medication. There are suggestions of a period of growth suppression. But over a long period of time, the loss of expected growth is made up. Information at present supports a *delay* in growth rather than a suppression of it.

When will I know if the medication is working?
Sometimes you can tell within a few hours after giving the child the medication. It may take a week to see the effects of Ritalin® and Dexedrine.® Improvement may not be evident until the third or fourth week with Cylert®and Ritalin-SR.®

Does medication interfere with healthy psychological development or handicap the child emotionally?
No. Medication gives the child more control, reduces the negative attention he receives and enhances satisfactory psychological development.

Significant emotional difficulties
Children whose overactivity results from emotional difficulties may respond to stimulant drugs. Because these drugs are usually safer than those used for emotional difficulties, the children may be given a trial on the medication, even though it probably won't decrease the level of activity.

The most commonly used drugs for treating the overactivity that results from emotional problems are Thorazine,® Mellaril® and Stelazine.® These medications are usually prescribed by a psychiatrist and should be given in conjunction with some type of psychotherapy.

Intelligence
Children who have a depressed level of intelligence often show symptoms of overactivity. The child's increased level of activity and short attention span usually result from brain damage. Sometimes drugs work with these children. Those used for children with emotional problems seem to be most effective.

Medication often does not seem to reduce the overactivity resulting from this cause. Parents must set up a very structured, consistent, predictable environment and may have to tolerate some overactive behaviors in this type of child.

Children whose overactive behavior results from high levels of intelligence are generally not managed by medication. Effective management techniques must be used and parents may have to tolerate some overactive behaviors in this type of child.

Management

Medication is not used with children whose overactive behavior results from a lack of management, ineffective management technique, personality characteristics, attitude and/or learned behavior patterns.

Combinations

When overactivity results from a combination of factors, medication may be used. Other techniques are tried first to reduce overactivity before drugs are used.

Other Approaches

During the past 50 years, reports have linked overactivity to food allergies. In recent years, a lot has been said about the management of overactive behaviors in children from a dietary or nutritional viewpoint. This specific management technique seems to be related to increased levels of activity and attentional problems caused by hyperactivity/hyperkinetic reaction of childhood or attention-deficit disorder. Below are some of the approaches receiving the most attention.

Feingold diet

For a more-detailed discussion of the diet, read Dr. Feingold's books—*Why Your Child Is Hyperactive* and *The Feingold Cookbook for Hyperactive Children,* both published by Random House. In the Feingold Diet, two groups of foods are eliminated.

Group-I foods

Almonds	Currants	Plums
Apples	Gooseberries	Prunes
Apricots	Grapes	Raisins
Blackberries	Nectarines	Raspberries
Boysenberries	Oranges	Strawberries
Cherries	Peaches	Tomatoes
Cucumbers	Pickles	

Group-I foods contain natural salicylates and are made up of several fruits and a couple of vegetables. The above list of fruits and vegetables must be *omitted* from the child's diet in all forms—fresh, frozen, canned, dried, as juice or as an ingredient of prepared food.

Group-II foods

Group II is made up of foods that contain synthetic or artificial color or flavors. This diet is *not* concerned with food preservatives except for butylated hydroxy toluene (BHT). Occasionally a child may show an adverse response to BHT. Eliminate all foods that contain artificial color and artificial flavors from the child's diet. To determine if a product contains artificial coloring or flavoring, *read the label carefully.*

Foods not permitted

The following is a list of those items that are *not* permitted on the Feingold Diet.

1. All cereals with artificial colors and flavors.
2. All instant-breakfast preparations.
3. All manufactured cakes, cookies, pastries, sweet rolls, doughnuts, pie crusts or other bakery products.
4. Frozen, baked goods and many packaged baking mixes.
5. Bologna, salami, frankfurters, meatloaf or any other artificially flavored or colored luncheon meats.
6. Artificially flavored or colored sausage, ham, bacon or pork.
7. All barbecued poultry and "self-basting" turkeys.
8. Frozen fish filets or fish sticks that are dyed or flavored.
9. All manufactured ice cream, sherbet, ices, gelatins and puddings, except when the label specifies no synthetic coloring or flavoring.
10. All powdered puddings, dessert mixes and flavored yogurts.
11. All manufactured candies, hard or soft.
12. Diet drinks, soft drinks, cider, all instant-breakfast drinks, all quick-mix powdered drinks, hot or cold tea and prepared chocolate milk.
13. Margarine, colored butter, mustard, catsup, colored cheeses, wine or cider vinegar, commercial chocolate syrup, cloves, chili sauce and mint-flavored items.
14. Medications and vitamins containing artificial flavors or colors, as well as over-the-counter medications that contain aspirin (Anacin,® Alka-Seltzer,® Bufferin,® Excedrin®).

15. All toothpastes, toothpowder, mouthwashes, cough drops, throat lozenges and antacid tablets.

Permitted foods

Group-II foods comprise the majority of the foods eaten by most children. Grocery shopping must be done carefully, and a number of foods must be "homemade" to avoid artificial flavoring and coloring. Dr. Feingold also provides a list of foods that *are permitted* on the diet. A summary of this list follows.

1. All meats, fresh fish and poultry (except stuffed).
2. All commercial breads except egg bread and whole wheat (usually dyed).
3. Any dry or cooked cereal without artificial colors or flavors.
4. Tapioca, plain yogurt, natural (white) cheese and honey.
5. Distilled white vinegar, all cooking oils and fats, and all flours.
6. Grapefruit and pineapple juice, pear and guava nectar, milk and 7-Up®.
7. Homemade items made *without* artificial colors, flavors or the foods listed in Group I, including:

bakery items	custards	lemonade
candies	gelatins	limeade
chocolate	ice cream	mayonnaise
syrup	jams & jellies	mustard

8. All other foods that do not contain natural salicylates (Group I) or artificial flavors or colors (Group II).

Restoring foods

If a child shows a favorable response to the Feingold Diet after 4 to 6 weeks, the foods in Group I may be restored *slowly*. Introduce new foods from Group I one at a time. Try them for 3 or 4 days. If no unfavorable reaction in the child's behavior is noted, another food item can be added. This procedure is followed until all items in Group I are tested.

Fruits and vegetables that don't affect the child can be included in his diet.

General instructions

Dr. Feingold offers some general instructions for parents who have children on his diet.

1. Keep a diet diary. *Everything* the child eats must be noted. Record the child's behavioral and academic responses. Whenever a change in behavior occurs, suspect an infraction.

2. The probability of success and eliminating resistance from the child is greatly increased if the whole family goes on the diet.

3. There must be strict adherence to the diet—100%. There cannot be any cheating.

4. No restrictions on homemade quantities of sweets.

5. Read all package and container labels carefully. When in doubt, do not use them.

6. If improvement occurs, it is usually observed within 7 to 21 days. For some children, improvement may not be seen until the child has been on the diet for 7 weeks.

7. In some cases, drugs used to control hyperactive behaviors can be discontinued after the child has been on the diet for 2 or 3 weeks. Always contact the child's doctor *before* the child's medication is changed.

Smith's nutritional approach

Dr. Lendon Smith feels everyone should follow a general eating pattern as part of a lifetime program of good nutrition. He calls this eating pattern the "Prevention Diet." He makes specific recommendations to control symptoms of overactivity. I'll summarize his views regarding nutrition as it relates to the management of overactivity in children. For more information regarding this area, read Dr. Lendon Smith's books *Feed Your Kids Right* and *Improving Your Child's Behavior Chemistry*.

The "prevention diet"

Dr. Smith's diet regimen consists of three parts.

Avoid anti-nutrients—Anti-nutrients are foods that have been packaged, processed, added to, stabilized, emulsified, colored or preserved. Avoid commercial products as much as possible. Sugar and "junk" foods are not permitted. Some of the sweet foods to eliminate include:

white and brown sugar
corn, cane or maple syrup
molasses or honey
commercial ice cream

boxed cereal
white flour
homogenized, pasteurized
 milk for 1 month

Natural foods—Eat natural foods 4 to 6 times a day, in small amounts. Natural foods include:

raw vegetables
eggs
fish, chicken
white cheeses (Jack, Swiss,
 Mozzarella)

nuts (especially almonds
 and peanuts)
vegetables (such as
 peas, beans, lentils)
raw fruits

Vitamins and minerals—These are taken if the child is behind in his requirements.

Vitamins
A—5,000 to 10,000 units
D—400 to 1,000 units
C—100 to 500mg
E—200 to 400 units
B-complex, 25 to 50mg of
  each of the B vitamins
  [Label should read: B1 25mg;
  B2 25mg; B3 (niacinamide)]

25mg; B6 (pyridoxine) 25mg;
 B12, 25mcg)
Inositol—25mg
Choline—25mg
PABA—25mg
Pantothenic acid—25mg
Biotin—250mcg
Folic acid—400mcg

Minerals
Calcium—500 to 1,000mg
Magnesium—250 to 500mg
Zinc—15mg

Iodine—0.1mg
Copper—1mg
Manganese—5mg

Hyperactivity

Dr. Smith believes some behaviors characterized as hyperactive can be managed by the following procedure, called the *Stress Formula*.

1. Eat no sugar, white flour or packaged cereals.
2. Nibble nutritious foods every 2 to 3 hours.
3. Vitamin C—500 to 10,000mg/day.
4. Vitamin-B complex—50 to 200mg of each of the B vitamins every day for 1 month, then a lower dose, perhaps for life.
5. Pantothenic acid—500 to 3,000mg/day. This can be varied up or down.
6. Pyridoxine B6—200 to 500mg/day.
7. Vitamin A—30,000 to 50,000 units/day for 1 month.

8. Calcium or a calcium salt—up to 1,000mg/day.

Dr. Smith also states some overactivity in children may be reduced by B-complex vitamin injections. B6 in 200 to 500mg doses may help. Often big doses of calcium (1,000 to 2,000mg/day) plus vitamin D (500 to 1000 units/day) result in improvement. Extra zinc (50 to 90mg/day) may be a partial answer.

Short attention span

To reduce the child's distractibility, attention problems and concentration deficits, Dr. Smith recommends the following:
1. Exclude salicylates (see Feingold Diet).
2. Increase B-complex vitamin intake to 100 to 200mg of each.
3. Increase intake of nutritious foods.
4. Increase calcium and magnesium intake.

Clumsiness

An increase in B-complex vitamins, especially B6 (100mg/day), may improve a child's coordination. Dr. Smith wrote:

"I have found if a child is hyperactive, I can help him achieve to the maximum of his potential if he/she exhibits the following: ticklishness, Jeckyll/Hyde behavior, food and carbohydrate cravings, deep or light sleep habits, bedwetting and some rhythmical-tension-relieving activity (thumbsucking, rocking, nail-biting).

"These indicate the child has a biochemical problem that can be solved with a nutritional approach. No sugar, white flour, boxed cereals, junk foods, additives or dairy products. The child may nibble wholesome foods and take extra vitamins and minerals, specifically vitamins C, B-complex (especially B6), calcium and magnesium. 80% will be 60 to 100% better in 3 weeks (based on 7,000 cases).

"If Ritalin® or Dexedrine® have a calming effect, I know the patient has a biochemical defect. A nutritional approach will help. I can usually guarantee medication dosage can be reduced or eliminated in 3 weeks."

In another correspondence from Dr. Smith, he wrote:

"I use the B-complex injections. Vitamin B6 seems to be the most important. Apparently these children have an absorption problem. Many of the children have allergies, and they can't absorb calcium and maybe the B vitamins. It appears they do not absorb the calcium from the milk. Many hyper children crave milk or sugar."

Sugar

Eliminate all sugar from the child's diet including candy, regular soft drinks, doughnuts, cookies.

Some people believe children who eat food with sugar show irritable moods, inability to concentrate, restlessness and other characteristics of overactive children. There is little research to support this position.

Some evidence supports the relationship between overactive behavior and sugar intake, but this relationship is not clear and requires further study. I have seen this approach work in some children but not in others. It may be worth trying this approach to keep the child from being put on medication. Some children also respond better to medication when sugar is removed from the diet. Consult the child's physician when considering any modification in diet.

Allergies

John Taylor, psychologist, stated in his book, *The Hyperactive Child and the Family* (New York: Everest House, 1980) allergic reactions to various substances in the environment may contribute to overactive behaviors. He lists over 50 possible sources of irritants that may produce allergic reactions in some children.

Drs. Sami Bahna and Douglas Heiner mention in their book, *Allergies to Milk* (New York, Grune & Stratton, 1980), some children who show allergic reactions to milk may also have overactive behaviors.

Their treatment approach is to remove the allergic substance from the child's environment or diet. There is some evidence to show some overactive children have more allergies than other children. But there is almost no evidence these allergic reactions are the cause of the overactive behaviors.

Some borderline overactive children who are allergic or have asthma show increased levels of activity as a result of the medications they take for the allergy. Sometimes medications can be changed or the dosage reduced. This may result in a decrease in activity and/or an increase in attention span. If this is the case, consult your child's physician.

Relaxation and biofeedback training

Some researchers have tried to train overactive children in the use of deep-muscle-relaxation techniques to reduce overactive behaviors. Studies indicate overactive children can learn to relax various muscle groups and calm down in the office or lab. But this reduction in behaviors doesn't generalize to other situations. The child can relax and slow down in the office or lab but does not show corresponding improvement at school and at home.

Relaxation and biofeedback training usually involves significant cost. It doesn't produce equal improvement outside the office to be considered as an effective method of treatment at this time.

General Comments

All the methods mentioned in this section have very little research evidence to support their claims. Some could be tried in an attempt to avoid medication, but avoid others. Consult your child's pediatrician when considering alternative methods of treatment. He or she may provide additional information and advice.

While there seems to be some relationship between what a child eats and his level of activity, research is limited. Attempts are being made to gather additional data. A child's body chemistry as it combines with certain food additives is very individual. Eliminating certain chemicals from one child's diet may work for him but not for another child. Some parents have told me a diet produced significant improvement in reducing their child's activity level. But it seems for every parent I've heard report positive results, a large number have told me diet didn't improve their child's overactivity.

Keep several things in mind when considering these methods.

A diet that eliminates certain color or flavor additives or one that provides nutritious foods seems to work on an individual basis. It results in positive improvement for some children but not for all.

The probability of success and eliminating resistance from the child is greatly increased if the whole family goes on the diet. It's difficult to tell a child he can't drink a soda if his sister is drinking one.

Diets are difficult to follow because most prepared food and some fresh fruits and vegetables must be eliminated. Meals must be made from scratch and use natural or raw foods. This may involve more of your time and may be viewed as too much trouble.

The dietary and nutritional management of overactive behavior in children is a relatively new concept, but it has received a great deal of attention in recent years. I haven't seen enough research or positive results from the people I come in contact with to make me a firm believer. However, I do not like to see children on medication and usually try every other alternative before I recommend drugs to control the symptoms of overactivity.

When parents ask me, "What about other types of treatment?" I believe some of the approaches discussed here may be worth a try.

Gather as much information as you can about any treatment approach before trying it or spending any money. Consult your child's doctor for further information and advice.

53

Physical Complaints

When a child voices recurring physical complaints or concerns, take him to a physician to see if there is a physical reason. If results are negative, the reason may have a *psychological* basis. Many bodily complaints, illnesses and pains don't have a *physical* basis. These include headaches, dizziness, stomachaches, nausea, muscle aches, sore throats, vomiting and stomach or chest pains. When complaints are seen that have no physical reason, they may have a psychological basis.

To say a child's headaches or chest pains are the result of psychological causes does *not* mean he is faking them or not experiencing pain. It means a *physical* reason doesn't exist. If you had a hard day and develop a headache as a result of the tension you experienced, you have a psychologically induced headache. This doesn't mean your head doesn't hurt or you're faking. It means a physical reason for your pain does not exist.

Children's physical complaints based on psychological tension fall into this category. When a child has a headache before school or a stomachache just before a big test, it's probably not the result of a conscious choice by the child.

Physical complaints with a psychological basis do not always show a pattern and cannot always be related to a specific event. They may occur in a random fashion or when they seem least likely to occur. A child who doesn't get headaches in school may complain about them while watching cartoons in the afternoon. Or the stomachache that occurs in school may also appear on weekends.

Some children show physical symptoms during a period

of calm when the child is not under pressure. If you can't identify a specific physical pattern behind the child's complaints, they may be psychological in nature.

There are several reasons why physical complaints occur that have no basis in physical disorders.

Somatization

This refers to psychological conflicts or frustrations expressed through the body. Some children express their psychological conflicts by physical complaints; others do not.

Physical symptoms and pain may represent psychological frustration, anger or insecurity. This may result from ambiguous, fluid and changing environments, such as an inconsistent home situation, a divorce or separation when the child is torn between both parents, a situation where the parents don't agree on methods of dealing with the child or any unpredictable environment.

Children also release psychological problems through their bodies when they have built up anger, resentment and hostility toward others they can't express. These bottled-up emotions are expressed through the body. Frustration in particular is a major psychological cause of physical symptoms.

Manipulation or avoidance

Some children use physical symptoms to avoid unpleasant duties, responsibilities or situations. Some children fake pain to avoid school, tests or chores. Most physical complaints used as manipulation or avoidance result from unconscious processes.

The child doesn't plan to have the headache to avoid school. He really experiences pain and has not consciously decided to use an avoidance maneuver. Physical complaints usually occur while the child is at school. They are used to avoid stressful situations by returning home. The child escapes punishment and unpleasant responsibilities.

Attention

When children are sick, they usually receive a significant amount of positive attention. Parents tend to be easier on them, give them their way and wait on them.

Some children learn one way to get positive attention is to

be sick. Physical symptoms occur because the child desires positive attention and affection.

Modeling

Some parents model physical complaints to their children. A mother frequently has headaches, a father uses physical complaints to avoid situations or grandparents emphasize physical problems. There's a strong probability that children exposed to these models will develop similar behavior.

Most of the time parents attribute this to heredity. But when children show physical symptoms similar to those of their parents, they result more frequently from a learning process than from heredity.

One-trial learning

Sometimes when a child is sick or has physical complaints, he may later develop similar symptoms. He learns there are considerable benefits from being sick. Consequently, symptoms appear again.

Faking

Although this doesn't occur as much as most parents think, some children fake physical symptoms to gain advantages, as mentioned above. Keep in mind most children do not fake sickness. Their pains and aches are psychologically caused and unplanned. They experience the pain, but the symptoms don't have a physical basis.

Dealing With Physical Complaints

Stop physical symptoms from working to the child's advantage. If a child receives a significant amount of attention for headaches or avoids unpleasant duties or situations, physical complaints may continue. If they fail to provide secondary gain, they usually decrease. There are basically two ways to accomplish this.

Natural consequences

This involves using natural consequence of a behavior to deal with the problem. If a child is sick, he must see a doctor. Most children dislike that.

A child frequently wants to come home from school because he has a headache or upset stomach. Tell him, "The doctor told me when you are sick, you have to stay in bed. You can't watch TV, play or read because that stimulates your brain and makes your headache worse. If you come home, you'll have to go to bed. What do you want to do?"

Your child feels ill in the morning and doesn't want to go to school. Tell her, "If you feel that bad and can't go to school, you also have to miss dance class this afternoon to stay home and rest."

By using natural consequences, you set up situations in which the advantages of being well outweigh the advantages of being sick. If the physical complaints have a psychological basis, they'll begin to diminish. Use this procedure for all causes of physical complaints described above.

A child was referred to me because she had been hospitalized twice for dehydration resulting from excessive vomiting. Medical test results were negative both times. When this child didn't get her way, she started gagging then vomited. Although several other methods were tried, the following procedure produced the best results.

One Sunday afternoon, her parents decided to take her and her brother to the movies. The children each wanted to see a different movie. When the parents decided to attend the show the brother selected, the little girl started vomiting. The parents treated it very matter-of-factly and gave the girl a towel. They told her to get in the car and take the towel. "If you feel you have to throw up, do it in the towel." On the way to the show, she gagged a few times but didn't throw up. After this was used a few times, the excessive vomiting was eliminated.

A teacher I worked with used a similar procedure to deal with a young child who vomited in the classroom. She told the child, "It's OK if you want to vomit in class. But if you must vomit, do it over there. Then wash your face, come back and clean it up." After this, the child vomited only once in the classroom. The behavior did not reappear.

Ignoring

By ignoring excessive physical complaints, you withdraw all attention from the behavior.

If a child frequently complains of stomachaches, ignore them. Don't respond to his excessive complaints. Another way to ignore a child's excessive ills or pains is to remove parental attention but deal with the behavior.

A question frequently asked by parents is, "How do I know the child isn't really sick?" Most parents and teachers who deal with a child on a daily basis can tell when a child is sick because his mood changes, and he isn't as active or alert. He's not himself. Depend on your knowledge of the child's total behavior to determine the basis of his complaints. If he's sick, you'll know it.

Reduce influence of models

When a significant person in the child's life (mother, father, grandparents) shows excessive concern and talks a lot about sickness or illness, there's a probability the child will model this behavior. Avoid discussions about physical problems in front of a child who shows excessive physical symptoms.

Provide structured, predictable, consistent environment

Some children who experience a changing, ambiguous or inconsistent environment develop physical symptoms. This often occurs in the case of a separation, conflict between parents or similar disruptive situations.

Use rewards and charts

When excessive physical concerns are seen in children, behavior charts and positive consequences can be used to correct the behavior. See Chapter 10, Using Charts to Change Behavior, for a detailed discussion.

I once worked with a 10-year-old who constantly said, "I think I'm going to throw up. I'm dizzy. My stomach hurts." This happened every 30 minutes at school and at home.

His mother set up a chart dividing the day into time periods of 30 minutes each. She told the child, "I'm going to set the timer on the stove. If you don't complain about being sick by the time the bell rings, I'll put a star on your chart. If you complain, I'll put an X on the chart."

The child liked to go hunting with his father, so stars on his chart were traded in for shotgun shells to be used on the weekend. As the child became involved with the chart, the time period was increased (he had to go 1 hour without complaining before he would receive a star, then 2 hours). After using the chart for about 5 weeks, the behavior significantly decreased.

Look for areas of difficulty

If a child's physical complaints form a pattern, they may represent an attempt to avoid frustration, failure, difficulty or situations he feels he can't deal with. When this pattern occurs, look beyond the physical symptoms.

A child who gets sick in the morning or complains of illness on school days but not the weekend may be having trouble with schoolwork, his teacher or schoolmates. Another child may show physical complaints only on the days he has a Boy Scout meeting. Further investigation might reveal the child isn't getting along with the other children at the meeting, one of the kids may be teasing him or he can't do what is expected.

When physical complaints occur and an area of difficulty can be related to them, try to eliminate the source of discomfort or difficulty before dealing directly with the pain, illness and aches.

Counseling and psychotherapy

When physical complaints are symptoms of an underlying psychological conflict, the above methods may not significantly reduce them. When this occurs, the child and family require professional intervention (individual or group therapy, counseling, family therapy). Consult your child's doctor for aid in identifying an appropriate mental-health professional.

54

Restlessness & Fidgeting

Some constant movement, excessive energy and inability to keep still may have to be tolerated. Other behaviors can be changed and/or procedures can be used to reduce the hassle, conflict and negative attention that center around these behaviors.

Rank the behavior in order of importance or severity. List the child's behaviors from those that can't be tolerated to those that aren't so bad. Overlook or tolerate those at the bottom of the list. Give more attention to the behaviors at the top of the list. You may not be able to overlook a child's running through the house, but you may be able to tolerate his squirming and fidgeting while looking at TV.

Allow the child to participate in physical play and games, to perform chores, to play and run, and engage in activities that "burn up" energy. This may help reduce his activity level when he is in the house. Try to give the child a cooling-off period to calm down or unwind before he comes inside. Keeping an overactive child "busy" and channeling his activity into some specific task may also help.

While some minor activity can be overlooked, you don't have to tolerate all the child's overactive behaviors. Other behaviors can be modified or reduced. Several procedures can be use to accomplish this. A few of these follow.

Behavior charts

Behavior charts can be used with these behaviors because they occur frequently during the day. A brief example gives you the general idea. Suppose you have a child who constantly runs through the house. After you analyze the behavior to see how frequently it occurs, you can set up a chart that breaks the day into time periods (every hour).

Identify a reward that is important to the child. Tell him, "For each time period that passes that you don't run through the house, you'll get a star on the chart. If you run, you won't get a star. You can trade every star for 10 minutes past your bedtime" or whatever the identified reward is.

As the running decreases and the child receives more stars, time periods can be increased (every 2 hours). Eventually the child gets a star if he doesn't run that day. Similar methods can be used on other behaviors that reflect increased levels of activity. See Chapter 10, Using Charts to Change Behavior, for a more detailed explanation.

Let's say you have a child who doesn't sit still during mealtime. He taps his fork, gets up from the table several times, fidgets, squirms. Mealtime is a hassle and usually results in indigestion for everyone. To decrease the child's activity level at the dinner table, identify a reward. Tell the child, "While we eat, we're going to give you warnings every time you fidget or get up (explain exactly what the child must do to get the warning). If you get fewer than 3 warnings, you'll get an ice cream after dinner (or whatever the identified reward is). If you get 3 or more warnings, you won't get ice cream." For some children, more warnings may have to be used, for others less.

Another child may not be able to play quietly. He constantly makes noise, jumps and runs. You want to decrease his inappropriate activity while playing. Tell him, "If you play quietly (explain exactly what you mean by this) for a few minutes, we'll play that game you like so much. If you run around and make a lot of noise, we won't play the game." At first, the time the child has to play quietly is very short. As he becomes successful and can play quietly for the given period, the time can be increased.

Review Methods and Techniques sections for additional ideas about reducing overactive behaviors. It's also a good idea to use positive consequences and reward when trying to modify this behavior. See Chapter 52, Overactivity, for more information.

55

Short Attention Span, Distractibility & Inability to Concentrate

Some children show deficits in attention and concentration. Descriptions are varied.

"Easily distracted."

"Unable to concentrate for more than a short period of time."

"A daydreamer."

"Takes 2 hours to do 10 minutes of homework."

"Not able to keep his mind on what he's doing."

Often total elimination of problems in this area is difficult. But several things can improve the child's ability to pay attention and concentrate and reduce the hassle produced by these weaknesses.

Reduce distractions

Let's say your child—who is easily distracted—tries to do his homework in the kitchen where you are cooking. His sister is doing her homework, and the baby is playing on the floor with his toys. He will experience problems. Many things are happening to take his attention away from his homework. It may appear he's never going to finish.

Imagine yourself at a party where 7 interesting people are talking at once. You're listening to person 1, but person 4 says something that gets your attention. Then person 6 starts telling an amusing story so you begin listening to him and so forth. After an hour, you may be totally confused and not fully understand what anyone is talking about. If you were trying to perform some task, you wouldn't have finished.

This is how an overactive child feels when he is bombarded with stimuli or is in a situation that involves many distractions.

When trying to get a child who has attentional problems to perform a task (homework), place him in a situation with minimal distraction. Do *not* put him in a room where other activity is going on, a TV is playing or where people or things can divert his attention. Put him in a quiet room or a place in the house that does not have much "people traffic." Reduce distractions that can be heard (voices of children playing outside, sound of TV) or seen (activity outside a window, favorite toys).

Break work into small units

Suppose a child has 15 minutes of homework that drags into hours because he can only concentrate for short periods of time. It may not be wise to try to get him to do it all at one time. Break it up into three 5-minute sessions.

The length of the sessions varies for each child. For some children use 30-second or 1-minute time periods. Tell a child, "We're going to break up your homework. We'll do some now and some later." Rather than for a 15-minute period, work on three 5-minute periods or whatever.

For some children, the use of positive consequences also helps them improve their ability to concentrate. Tell the child the same thing but add, "I'm going to set the timer on the stove for 5 minutes. If you work till the bell rings, I'll play that game you like to play" or "you'll earn 5 minutes past your bedtime," or whatever reward is important to the child. As the child improves or if small periods of time are used at first, increase the length of the sessions. Start off with 1-minute sessions for several days. When the child is doing well, increase the time to 2 minutes. Do this until you reach the maximum time the child can concentrate at one sitting.

The task can also be broken up. Suppose a child's room has been messed up for days, and you tell him, "Go clean up your room." The child goes in the room and starts picking up. After he's made his bed and put his shoes away, he finds a toy that has been lost for weeks. He stops what he's doing and starts playing. Fifteen minutes later you check on him and find the room is still a mess.

The task of cleaning the room may involve several separate duties (making a bed, putting away toys, hanging up clothes, picking up shoes, putting dirty clothes where they belong). Children who have attentional problems usually have trouble with this type of situation.

To make the task easier and to increase the probability of success, give the child cleaning duties one at a time. Tell him, "Make your bed." After a period of time, tell him, "Hang up your clothes," and so forth.

Use consequences in this situation.

"You can't go play until your bed is made."

"I'll play pitch and catch with you when all your clothes are hung up."

The number of duties the child must do at one time can be increased as the child improves. You may never get to the point where you can tell him, "Go clean your room."

Give instructions one at a time

A child with attentional problems is told, "Go outside and take this food to the dog. While you're outside, bring in the mop. Tell your brother to come inside." He goes outside and while putting down the dog food, he spots a bug crawling on the side of the house. He starts following it; 5 minutes later he comes inside without the mop or his brother. You ask, "Where's the mop? Did you tell your brother to come inside?"

The child responds with, "I forgot."

Children with these problems can't handle a series of instructions or directions. They are told, "Go put your pajamas on, brush your teeth and bring me the newspaper from the kitchen." The child may finish the first but forget about the other two. Something distracts the child before he's able to get to the second task, and he "forgets" about it. Have him repeat the instructions in his own words.

Another technique to use when giving children directions or instructions is to be sure they hear and/or understand what is being said. Often the reason directions are not completed is they are never heard or fully understood. Because of attention problems, the child may not be listening to what you say. Be sure you have the child's attention before giving instructions. Look him in the face and have him look at you.

See Chapter 52, Overactivity, Attention-Deficit Disorder & Hyperactivity, for more information.

56

Shy Children

Shy children are described in many ways—sensitive, reserved, reclusive, withdrawn, bashful, timid, backward, introverted, hesitant, modest, easily frightened, avoids contact with others, has difficulty meeting new people. These children aren't usually verbal, have difficulty expressing feelings, have trouble with social interaction and are usually in the background or on the fringe in social situations. There seem to be several situations where this behavior is more likely to occur. They are described below.

Causes of Shyness

Genetic or heredity?

There is a possibility children inherit personality characteristics. Many shy children are described by parents as being shy like their father or mother. Or a parent might say, "I tend to be a loner and I don't have too many friends and stay to myself." These same characteristics are observed in the child.

Modeling

Children learn and develop behaviors if they see other significant people in their environment modeling the same behaviors. The parents are socially isolated, have trouble interacting with others and avoid social situations. The child will probably also learn these behaviors.

Lack of confidence

Some children who lack confidence or have a negative self-concept may show this behavior. They don't readily verbalize with others, do not commit themselves or put themselves in a situation where failure may occur. This usually means avoiding people. This child is saying, "The less I do, the fewer mistakes I'll make."

Excessive negative attention or punishment

Some children are exposed to yelling, screaming and emphasis on mistakes. More attention is paid to what they do wrong than what they do right. They may deal with this situation by withdrawing or showing other shy-type behaviors.

If excessive punishment or control by fear is used, some children show a timid, hesitant, fearful approach to the environment. They often look like "scared rabbits" and are very much aware of and concerned about negative consequences, failure or being wrong.

Changing environments

Fluid, unpredictable, inconsistent or unstructured situations may promote shy behavior in some children. This could be a result of significant changes in the child's life (parental separation, change of schools, death of a parent), or it could result from inconsistent behavior-management techniques.

Dependency

Some children who are dependent on others to aid and guide them have difficulty demonstrating independent behavior. When it's necessary for this child to function independently, he may appear timid, reserved and hesitant. He may be described as "shy."

Lack of socialization

Some children do not have the opportunity to interact or play with others their age. They may develop inappropriate or immature patterns of interaction. Because of this lack of experience, other children tend to withdraw from them because they don't have confidence in their skills to relate to others. Or they don't know how to interact with others.

Emotional problems

Children who have significant emotional problems may show withdrawn behavior and difficulty relating to people. This child often makes marginal adjustments in many areas of his life. He doesn't have a need to interact with people. He'd much rather be alone or in his own secure environment than with other people.

Dealing with Shyness

If you have a child with shy characteristics, it doesn't mean you're doing anything wrong or that you caused this behavior. Some genetic or heredity factors contribute to certain personality characteristics.

I could describe one of my children as being very talkative, extroverted, outgoing and able to converse with anyone he meets. Another of my children may be timid, introverted and a "man of few words." If behavior was directly related to the patterns of family interaction, both children should show similar characteristics. However, the situation I described above is very typical in many families.

Don't try to change the introvert into an extrovert or make a timid, reserved child the life of the party. The shy child may always remain shy. But the severity of the shyness or the extent to which it will significantly interfere with his life can possibly be reduced. Try the following methods and techniques to reduce the child's shyness and improve his verbal interaction in social skills.

Increase socialization

Children learn to deal with other children by being with them. A child who is shy and lacking in social skills needs to increase his interaction with children his own age. In the beginning, it's better to have him interact with one child and not in a group or with several children. See Chapter 45, Getting Along with Other Children, for more information.

Use positive interaction and consequences

Get off his back! Don't yell, scream, criticize or use negative attention. Use rewards and incentives for good behavior rather than punishment for bad behavior. Increase the positive interaction you have with the child, and talk with him about his interests, accomplishments and good behaviors. See Chapter 7, Reward; Chapter 8, Punishment; and Chapter 14, Communication Between Parent & Child, for additional techniques.

Promote independent behavior

Don't foster dependent behavior or make your child rely on you to function. Let him do things he should be doing at his age level. Avoid excessive restrictions and doing for him. Read Chapter 39, Dependent Children.

Build confidence

Try to identify areas or events and situations that may contribute to the development of a negative self-image and a lack of confidence. Accentuate the positive. Get the child involved in activities in which he will succeed. Promote other situations that will strengthen confidence. See Chapter 36, Building Confidence, for additional methods and a more-detailed discussion.

Stabilize environment

There may have been major changes in the child's life or other situations that produce an unpredictable environment. Try to increase the structure, consistency and predictability. This may involve many things, from major environmental changes to inconsistent behavior-management techniques. Chapter 19, Effects of Divorce, Separation, Parental Conflict & Other Environmental Changes on Behavior, discusses the situation in great detail.

Counseling and psychotherapy

For children who experience significant emotional problems, counseling may be the best avenue to follow. I mention some of the characteristics of the child with significant emotional problems in Chapter 52, Overactivity, Attention-Deficit Disorder, Hyperactivity. Review this.

If you've tried some of the above techniques and aren't successful, it may be wise to seek professional help, even if you don't feel the child has significant emotional problems. A therapist or counselor may be able to work with the child to help him improve his behavior. Or the professional may be able to help you have a positive influence on changing the behavior.

57

Sibling Conflict

Parents with one child miss some aspects of parenting. One is mystery. I was recently cutting the grass and found one of my wrenches rusting in the mud. It had been there awhile and was ruined. I knew my wife didn't use the wrench, and I didn't remember using it. So I went inside and asked my sons who had used the wrench. Neither had used the wrench or knew anything about it.

In situations like this, a mystery is created, and you have to find out who did what. If you only had one child and you assume you or your wife didn't use the wrench, it's obvious who the culprit is. If a bag of potato chips is missing and you have more than one child, you may have to bring in Sherlock Holmes to solve the mystery of the missing potato chips.

The other thing one-child parents don't experience is disagreements, arguing and conflicts between brothers and sisters.

"Mom, Jason's looking at me—tell him to stop looking at me."

"She's hitting me."

"He's calling me retarded."

"He keeps borrowing my brush and never puts it back."

The conflict in many situations involves name calling, teasing, aggravation and sometimes fighting.

No matter what you do, you probably won't be able to eliminate ALL fighting or competition between siblings. You can do several things to reduce the amount of conflict and its effects on the general atmosphere around your home.

Treat children the same but differently

Children have different personalities. Even though you try, there's no way to treat all your children the same. One child may be very talkative, another quiet. Your daughter may be very affectionate and loving, while your son is somewhat distant. Try to give all your children the same amount of attention, but you may have to give it in different ways.

Avoid situations where you do the same thing for both children. Every time you come home, you bring both children a candy. If you buy one child a T-shirt, you feel you must buy the other the same shirt.

Try to create a situation to get the child to realize he is the same as his siblings but in a different manner. Get the child thinking, "She bought something for my sister today and didn't buy me anything. But last week she bought a pair of tennis shoes for me, and my sister didn't get anything."

"Mary got some candy at the store today, and I didn't get any. But I got ice cream last week, and she didn't."

If you constantly do the same thing for both children, you may create a situation in which the child feels he must be like the other child or do everything the other child does. This causes problems later when the 12-year-old may feel he should be able to do exactly the same things as a 16-year-old.

Don't be an arbitrator

Deal with things when you can determine who is at fault. Your children are playing in the back room. All of a sudden an argument breaks out. One runs into the kitchen and starts telling you what happened. A couple of minutes later, the other one comes in and gives you an entirely different story.

You have to become a detective to decide who's at fault, who started the conflict and who must be disciplined.

Most of the time when you become an arbitrator, *you* lose. If this occurs frequently in your home, one child may feel unjustly treated. Only deal with things you *see*. Have the children come to some kind of resolution or solve the problem themselves. If they fight over what TV program to watch, say, "Go to your room, and figure out which program you want to see. When you come to a conclusion, come out and watch it." Try to have the children resolve the conflicts themselves.

Don't create competitive situations

There will always be competition among siblings, no matter what you do. But don't create situations that add to this. One child gives no trouble with homework. The other child creates problems every night. There's usually a fight and hassles over homework. Don't tell both children, "Anyone who does their homework will be able to stay up 15 minutes past their bedtime. Anyone who gives me trouble will go to bed at the same time."

If you do this, you'll create unfair competition. The child who doesn't give any trouble with homework will usually receive the reward, and the other one may not.

Try to identify something that needs improvement in the child who isn't giving you trouble with homework. One child may be able to stay up past his bedtime for cooperating with the homework. The other child may earn the same or similar privilege for cleaning his room or the bathroom after he takes a bath.

See your children's strengths and weaknesses. A weakness in some children may be a strength in others. You create an unfair competitive situation by dealing with the same behavior. Look for each child's weaknesses, and try to improve these.

This also involves getting your children involved in the same activities (dancing, music, football). This brings us to the next consideration.

Develop individual achievements and interests

In many families, the child who gets the best grades is also the child who catches the biggest fish when fishing, plays baseball better, has a higher degree belt in karate and plays a musical instrument with more skill. To involve your children in the same activities may create a competitive situation in which one child *always* loses.

Individualize interests, and involve them in different things. It's much easier for a child to think, "My brother is a better baseball player than I am, but I know more about fishing than he does." Or "My sister dances much better than I do, but I know more about music and can play the piano much better than she can."

Develop a seniority system

In most families more is expected from the older children. An older child and his sister are watching television. The younger child starts jumping all over the furniture or turning chairs over. You come into the room and tell the older one, "You know better than that. You shouldn't have let your sister jump all over the couch." The older child usually has more responsibilities and duties around the home.

If more is expected from a child and you give him more responsibility, he should have more privileges. Older children have built-in privileges. The 10-year-old may be able to ride his bike farther than the 6-year-old. He may be able to cross certain streets the younger child cannot. You should also create a seniority system in the sense the older child can stay up later. The older child should get more allowance than the younger child.

If all the children have the same privileges, but one has more responsibility, problems may arise.

Develop outside friendships and different playmates

Who are the sibling's primary playmates? If the child's primary playmate is his brother, there may be more conflict than if the child's primary playmate is someone else. If your children play with one another more than 50% of the time, encourage them to develop other friendships. Brothers and sisters get along better if they play more with other children than with each other.

This also involves children who play with the same playmates. If two sisters are close in age and have common friends, they're more apt to have conflicts than if they have different friends. Encourage them to develop individual friendships and relationships. Have them play more with other children than with each other.

Is one child being favored?

Problems may arise between siblings in two general situations. First, is the "good" child receiving more favoritism and attention than another child? If so, conflict may develop. If a child receives a great deal of negative attention (hyperactivity, has trouble in school, stubbornness), the child may feel his sibling is favored because he receives less negative attention. The obvious solution is to avoid favoritism.

For the child who receives more negative attention, place as much emphasis on good behavior, achievements and successes as you do on his misbehaviors, failures and mistakes. You may not be able to reduce the negative attention, but you *can* increase the positive attention. When you turn the lights out to go to bed and review the day, be sure you have spent as much time (maybe more) looking at your child's good behavior as you have spent in emphasizing the bad.

Prevent conflict from escalating

Deal with the fight before it becomes a full-blown battle. In most children, you can see a conflict starting to escalate. At first there is some name-calling and teasing. Then it moves into more screaming and hollering. Then it becomes pushing and shoving, and finally there's a full-blown fight.

Rather than deal with the fight when it occurs, look at the conflicts your children have to see how they develop. Prevent the conflict from escalating by dealing with behaviors that occur early in the process. Deal with the name-calling rather than the fight.

A reward system can be set up for not calling names. Or discipline may be used when name-calling occurs.

You may want to review Chapter 45, Getting Along with Other Children.

58

Spoiling

Spoiling is a troublesome word because most parents don't like to hear other people call their child *spoiled*. It's usually OK for a parent to say, "My child is spoiled." Most people define this child as one who has everything or gets anything he wants. They usually define spoiling in terms of material things. Parents buy the child a great deal. This may be true in some cases, but there is much more to spoiling than buying a child material things. A child could have every toy imaginable and not be spoiled, while a child with few material possessions could be very spoiled.

Spoiled children manipulate their parents to get what they want (staying up late, going outside to play after they have been told no). The child is in control.

A general description of the spoiled child is *one who is more in control than the parents*. Control may involve material things, but more often it includes a variety of behavioral activities. There is usually a lack of effective discipline or parental control. The child is allowed to do his own thing, get what he wants and has a great deal of control over his environment.

Relate consequences to behavior

Whatever happens to a child should be related to his behavior. A child goes shopping with you. You tell him, "If you're bad in the store, you won't get a candy." The child is bad and still gets the candy. The candy had nothing to do with his behavior. It just appeared.

Another child comes home and says, "I want a basketball like Jeff has." His father gets him one. Again, the basketball is not related to behavior.

The consequences of the child's behavior should be directly tied to him. A child should earn the consequences of his actions. It's not important how many toys or privileges a child has, but how he gets them. Read Chapter 40, Developing Responsible Behavior, for suggestions on how to avoid spoiling and how to deal with it when it occurs.

Parents in control

Parents need to be in control. Children need structure, predictability, discipline and external controls in their environment. When spoiling occurs, these are usually absent. Their absence produces an ambiguous, unpredictable environment for the child. See Chapter 31, Who's in Control?

The child may be confused and try to gain more control over the environment by becoming rebellious, self-centered, demanding and selfish. Chapter 19, Effects of Divorce, Separation, Parental Conflict & Other Environmental Changes on Behavior, discusses the results of an unstructured environment and how to deal with behavior that may result from it. You may want to reread this chapter because spoiling often produces a similar situation for the child as that produced by changes in his environment or a lack of structure or limits.

Avoid spoiling, catering to a child, giving him his way, meeting all his needs or allowing him to control you. Spoiled children often develop a self-centered, pleasure-orientation to their environment, have problems in their peer relationships because they're bossy, fail to develop responsibility, have difficulties at school because they do their own thing, become rebellious, don't develop self-discipline and do only what they want. See Chapter 60, Stubborn, Strong-Willed, Pleasure-Oriented Children, for more information. This behavior pattern will result in future problems for most children.

59

Stealing

Somewhere between 4 and 6, children learn about taking something that doesn't belong to them. Most children steal at some time in their lives. Whether it becomes a problem depends on how frequently it occurs and how you deal with it.

When stealing occurs, the best possible way to initially deal with it is to stop it from working. If your child comes home with something that doesn't belong to him, make him bring it back to the store and talk to the manager. Or return it to his friend's house or give it to the teacher if he "found" it in school. A good rule for a young child is you will return anything you don't buy for him or anything that isn't his. If your child says someone gave it to him or "It is Joey's bike. I'm only keeping it for him," check it out. See if he is telling the truth.

Some children trade or swap their possessions for other children's things. Some children buy and sell things. If your child is taking things that don't belong to him, discourage this type of behavior.

Causes of Stealing

It works

Some children steal because they get away with it. They bring something home that doesn't belong to them and are able to keep it. They continue to take things because it works.

The child brings a watch home from school and tells you, "Jason gave it to me," and he keeps it. Or a child has a bike that supposedly belongs to his friend. He keeps it at the house for 6 months.

Models

If parents, grandparents or other close adults model this behavior, the child is apt to show a similar pattern. If every time I take my children fishing, I take crabs from someone else's crab traps, I show them this is acceptable behavior. Talking to your spouse in front of your child about how you put something over on someone on a business transaction or the cashier gave you change for a $20 bill when you give her $10 teaches them the behavior works, and it's OK to do it.

Peer groups may also influence children or serve as models for behavior. If your child belongs to a peer group or has friends who steal, he's more likely to show this behavior than if his friends don't show similar behaviors. Characters he sees on TV and in the movies may also influence his behavior.

Personality characteristics

The con artist, manipulator or pleasure-oriented child is more likely to engage in this behavior than other children.

Need

Some children steal because that's the only way they get what they want. The extreme case is a child who takes food because he's hungry. This cause primarily exists in families with financial problems. However, I have seen children from middle-class families steal designer clothes to keep up with their schoolmates because their parents couldn't afford the clothes.

Emotional closeness to parent

My approach to children is more behavioral than psychoanalytical. I look for underlying causes, events in childhood, flaws in relationships and other reasons to explain behavior.

There are several aspects of this theory that make sense to me that I have seen work. One relates to stealing in young children under 10. After trying several things with no success, we increased the quality time with the parent, specifically the mother. Behavior was eliminated.

Methods of Treatment

Develop responsible behavior

Rather than focus directly on stealing, work to develop

more responsible behaviors in many situations. Have the child learn there are many things you must do because you have to. This might involve many different things—taking a bath when told, putting his bike in the garage, using his brother's basketball after asking him first, cooperating with homework and other behaviors that reflect responsibility.

This will also help the child think before he acts and weigh the consequences of his actions before he does something. See Chapter 40, Developing Responsible Behavior.

Stop stealing from working

Don't let the child get away with it. Catch him. Stop it from working. A good general rule is, "You don't keep anything you bring home that I don't know where you got it. Everything you find will be returned to the place where you found it, or it will be mine to keep."

If the child says his friend gave him the watch or toy, check it out. This may also involve searching his room, looking through his school bag and checking his hiding places.

Reduce models

Don't model the behavior for the child. Avoid discussing this type of activity in front of the child. Minimize contact with relatives, peers and TV programs that approve of or promote taking property that doesn't belong to you.

Deal with child's personality

Some personality types are more likely to engage in this behavior than other personality types. See Chapter 37, Con Artist—Manipulative Children; Chapter 50, Lying; Chapter 40, Developing Responsibility; and Chapter 60, Stubborn, Strong-Willed, Pleasure-Oriented Children, for more information.

Try to eliminate need

This might involve "getting a job" for the child or identifying areas of support or financial aid for the family. Perhaps children at your child's school or in his peer group have values and material possessions that are inconsistent with yours or you can't financially compete with the other parents. Maybe your child should be in a different school or be a member of a peer group with values and means similar to yours.

Increase quality time

This seems to work better when the involvement is with the mother. Increase the quality time you spend with the child. Use a reward system for not stealing; the reward could involve time with you. You can kill two birds with one stone—you give the child time and have a system to modify his behavior.

"I'm going to check with your teacher at school and look through your school bag and pockets. On the days you haven't taken anything, we'll play that game you like."

The increase in emotional closeness or quality time could involve many things (reading the child an extra story at night, going for a bike ride, playing together, taking the child out to eat, talking with him). Time spent with the child and the activity should only be for the child. Don't include siblings or the father. This time is just for you and your child.

60

Stubborn, Strong-Willed & Pleasure-Oriented Children

When I graduated from college, I was young, very idealistic and thought I knew everything. I believed the environment was *the* factor in determining and shaping behavior and personalities. Since then, I've aged, and I hope I've gotten wiser. I realize there's a lot I don't know. I've also developed a greater respect for the effects of heredity on personality characteristics. See Chapter 15, Children Have Personalities, for additional comments.

Environment and the way you deal with your children can shape personalities and develop behaviors. Some children's personalities can be seen at a very young age. This is often true of the strong-willed, pleasure-oriented child. She may be a difficult infant, give trouble nursing and have days and nights mixed up.

Some children want to bathe and dress themselves at an early age; others would let you dress them until they're 16. Some children with 15 minutes of homework come home, do the homework and go out to play. Others spend 3-1/2 hours trying to get out of the 15 minutes of homework.

Some children are stubborn and want to do it their way. They'll buck the system every chance they get. They want to do what they want, for as long they want, when they want. These are also strong-willed, pleasure-oriented children.

A strong-willed, pleasure-oriented child is primarily concerned with satisfying his own needs and wishes. He's more concerned with the pleasure he derives from his behavior than any punishment. He may know he's not supposed to do something and will be punished if he does. But if it's fun, he'll do it and worry about punishment later. He starts doing what he pleases and disregards rules and responsibilities imposed by others.

If you ask him to do something, no matter how difficult, and he wants to do it, it'll be done. If you ask him to do something, no matter how small, and he doesn't want to, it's like trying to run through a brick wall.

It may look as if this child acts before he thinks. But this isn't true. He behaves this way because he's more concerned with what he wants to do than what will happen to him.

Routines

These children have a lot of difficulty with routines. If you look at what most adults do every day, as much as 90% of the day, involves doing things you *have* to do, not things you *want* to do. You have to go to work, cut grass, wash clothes, cook, help kids with homework. If you had your choice, you probably wouldn't do any of those things. But most of us don't have a choice. Our daily routines have to be done.

Although a child's level of responsibility is nowhere close to yours, he still has a lot of things he has to do. A child has to pick up his clothes, do homework, come in from playing when it is dark, take a bath, brush his teeth.

The strong-willed child has trouble with routines and responsibilities. He wants to do what he wants to do. You may have trouble getting a child out of bed in the morning, in bed at night and all the routines in between. This child's attitude is, "If it fits what I'm supposed to do, that's great. If it doesn't, that's OK, too." This attitude drives self-motivated, high-achieving parents crazy!

On the top of his list of important things to do is playing, having a good time, doing what he wants, having fun. Cleaning his room, feeding the dog, doing schoolwork, putting out the garbage falls at the bottom of the list. He cleans his room halfway by hiding stuff under and behind things. He does his homework and classwork in the fastest possible way. He may put down any answer—right or wrong—just to have an answer. At times, he "forgets" books in school or homework assignments, so he won't have to do the work or study for a test.

Problems in school

In school, many problems are seen, usually characterized by an inability to follow classroom procedure. The child often does what he wants to do in the classroom and doesn't do what he's supposed to do. He may daydream and be inattentive and overactive. He has not developed internal control, self-discipline or responsibility.

Skilled con artists

These children are usually very skilled con artists who are aware of inconsistencies in the environment. They are quick to manipulate people and events to satisfy their own needs and wishes or to avoid unpleasant duties and responsibilities. The manipulation is pleasure-oriented because he wants something, but someone or something is preventing him from getting it. He knows what he has to do to get around what blocks him so his needs will be fulfilled.

Although these children can be polite, charming and affable when it is to their advantage, they often have problems with authority or those in a position of supervision or direction over them. They are often rebellious, stubborn, oppositional and resistant. People they give the most trouble to are usually their parents. Most neighbors, friends and people who meet this child think he's a great kid who is a pleasure to have at their house. They say he's polite, helpful and cooperative. Most parents think, "Are they talking about the same kid who lives at our house?"

Dealing with the Strong-Willed, Pleasure-Oriented Child

Several techniques work well with this child. Many parents have trouble dealing with the strong-willed child because the methods that work effectively with most children don't work with this child.

Use goals, incentives and rewards

Punishment doesn't work well—often not at all—with this child. Negative consequences, when they do work, affect him only temporarily—a few minutes, at best a few days.

Let's say two children are sitting on your front porch, and you ordered a load of mud for your garden. The dump truck arrives and drops the mud on your lawn. You go outside and tell these two children, "Don't go in the pile of mud. If you do, you'll be punished for a week in your room. No TV. No playing with your toys or friends. No riding your bike."

One child thinks, "It's boring in my room. I'll miss my favorite cartoons and TV programs. I won't see my friends or be able to ride my new bike!" So he stays on the front porch.

The strong-willed, pleasure-oriented child thinks, "I could go in that pile of mud and make some tunnels or make mud balls and throw them. I could jump off the pile or roll down it. Ride my bike on it. The heck with the punishment." So he's in the pile of mud.

In this example, the first child is concerned about the negative consequences of his behavior—what will happen to him. This child shows some fear or worry about punishment. He can be motivated away from things.

"I'll stay on the front porch to avoid missing my cartoons." Punishment works well with this child.

The pleasure-oriented child is more motivated toward things. "What's in it for me? How much fun I will have? What am I going to get out of this?"

Punishment is meaningless to the pleasure-oriented child because he isn't concerned about what will happen to him. He's more concerned with what is in it for him. His choice is between pleasure and no pleasure. Nine out of 10 times, he'll choose the pleasurable activity.

Rewards are better

A better approach for this child is to use an incentive, goal or reward. Tell him, "I'm going to the store in 30 minutes. Anyone who doesn't go in the mud will get an ice cream. Anyone who goes in the mud won't get one." Now the child has a choice between two pleasures—playing in the mud and ice cream. You're more likely to get him to make the choice of staying on the porch with this approach. See Chapter 7, Reward, for more information on this consequence. Often reward for appropriate behavior will get better results than punishment for misconduct for this type of child.

Don't rely on reasoning, explaining or lectures

Some children are born with characteristics of self-discipline, responsibility and doing what they're supposed to do.

With other children, you can develop these behaviors by talking to them and establishing or changing an attitude. By giving them information, explaining things to them, being logical or getting them to see the situation from a different angle, an attitude develops and behavior follows.

It's almost like a light bulb comes on! You might say, "You have to brush your teeth to prevent cavities. If you don't, you will have rotten and ugly teeth and will have to go to the dentist. That will cost money and I won't be able to buy you as many toys, etc." After telling him this, the child brushes his teeth every night without your telling him.

You might explain the importance of homework, why he should not ride his bike on the highway, etc. and the child behaves accordingly. "Don't touch the pot on the stove. It's hot. You will get burned and that will hurt." Or, he could see his sister get burned by doing that and he does not touch the pot.

These techniques don't work effectively with a strong-willed, pleasure-oriented child. Talking, reasoning, explaining, lectures, yelling and screaming are ineffective. He develops attitudes and responsible behavior by experiencing consequences. What you do is more important than what you say. You can explain to a pleasure-oriented child, but the information or lecture will go in one ear and out the other. He'll do what he wants to do.

With the child mentioned earlier, a light bulb comes on (the attitude is established) and the behavior follows. The strong-willed child's light bulb comes on, but it is very dim. It increases with intensity each time you are able to get him to perform the behavior. The attitude develops gradually over time as he repeats the behavior. The more we can get him to behave in a certain way and something happens that he likes or doesn't like, the faster the attitude develops. He has to experience the consequences of his behavior. He has to touch the pot to learn that hot pots cause pain. It may be all right to explain why a child needs to do his homework, but the most important thing with this child is what is going to happen if he does it and what is going to happen if he does not do it. You might say, "You have been giving me a hassle every night with your homework. You complain, whine, etc. Every night your homework is done and you cooperate and are pleasant, you can stay up 30 minutes past your bedtime. If you give me trouble, you'll go to bed at the regular time."

If someone said to me, "You can go to work and I will pay you or you can stay home and I will pay you," I'd be fishing instead of working! I would have to be stupid to go to work. Many pleasure-oriented children approach or see the environment in this fashion. Or, they feel if they get in a jam, they will be able to con or manipulate themselves out of the situation. You have to make the consequences different for this child if you expect to change his behavior or have him develop an attitude.

Explanations don't work

Many parents talk, explain, reason or lecture too much. The strong-willed child frequently doesn't accept explanations for why he can't do what he wants to do. The only thing that will please him is what he wants to hear.

One, ten, one-hundred or a thousand explanations will not satisfy him. The only thing that will please him is what he wants to hear. Your child may ask, "Can I go to Robbie's house?" You say, "No." He asks, "Why?" After numerous logical reasons and explanations of why he can't go to his friend's house, he is still giving you a hassle. The only thing that will satisfy him is for you to say, "Yes, you can go to Robbie's."

Sometimes the only reason that is necessary is, "Because I said so!"

Suppose I tell my boss, "The person who made the rule that I have to work 5 days and have 2 days off is stupid. I think I should work 3-1/2 days and take off 3-1/2 days. That makes more sense to me. Now he can explain to me that people used to work 7 days a week and I have it easier than they did. The only response that will satisfy me is, "You're right. Work 3-1/2 days and take off 3-1/2 days." My boss does not have to go into elaborate and detailed explanations. He says, "Come to work 5 days and take off 2 days because you're working for me and I said so. If you don't like it, find another job."

Kids often ask questions that don't have logical answers. Give me a good reason for, "Why do I have to make my bed every morning if I am going to mess it up every night?" There is none. The only answer is, "I have the job. I pay the rent, electricity, phone, etc., and I bought your furniture. Because I said so you will not be able to watch TV when you come home from school until your bed has been made."

Maintain a business-like approach

Some people do things for you because of a relationship that has been formed or you have been nice to them. Other people would see this as a weakness to exploit.

Suppose you've done 10 favors for me. You ask me to drive you to pick up your car. I'm busy, but 10 flags pop up in my head. I remember the favors. So I say, "Come on, I'll take you." The pleasure-oriented personality may think he has put something over on the person 10 times and say, "No, I can't take you. I'm busy."

Never say, "I'm going to buy you this candy. I want you to be good the rest of the time we're shopping." The good behavior will last until the candy is eaten!

You should say, "We're going shopping. I usually have to correct you many times. Each time I have to tell you something, I'll give you a warning. If you do not have 3 warnings when we're finished, you'll get the candy. If you have 3 or more warnings, no candy."

This child needs the rules or expectations and consequences spelled out ahead of time. Consequences should occur *after* he fulfills the expectations.

Severe, harsh, long or big consequences don't work

With the pleasure-oriented child, long or severe punishments or big rewards don't effectively change behavior. Suppose you have a child who loves Saturday morning cartoons. It is 7:30 am and he's jumping on the furniture in the den. You say, "If you jump on the couch again, you have to go to your room for the rest of the morning. You'll miss all your cartoons."

At 7:35, he jumps on the couch again. You send him to his room for 3 or 4 hours. This is *not* the best way to discipline the pleasure-oriented child. This works best with the "attitude kid"—the one you can talk to and reason with to produce behavioral change. The "attitude kid" goes to his room and starts thinking, "I missed my favorite cartoons. It's boring in my room. What I did was stupid. It wasn't worth it!" He goes in his room and starts thinking. The wheels start turning in his head and he develops changes in his attitude. The correct or expected behavior follows.

If you send the strong-willed child to his room for 3 or 4 hours, he will holler, cry and pout for 5 or 10 minutes. Then he will find something to entertain himself. The big consequence makes no impact. This is why failing a grade or having to go to summer school does not significantly change this child's behavior. He got away without doing homework 89 times. The big consequences of failing or going to summer school do not change his attitude. It is better for this child to check with the teacher every Friday. If he has completed all his homework, some consequences will follow. If has has not completed all of his homework, a different consequence will occur. Doing this 20 times a year is more effective than one big consequence.

For the pleasure-oriented child, it's better to say, "If you jump on the furniture, you have to go to your room for 5 minutes." He jumps. You send him to his room for 5 minutes. After the time passes, he comes back into the den and jumps again. You send him back to his room for 5 more minutes. This procedure is repeated if he jumps again.

For this child, it's better to send him to his room 50 times for 5 minutes than 1 time for 3 or 4 hours. Don't let something slide 49 times and then come down with a really big consequence. It is more effective to give the pleasure-oriented child 48 small consequences. You have to establish a cause-and-effect relationship.

Big consequences do not significantly affect behavior. The more you can get him to do something and something happens that he likes or doesn't like, the faster the behavior will change.

Big incentives or rewards that occur after a long period don't work well with this child. In January, you say, "If you pass all your classes this year, we'll go to Disney World this summer." Or "If you don't get suspended again for the rest of the school year, I'll buy you a motorcycle."

If you set up a long-term incentive for the pleasure-oriented child, he'll work like crazy for 3 days but rapidly slides back into his old behavior. Or he won't show any behavioral change until 3 days before the report card. Then he'll study 24 hours a day.

It's better to get a weekly report from the school and base weekend privileges on his performance at school for the week. Or get a weekly report from school; if there's a long-term goal, he can earn points toward that goal on a weekly basis.

Sentencing the child

Don't give the child a sentence.

"Go to your room; you are punished all day."

"You can't use the phone for a week."

"You will not be able to play for the whole week."

These "sentence kids" go in their room and serve their sentence. Then they come out and do the same thing again.

Sentences are given to change an attitude or get a child to think differently. They do *not* work with pleasure-oriented children. These children work better when there are goals or incentives. If you give them a sentence, give them something they can work toward.

"Because you've been doing poorly in school, you can't talk on the phone this week. However, each evening you do your homework and don't give me any trouble, you can talk on the phone that night."

If you give this child a sentence, the only thing you're positive of is he won't talk on the phone for a week. If you give him something to work toward (way to work out of the sentence), you may get some homework completed.

Avoid being manipulated

These children are good con artists and are skilled at manipulation. Don't be too generous with your trust. They know exactly what you want to hear. You need to prevent them from getting away with things.

You ask your daughter, "Do you have any homework?"

She says, "No," and goes outside to play. At the end of the week, you receive a note from her teacher indicating she didn't turn in her homework for the week.

Don't believe these children too readily. They have to earn your trust. Check on them to see if what they told you is correct.

Accentuate child's achievement and good behavior

The child bucks the system, wants to do what he wants to do and doesn't listen as well as other children. He tends to get more negative attention than the average child. He needs more positive attention given to his good behavior to balance or offset the negative attention.

Avoid power struggles

The pleasure-oriented child likes to be in control. He doesn't readily accept no for an answer. He's good at enticing you into a power struggle, a screaming match or saying things to start a heated discussion.

"I think I'm going to quit school."

Avoid getting involved in a conversation about something like this. Deal with him in a calm, business-like manner.

Sometimes it is more important for the child to experience consequences of his behavior than for you to get the task accomplished. You know a child loves to go outside to play. You tell him, "You can't go outside to play until your room is cleaned."

He says, "I don't care. I didn't want to go outside and play. I'm going to watch TV."

You think, "What am I going to do now?"

The answer—nothing. The rule sticks. With this example, getting the room clean is actually the *fourth* thing you're trying to accomplish. The first thing you are trying to achieve is to make him aware that a consequence will occur if he cleans the room and an entirely different one will occur if he does not.

The second thing we are trying to achieve is to teach the child that he is responsible for his behavior. "Only you can determine when you go outside to play. You are responsible for what happens to you."

The third thing you're trying to accomplish is to teach him that you're going to do what he tells you to do. You're going to follow through consistently with consequences. The consequences depend on his actions.

"If you don't clean your room, you're telling me you don't

want to play. I'm going to be sure it happens. If you clean your room, you're telling me you want to go outside. I'll follow through with that."

Getting the room cleaned is actually the fourth thing you are trying to accomplish.

Sometimes you battle with your child all day—homework, bath time, picking up. If you try to win each battle by forcing the child to do what you want, you'll be fighting the same battles until the child leaves home. You win each battle, but your child doesn't develop any independent or responsible behavior. It's better to lose a few battles but win the war. Experiencing consequences today gets more cooperation tomorrow.

You tell your daughter to take her bath, "If you are in and out of the bath tub by 7 pm, you can watch TV. If you do not bathe, you will go straight to bed at 7 pm. She refuses to bathe and goes straight to bed. You think, "I've lost. She won." But it is more important that she experiences the consequences of not taking her bath than for you to win the bath battle. Your child won't die if she doesn't take a bath, do her homework or clean her room. Experiencing the consequences today will get you more cooperation tomorrow.

For behaviors that are dangerous or may produce injury, you may have to control her or get her to do what you request when you request it. But most of the time you can forget about the battles and focus on the war.

Certain environments accentuate problems

Many children inherit their pleasure-oriented personality characteristics. But certain environments produce or accentuate existing stubborn and strong-willed personality aspects.

Children who are in more control than their parents may show these features. This may occur in situations when there is a lack of supervision. The parent isn't around, and the child sets his own limits and restrictions. In other environments, the parents may be present, but they don't set limits. Spoiling, giving into him and catering to his every need also produces a situation in which the child has no limits. He can do whatever he pleases. See Spoiling, Chapter 58; Developing Responsible Behavior, Chapter 40; and Who's In Control? Chapter 31, for more information.

A child in an inconsistent environment may also show some of these personality characteristics. Separations or moving to a new house may affect some children. An inconsistent approach to discipline may also result in an increase in these personality characteristics. See Chapter 19, Effects of Divorce, Separation, Parental Conflict & Other Environmental Changes on Behavior, for more information.

What Have I Done to Cause This Behavior?

Heredity may have had a large part in your child's behavior. This is usually evident in a family with more than one child. Other children in the same family may have totally opposite personality characteristics. See Chapter 15, Children Have Personalities, for additional information. The most important question is not, "Why?" the child is like he is, but "How do I deal with his personality and behavior?"

61

Temper Tantrums, Whining & Similar Behavior

A particular cluster of behavior patterns in children occurs. Behavior ranges from severe temper tantrums to silly facial expressions. It includes whining, pouting, crying and repeatedly asking similar questions or making statements ("Why can't I do it? Please let me go. I'll be good. Come on, give me one more chance."). It occurs for one of two reasons; the behavior gets a reaction from the parent, or the behavior manipulates others so the child gets his way.

Analyze behavior to find what the child gets out of it. Is he getting you mad, upset, angry or nervous? Is he getting his way? Is the answer is yes, ignore the behavior. When these actions are first seen, immediately withdraw all attention from the child so his misbehavior receives no reinforcement.

If ignoring is used but the behavior doesn't change, try other consequences. Deal with behavior in a calm manner, withdrawing all negative attention. Set up a behavior chart using reward for appropriate behavior or response-cost punishment for the target behavior. See Chapters 9 and 10, Ignoring Specific Behavior and Using Charts to Change Behavior.

62

Thumb-Sucking

Thumb-sucking or finger-sucking is common among young children. Some believe this behavior results from a lack of sufficient sucking experiences in infancy. Other theories say it also results in children who are allowed to suck. Other explanations have also been given. Although there are many theories to explain the behavior, thumb-sucking occurs in two general situations.

Child is born sucking thumb

Some children are born sucking their thumbs or fingers. Other children start sucking their thumbs early. It seems as if they have always sucked their thumbs. They have a strong habit, and the behavior continues past an acceptable age.

Behavior appears later

Other children have not sucked their thumbs or stopped for a long period of time. Then the behavior appears later.

Causes

Habit

A child may be brought to you in the hospital sucking his thumb and continue as he grows older. Some start at an early age and continue.

Regressive behavior

A child goes back to an earlier form of behavior or level of development. This may occur when the child experiences trauma, emotional upset or changes or significant shifts in his or the family's routines. It could be major changes (divorce, birth of a sibling, death in the family) or other changes (the child he used to play with moves, change in parents' work hours).

It doesn't have to be a "negative" or obviously upsetting change (separation, marital conflict). It could involve "positive" changes (move to a new house with a swimming pool, Mom stops working).

The fact a shift in the routine or the child's environment occurred is the important factor. Some children respond to unpredictable, changing environments by going back to an earlier form of behavior where they experienced less pressure or stress. A child may not have sucked his thumb at all. When he is 3, a brother is born, and he starts sucking his thumb. A child may first show this behavior at 5, when his parent's marital conflict became more intense.

An unstructured environment can also exist in situations where consistent limits are not placed on a child's behavior. This occurs when there is a lack of discipline, spoiling, one parent telling the child one thing and the other contradicting it, inconsistency in the parent's interaction with the child. The insecurity or uncertainty the child experiences in this situation is expressed through this type of regressive behavior.

Dependency

Children who are excessively dependent on their parents or siblings, overprotected and babied often fail to develop age-appropriate behavior. These children appear to resist growing up in many areas. This behavior may be included along with others.

Models

If a child's older sibling sucks his thumb, the younger brother or sister may learn this behavior.

Treatment

Treat the behavior matter-of-factly. Don't punish, yell, criticize, belittle or embarrass the child. Deal with this behavior in a calm, rational way. Ignoring it may be the best way to deal with it initially. Other techniques can be tried if this is ineffective. Stay calm.

Most children reduce the behavior when they start school

or their interaction with their peers increases. Many children also stop thumb-sucking when their permanent teeth appear.

Stabilize environment

Look for areas of upset, and try to stabilize the child's environment. A new home, change of school or parental conflict may contribute to the child's behavior. Provide more structure, consistency and predictability in the overall environment. See Chapter 4, Being a Consistent Parent; Chapter 5, Setting Rules for Behavior; and Chapter 19, Effects of Divorce, Separation, Parental Conflict & Other Environmental Changes.

Let the child grow up

Treat the child according to his age. Do *not* baby the child or allow him to be excessively dependent on you. Don't do things for him you know he can do for himself.

Avoid overprotection. Promote independent and age-appropriate behavior in many areas. See Dependent Behavior, Chapter 39, and Spoiling, Chapter 58, for more information.

Use positive consequences

Use rewards for the child when he doesn't suck his thumb. Identify times when the child sucks his thumb (quiet time, watching TV, before he goes to sleep). Then set up a chart. The periods he doesn't suck his thumb, something positive will happen. See Chapter 10, Using Charts to Change Behavior, for additional techniques.

Although ignoring is the best method to deal with this behavior initially, thumb-sucking may interfere with the growth of the child's teeth. If this occurs, the child may need braces. Although this behavior may not be significant, the cost of braces may be. It's wise to try to modify this behavior before it interferes with the normal development of his teeth.

Counseling and psychotherapy

Counseling the child with this problem is ineffective. Counseling for you may be beneficial to learn effective behavior-modification techniques to deal with this behavior.

Consult dentist who is familiar with problem

In extreme cases, orthodontic devices can be placed in the mouth to reduce thumb-sucking.

Security objects

Some children may have security objects associated with some of their routines (going to sleep, sucking a thumb). These objects usually associated with this behavior are stuffed animals, blankets or smooth material (satin on the end of a blanket).

Try to eliminate these security objects at an early age (before 18 months). But if the security objects are not offensive to you and not harmful to your child, you may decide to let them persist until he gives them up on his own.

There is no hard-and-fast rule about when children should abandon security objects. If the security object is associated with the thumb-sucking, it may be easier to change the behavior if the security object is no longer present. For example, if a child always sucks his thumb when he has his favorite blanket, it may be easier to reduce thumb-sucking if the need for the blanket is eliminated.

Positive consequences can also be used to modify the need for security objects are associated with the behavior that you are trying to reduce. See the appropriate chapters under Ssection I, Methods and Techniques, for more information.

63

Tics, Nervous Habits
& Tourette Syndrome

Tic disorders usually appear in childhood. The average age of onset is 7. They often begin suddenly with a single tic. Eye-blinking and head movements are most common. *Tics* are spasmodic, frequently repeated, stereotyped movements that are not rhythmic. Although they can sometimes be suppressed for short periods, tics are not under the child's voluntary control. Movements are purposeless and usually stop with sleep. They typically become worse with emotional stress. The eyes, face, neck and shoulders are most often affected. Other muscles or muscle groups may be involved.

Tics may be fleeting, episodic or chronic. A single tic may vanish, sometimes to be replaced by a different one. Several tics may develop at the same time, one after the other.

Until fairly recently, tics were considered psychological or emotional. Neurological and genetic factors are now believed to be of major importance.

Disorders involving tics are generally divided into categories according to the age they begin, how long they last and the presence of vocal or phonic tics in addition to motor tics.

Types of Tic Disorders

Transient tic disorders

Temporary tics often begin during the early school years. Common tics include eye blinking, nose puckering, grimacing and squinting. Temporary vocalizations *(phonations)* are less common and include various throat sounds, sniffing, humming or other distracting noises. Childhood tics may be bizarre, such as licking the palm or poking and pinching the genitals.

These temporary tics may last only weeks or a few months. They are usually not associated with specific behavioral or school problems. They are noticeable with heightened excitement or fatigue.

As with all tic syndromes, boys are 3 to 4 times more often affected than girls. While transient tics do not persist for more than 1 year, it is not uncommon for a child to have a series of temporary tics over several years.

Chronic tic disorders

These tics are differentiated from transient ones by their relatively unchanging character and their duration over many years.

Chronic multiple tics

An individual has several chronic motor tics. It isn't easy to draw the lines between transient, chronic and chronic multiple tics.

Tourette Syndrome

Gilles de la Tourette Syndrome (Tourette Syndrome) is a tic condition that begins in early childhood or adolescence. The first symptoms usually are frequent and repetitive motor or involuntary movements of the face, arms, limbs, and/or trunk.

The most common first symptom is a facial tic (eye blink, nose twitch, grimace). It is replaced or added to by other tics of the neck, trunk and/or limbs. In most cases there are multiple tics.

Involuntary movements may be complicated, involving the entire body, such as kicking, stamping or hopping. Other symptoms, such as touching and repetitive thoughts and movements, can also occur. Compulsive behavior, such as breaking objects, checking repeatedly to see if doors are locked or the stove is off, may appear.

There are also verbal or phonic tics. Phonic tics (noises) are usually added to the involuntary movements or may replace one or more of the motor tics. They may include a wide variety of sounds, such as grunting, throat clearing, shouting, barking, inarticulate sounds, sniffing, snorting and hissing.

Echo phenomena are also reported. These may include repeating words of others, repeating your own words or repeating movements of others. This is called *echolalia*.

Phonic tics are also called *coprolalia* (saying obscene words involuntarily). Researchers estimate coprolalia occurs in less than 25% of Tourette patients at some time in their lives. Neither *echolalia* nor *coprolalia* are essential for the diagnosis. However, all Tourette patients exhibit involuntary movements and some sounds.

A motor tic usually appears first. Involuntary sounds may be the first symptom, or movements and sounds may occur together. For all patients, the development and course of the symptoms follow the same pattern.

Symptoms wax and wane. Old symptoms are replaced by new ones, or new symptoms are added to old ones. Symptoms may lessen during periods of pleasurable concentration. In many cases, the symptoms may disappear for a while (remission). There have been reported cases of complete remission occurring after adolescence.

Children with Tourette Syndrome can expect to live a normal life span. Although the condition is often lifelong and chronic, Tourette Syndrome is not a degenerative disorder.

The disorder is called a *syndrome* rather than a *disease* because its cause is unknown and diagnosis is based on a group of symptoms.

Nervous Habits

Some habits or behaviors people see as "nervous" are not caused by psychological or emotional factors. They have more of a physical, genetic or neurological basis. These tic disorders are described above. Other "nervous behavior" may be the result of pressure, stress or emotional factors. Some behaviors may be seen as habits that have developed over time. These include nail-biting, knuckle-cracking, chewing on clothing, hair twisting or curling, picking sores, pulling out hair and other obsessive-compulsive behaviors (rituals).

These behaviors seem to occur in two ways. First, the child has had the behavior a long time or since you can remember.

The behavior may have started when the child was young or he was born with it (a child may have twisted his hair in the nursery at the hospital or another child has been biting his fingernails or finger since he was an infant).

The second situation occurs when a child who has not shown the behavior starts exhibiting it (a 9-year-old starts biting his fingernails, a 7-year-old starts pulling out hair).

Emotional and psychological factors

When a child has not shown a behavior then starts exhibiting it, the behaviors are more likely to be a result of emotional factors (stress, pressure, frustration, conflict, unstable home-situation, insecurity, uncertainty).

When a child begins to show a behavior, try to identify possible changes in the environment or other things that might be causing stress (marital conflict, school difficulties, peer problems, lack of confidence). The first attempt to deal with a nervous habit is to stabilize the environment or try to eliminate or reduce the stress of frustration.

Obsessive-compulsive behavior

Another "nervous habit" related to emotional difficulties is obsessive-compulsive behavior. This behavior includes unpleasant thoughts or repetitive impulses performed in a meaningless or ritualistic way. An *obsession* is a constant preoccupation with a given thought or a complex of related thoughts a person cannot "shake." A *compulsion* is an irresistible urge to do some kind of action.

Obsessive-compulsive symptoms vary in complexity from ordinary trivial little acts (tapping, counting, snapping the fingers, saying a set word or phrase over and over, imagining a sound or scene) to complex ceremonials carried out in fixed, unvarying sequences (handwashing, having to do the exact same routine every morning, retracing your steps, repeating opening and closing doors, locking and relocking doors).

The thoughts or rituals occur to deal with anxiety and/or to prevent something terrible from happening. Psychological intervention is usually needed.

Habits

Some behaviors can be seen as habits. These behaviors

occur in two situations. First, the actions seem to have always existed. Secondly, some habits are established as a result of pressure or change and continue after the stress has disappeared. A child might start biting his fingernails because of difficulties at school. When school is over and he doesn't fail, he continues to show this.

Several things can be done to deal with nervous habits that do not have a physical basis.

Counseling and psychotherapy

For the behaviors associated with Tourette Syndrome or neurological problems, this form of treatment is very ineffective. Counseling may be beneficial for children showing behaviors that have an emotional basis. A mental-health professional may be able to help you set up a behavior modification to reduce or change the habit.

See Chapter 23, Selecting Psychological Services, and the ones under the section on Methods and Techniques for additional information.

Reduce models

When your child shows a behavior similar to yours, your spouse's or his sibling's, he may have learned it from the model. Change your behavior, or don't model the behavior in front of the child.

Identify stress and change

If there is new pressure or instability in the environment (move, marital conflict, divorce) and it can be identified and changed, the behavior in the child may also change.

Use positive consequences

Avoid the use of criticism, guilt, ridicule or excessive punishment to deal with this behavior. Use reward, positive consequences and incentives for showing appropriate behavior rather than negative consequences when the undesirable behavior occurs.

Tourette Syndrome

Many children who have Tourette Syndrome have trouble in school, are difficult to manage and show symptoms of overactivity/attention-deficit disorder.

Tourette Syndrome, mentioned in medical journals since Dr. Gilles de la Tourette identified it in 1885, is still poorly understood and constantly misdiagnosed. It is most often misdiagnosed as an emotional problem, which it is not. It is difficult to live with bizarre symptoms at home and in a school environment. Imagine how it must feel to twitch, jerk and yelp uncontrollably without even knowing why your body is doing such strange things. People with Tourette Syndrome suffer for 7 to 10 years, often through high school, before they are properly identified.

Although more doctors are able to accurately diagnose the syndrome (due in great part to the recent efforts of the Tourette Syndrome Association), about 60% of all newly diagnosed patients diagnose themselves after reading a popular article or viewing a program about Tourette Syndrome. Hopefully, the information in this chapter will help identify other cases.

Characteristics of Tourette Syndrome

A Tourette patient may exhibit one or more of these tics, depending on the severity of the case.

eyeblinking	grunting	picking at things
facial twitches	inarticulate sounds	(clothing)
sniffing	stuttering	obsessive thinking
head jerks	blocking	(recurring
shoulder jerks	touching part	thoughts)
arm movements	of body	repetition (saying
finger or hand	touching other	words or phrases
movements	people	over and over)
stomach jerks	touching objects	echolalia
kicking	self-abusive	(repeating what
leg movements	behavior	someone else
low noises	emotional ups	just said)
loud noises	and downs	
coprolalia	low frustration	
(obscene words)	tolerance	
words out of	anger, temper fits	
context	compulsive	
throat clearing	behaviors (rituals)	

Behavior problems

Many children with the syndrome have behavioral problems. Sometimes their difficulties in behavior can be more disabling than the tics. There are three general areas of difficulty.

Behaviors that are part of the neurological syndrome— These include many characteristics of overactivity (irritability, impulsiveness, low frustration tolerance, attentional problems, overactivity). Also included is obsessive thinking, with thought intrusions and compulsive ritualistic behaviors. Occasional self-destructive behaviors are also seen.

Complications or side effects of medication—When drugs are given to treat the tics, sedation, intellectual dulling, mental clouding, memory problems, lack of motivation, restlessness, irritability or depression are some side effects. School avoidance or phobia and related behavior may occur at times.

Personality and environmental factors—This group is more difficult to define because it may involve many problems. These behaviors develop as a reaction to having to grow up and live with a handicap. In addition, symptoms wax and wane. This may be a source of stress itself. The teased child may become aggressive, withdrawn or develop a poor self-concept, depending on his personality.

Adolescence is a time of significant emotional turmoil. Unfortunately, this is often the time when Tourette symptoms intensify and become worse. It isn't hard to imagine how difficult this time may be for the adolescent. Psychological reaction may include social withdrawal, depression, anger, rage and a general sense of frustration. Often this is expressed as anger toward the family. Special care must be taken in trying to understand the stresses, particularly during this period.

Treating behavioral difficulties

Some behavior problems associated with the neurological disorder can be treated with medication. Disorders relating to medication side effects can often be dealt with and minimized by careful monitoring of dose and schedule.

The most difficult behavioral problems are those resulting from psychological factors. The best way to handle this is from a combined medical/psychological approach. Support of family and friends may be sufficient to help the child cope with the stress. Psychological counseling should be considered.

Extra help is needed because family support alone may not be sufficient to deal with the pressures of having the syndrome. Psychological counseling, psychotherapy, relaxation and similar forms of treatment do *not* improve the neurological components (tics, overactivity, attention deficits) of this syndrome, but this counseling may help the child deal with socialization problems, a lack of confidence and anger. Be sure the therapist is very familiar with this syndrome.

Overactivity/attention-deficit disorder

Parents of many children with this syndrome initially become concerned with their child because of increased levels of activity or attention problems. They are contacted by their child's teacher, or they consult a pediatrician or mental-health professional because of some of the overactivity symptoms. See Chapter 52, Overactivity, Attention-deficit Disorder & Hyperactivity, for more information on characteristics of this behavior.

I have seen children in kindergarten with overactivity symptoms who showed no symptoms of Tourette Syndrome. However, characteristics of the syndrome emerged as they got older. Some overactive children may show some of the symptoms of Tourette Syndrome, such as tics, when placed on stimulant medication.

The most-common behavioral problems associated with Tourette Syndrome involve the regulation of attention and activity. At least 50% of children with the syndrome exhibit diagnostic criteria for attention-deficit disorder (poor attention, difficulty concentrating, distractibility, impulsivity) and/or hyperactivity (fidgety movements, increased levels of activity).

Overactive characteristics may originate early in the preschool years and precede the onset of tics. Overactive characteristics tend to worsen with the tics. Attention problems and hyperactivity are the primary factors that affect school achievement in children with this syndrome. Learning disabilities are also very common.

Medication

Medication is the only proven effective treatment for Tourette Syndrome. Psychotherapy may be useful in relation to personality and adjustment difficulties and peer relations. But as a rule, tics are not responsive to psychotherapy.

Tourette Syndrome symptoms can be reduced in many cases through careful use of drugs. Medication can control about 70% of symptoms for most patients while they take the medication. In about 5% of all cases, there has been complete remission, with medication no longer required.

Haloperidol (Haldol®)—Since the 1960s, haloperidol has been the drug of choice for treating Tourette Syndrome. Haloperidol is most effective at low doses.

Those who don't respond to low doses of haloperidol may sustain a reduction of symptoms at higher doses. But results are never as satisfying, and side effects limit the drug's usefulness.

Up to 80% of patients with Tourette Syndrome initially benefit from haloperidol, sometimes dramatically. However, long-term follow-up suggests a smaller number, perhaps 20 to 30%, continue haloperidol for an extended period of time. Patients often discontinue haloperidol because of side effects.

School phobias may appear during the first weeks of treatment with low doses of haloperidol. While the tic symptoms improve, social phobias may involve acute anxiety about going to school or performing at school. This can be extremely disabling. When these phobias are not recognized as drug side effects, they can continue for months. They remit within weeks of stopping haloperidol.

Intellectual dulling leads to marked worsening of school and work performance. Children who are A students and have many friends may become C students, show a lack of interest and become isolated. School avoidance may become extreme.

School avoidance may be improved by reducing the dosage. But tics may emerge. It may be better to have the tics and reduce the side effect of school avoidance. If the tics must be minimized, a change in medication may be necessary.

Long-term use of medication often complicates the understanding of the emergence of social and personality difficulties. Side effects may have considerable impact on a child's sense of self-control, autonomy, self-esteem and cognitive and social competence.

Medication may alter how a child's body feels to himself and how he experiences the working of his mind. Additionally, the use of any medication may alter a child's daily schedule and focus parental and other adult concern on small changes in symptoms and side effects. It ties the child to the care and attention of many adults.

Clonidine (Catapres®)—Clonidine seems useful in reducing simple motor and phonic symptoms. At times it may help to improve attention problems and helping complex motor and phonic symptoms.

Clonidine is started at low doses and slowly increased over several weeks. It tends to work more slowly than haloperidol. When large doses are used earlier, improvement may occur sooner, but there may be more sedation. With a slower increase, clonidine may take 3 weeks or longer to show a beneficial effect.

The patient may experience a reduction in tension, a feeling of being calm or a sense of having a "longer fuse" before tics are reduced. A gradual decrease in complex motor tics and compulsions also may precede improvement in simple tics. Evaluation of the medication's effectiveness may not be possible before 3 to 4 months.

When there is a positive response, improvement may progressively appear many months and even up to a year or more later. Patients gain confidence in themselves, adjust better to school, feel less irritable and have fewer tic symptoms. These therapeutic benefits reinforce each other.

Clonidine has only recently been used in Tourette Syndrome. The longest individual treatment has lasted about 5 years. Children with extremely severe Tourette Syndrome have benefited from treatment over this length of time. Only very slight increases in medication have been required at times.

The major side effect of clonidine is sedation, which appears early in the course of treatment, especially if the dose is increased quickly. It tends to lessen after several weeks. A few patients have dry mouth, but children seem to have this less often than adults. Rarely, patients will feel that things are "too bright," perhaps because of impairment of pupillary contraction.

At high doses, there may be hypotension and dizziness. This is more likely if clonidine is given at high doses quite early. At lower doses, blood pressure is not clinically affected, although a fall of pressure can be detected. Increased irritability, nightmares and insomnia have also been reported.

Pimozide (Orap®)—Pimozide has been shown to be at least as effective as haloperidol in treating Tourette Syndrome and is probably less sedating. Major side effects are similar to haloperidol.

Pimozide causes EKG changes in up to 25% of patients. Those receiving pimozide should receive an EKG before treatment, every several months and at points of dosage increase. This medication is approved for use in children over 12. Data is limited for younger children.

Phenothiazines—Some patients respond well to phenothiazines (fluphenazine). For the patient who cannot tolerate haloperidol, a trial with phenothiazine may be indicated. Side effects are similar to haloperidol.

Stimulants—A particularly important risk factor in tics and Tourette Syndrome is the use of stimulant medication. Over 25% of all Tourette Syndrome patients have had a course of stimulant medication early in the emergence of their behavioral or tic symptoms. They are incorrectly diagnosed as having attention-deficit disorder and hyperactivity. Over the last several years, series of cases have been reported in which the use of stimulants correlated with the onset of motor and phonic tics.

A small number of all children treated with stimulant medication develop simple motor tics (eye blinking, nose puckering) that disappear with reduction or termination of the medication. It is controversial whether stimulants can actually trigger or produce prolonged chronic multiple tics or Tourette Syndrome. However, this seems to have occurred in many cases. Stimulants may merely "unmask" an underlying and pre-existing tendency to tics.

Stimulants must be used cautiously with attention-deficit-disorder children who have a close relative with tics. Do not use stimulants with attention-deficit-disorder children who have a close relative with Tourette Syndrome. Stop stimulant use if tics develop in children who previously were tic-free.

Stimulant medications most frequently used include Dexedrine,[®] Ritalin,[®] Cylert[®] and Ritalin-SR.[®] See Chapter 52, Overactivity, Attention-deficit Disorder & Hyperactivity, for a detailed discussion of these medications.

Things to consider

1. Follow your doctor's instructions about medication for your child. There are many things your doctor may not tell you.
2. Let your child be responsible for taking his own medication if he is old enough. Buy him a pill container with sections for each day.
3. The medication may make your child tire easily. An earlier bedtime may be needed.
4. Check with your doctor about medication interactions.
5. Don't overmedicate your child. No medication will eliminate 100% of the child's symptoms. No pill will remove all traces of the disorder.

Alternative or different treatments

Some parents seek alternative treatments for their child when commonly used therapies don't work. People afflicted with any chronic illness may seek unconventional treatments, services or devices.

Every time you take your child to a different doctor or try a different medication, you reinforce the child's feeling he is "different" or "sick." He may become a perpetual patient.

Since 1825, when leeches were used to try to reduce the tics of Tourette Syndrome, other treatments have been tried with little or no success. Other medications are being tested for controlling the tics of Tourette Syndrome. Becoming involved with the Tourette Syndrome Association will keep you informed of new research and treatments.

School Concerns for
the Child with Tourette Syndrome

At least 30 to 40% of children with Tourette Syndrome have

serious school-performance handicaps that require special intervention. Teachers, nurses, psychologists, guidance counselors and administrators can play a vital role in the lives of these students in two very distinct ways. One is to help identify new cases and refer them for help. The second is in skillfully handling the child in the educational setting.

The first is easier to achieve. Teachers are in an excellent position to save many children from years of torment and embarrassment.

The second way educators can dramatically affect the lives of students with Tourette Syndrome is how they handle this special child in the classroom situation.

Confidence

The most important thing a teacher can do for a child with Tourette is to foster feelings of self-worth and self-esteem. It is difficult to get past the twitches and yelps to the "real" child, but it is worth the effort. Tourette children have redeeming positive qualities that can be tapped to bolster their self-image.

A teacher sensitive to a child's need to feel good about himself can find many opportunities to promote these feelings. Treating a child with sensitivity and respect will have an indelible and positive effect on his life.

Let the child know he is doing a good job. Praise him for things you might take for granted with another child. Stress the positive things he does, not the negative.

Compassion

Tolerance and compassion can be taught to students. When the classroom atmosphere encourages feelings of human kindness, tolerance and compassion, benefits accrue to society as a whole. The lesson isn't learned overnight, but it is well worth the extended effort.

Very often dislike or rejection of another person is based on fear of the unknown. A teacher who takes the trouble to educate himself concerning the limitations or symptoms of a particular disability can share with his class his knowledge. This can help the entire group to overcome a major stumbling block to acceptance. An older Tourette student expressed this thought, "All I ever wanted was for my teachers to understand

and accept me. Underneath my tics and noises, I'm a person just like anyone else."

Learning problems

Some Tourette Syndrome students have accompanying learning disabilities. Understanding how to deal with the learning-disabled child can often be confusing for a teacher, even without the added complication of Tourette Syndrome.

Teachers and parents consistently note characteristics of impulsivity among Tourette Syndrome children. Another frequently reported problem is a student may appear to "get stuck" with an activity or an action. When teachers understand, they are more likely to have the patience to cope. Some Tourette Syndrome children have problems "getting started" and may need individualized encouragement.

Most students have difficulty concentrating. This is especially true for Tourette students taking medication. Many Tourette children have difficulty in school because of attentional problems and overactivity. This is the source of most of their academic trouble.

The pace must be modified for these learners so they are not penalized for patterns of behavior that are out of their control. Methods of evaluating and reporting such students should also be modified to meet their individual needs. Progress and learning for a child with Tourette Syndrome should be measured according to his own potential and abilities.

Students sensitive about their learning problems and fearing they will be laughed at often develop the defensive posture of "class clown." They deliberately act funny and call attention to themselves for silly behavior in the hopes others won't notice their true shortcomings. Teachers should be sensitive to this pattern of behavior and deal with it firmly but kindly.

Getting along with other children

Many children with Tourette Syndrome have problems with socialization or peer interaction. A teacher can often create situations that promote appropriate interaction or the development of friendships. See Chapter 45, Getting Along with Other Children, for more ideas.

Anger

Feelings of anger and frustration may be present in some children. They can be expressed directly or indirectly. For tips on dealing with these emotions, see Chapter 32, Anger—Aggressive and Rebellious Behaviors.

Parental Questions About Tourette Syndrome

How should I react to the news "My child has Tourette Syndrome?" Each parent reacts differently. Some feel relief that there was a name for the disorder. Others feel anger and disbelief.

Share the diagnosis! Once you learn the true nature of your child's condition, use that information to help him. Share it with your child's teachers. Don't feel shame or guilt for your child's condition. Let the grandparents know. Tell the parents of your child's friends so they can be more understanding. Call it by its real name—Tourette Syndrome not "a habit."

Can the tics be controlled? A patient can hold back the tics for a short time, but eventually they burst through. A child may try to control the tics while in school then relax at home. For this reason, the tics often appear worse at home than in the school situation.

Don't ask your child to "try to stop making those noises." It only puts more pressure on him, causing additional stress, which in the long run, may cause him to tic more!

How do I explain what's wrong with my child? It depends on the person with whom you're talking. If you're at a movie and your child is sniffing and hooting, the people in front of you may turn around and say, "Shhh." This isn't the time to get into a discussion about Tourette Syndrome. But if you're at a grocery store and your child begins to shout obscenities to the horror of the little old lady in front of you, it might be appropriate to say, "I'm sorry. He can't help it. It's a neurological disorder." You'll feel better; your child, though self-conscious, will feel better, and the woman may have learned something.

What about family stress? Tourette Syndrome is a family affair. It affects all members of a family. For most, finally having the child diagnosed comes after years of wondering what was wrong, blaming yourselves, each other, the child. Once diagnosed, you begin to come to grips with the situation as individuals and as a family.

Lucky is the child whose parents can talk, acknowledge the tensions and occupy their minds with other things.

But many parents find it difficult to acknowledge their child has an illness. They feel powerless because they "can't make it better." Some react by ignoring the problem. Others stay away from the child; still others want to overprotect the child.

1. *Do* try to encourage your mate to talk out his feelings.

2. *Do* arrange for some time alone as a couple.

3. *Do* continue to develop other interests so your life isn't focused on your child.

What do I tell my other children? Explain the disorder to your other children. They need to understand why their sibling behaves as he does. If they can be frank and unembarrassed, they can help ease the way for the youngster with Tourette Syndrome.

How do I deal with relatives? Often your family is the most difficult to handle. Grandparents may feel the child needs a good spanking, even though you've explained what is wrong. Continue to sound like a broken record! "He can't help sniffing, Grandma. It's not his adenoids; it's Tourette Syndrome that causes him to make all those noises." If you say nothing, your child may feel you think he *could* stop if he wanted to. He needs to know you support him at all times.

How can I help my child? By being understanding and showing you still love and care for him. Listen to his hurts and encourage him to talk out his embarrassments. Your child knows he's making noises and jerking. He wants to stop even more than you want him to!

Include him in all family activities. Encourage him to participate in normal interpersonal relationships and to tell friends about his disorder. *Don't* allow your child to hide from people. *Don't* let him refer to his tics as a "habit." That suggests that he could stop with self-control. He can't!

What about discipline? Don't punish your child for any of his tics. But many parents are torn between symptoms of Tourette Syndrome or the effects of the medications, and what is simply being naughty. "What is him, and what's the disorder?" asked one mother.

Fatigue or stress worsen some Tourette symptoms and make the child irritable. Children with Tourette Syndrome or any other chronic condition soon learn how to manipulate their parents by playing on their concern.

Scientific evidence suggests some extreme ranges of emotion may be part of the Tourette symptoms. There might be a subcategory of Tourette children who have difficulty inhibiting their moods. Some have difficulty "cooling down." Their anger grows out of proportion and becomes a temper tantrum. They may also have spells of laughter or silliness they can't control.

Any behavior that is unacceptable must be controlled. If you don't maintain discipline, you'll have a spoiled youngster. Use positive methods of discipline to determine what behaviors he can and can't control. See chapters listed under the Methods and Techniques section for more information.

What do I tell the teacher? Learn all you can about Tourette Syndrome. Teach those who come in contact with your child about Tourette Syndrome—the teachers, school nurses, counselors, physical education instructors.

If the teacher is understanding and explains the problems to the other students, chances are your child will be more readily accepted by his peers.

Intelligence is not affected by this disorder, nor does the child deteriorate mentally. IQ scores of children with Tourette Syndrome run the same as the general public. However, some medications may cause a dulling effect. Achievement in school may be affected. In some cases, IQ-testing procedures must be modified for the Tourette child.

Your child may have difficulty concentrating, suffer from fatigue and fall asleep in class until he is used to the medication. If your child has poor concentration, he should be given extra time on tests. If your child has an arm tic, suggest that he be seated on the opposite side of classmates so he won't hit them. If it bothers him to have children sitting in back of him, ask that he be seated in the back of the classroom.

Some children have added difficulty in the classroom because they also suffer from hyperactivity and/or learning disabilities. Some teachers can't tolerate the child's behavior in the classroom because the symptoms are so disruptive. Many children were excluded from the classroom and were taught at home or sent to special schools or classes.

But times have changed. Federal Law P.L. 94-142, the Education for All Handicapped Children Act, mandates a "free, appropriate education" for all handicapped children in the United States. A child with Tourette Syndrome can and should be educated in the "least-restrictive environment," using supplementary aids and services.

Conclusion

Each case of Tourette Syndrome is unique to the person who has it. It's important to realize you're not alone, and your child is not the only one who suffers from this unusual disorder. If other people know your child suffers from a physical disorder, they tend to be understanding and sympathetic.

If you feel your child shows some of the symptoms of this syndrome, contact your pediatrician or a pediatric neurologist. Contact the Tourette Syndrome Association; they'll send you a list of physicians and mental-health professionals in your area who are familiar with this syndrome.

For more information write or call:

Tourette Syndrome Association
42-40 Bell Blvd.
Bayside, NY 11361-2857
(718) 224-2999
(800) 237-0717

64

Toilet Training

W hen you begin toilet-training your child, how long it takes to complete and how many mistakes your child will make aren't particularly important. It's important for toilet training to be completed in a positive, cooperative manner. Avoid using punishment, criticism, getting upset, screaming, yelling or other negative methods to deal with the situation.

When Do I Start Toilet Training?

There are many opinions about when to start toilet training. One rule is the earlier you begin, the more time it will take to complete training. One mother may begin training when her child is 13 months old and complete it when he is 19 months old (training time—6 months). Another mother might start at 19 months and complete the training when the child is 21 months old (training time—2 months). However, this rule is generally true when applied within reasonable limits. It wouldn't apply if you started training when the child was 5 years old!

When your child is about 15 months old—certainly by 20 months—he may start to give you signals he is ready to begin toilet training. Children vary in their physical and mental development, as well as in bladder control. There are three general areas you can assess to help you determine whether the child is ready to begin toilet training.

Does he seem to have bladder control? Is he aware when he is about to or has wet or soiled?

His diaper may be dry for longer periods of time (2 or 3

hours). He may urinate a good deal at one time rather than small amounts frequently throughout the day. He may indicate he wants his diaper changed as soon as it is wet or soiled. He may pull at his diaper or show facial or bodily expressions when he knows he is about to urinate.

If he shows any of these signs or any other signs that suggest to you he is aware of his toileting behavior, he probably has enough bladder control to begin training.

Is he developed physically?

The child is able to walk fairly well without the need of assistance. He appears to have good finger and hand coordination so he can pick up objects easily.

Can he follow instructions?

He knows or can point to parts of his body when asked (nose, eyes, mouth, hair). He follows simple directions, such as "Sit down in the chair. Come to Mama. Get that book. Come with Mama to the refrigerator to get a drink."

He will imitate behaviors you show to him (playing patty cake) and may place one familiar object into another or put blocks in a box. If he's able to follow most instructions, he is intellectually capable to begin training.

If the child doesn't show sufficient bladder control, awareness of when he has wet or soiled or doesn't have sufficient physical development, delay toilet training. These aspects are highly dependent on physical maturation, and time will tend to improve these skills.

If your child has difficulty following instructions, you might want to work on trying to develop these skills before you begin toilet training. Once he can follow simple directions and has the other aspects, you could begin toilet training.

There are some situations where a child will show adequate behaviors in all three areas but still resists toilet training. If this happens, delay toilet training. If the child shows stubborn, strong-willed behaviors in many areas of his life, help him develop more cooperative behaviors before you begin toilet training.

Training with Models

Several things can be done before starting toilet training. These indirectly help the child learn this process.

Have the child assist you when you are dressing him, especially in pulling his pants up and down. He may not able to do this on his own and may require some assistance from you (you pull up his pants to a certain spot and let him complete the process).

Have the child watch others (mom, dad, brother, sister) successfully use the toilet. Go through each step with him. Teach him words to use in potty training (wet, dry, sit down, pull down your pants, urination, pee, wee wee, poo poo) or any words you will use in trying to train him. Try to teach him to be cooperative with you and follow simple instructions. Use reward and praise when he follows directions.

Training

Usually the mother is the one who initiates training with the child. But anyone who has a relationship with the child can do the toilet training. This could be a grandparent, older sibling, nursery-school teacher, neighbor. The most important thing for the person to keep in mind is this process has to be followed very consistently, in a very positive manner. Avoid confrontation, getting upset and excessive negative attention.

Toilet training should take place in the most convenient location of the house (the kitchen, the den, the room where more time is spent). The process may be made a little easier by starting toilet training in a room where much time is spent, it isn't carpeted and rewards are readily accessible.

Once the child is successful in this setting, move the potty closer to the bathroom and eventually into the bathroom. Identify appropriate rewards or incentives for the child. They could be material things (candy, drinks) or activities (going outside, reading a story, riding a bike, playing a game). They should be small and of short duration (a small piece of candy, an activity that is over in a few minutes). Try to identify things that are important to the child. It may involve using the same thing most of the time or it may be a variety of activities.

Have the child wear toilet-training pants a few sizes too

large so he'll be able to get them on and off easily.

Eliminate as many distractions as possible during the training procedure. Minimize toys, TV and your involvement in other activities (cooking). Focus your attention on the training procedures. Give your child undivided attention. Don't allow any event or person to interrupt this process. If the child shows many of the above characteristics, training won't take long.

Use models

Before beginning toilet training, have a model go through the exact procedures required of the child and what the consequences for certain behaviors and actions will be. Ideally the child will learn best from a model who is similar to him (a sibling or another child close to his age). Older siblings, adults or a doll can also be used.

Some books recommend you use a doll that wets to teach the child what specific actions he should learn in toileting and what types of social approval and rewards he can expect to receive for these actions. This can also be done with a sibling who has already been toilet trained.

Complete the procedure with the doll or other sibling. After your child is aware of the procedure, have him ask the questions, take the doll or child through the required motions and give up the verbal approval and reward to the doll.

Now tell the child the doll has to pee pee. Instruct the child to help the doll to the potty chair, lower her pants, sit on the potty and remain quietly on the chair. Help the child when he doesn't follow the instructions appropriately.

When the doll or sibling is on the potty, tell the child to look between the child's legs to see if they are about to pee pee. Then cause the doll to wet or distract the child and do some other method to indicate the child has wet. As soon as this occurs, encourage your child to praise the behavior. "You're a big boy." Have him get excited, clap his hands and use verbal reward and positive attention.

At the same time, tell the child to give the doll the reward (candy, read them a story) as soon as possible. If it is a material reward (candy), have the child give it to the doll as soon as the doll goes in the potty. If it is an activity reward, the child should complete the remainder of the toileting procedure before giving the child the reward. He should help the doll or brother pull up his pants, empty the potty into the toilet and flush the toilet.

After the procedure has been completed, work on emphasizing the importance of being dry. Have the child ask the doll or his brother if they are dry. When the child makes a dry check and the doll is dry, some type of reward can be given. When using this procedure with the child himself, use some type of liquid or favorite drink of the child.

After several dry-pants checks, try to distract the child and spill some water on the doll's training pants. Tell the child to tell the doll he is displeased with the wet pants. If the child hasn't begun talking, use some other method or you could indicate disapproval along with the child. Tell your child to help the doll practice going to the potty by repeating the procedure described above.

Training with the Child

After you complete these procedures with your child several times and he appears to have them down pat, start asking him if his own pants are dry. If they are, give him a reward.

When your child clearly understands the steps involved in toileting, you can discontinue the use of the model and focus more on the child. Start asking him if his pants are dry and make dry-pants checks frequently. Have the child feel his pants to see if they are dry and indicate to you in some way they are. Give a lot of praise and approval for the dry pants, and give him a reward. The reward for dry pants could be extra drinks to create more of a desire to urinate.

Try to establish a time the child goes to the potty and sits. Look for bodily cues to indicate the child has a need to urinate; take him to the potty then.

The first few times you take the child to the potty, you will want him to remain there for a fairly long—maybe 10 minutes. The purpose is to have him urinate in the potty so you can administer the reward. After he has urinated in the potty a few times and receives the reward and praise, he should begin to realize he *should* do this. As the urination becomes more frequent, the time required on the potty should be decreased.

After this is done with a fair amount of success, try to have the child initiate the toileting sequence without having to be told or without you with him. To create this independence, start with a direct instruction. "Alan go to the potty." Then change it to a question. "Alan, do you want to potty?"

Ask him frequently whether he must pee pee. Or show him where you potty and continue the statements about his dry pants.

Rewards

After the child has begun to urinate in the potty, use a significant amount of reward and praise for the behavior.

When an accident occurs and he wets his pants, show your disapproval for the wet pants. Then take the child and rehearse or practice the procedure that would have prevented him from wetting his pants. Have him sit on the potty. If possible, have him assume the responsibility for his wet pants. The natural consequence of wetting your pants is you have to take them off and put them where they belong and put on a clean pair.

After the child goes to the potty without a reminder and completes the entire toilet-training experience without instructions or guidance several times, you may consider this behavior is starting to be established. You may want to decrease the emphasis on dry pants and rewards for this behavior. Maintain rewards for going to the potty.

Conclusion

I have given you a very brief outline and steps for successful toilet training. The emphasis is on consistency and being positive with the child. I haven't gone into great detail because you can buy an excellent book, *Toilet Training In Less Than A Day* by N. H. Azrin and R. M. Foxx (1976, Pocketbooks, New York). If you need additional help in this area of behavior, buy a copy.

You may not be able to complete the toilet training in less than a day, but the general methods, procedures and techniques are excellent. If they are followed, it will minimize the problems you experience with your child.

65

Academic & Behavior Problems

Problems that occur in school are often related to academic performance, behavior or a combination of the two. Communication between the parent and teacher or administration is an absolute necessity to deal with problems effectively, such as trouble completing work, passing tests, getting along with other children, paying attention in class, following classroom procedure.

The first step in eliminating the problem is to establish an open line of communication between you and the appropriate school personnel—counselor, teacher, principal. This helps you stay informed about the problem so you can deal with it before it gets out of hand.

I frequently hear parents say, "Why did the teacher wait till Christmas to tell me he wasn't turning in his homework? They didn't tell me he was in danger of failing until the end of the year. If he has been a behavior problem since September, why didn't I know about it sooner? If we had known about this problem when it started, we could have done something about it. Now it's out of hand." Or parents wait 2 to 4 months into the school year or until the first P.T.A. meeting or parent-teacher conference to make contact with the school.

You may have to make first contact

Waiting for the first meeting or for the teacher to contact you is a bad practice, especially if you have a child with a history of difficulty in school or if you suspect some type of problem. You have one child in Mrs. Smith's class, but Mrs. Smith has 30 to 175 other students. Her time for dealing with one student is limited.

Teachers don't always get a positive reaction when they call parents. Parents may be uncooperative, disinterested, blame the school or teacher for the problems or defend the child and not listen to details of the problem. Parent contact often is a negative experience or a waste of time for the teacher, so it may be avoided.

When a teacher encounters a cooperative, concerned parent, he usually makes every effort to open the lines of communication. Even so, it is usually better if you initiate the call or visit rather than waiting for the teacher to call.

Don't assume no news is good news. I often suggest a parent put an "X" on a calendar every 2 or 3 weeks to remind them to talk with the teacher.

Academic Problems

Many parents explain a child's academic troubles by saying, "He's lazy. He's not interested in school. He does not want to work." But there are many other reasons children have difficulty with schoolwork. Some problems may be related to behavior; before one can say a child has a true academic problem, the behavior must be controlled.

Almost all children who have learning difficulties eventually develop behavior problems. A child may have only academic trouble, but after a few months or years of not being able to grasp the material, he won't be able to keep up. He finds himself in a situation where he doesn't understand what's going on in the class. Very little makes sense.

Children who have trouble learning experience a great deal of failure, frustration and negative attention. They are eventually identified as having behavior problems. A discussion of methods for dealing with school-related behavior appears later in this section.

Deal with problems early

Establish good communication between you and the teacher to become aware of and deal with school problems early, before they get out of hand. This is extremely important in effectively correcting academic difficulties. The sooner the problem can be identified, diagnosed and appropriate recommendations made, the easier it is to treat. And it's unlikely that future problems will develop. Many times I see children in fifth or sixth grade who have had academic problems since kindergarten or first grade but for some reason nothing has been done earlier.

Seek professional help

If a child has problems with his schoolwork, seek professional help and get an evaluation as soon as possible. Most school systems have evaluation teams that test and diagnose children who experience learning difficulties. The evaluator should also make recommendations about what can be done to minimize the child's difficulties.

Evaluations can also be obtained from mental-health centers, state agencies or private psychologists. When selecting a person or team to evaluate your child, be sure they are licensed, certified or have the appropriate credentials. You can also ask the child's pediatrician, teacher or school to recommend someone.

Evaluations are extremely helpful in assisting children with learning problems. There are many reasons children have trouble with schoolwork. They may have learning problems due to perceptual-motor deficiencies, to auditory- or visual-processing problems or to poor memory. They may have a poor learning foundation, an achievement level below their grade placement (in fifth grade but reading at a third-grade level) or be slow learners. Appropriate testing will help pinpoint the area of difficulty.

Always having a child evaluated *before* he repeats a grade. Some children may benefit from repeating a grade, but for others special education is necessary to correct their learning problems. See Chapter 75, Learning Disabilities, Chapter 81, Should my Child Repeat the Grade? and Chapter 82, Special Education.

Behavioral Problems

When a child shows behavioral and academic problems, first attend to the behavior before trying to make an accurate assessment of the learning problem. If a child is doing poorly but is not completing his work and not paying attention in class, try to eliminate the interfering behavior.

Look beyond school behavior

The greatest mistake most parents make is they *only* zero in on school behavior. The major problem for Joey is he doesn't follow classroom procedure. You set up a program to deal with this school behavior, but it doesn't work. Why? Because behavior seen at school is only part of a larger behavioral pattern. Taking a broader look at Joey, we see this behavior is typical in many other situations.

A child's behavior is part of his *total* environment. To produce change in one area (school), other areas must also be dealt with. If you isolate only 10% of the behavior and try to change it, there's a strong probability your attempts will fail.

Examine child's total environment

When I work on a child's school-behavior problems, I get the parents to identify situations in the child's total environment where this behavior is also seen. When first trying to produce change, we focus on the behavior at home and in the neighborhood rather than at school. If not listening in school is his major difficulty, we try to get him listening at home before we deal with his academic behavior. If irresponsibility is the source of trouble, we first try to build and establish responsible action at home.

There are several reasons for taking this approach. First, you have more control of the child's behavior at home than at school. You are much closer to the source of the problem. And you deal with a greater variety of situations where the behavior is seen.

Second, in trying to promote change in this fashion, you can deal with a larger portion of the total behavior pattern. The child's irresponsible behavior in school may represent only 10% of the total pattern. By dealing with the behavior at home and in the neighborhood, you may influence 90% of the pattern.

Finally, patterns of behavior develop elsewhere and get transferred to school. If a child has learned to manipulate you to satisfy his needs, there's a strong probability this behavior will be seen at school. The child may do what he pleases, refuse to work when he doesn't feel like it and ignore classroom procedure. Bad behavior developed at home is transferred to school. Get the reverse process to occur.

Produce changes at home

By producing change at home, the new or good behavior can be extended to school. Often we see the child's behavior improve at school without directly working on it. By getting him to listen better or show more responsibility at home, the child's school behavior may improve at the same time. When trying to change any behavior, work with it in the context of its *total environment*. When it starts to change, you may see improvement in areas you have not directly tried to change.

Once a behavior shows significant improvement at home, about 2 weeks later the changes often extend to school. However, sometimes this process doesn't occur easily, and further steps must be taken to help the behavior be seen in school. When you start working directly with the school behavior, increase communication between you and the school.

If you establish some control or change at home but a corresponding improvement at school has not occurred, several techniques can be used. Behavioral charts or some communication procedure may be helpful. Keep the system simple.

Several procedures are described in Chapter 76, Monitoring School Behavior & Performance. Review the chapters in the sections that pertain to the difficulties your child may be having in the academic setting or with schoolwork. These will provide additional techniques to deal with the behavior.

Try positive attention

Children attend school about half of the time they're awake. If you add homework, class projects and school-related activities, it involves 60 to 70% of a child's life. When a child has trouble in school, a large portion of his life involves negative attention. It's very important for you to provide positive attention to children who have school difficulties. These children should receive more positive attention at home than the child who is not experiencing difficulty at school. This is needed to offset the excessive negative attention.

66

Bringing Home Assignments, Books, Tests & Notes

Most children learn quickly if they don't write part of the assignment, they'll have to spend less time on their homework. They'll have more time to play. If they "forget" a book in school, they won't have to study that subject. If a test paper with a failing grade or a bad note from the teacher gets lost, they won't get yelled at or punished. If they lose or "forget" to show a detention until 2 minutes before school on Monday morning, they'll probably be able to play all weekend.

"Mom, a band of gypsies attacked me on the way home from school and took my science test. I don't remember what grade I received."

I often see children a day after they received their report cards. They have "forgotten" the grades they got. Many kids use these behaviors because they work. Other kids are disorganized, distractible and genuinely forgetful. Still other children have trouble in this area because they are irresponsible, lack self-discipline or can't function independently.

Causes

It works

Many children continue to engage in these behaviors because they get away with it. It's more to their advantage not to bring home the required books than to bring them home. The child may see the situation as, "If I bring home my math homework, I'll have to do homework. It'll cut into my play time. If I leave it at school, I'll have more time to play." The consequences of leaving the book at school are much better than those of remembering to bring it home.

The first thing to do in dealing with this type of behavior is you have to stop it from working. Don't let the child get away with it. Make the consequences of his behavior different. The consequences of showing you a math paper at night are better than showing you a math paper in the morning 2 minutes before the bus arrives to take him to school. See Chapter 5, Setting Rules for Behavior, for more information.

Negative attention or punishment centers around schoolwork

If every time I sit down to do homework you yell at me or criticize me, I'm apt to forget what I had for homework or not bring the necessary books home. If I know a failing test gets me restricted for a month, I might lose it.

If your child frequently forgets, loses or doesn't bring home school-related work or materials, look at your method of discipline. If discipline primarily involves negative attention or restrictions, use other methods of discipline. See Chapter 7, Reward, and Chapter 9, Ignoring, for additional types of disciplinary tactics.

Attention-deficit disorder or overactivity

Children with attention problems and/or increased levels of activity forget because of their inability to concentrate and their distractibility. They may have difficulty following directions and tend to be disorganized. See Chapter 52.

Dependent children

These children have a great deal of trouble functioning independently and rely heavily on others for aid and guidance in problem solving, decision making and daily functioning. If your child has some difficulty in this area and shows these characteristics, try to develop an overall level of more independence and self-reliance in many areas of their life. See Chapter 39, Dependent Children, for more information.

Lack of responsibility or self-discipline

Children who are irresponsible in many areas of their life usually show the same behavior in their approach to school-related activities and work. Try to develop an overall level of responsibility in these children. See Chapter 40, Developing Responsible Behavior, for more information.

School not important

Adults realize the importance of education and how doing what you're supposed to do in school directly relates to this. Children don't have the same beliefs. Some children could care less about school and take school as seriously as you and I take Saturday-morning cartoons. They don't care if they receive an A or an F, 0% or 100%. They see school as something they must put up with until it's no longer necessary. For this child, try to develop other incentives to get him to perform the necessary task regarding school. See Chapter 60, Stubborn, Strong-Willed, Pleasure-Oriented Children, for more information.

What Can You Do?

Assignments

A common statement made by some parents is, "The teacher says he's doing poorly because he isn't prepared for class and doesn't do all his homework. I don't know what he has to study or what he has for homework. When I ask him about it, he tells me he finished it at school or has completed everything he has to do."

To help a child do the required assignments, you must know what he has to do to see that it gets done. With some children, this is no problem. But with others, it's a daily mystery. There are several ways to deal with situation. Below are some suggestions.

An assignment book—Provide an assignment book. Have the child write down all the assignments as they are given by the teacher(s). At the end of the period or day, he brings the book to the teacher(s). The teacher writes a name or initials through the assignment. Be sure the teacher marks the assignment so the child can't erase or change what is required. If the child doesn't have any homework or assignment, he should write "no homework" and have the teacher also initial that. (See next page.)

Using this procedure, which requires only a few seconds of the teacher's time, the child is responsible for the entries and having the teacher sign it. This procedure provides *exact*

Reading: PAGES 20-24
Math: problems 4-30, page 40
Science: study Chapter 4

information about the work to be done each night.

Often when I discuss this with a parent, he tells me he tried this method. The teacher agreed to be involved. However, the child forgot or didn't get the assignments signed by the teacher. I usually ask the parent, "What happened to the child when he didn't get the assignment signed?"

In most cases when the system didn't work, the parents did nothing. I then tell them, "The child would have to be stupid to bring it home signed because that would mean he'd have to do the work. By not getting it signed, he didn't have to do the work. The consequences of getting it signed was more to his disadvantage than to his advantage."

If you use this type of system, establish one consequence for getting the assignments signed and a different consequence for not getting it signed. You could establish appropriate rewards or negative consequences for bringing or not bringing home the assignment properly signed. On the days when the assignment is brought home signed, the child might earn extra play time or TV time. When he doesn't, the child does not earn the extra privilege. Or use negative consequences. When assignments are signed, the child can watch TV or play. If they aren't signed, he doesn't watch TV or play.

Home-school communication system—This is similar to the system described in Chapter 76, Monitoring School Behavior and Performance. It can be established to monitor the child on a daily or weekly basis. By using this system, you can tell if the child is doing the required assignments.

Look at all work—If a child tells you he completed a certain assignment in school but the teacher tells you he isn't doing the required assignments, establish a general rule. He must show you *all* completed work; nothing is to be left at school. If something is left in school, you must assume he didn't do it.

This means he has to do it again at home. You must see all completed assignments for them to be considered completed.

School programs—Some schools have programs established where children who do not complete the required assignments stay in at recess or after school to complete the required work. If your school has such a program, utilize it.

Teacher sends home incomplete work—In some situations, have the teacher send home on Friday all the work or assignments that weren't completed during the week. Establish a work time for the child on Saturday before he goes out to play or watch cartoons. The child learns he will have to do the assignment. He can do them when they are supposed to be done, or he can complete them when he should be playing.

Too much negative attention—See if there is an excessive amount of negative attention centering around homework time. If there is, the child may be avoiding the homework to avoid the hassle or negative attention. Try to create a calm, positive atmosphere centering around homework. See Chapter 72, Homework, for additional information.

Help him be organized—If the child is disorganized, distractible, dependent and irresponsible, try to develop and improve these behaviors in other areas of his life.

Don't assume responsibility—Don't assume responsibility for getting the child's assignment. Don't go to school and copy the assignment off the board or have his older sister go in the classroom and copy it. Don't call a friend who has a child in class to find out the assignment. Have the child make the phone call and find out. Or have him go back to school to copy the assignment off the board.

Stop behavior from working—Establish consequences that are different for completing and bringing home assignments and other consequences for not doing these required tasks.

Tests and notes

One school year I got a call from my oldest son's teacher. She told me he was doing poorly in math. It was a surprise to my wife and me. I asked the teacher, "How can that be? He's getting good grades on his tests." The teacher told me this wasn't true and he had failed about half of the math tests he had taken during the grading period. I hadn't seen them.

When I questioned my son, he said he had lost the tests or had put then in his desk and forgotten to tell us about them. We weren't seeing the bad test papers so we didn't know of his poor performance or that he needed help in certain areas.

Some children don't bring home notes from school, whether good or bad, or other communications from the school regarding PTA meetings, penny parties, skating events. Several procedures can be used to increase the probability you will see more of the tests and notes coming from school. Let's look at a few of these.

Reduce negative attention—Reduce the negative attention given to poor test grades or bad notes from school. Reward good performance and good notes rather than punishing poor grades and notes indicating misbehavior.

Use behavior charts—Set up a behavior chart, and put it on the refrigerator. The child can earn points for *every* test or note brought home from school. He will receive more points for A's than B's, etc., but he will receive points for *all* test papers, even a failed one. Points are given for *all* notes that come home from school. Notes indicating good behavior provide more points than those indicating misconduct or notes involving a general communication from the school regarding the penny party or early dismissal. Points the child earns can be used to receive a reward or other desired activity or thing.

School policies—Some schools have a policy; they require children to have all test papers signed. Other schools have only failing grades signed. Still others do not require the parents to sign any test papers.

If your child is not bringing home tests and notes, talk with the teacher. Establish a system so you sign all your child's test papers or notes. You, the teacher and child are then aware of the fact every test must be signed by you and returned to school for the teacher to see it. It's best to set up different consequences for when the child brings the paper home to be signed and an entirely different consequences if he does not bring the paper.

Celebrate passing grades—Make a big deal about all your child's passing grades. Post them on a bulletin board so everyone can see or on the front of the refrigerator. That way grandparents, relatives and friends can see them and make positive comments about the test grades.

Books

Some children don't bring home any books; others only bring home the books in subjects in which they don't have any homework. They forget to bring home the required material to complete the homework or assignment. Techniques similar to the ones discussed above can also be used in this area. Here are a few additional ideas.

Bring home all books—The child who forgets the appropriate books may be required to bring home *all* of his books every day from school. Set up consequences for bringing home *all* his books. Other consequences can be set up for days he doesn't bring his books. After he does this for a while, you may allow him to bring home just the appropriate books.

Set up a situation where he can play or watch television when the appropriate books come home and he is not able to engage in the activity if he forgets a book. If he has trouble remembering again, have him bring home all his books.

Know his schedule—If you know your child has a spelling test every Thursday or a science test on Friday, set up a situation where he receives a point every time he brings home the science book or spelling book. Points can be traded for a treat.

Extra work—A child who doesn't bring home books may be given an option. On days he has homework and doesn't bring home the required book, you will give him work to do. The work will be twice as much as he would have to do if he brought the books home from school. If the child's homework is 10 math problems and he doesn't bring the book home, you might give him 20 problems to do.

Another set of books—You might get another set of books from school. Tell the child if he brings the appropriate books home and does his homework, a consequence will happen. If he doesn't, you'll have a book handy. He still has to do his homework but an entirely different consequence will happen.

Create a situation in which leaving his books in school does not allow him to get away with not doing the homework. Make it to his advantage to bring home the required materials.

67

Children Who Need a Smaller Classroom Setting or a Smaller Pupil-Teacher Ratio

Most schools average about 30 children in a class. Some children can handle this setting fine. Others need a smaller setting because of academic and/or behavioral difficulties. A smaller pupil-teacher ratio enables a child to receive more individual attention. Work can be presented at a level commensurate with his ability. Frustration and failure can be minimized. In some cases, it's better to try to fit the school to the child's needs rather than trying to fit the child to the school.

Academic concerns

Children who have problems with schoolwork may not be able to handle the academic expectations in a large classroom. This may involve a poor foundation (the child is in sixth grade but reading on a second-grade level). A depressed level of intelligence or developmental lags (learning disability, perceptual motor deficits, auditory-processing problems) may also cause problems. The child can't keep up with the other children in the large classroom.

Behavioral concerns

The child may display "bad" behavior, such as disrupting the classroom, acting out, difficulty with authority. Or it may involve other behaviors that interfere with the child's performance (attention deficits, overactivity, lack of responsibility, independent behavior and self-discipline). In a large classroom, the child can't receive the individual attention that may be necessary for him to function.

Some children need a special-education class or a specialized school. Most can function in a regular school if classes have a small pupil-teacher ratio. In some areas, a school with 10 to 20 children in a class may be difficult to find. In areas where there are many schools, this academic setting is usually available.

Determining if a school can help your child

To determine if a school can help your child, look at a couple of things. First, contact a mental-health professional, educational specialist or someone who is familiar with the schools in your area. Have them try to identify the needs of your child and generate a list of possible schools.

Once schools have been identified, the second step is to visit each school and talk with the principal or counselor. Describe the needs of the child and the approach that is needed to maximize the probability of success. School personnel must make a decision as to whether they feel they can provide the necessary services.

For children I work with, I have the parents contact the school to see if there is an opening in a specific grade. If there is, I contact the school and describe what I feel the child needs and get some type of feedback from the administration. Then the parents and I try to make a decision regarding the appropriateness of the school.

Ask the school to give you the names of parents who have children with similar difficulties. Contact them for feedback about their perceptions of the school and the help received.

Grade placement is important

In a smaller school setting, grade placement of the child often determines if the school can help. You may have a third grader who is academically behind. When considering the child, the school may say their third-grade class is advanced. If he was in fourth grade, they could help him because several children in that grade receive special help and have a poor foundation.

You may have to look at the child's grade in the school rather than the overall school.

68

Classwork

"The teacher says my child isn't doing his work in class. What am I supposed to do? I'm not in school with him."

I hear this frequently. Although you don't attend school with your children, you can do some things to help your child deal with work in the classroom setting. Before trying to change behavior, identify the possible cause of the incomplete or inadequate classwork. In most cases, this refers to the child's written work. But it may also pertain to attention in class, participation in verbal discussions or activities or other behaviors indicating the child doesn't follow classroom procedure.

The child may not complete any work. Or he may rush through the work and finish it in a sloppy, impulsive way. He may put down any answer just to have something on the paper. Or it may be incorrect, even though he has put forth significant effort.

Attention problems or overactivity

Children who are distractible, have attention problems, cannot concentrate or cannot stay still, often have difficulty completing classwork. They don't finish seatwork or tests because they can't force themselves to concentrate to complete the task. They have difficulty sustaining effort. Children with these characteristics will experience difficulty in this area.

Perhaps your child is having problems with attention and/or overactivity. You have tried to improve the behavior but have experienced little success. It may be appropriate to have the child evaluated or seen by a mental-health professional who specializes in child behavior. By doing this, you can get a better idea if the child can or can't control specific behavior. If he cannot sustain his attention or decrease activity level, even though he tries very hard, other steps must be taken to deal with the classroom behavior.

Perceptual-motor problems

Some children who have eye-hand coordination difficulties or weakness in fine-motor coordination have difficulty manipulating a pencil or copying from the board. Handwriting is extremely difficult, takes a long time and involves a significant amount of effort. Written activities are difficult, and usually the child doesn't complete the work.

Academic problems

If a child is in seventh grade but only has the academic skills of a fourth grader, he's going to have trouble with classwork. If a specific learning disability or reading problem exists, classwork may often be incomplete or inadequate. Because of the difficulty this child experiences with schoolwork, he may also show a lack of motivation or a tendency to give up.

Lack of responsible behaviors

Some children have not learned there are certain things you must do because you have to do them, whether you want to or not. If seatwork is presented and they're interested in the work, they usually complete it quickly and correctly. However, if given information they aren't interested in, they don't do the work or they complete it quickly just to get it done. These children lack responsibility, self-discipline and internal controls. They want to do what *they* want to do when *they* want to do it for as long as *they* want to do it. They usually don't complete classwork because they don't want to.

Lack of independent behavior

If the teacher stands over the child or works with him in a one-on-one situation, work is usually completed. However, if independent work habits are required, the child doesn't produce. The teacher may tell the class, "I'm going to work with this reading group for a while. While I'm doing this, I want you to complete page 5 and 6 in your English workbook." In these situations, the child doesn't perform. These are usually dependent children or those who have not developed independent behaviors.

Dealing with Classwork

You can do several things to help the teacher. This may result in an increase of classwork finished, complete activities or participation and attention in class.

Identify cause of problem

This is the first thing to try. Talk with the child's teacher. Try to identify the exact situations and/or activities where this behavior is seen. Have the teacher tell you specifically what the child is or is not doing and how he approaches the task.

If motivation seems to be present, does she feel he can do the work and isn't trying, or does she question his ability?

Does the lack of attention or incomplete work pertain only to written work?

Does he have trouble completing certain types of tests but does well when tested in a different fashion?

Can he attend to some activities but not others? Or is his attention problem apparent in all activities?

Once you define in detail what is happening in the classroom, you may be able to figure out why the problem is occurring.

Causes of incomplete or ineffective classwork are discussed in other chapters. Review the chapter or chapters that seem appropriate for your child.

Develop other behaviors

Many children who show attention problems, overactivity, irresponsible behavior and lack of independent skills in school show very similar behaviors in other areas of their lives. Parents usually focus only on school because it's the most important behavior. When trying to develop more responsibility in a child regarding his schoolwork, you must also develop responsibility in behaviors that occur around the home and in the neighborhood.

An irresponsible child may buck routine situations and give you trouble when it's time to take a bath, go to bed or pick up his clothes. If you can establish more cooperation and responsibility in these areas, it is easier to develop responsibility regarding school behavior.

The child who lacks independent skills and depends on you must learn independent skills at home before these skills can develop in school. Don't work only on school behavior if your child's classroom problems are similar to home problems.

Evaluate academic problems

Does your child have trouble because of a lack of foundation, ability problems or the possibility of a specific-learning difficulty? It might be beneficial to have him evaluated so the specific area of difficulty can be identified.

Evaluation results should provide some recommendations for dealing with the situation. The school may be too advanced for the child, or he may need tutoring. A smaller class setting may be appropriate, or he may need to repeat the grade. Some form of therapy or outside assistance may be appropriate.

Establish home-school communication system

Do this so you have a daily or weekly report on the child's progress in the classroom. Review Chapter 76, Monitoring School Behavior and Performance, Home-School Communications. This will give you some ideas of communication systems to use.

You must have feedback from the school so you can administer consequences at home that may motivate the child to complete his work. Communication from school must be simple and involve a minimal amount of the teacher's time. It should be more frequent than interim reports or report cards.

69

Following Directions & Auditory-Processing Problems

When you're looking for services for your child, be sure to locate someone who has experience and is a specialist in the area of need. I wanted to include this chapter in the revised book, but this area is not consistent with my training. So I asked Dr. Annell McGee, a speech and language pathologist, to provide assistance. Most of this chapter was prepared by Dr. McGee.

Auditory Processing

Auditory processing can be defined as *what the brain does with what the ear hears.* A normal ear hears sound and can reflexively respond to it without the sound meaning anything to the person hearing it. For one sound to be distinguished from another, to be remembered and to be understood, the brain must process it. When an auditory-processing problem exists, there is some interruption in the flow of information to the part of the brain that interprets the particular sounds.

There are many sounds in our environment. We attach meaning to them due to past experience. Some of the most important sounds we hear are speech sounds.

Speech

Speech has meaning to you based on past experience and learning. When you listen to someone speaking a foreign language, you are aware he is talking. But the words mean nothing if you haven't learned that particular language.

Speech and language are intimately interrelated, but a

distinction should be made between them. Language is made up of words and combinations of words that are spoken and listened to. Speech is *the vehicle or mechanism that carries or expresses the language.* This chapter focuses on the speech and language that is listened to and understood. This is the aspect of speech and language that is affected in auditory-processing problems.

Auditory processing

Auditory processing is usually thought of in terms of specific abilities that involve attention, discrimination, sequencing, association and memory. These abilities must be adequately developed before a child can understand language in the classroom. Development of these skills occurs almost automatically if the child has a pair of normally hearing ears, a normally developed brain and exposure to a normally stimulating environment.

Attention—Attention involves paying attention to what is being taught in the classroom. It also involves *figure-ground.* This is the ability to select and attend to the most important message from a background of extraneous sights and sounds.

Discrimination—This is the ability of the various senses to recognize differences in things that are similar. Auditory discrimination refers to the ability to hear the fine differences in sounds that are almost the same. The child may be able to distinguish between the sounds of "f" and the quiet "th," as may be heard in the words "fie" and "thigh" or between the short "e" and "i" vowels, such as in "pet" and "pit."

Sequencing—This process requires the child to hold information in a particular order, such as being able to remember the names of the days of the week in the order they occur.

Association—Association refers to the ability to "make connections" between and among things. It involves categorizing things that have common characteristics and being able to learn something new by "connecting it up" with something already learned. Associations can be very simple and concrete. Or they can be very complex and abstract. There is also a continuous range from very simple-concrete to very complex-abstract, within which any concept may fall.

Memory—There are two important aspects of memory.

Auditory short-term memory involves the ability to listen to, remember and immediately respond to a message. It is closely related to auditory sequencing because auditory signals are usually expected to be remembered in a particular order. The sequential aspects of auditory signals are very "fleeting."

Auditory long-term memory involves the ability to "store" information and retrieve it from "storage" when needed. Beyond these skills, the child must learn to understand and use vocabulary and grammar appropriate for his age and grade level.

Vocabulary—Vocabulary refers to the words and their meanings that we use to express our thoughts, ideas, feelings or whatever else we have to say.

Grammar—Grammar is the organized way in which we put words together into phrases, sentences, paragraphs and dialogue that can be understood by others. Language is very complex. A thorough explanation of its varied aspects is beyond the scope of this chapter.

Causes of Problems

Auditory-processing problems may result from one or a combination of several causes. Often the cause of the problem can't be clearly detected. In these cases, there is a developmental lag or a delay in the development of these skills. Even when causes are known, the result is a developmental delay because skills don't develop automatically at the age levels they should. In some cases, there is a history of infant prematurity, illnesses of the mother during pregnancy, jaundice at birth or an early childhood disease, heart condition or other medical problem. These and other similar causes may result in a very subtle form of brain injury that is difficult, if not impossible, to detect in the usual pediatric-neurological examination.

Environmental deprivation or variation may also cause auditory-processing problems. If the child is not exposed to normal preschool opportunities and experiences, his auditory-processing skills may not develop correctly. If a child is raised in a culture whose native language is different from the language of the classroom, he may have difficulty learning the differences in the sounds of the classroom language.

Ear infections

Perhaps the major cause of auditory-processing problems is a history of early childhood middle-ear infections. These infections rarely result in permanent damage to the peripheral hearing mechanism—the middle and inner ear where listening begins. But they cause mild to moderate hearing losses. When periods of hearing loss occur, the infant's and young child's brain doesn't receive the information from its environment that it needs for auditory processing to develop normally.

The auditory-processing problems discussed here are not associated with major problems, such as significant and permanent hearing loss, brain damage or mental retardation. These children have difficulty processing auditory information. But they are not included in this discussion.

Effects on Learning

Auditory-processing problems can affect learning in many ways. To learn, a child must first be able to remain reasonably still and pay attention. Next, he must be able to pick out the important messages from the noisy background of sounds that occur in a classroom. If he can't select important sounds, he can't begin to learn at the level he should for his age.

Academic skills that appear to be most affected by poor auditory-processing abilities are language arts—phonics, reading, spelling and English.

The inability to follow directions and comprehend classroom instructions may also result from an auditory-processing problem. In this case, all aspects of academic learning could be affected. In addition, not all language-arts subjects may be affected.

Word-attack skills

The child must be able to make sound-symbol associations—know what sound the written letter makes. Then he can "sound out" letters when reading a new word he doesn't recognize. This is called "word-attack" skill. Children with auditory-processing problems may have difficulty developing this skill.

Sound blending

The ability to blend sounds into words depends on discrimination synthesis, which is a form of sequencing and association. In sound blending, the child must know the sounds of the letters and be able to say them in sequential order as he reads them. His brain must make the association so those word parts can be blended into a whole, meaningful word.

Many children are able to blend word parts into whole words when the word parts are spoken by another person, such as a teacher or other adult. However, the same child may not be able to blend the parts into wholes when "sounding out" the letters by himself. The ability to make sound-symbol associations and the use of sound-blending skills are essential for learning how to read.

Reading

Some children learn to read through the visual system. Others are more auditory learners. Reading involves *both* auditory and visual skills. The learning of language through the auditory system is essential to learning how to read. Children with auditory-processing problems have difficulty learning that skill.

The degree to which problems in auditory processing affect the ability to learn to read depends on how well the student can use his strengths in the visual system to compensate for his auditory weaknesses.

Spelling

The ability to learn to spell depends on auditory discrimination, sound-symbol association, sequencing and memory. The child must be able to hear or discriminate the spelling word as it is said by the teacher. If the teacher says "cat" and the child thinks the teacher said "cap," he will make a spelling error.

Not all words are spelled as they sound. The child must be able to perform a quick sequential task which is the opposite of blending. He must be able to break down the word into parts and write the individual letters in the word he hears. He must be able to get the letters in the correct sequential order. When he is studying the spelling words, he must be able to make a visual and auditory mental picture of each word. He has to be able to store it in his long-term memory bank and retrieve it when taking the spelling test or writing his compositions.

English

Learning the vocabulary and grammatical structures taught in English depends on all of the auditory-processing skills. These skills are basic to the understanding and use of all aspects of language.

Characteristics of Problems

Most auditory-processing problems go undetected until the child enters school. Skills should develop automatically from the time a child is born and exposed to his environment. They should continue to mature up to a certain point as he gets older. They aren't usually fully developed when the child enters school, but their development should be adequate for the child's age level.

Development of auditory-processing skills is not usually put "to the test" until a child begins to be taught academic skills. Normal academic-skills learning depends on the normal development of auditory-processing skills. The child with an auditory-processing problem may begin to lag behind other students even as early as kindergarten.

Some words of caution—Not all children with learning problems have auditory-processing problems. But don't rule out these problems in cases of academic failure. Not all children who lag slightly behind their fellow students have an auditory-processing problem. There is variation in the development and maturation of these skills and all skills required to learn.

Detection and treatment

Early detection and treatment of these problems is very important. Children who show tendencies toward the presence of such difficulties should be screened and observed over time. Early detection and treatment is important. There are some things you can look for in your preschool child. Specific characteristics exhibited by children with auditory-processing problems are described on the following pages. Familiarize yourself with these characteristics; take note if your child behaves in these ways. Be aware that many of these behaviors are on a continuum of development and may not be considered abnormal or unusual at a certain age. Take care of middle-ear infections in your child promptly.

Delays or difficulties in speech

If a child's speech doesn't develop as it should, the lag may be due to an auditory-processing problem. An example is the child who has difficulty pronouncing his words or saying letter sounds correctly. His speech is difficult to understand.

Some children with auditory-processing problems are excessively verbal and don't give themselves the chance to listen. Their connected speech may be full of mispronounced words. When listened to carefully, these words are usually several syllables in length. Some syllables may be omitted or out of order. Often the child can pronounce the word correctly if taken out of context, but sometimes he can't.

Older children may make errors pronouncing certain speech sounds well beyond the age when their speech should be free of such errors.

Abnormal voice quality

A voice that is too loud or too soft, one that is harsh or unpleasant to listen to or one that sounds like it's coming through the child's nose may signify upper-respiratory problems, allergies or even structural abnormalities associated with middle-ear infections. Infections could be the cause of an auditory-processing problem.

Difficulty expressing thoughts

A child may not express himself well in words or complete sentences. He may have this problem because he can't process language through his auditory system.

Inability to attend to or tell difference between auditory signals

Some preschool children seem not to hear, do not attend to auditory signals or can't tell the difference between signals such as telephone and doorbell rings. They may be exhibiting early signs of an auditory-processing problem. The inability to distinguish between pleasant and unpleasant vocal tones or to respond to sounds by turning to the object or person who is making the sound may be signs of problems.

Difficulty following simple commands

A preschool child who has difficulty learning rhythm games, such as "patty cake," is unable to follow simple commands, can't listen to simple stories, can't repeat a certain number of digits, words or sentences of certain lengths may have an auditory-processing problem.

The child of 2-1/2 to 3 should be able to follow simple, two-level commands. By 4 to 5, he should be able to follow more complicated directions involving 2 to 3 actions; the 2- to 2-1/2-year-old should be able to listen to a simple story for 5 to 10 minutes. By 2-1/2, he should listen for 20 minutes.

The ability to repeat numbers from short-term memory varies from two at age 2 to 2-1/2, to three at age 2-1/2 to 3. Repeating four numbers is appropriate for 4 to 4-1/2 and five digits at 6 to 7 years.

The 2- to 2-1/2-year-old should be able to repeat six- to eight-syllable sentences. A 3-1/2-to-4-year-old should be able to repeat 12-syllable sentences.

Use developmental charts as a guideline. Obvious lack of awareness of auditory signals and significant delays in language development could indicate more serious and permanent problems, which can be identified through evaluation procedures.

School-age children may not have learned how to tell left from right or how to do serial activities, such as saying the alphabet, days of the week or months of the year. Some can't report personal information, such as birthdate, age, address and phone number. They may have difficulty learning to tell time or following instructions that involve space and/or time directions.

Academic difficulties

Parents of school-age children may not have seen any difference in their child's behavior before he enters school. Consider the possibility of an auditory-processing problem if your child begins to have difficulty in the classroom. This is particularly true with following directions and/or language arts subjects, such as phonics, reading and spelling.

In kindergarten, the child begins to learn to follow classroom instructions and is introduced to basic phonics skills. The more-advanced student may begin to do some simple sight reading.

The first grader is expected to begin to use some simple word-attack skills. Complexity of expectations increases as the child advances in school. An auditory-processing problem usually shows up by first or second grade, but it can go undetected until the student is more advanced in school. It depends on the degree of the problem and the complexity of the learning material. It also depends on the alertness of the school personnel and the parents to the fact that the student isn't learning at the rate he should be.

To detect the possibility of an auditory-processing problem, keep abreast of his academic progress. Be aware of academic behaviors that are exhibited with auditory-processing problems. A description of those behaviors follows.

Behavioral difficulties

In extreme cases, a child with an auditory-processing problem may be a behavior problem in the classroom and/or at home. His acting-out behavior may be due to his inability to control his behavior or the frustration he experiences because of his academic failure. Or the child may be very subdued or depressed because of his failure. He may have difficulty paying attention in class and doing homework. He may be "all over the place" with gross body movements or fidgetiness and hand movements. He "can't sit still." He has to handle everything in front of him.

These behaviors are often labeled as "distracted" and "disinhibited." His responses to lessons may be inconsistent. He may know them one day and not the next. He may know the lessons at home but not when he reaches school.

He usually likes activities that don't require auditory learning. He may focus so intensely on these activities that it is difficult to get his attention.

He may be physically clumsy. He may find playing alone difficult because he lacks the imagination needed for creative play. The child who reports he is "bored" may have an auditory-processing problem because he lacks the self-direction to involve himself very long in interesting activities.

He may feel anxious and tense because of his eager attempts to perform tasks that are too difficult for him. Some become discouraged and give up sooner than the average child. Some are insecure because of the failures they experience. These feelings can lead to developing a poor self-image and poor self-esteem, which is the most devastating outcome of an auditory-processing problem. Begin evaluation and remedial procedures as soon as possible if a problem in this area is suspected. This will help prevent the child from developing negative feelings about himself and encourages the development of his delayed auditory-processing skills.

Self-cuing and work habits

Children who show auditory-processing problems may use self-cuing behaviors, such as verbally repeating or finger-writing the statement or question. These behaviors are compensatory. They are not bad in themselves but may tend to slow the student down so he can't keep up with the normal pace of the classroom.

Other behaviors interfere with his ability to keep up. Responses may be delayed, he may self-correct his errors or he may need to have instructions repeated.

Although some children may be slow because of their need to be overly neat, most display messy work habits and writing skills.

Many require more individual attention in the classroom than the average child. They may have difficulty following directions because they cannot track the information being given to them. Or they may begin to respond before they have received all the information because of their inability to control their responses. Many children tire easily, particularly when required to pay attention to auditory information.

Not all children with an auditory-processing problem exhibit all the characteristics of the disorder. Some children exhibit few, if any, but most exhibit at least some. On the other hand, just because a child may exhibit some of the behaviors doesn't mean he has an auditory-processing problem.

What to Do?

Hearing examination

Have the child's auditory sensitivity checked to see if the peripheral hearing mechanisms (middle and inner ear) are normal.

A screening test should involve the use of an audiometer. Each ear should be tested. Anyone trained in the use of an audiometer can administer a hearing screening test.

If the child fails the test, have him rechecked within a week. If he fails the recheck, further testing is necessary. Have this done by a certified and/or licensed audiologist who has special training to test hearing sensitivity and determine the hearing problem.

Have a child with a hearing problem, whether permanent or temporary, examined by an otologist (a physician who specializes in diseases and disorders of the ear). A temporary hearing loss can be treated and usually cured. This type of hearing loss may cause an auditory-processing problem.

Psycho-educational evaluation

If some other type of learning problem, such as a learning disability, mental retardation or emotional disturbance, is suspected, have the child tested by a psychologist. The child's educational performance and progress in the classroom should be reported by the teacher. Rule out any possible physical problems, such as gross-motor or fine-motor problems or visual problems. It may be necessary for an educational specialist to test the child or work with him to determine his learning style.

Speech and language evaluation

The professional who most commonly evaluates and provides remedial services to children with auditory-processing problems is the speech-and-language pathologist. If a problem is suspected, have the child seen by a qualified specialist who can evaluate the problem. He or she will explain the evaluation results to you and make appropriate recommendations for dealing with the problem.

Evaluation of the problem should involve administering tests designed to measure the child's functioning level in the following skills:

1. Receptive and expressive vocabulary and grammar. This involves the child's ability to understand and use words and grammatical structures, and to follow oral directions and commands.
2. Auditory discrimination in quiet and noise.
3. Auditory closure, which involves the ability to fill in information that is missing from an auditory signal.
4. Sound-symbol association.
5. Sound blending when listening to the signal and when saying the sound himself.
6. Auditory short-term memory.
7. Auditory association.

A thorough evaluation should include the administration of one or more tests to assess each skill. Even certain visual-perceptual skills, such as association, memory and closure, should be evaluated to determine if possible strengths in these skills can be used to compensate for or improve weak auditory skills. If there is evidence of a problem in the child's speech production, such as an articulation, stuttering or voice problem, evaluation of the problem should also be included.

School and home interventions

When an auditory-processing problem is detected, the child usually needs remedial services as soon as possible. Some classroom interventions and/or parent assistance may be all that is necessary if the problem is mild and hasn't affected the child's educational performance and progress significantly.

In the classroom, put the child in a setting that is as distraction-free and noise-free as possible. He should be seated where he can see the teacher at all times and be encouraged to move in his seat to see any student who is directly involved in a lesson. He should be encouraged to "use his eyes to help him listen."

The teacher should speak clearly to him at all times and give him directions that are broken down into fewer steps. She should allow and encourage him to ask to have directions and instructions repeated if he doesn't think he understands. She should seek advice from the school speech-and-language pathologist for specific activities that will help the child. You can also contact a speech-and-language pathologist for specific suggestions and activities to practice with your child.

At home, eliminate noise and other distractions when talking to your child. Be sure he pays attention. Position yourself close to him. Use simple language. Provide a general atmosphere of structure and order in the home.

Not all skills may be affected; the degree to which any skill is affected also varies. It's important for teacher and parents to have some guidance as to the type and level of activity most appropriate for the child. School-supply houses sell materials to use with these children. Seek advice on appropriateness of the material.

Some children with auditory-processing problems function better in a smaller classroom where there is a lower pupil-teacher ratio. Some may need to be taught in a special-education classroom.

An auditory-processing problem may be part of a more complex problem called *learning disability*. A child with a learning disability may require special education. The learning-disabled child's eligibility for special education in a public-school program depends on criteria for placement established by the school system.

Some children with an auditory-processing problem are not eligible for education in a special classroom. These children may be able to receive services from the school speech-and-language pathologist. You may wish to seek private therapy.

When the child is enrolled in a school where these services are unavailable, seek private therapy through an individual, university, hospital or community agency.

What to Look for in Therapy

The child who is enrolled in therapy for an auditory-processing problem should have an individually designed program tailored to his particular needs. Activities should be appropriate to the skills in which he exhibits weaknesses. The level of difficulty should be commensurate with his ability level. A high degree of possible success should be built into the program so he can receive the maximum amount of positive reinforcement. He needs to find the experience rewarding. He needs to have his self-confidence restored. At the same time, he should be encouraged to "check his work" for any errors he may have made so he can learn to be aware of and correct errors in his schoolwork.

Repeated practice should result in responses becoming more automatic so he won't require extra time to respond or need to have instructions repeated. Compensatory practices should be discovered and developed. If his visual skills are stronger than his auditory skills, encourage him to use his stronger visual skills while he learns to develop auditory abilities. Learning strategies should also be discovered and developed so his learning style is more organized. Distracting sights and sounds should be introduced gradually so he builds up a tolerance for distractions.

Authorities disagree as to whether or not specific skills, such as memory, can be improved through training. Many believe they can't. But therapy *can* serve to help the child learn to pay attention and listen. It can help develop compensatory behaviors and teach him strategies to improve classroom learning. It may relieve his tension and frustration and restore some of his self-confidence.

Don't confuse therapy for an auditory-processing problem with academic tutoring. Therapy develops skills that are preliminary to academic skills; these should be developed at the automatic level by the time a child is old enough to need them. He shouldn't have to think about it too much before carrying out an activity that requires one or more of these skills.

Some activities used by therapists to deal with certain auditory-processing skills, such as discrimination, sound-symbol association and blending, are similar to some academic activities. Some activities used to train auditory-association skills may be academically oriented. It isn't always possible to separate the perceptual from the academic because of their interrelationship. The therapist should relate activities as closely as possible to the child's school program. But the speech-and-language pathologist is not a reading, spelling or English teacher!

If the child's therapy is effective, it is reflected in improved performance in school. The child will begin to pay more attention and more opportunity for learning will occur. The individual attention he receives tells him he is important and he can learn. His motivation will improve. Interest in schoolwork usually results in improvement. Practicing auditory-processing activities results in more automatic use of these skills. The child won't be so slow to respond or require extra information and attention. His grades should improve in academics and conduct.

Although some positive changes may be seen right away, it usually takes some time for effects of the program to have a significant impact. Progress in therapy depends on the severity of the problem, the child's age, his motivational level and how much time you can help the child at home.

However, 6 months is a fair time to allow to determine if therapy will be effective. If improvement does not occur, seek help elsewhere or try different interventions. See Chapter 80, Should My Child Change Schools? and Chapter 67, Children Who Need a Smaller Classroom Setting or Smaller Pupil-Teacher Ratio.

How effective is therapy?

Therapy is almost always effective to some degree. When it is effective, you must judge the value of the amount of improvement versus the time and money spent when a fee for services is involved.

The number of therapy sessions needed each week is recommended by the speech-and-language pathologist. Therapy should also include a home program designed by the therapist. The therapist should also give you specific details about how to use the program. The total amount of time in terms of months and years required for auditory-processing therapy varies.

The goal of therapy is the realization of the child's full potential. Potential varies. Learning potential or intelligence is usually determined by psychological evaluations. If the child has normal potential, achievement of average functioning at the child's expected grade level could be a realistic goal. Variations of this goal are determined by the child's learning potential if it isn't normal and by other complicating factors.

Many children receive the therapy, achieve the goal and are dismissed from therapy in a year or two. Some children in special education need services for many years. The child with an auditory-processing problem may need therapy through most of his school years to be able to achieve and maintain his full potential.

When behavior is being dealt with, there are no absolutes or guarantees. Auditory-processing skills mature, and compensatory behaviors develop over time. A child's skills will eventually become commensurate with his learning potential at times, even without therapy. However, the years of failure and frustration before the child's skills fully develop can be devastating to the child. Therapy for an auditory-processing problem can help alleviate this devastation.

Annell McGee, Ph.D.

Annell McGee received her Ph.D. in speech and language pathology from the University of Denver, where she specialized in studying neurologically based communication disorders and disorders of the auditory nervous system. She began her career as a speech-language pathologist 25 years ago, working with neurologically impaired preschool cerebral-palsied children.

Dr. McGee has diagnosed and treated thousands of children and adults with neurologically based communication disorders many of who exhibited an auditory-processing problem. She has also taught courses in language and language-based learning disabilities to graduate students at Louisiana State University and Tulane University Medical Centers. She is currently in private practice in Metairie and Chalmette, Louisiana and is employed as a speech-language pathologist for the public-school system of Jefferson Parish, Louisiana.

70

Grades

For some parents, high grades in school are a must. Others just hope their child receives passing grades. Parents make some mistakes about grades and school performance.

Consider intellectual ability

Some parents expect too much from their child in terms of grades. About 50% of all children have average intellectual ability. Their learning potential is in the average range. For half the children in the United States, doing their best means C-level work. However, many parents view a C as an unacceptable grade and demand A's and B's. If you took 100 children and placed them in a room, you'd find 50 of them have average intellectual potential, 25 are above-average and 25 are below-average.

Suppose you have no idea of a child's intelligence. If you assume he's average, you have a 75% chance of not overestimating his ability. However, if you expect above-average intellectual ability, you have a 25% chance of not overestimating his ability. If you were a betting person, you'd have a better chance to win if you expected average work than above-average work.

But most parents expect and sometimes demand above-average school performance from their children. They don't accept C-level work.

There's nothing wrong with being average. If C-level work was unacceptable, schools wouldn't have grading systems that indicated above-average, average and below-average work.

See Chapter 73, Intelligence.

Same performance

Another mistake some parents make is to expect the same performance all the time. Everybody has trouble learning something and makes a mistake. No one is perfect. A ninth grader was expected to get straight A's on her final report card to go on a summer trip. She didn't and wasn't able to go. She told me she had some trouble understanding algebra and didn't do well in that subject. Her inadequate report card showed all A's and a B in algebra!

Allow your child some margin for error. Look at the child's overall performance. He may like a particular subject and get an A or a B but get a D in another subject. The remaining grades are all C's. Rather than place a lot of negative emphasis on the D, look at the child's overall *average* performance.

There are some periods in a child's life when his grades may drop. In the lower grades (first and second grade), it isn't that hard for an average child to overachieve and receive all A's or mostly A's and a few B's. As the child progresses in school it may be more difficult to overachieve and the A-B student may become a C student around third or fourth grade. His decrease in grades may not reflect a problem. It may show it is more difficult for this child to overachieve. Grades now reflect his average ability.

In preadolescence or adolescence, grades may also show decline. The 8-, 9- or 10-year-old may have a 5-pound bag with 3 pounds of activities to put in it. The seventh, eighth or ninth grader still has the same 5-pound bag, but now he has 25 pounds of activities to put in it. At this age, important things are talking on the phone, the opposite sex, going out, looking good and going to football games. You can only put so much in a 5-pound bag. Grades and schoolwork are usually placed on the bottom of the list of important things to do. Grades may decline.

Don't make time period too long

Another general mistake some parents make is trying to improve their child's grades over too long a period of time. Most schools have grading periods of 6 or 9 weeks. Often disciplinary measures are put into effect until the next report card. For most children, this is too long, and several problems are apt to arise.

Let's say you have a child who failed two subjects because he wasn't prepared for tests and didn't turn in the required work. You tell him, "You have to spend 2 hours in your room each day doing homework and studying. You won't be allowed to go outside and play until your grades improve."

If this means till the next report card or 4-1/2 weeks until progress reports are issued, several things may occur. This child will probably go sit in his room each day and daydream, draw, play with something, count the dots on the ceiling or do anything but study.

Secondly, when long punishment is used to improve grades, one of two typical patterns results. Some children work very hard in the beginning and keep at it for about 2 or 3 weeks. But because there is no immediate reward, they give up, go back to their old ways and grades don't improve. Other children play around during most of the punishment period and work very hard only the last week or 2 before the report card. This last-minute burst of studying doesn't improve overall grades, and they remain punished. They actually feel punished for working hard, based on the principle of immediacy of consequences.

The most important thing about a reward or a punishment is it follows the behavior you're trying to control. Whatever behavior occurs immediately *before* the consequence is the one that is affected by punishment. Because of this principle, don't use methods that continue until the next report card.

When working with grades, set short-term goals. Deal with the situation on a *daily* or *weekly* basis rather over a long period of time. A home/school communication system can be established to monitor the child's behavior or performance.

Look beyond grades

Another problem is you may only look at the poor grades and not the reason for the deficient grades. Emphasis is placed on *grades*.

"If you get a C average, you can talk on the phone."

"I know he's capable of A and B work. I won't accept anything below that."

Forget about grades! Focus on the behavior that causes

poor grades. Look at the child's effort rather than grades. Let's say you get your child's report card and find he has failed math. The first question to ask yourself is, "Why has he failed?" This may be answered by having a meeting with his teacher.

You may find he did poorly because he hasn't turned in his homework and hasn't completed math classwork. Now that you have the reason for his poor performance, focus on improving this. Improvement in his grades will follow.

Rather than saying, "Until your grades improve" say, "Until the behavior that is contributing to your poor grades improves." If a child does poorly in a subject because he hasn't done his homework or class assignments, assume if his work habits improve, his grades will also change. Focus on the *behavior* not on the grades.

You might say, "Each day you complete your classwork and turn in your homework, you can stay up 30 minutes past your bedtime" or some other reward.

Establish a communication system with the school, and use a behavior chart to deal with the behavior. If you can get the child to turn in all his homework and complete classwork on a daily basis, his grades will improve at the end of the 9-week period.

Focus on your child's effort and not the grades. Often this will reduce some of the pressure your child feels. If your child has average or above-average ability and you focus on improving the behavior that is producing the poor grades, an improvement in this behavior will result in an improvement in his grades.

The three general behaviors to focus on are homework, classwork and participation or paying attention in class.

I tell children, "You and I could take a senior-level advanced chemistry class at the local university and may fail every test. However, we could get an A in doing homework and classwork and paying attention in class."

If your child gets a D or F in a class and his teacher tells you, "He's turned in all his homework. He pays attention in class and does all the seat work. He looks like he's trying." Your child has earned the D or F and this might indicate he needs a tutor.

However, if the teacher says, "He's missed 6 of 10 homework assignments, seems to be daydreaming in class and does not take notes." He hasn't earned any grade. This indicates that you need to help improve his effort and motivation.

We all tell our children, "All I want is for you to do your best. If you give it 100%, that's all that matters." Therefore, effort is much more important than grades.

71

Helping Your Child Achieve in School

How can you encourage your child to study and learn? What can you do to develop a positive attitude toward schoolwork or get your child to realize homework and studying are things he has to do whether he wants to or not?

Some children are born with a great deal of interest in school and self-discipline. If you have one of these children, you probably wouldn't be reading this chapter. Many kids could care less about school and view it as something to avoid. A child's school success often depends less on his level of intelligence than it does on what you do at home to help him achieve. You might want to review Chapter 40, Developing Responsible Behavior, and other chapters in the School Concerns section.

Life shouldn't revolve around school

Your child's entire life shouldn't revolve around school and schoolwork. Does your child go to school, come home and do homework, then go to bed? He can't maintain this pace throughout his school career. If you feel your child is involved with schoolwork 24 hours a day, his motivation and willingness to become involved in schoolwork will dramatically decrease as time passes. Involvement in outside activities is important. You can possibly use this as a consequence or motivational factor. "You can go to basketball practice or karate classes only if your homework has been completed before it is time to go."

Be positive

Avoid hassles, confrontations, power struggles and screaming matches centering around homework or school-related work. If your child sits down every night to do his homework and it's a hassle, he'll learn to avoid the situation. Try to be positive and minimize negative attention to his behavior. This may be accomplished by setting rules and consequences ahead of time. Provide structure without being a nag or constantly on the child's back.

Use his "best" time

Find out what time your child does his best work. Adjust his study time accordingly. Some children complete homework better right after school. Others do better if they're allowed to play first then do their homework. Some children do well studying in the morning. Try several schedules to see what fits him the best and which particular study time involves less hassle and confrontation.

Teach him to be organized

Help him organize his notebooks. Have a place for him to place his homework assignments and the completed work. Help him develop a plan of study and what should be done each night.

Where to study

Some children study better in their rooms. Others perform more effectively in the kitchen while you prepare dinner or help your other children with their homework. The place where a child studies or under what conditions he studies more effectively depends on many factors. It's different for different children.

Watch your child to decide what is best. Most children don't learn effectively if they study or do their homework in front of the TV or listening to a stereo.

Eliminate distractions during study time

For some children, this involves turning off the TV and stereo, avoiding the commotion caused by younger brothers and sisters, and being in a situation free from noise, activity and commotion. A clear desk is more conducive to studying.

Work on one assignment

Encourage your child to work on one assignment at a time. He might attack the toughest subject or the one he has the most difficulty in first. Leave the easiest subjects until later. He might study before doing written homework.

Setting goals

Help your child set specific goals. He might use 10 to 15 minutes each night to review notes he took that day in each subject. If there's a test on Thursday, he might study a third of the material on Monday, a third on Tuesday and the remainder on Wednesday. The more specific you can make a goal, the better his study habits will be.

Don't sit with your child

Avoid having to sit with your child while he does his homework. If the only way your child will work is with you sitting by him and forcing him to do it, he isn't developing responsible or independent behaviors.

Try to develop independent work habits. Have the child depend on you only for activities he doesn't understand or when he needs help studying. Don't have him depend on you to complete his homework assignment.

Don't do his homework

It's a big mistake to do your child's homework. Don't allow him to manipulate you so you provide more of the information and do more of the work than he does. Take time to explain how he can approach the problem. Set limits on his behavior with appropriate consequences to help him develop more self-discipline and independent behavior.

No procrastination

Encourage your child to complete projects ahead of time and not procrastinate. The use of rewards and positive consequences may be beneficial in accomplishing this.

Break large projects into smaller ones

Teach your child how to break large projects into smaller ones. A large task might be accomplished by studying one chapter each night, or a book report might be easily attacked by doing one section every few days.

If your child has trouble with a subject, it might be best if he skips that subject for a while and moves onto another subject. The frustration and time it takes to tackle one problem may interfere with the remainder of his study time or homework.

Short study periods
Some children do better with homework if it's broken into periods of study divided by short breaks. Establish the best method of doing homework with your child.

General Study Tips

1. Before reading a chapter, have your child look over it and notice the headings, italicized words, summary, review questions and charts.
2. Have him read small sections. Then discuss the section or ask him questions about what he has read. Or have him verbally summarize what he has read.
3. Some children learn better if they read out loud, write their material or hear it. Use as many senses as possible in homework and study activities.
4. Teach your child to use tricks or methods to memorize things. Look for ways to associate the unknown with the known. Spelling "geography" might be seen as **George** ran **a pig home y**esterday. The difference between princi**ple** and princi**pal** is the person who is the princi**pal** of your school is a "pal." Use devices and memory tricks to aid studying.
5. In subjects, such as math, where there is sequential learning, be sure your child knows one area before he moves on to the next. If he doesn't know the appropriate concepts by the time the class changes to other concepts, spend extra time reviewing the material.
6. Teach him not to cram for tests. Study a little bit each night.
7. Talk about current events. Encourage him to read the newspaper each day. Talk about programs, events and activities he sees on TV.
8. When working on projects or repairing things around the house, talk to the child about methods of problem solving and the approaches you use to solve the particular problem.
9. Encourage your child to read. Obtain high-interest reading material, such as magazines about skateboards, baseball, foot-

ball, rock groups or other interests of your child.

10. Expose your child to different experiences. Take him to activities, visit museums and talk about things you see when visiting the zoo or park. Relate school assignments to his interests. A particular child who is enthusiastic about baseball might write a report on the history of baseball. Another child who is interested in music or singing might do a research paper on a particular instrument, composer or singer.

11. Children have good days and bad days and sometimes good weeks and bad weeks. Don't get upset and critical of a failed test. Become concerned only if a pattern develops. If your child generally performs well, overlook mistakes, failures and weaknesses that are seen infrequently.

12. Encourage outside activities. Although school is the most important thing in your child's life, there are other things that result in development of confidence and self-esteem. Allow him to become involved in extracurricular activities, events and activities that develop self-esteem.

13. Don't set expectations too high. Look for gradual improvements. A child who is consistently making D's may find it very difficult to make an A or B to go on a hunting trip. It might be more appropriate to set the goal of C work.

14. When your child comes home from school, don't give him the third degree and ask him 400 questions about what happened at school today. Let it flow smoothly. When the child starts communicating about his day at school, stop what you're doing and give him your full attention.

15. Don't push your child to top his previous achievements. If success brings pressure, your child may find it easier to fail.

16. Don't call your child's questions *stupid*. Show him how to find the answer. Children learn by asking questions.

17. Encourage independence and self-discipline. You won't always be there to help, pamper or force your child into completing his assignments. You don't want to be there all the time either. Help your child set his own standards, and help him develop responsible behaviors.

72

Homework

Some parents are happy to have the summer end so the children are back in school. Others dread the end of summer because school means grades and homework. For them, school brings arguing, fighting and repeated attempts to have their child do his homework, study for a test and make adequate grades.

Getting children to do their homework is a never-ending battle for some parents. I have provided some suggestions to make this job a little easier. Some other chapters under this section on School Concerns, as well as the section on Methods and Techniques, will give you additional tips.

Establish a routine

Children who do homework after school on some days, after dinner on others or late at night at other times are more likely to give you trouble at homework time than children who do homework the same time each day. Establish a time each day when homework is done (after school, after dinner, before watching TV at night, 5 o'clock). Stick to it.

Try to establish a routine regarding how your child does his homework (have the child do his most difficult subjects first, study before doing the written work). The method depends on the individual child. What works with his sister may not work with him.

Establishing a routine may help your child learn to be organized. Discuss what needs to be done and ways to get it done. A calendar, list or visual of the routine may make sense out of jumbled assignments and may make them seem easier.

When should child do homework?

A question I am frequently asked is, "When should I have my child do his homework? As soon as he comes from school? Should I let him have a break to play first ?"

There is no standard answer. Some children can go out to play then come in to do the required work. Other children who get excited and stimulated by play find it impossible to calm down and study effectively. The answer depends on your child. Use the method that works best with your child.

Some children complain strongly about doing homework after coming home from school if they can't play first. Tell your child, "You can go outside and play today before doing your homework. If you come in when I call and don't give me any problems about the homework, tomorrow you can play before you do the homework. If you give me trouble and I have to fight you to get the work done, tomorrow you'll do it first then go play."

Put the responsibility of when homework is done on the child. He decides when it will be done. If he goes out to play and then homework runs smoothly, he's telling you, "I can handle this. Let me go play first tomorrow." If he gives a lot of trouble, he's telling you, "I can't handle this. Make me do my homework before I go play."

For a child who attends afterschool care or goes to grandma's house, try to get him to do his written work before you pick him up. Some grandparents and afterschool-care programs have homework time set up. They work with the children to see some homework is completed. Other programs do not, and the child is on his own. If this is the case, it may be better to let your child play or watch TV and do homework later.

For others, you might want them to get some work done. For them, and children who go home and are on their own until a parent gets home, use something different. Identify an appropriate incentive and tell the child, "When I pick you up or come home from work, you receive a point for every written assignment completed correctly and neatly. For every point you get, you can stay up 10 minutes past your bedtime." Or "You have been wanting Chris to sleep over on Friday night. If you have

10 points by Friday, he can sleep over."

For some children, it may be best to break up the homework period. They work 15 minutes before they go out to play and another 15 minutes before they get their snack. Other children may require three separate work periods. This procedure is good for children who have short attention spans.

Where should child do homework?

It depends on the child. Minimize distractions. Avoid watching TV or listening to the stereo while doing homework. Some children can do their homework at the kitchen table with others. Others do better when working alone or in their room. Try several different locations or situations. Use the one that works best for your child.

How much time should be spent on homework?

It depends on the school he attends and how much homework is given. Check with your child's teacher to get an estimate of how long the homework should take. Problems arise in this area when 20 minutes of homework takes 3 hours or the child comes home from school and does homework until it's time to go to bed. Several situations contribute to problems in this area. Let's look at some of these and methods to deal with them.

Some children spend 3-1/2 hours trying to get out of 15 minutes of homework. They try to avoid homework instead of doing it. Children may show this type of behavior in other areas of their life.

Some schools send home classwork to be done as homework if it isn't finished in school. If your child's homework takes many hours to complete because he didn't do his classwork, something needs to be done to get the classwork completed in school. Set up a home-school communication system.

Attention problems may cause child to take longer

Overactive children and/or those who have problems with attention and concentration may take a long time to do homework. They can't sit still or they don't have enough control for sustained attention. Make attempts to decrease the child's level of activity and increase his attention span. See Chapter 52,

Overactivity, Attention-Deficit Disorder & Hyperactivity, for techniques to will help accomplish this.

Academic problems

Children who have academic problems may require more time for homework. This occurs in several different situations. The school may be too different for the child. A child with average intellectual ability has difficulty in a school geared toward above-average children. The low-average child may have difficulty keeping up in an average school. A child who has a poor foundation, a learning disability or a specific developmental lag may also have to spend an excessive amount of time on homework.

In these cases, the school may have to make adjustments for the child (less homework, less written and more verbal homework, put him in lower-level class, place him in a reading lab or resource room). Or you may need to look for another school. See the appropriate chapters under School Concerns for more information.

Use a timer

Use a timer or set a specific time when homework has to be finished. Identify an incentive, and estimate how long it will take to do the homework. Maybe you estimate 30 to 40 minutes. Set the timer on the stove for 60 minutes. Tell the child, "If you finish all your homework by the time the bell rings and it's neat, we can play your favorite game tonight. If not, we won't play."

Another method to use to reduce homework time on weekdays is to talk with your child's teacher. Tell her you're going to set a time limit for homework. After a certain period of time, you'll shut it down and not allow your child to do any more. The child will experience whatever consequences the teacher or school has set for no homework. Or the child has to do all the homework he didn't complete during the week on Saturday morning before he watches cartoons or goes out to play.

Your child seems to be putting forth an effort with homework and studying, and it still takes a long time and/or he has trouble grasping the material. It may be wise to have him evaluated to see if a learning problem exists or another school might be more appropriate.

A child who spends an excessive amount of time doing homework may feel like school is his whole life. He's involved with school the entire time he's awake. He can't maintain this pace for long—neither can you. He'll burn out, shut down and lose motivation. Do something quickly to change this situation!

Don't foster dependency

Try to develop independent homework behaviors. For some parents, homework means sitting with their child the entire time to get the homework done. If they're not physically close while their child works, nothing happens.

Although it's good to help your children with homework, it isn't necessary for the child to become excessively dependent on you to do it.

If you develop this habit, you may have to continue indefinitely. You also run into a lot of trouble if you have two or more children who require this. Children dealt with this way may also show a lack of independent behavior in school. The teacher may say, "If I'm standing right over him or it's a one-on-one situation, he does fine. However, if I give him some independent work, he doesn't finish it."

In some instances, sitting with the child can serve as the reward. Your child has 10 math problems for homework. Usually you have to sit with him to get them done. Tell him, "I have something to do. Do the first 2 by yourself and I'll sit with you while you do the rest." After a week, require him to do 3 or 4 math problems before you sit with him. The amount of work can be increased every few days.

Many children who show dependent homework behavior lack independence in many areas of their life. Don't foster dependency in other areas. Require more independence. See Chapter 39, Dependent Behavior, for additional suggestions.

Another way dependency is developed around homework is when the child manipulates you. You provide the correct answers or do the work for the child. *Don't do this!*

Avoid excessive negative attention

Some children try to put off homework because they

receive negative attention at that time. Homework time for some children means their mother gets upset or they get hollered at, criticized or slapped. They try every trick they know to prevent this from happening.

Most parents become too emotional when helping their children with schoolwork. They get upset, frustrated and lose control. The learning situation becomes a negative experience for parents and children. This is the main reason parents don't make good tutors, even if they are teachers.

Although it's easier said than done, try to deal with homework in a calm, matter-of-fact way to reduce the amount of negative attention the child receives. Deal with the child and his various behaviors in a *positive* way.

Don't force child to do homework

If you have to battle the child every night or fight with him to do homework, negative attention builds up on this activity and behavior. If you have to tie the child in a chair and make him to do the work, you may get the homework finished each night. But nothing is done to develop any responsibility or self-discipline.

If this is the procedure you use, you'll have to do it every night—probably until the child finishes school. If you are more responsible for the child doing his homework than he is, you're in for trouble. Put the responsibility on the child. Set rules and consequences and enforce them consistently. See Chapter 39, Developing Responsible Behavior.

General Techniques to Deal with Homework

I have provided a few examples of how the concepts discussed in the section on Method and Techniques can be applied to homework.

Some behavior carries its own consequences

"Go do your homework. It should take 30 minutes to do if you apply yourself. If you fool around, it'll take 3 hours. That means you'll have less play time."

"Your sister and I are going to Grandmother's house at 7 o'clock. If you finish your homework, you can come with us. If you aren't finished, you'll have to stay home with your father and finish it."

Do what I want, then you can do what you want to do

"You can't go outside and play until homework is done."

"You can watch TV when you complete your work."

"Homework must be done before you go to baseball practice."

Set expectations using a consequence
that is important to him

"If you do your homework without complaining or giving me a fight, you can stay up past your bedtime. If you give me trouble, you'll go to bed at the same time."

"If you finish your homework by 7 o'clock 3 of the next 4 nights, on Saturday we'll get those handle grips you've been wanting. If you don't, we'll try again next week."

Work on other behaviors

Many children who show trouble with homework show similar behavior in other areas of their life. Try to develop other behaviors (independence, cooperation, responsibility, self-discipline) to help produce more cooperation and less hassle at homework time.

73

Intelligence

Some parents have an inaccurate idea of what intelligence is. As a result, they set excessive expectations for school performance. If their child is unable to meet the expectations, he receives unnecessary negative attention.

What Is Intelligence?

There is a great deal of disagreement among professionals about what constitutes "intelligence." For our purposes, intelligence is a child's capability, his potential, how smart he is and his ability to learn.

Intelligence is inherited. A child is born with a certain level of intelligence. For all practical purposes, it does not change throughout his life. The child's capacity to learn is inherited primarily from his parents and grandparents.

It's possible for a child to inherit characteristics from any generation of his family tree. An example pertaining to height serves to make several points. My mother is 4' 10" and my father is 5' 5". I was unlikely to be tall. I am about 5' 5"; this was set at birth. When I was born, I had a certain genetic capacity for height. No matter what I did or how hard I tried, I wouldn't grow taller than 5' 5". If I had been sick, had an accident or didn't eat properly, I might not have reached this height.

Intelligence is determined the same way. It is fixed at birth. No individual can get smarter with time. But his capacity might be decreased if something interfered with his development.

Measuring Intelligence

Intelligence is measured by various tests. A child is given

a test that has been given to thousands of children his age in years and months. His score is compared to the scores of the other children to determine a relative level of intelligence. Individual tests, given on a one-on-one basis, yield more accurate results than tests given in a group.

Intelligence is often described in terms of an Intelligence Quotient (IQ). This is simply a child's mental age (as determined by a test) divided by his chronological age, multiplied by 100.

$$\frac{\text{Mental Age}}{\text{Chronological Age}} \times 100 = \text{IQ}$$

Some problems were encountered with this method of determining IQ. Most modern tests use a deviation IQ. This obtains IQ by statistical comparison. Each child's test performance is compared with scores earned by children in his or her own age group.

The actual IQ number is not very important. What should be considered is the range of a child's intelligence. The distribution and ranges of intelligence are shown in this graph.

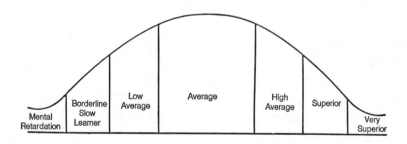

An *average* range of intelligence includes about 50% of the children in the United States. On each side of the average range, there are various levels of intelligence. About 25% of the children are *above average,* and about 25% of children are *below average* in their ability.

One way of viewing intelligence is to think of each child as being born with a certain-size bucket. Children falling in the *superior* range of intelligence have very large buckets. Children in the *mental-retardation* range of intelligence have small buckets. Most children fall within the *average* range and have average-size buckets.

Expectations for Performance

Regardless of your child's range of intelligence, your primary concern should be, "Is he doing his best? Is he working up to his capacity?"

Some parents don't look at it this way. They want, expect and demand above-average work, even though the majority of children have only average ability. Look at 100 children in school, and you'll find 50 with average intelligence, 25 above average and 25 below average.

Let's say you have no idea of your child's range of ability. If you assume he is average, the chances are 7-1/2 out of 10 you have not overestimated his ability. However, if you assume he is above average, the chances drop to 2-1/2 out of 10 that you have not overestimated his ability. If you were betting, you'd have a better chance to win if you guessed *average*. But most parents expect above-average school performance from their children and don't accept C-level work.

What happens if you expect more from your child than he is capable of giving? He is certain to fail. If he isn't capable of attaining the expectations set for him, whatever he does will become a negative experience. We all tend to stay away from things that are difficult or negative for us. If high expectations make schoolwork negative, the child will avoid duties and tasks related to school.

You have a much better chance of being correct if you assume your child has an average intellect. If you assume a child is average when he is above average, he will eventually perform on his actual (above-average) level. Schoolwork involves success, praise and accomplishment. He will engage in things that involve positive attention.

On the other hand, if you expect above-average work and the child is average, he will perform on a below-average level because schoolwork involves failure, punishment and frustration.

74

Is My Child Ready for Kindergarten?

Before proceeding with this chapter, I suggest reading Chapter 47, Immaturity, and Chapter 81, Should My Child Repeat the Grade?

Many schools evaluate a child's readiness for kindergarten solely on intellectual and academic skills. However, academic maturity is only one of the five general areas to assess. In determining whether a child is ready for school, one must assess his academic maturity and his physical, social, emotional and behavioral maturity. Deficits in any area may interfere with adequate performance in a kindergarten setting.

Many well-meaning but ill-informed parents and educators push young children into school too soon. Being bright and being ready to begin formal schooling are two separate issues. When children enter school before they are developmentally ready or mature enough to cope with it, their chances for failure dramatically increase.

Age is an important factor

In determining whether a child is ready for school, assess all areas of maturity. An important factor in overall maturity is *age*. Children with late birthdays (significantly younger than most of the children in the class) tend to have more difficulty in school than those with early birthdays. There is a national trend to move the cutoff date for school entrance from late fall—early winter to much earlier in the fall or even late summer. Findings of research in this area are the major reason for this trend.

1. Older children in a grade tend to receive more above-average grades from teachers than do younger children in the same grade.
2. Older children are more likely to score in the above-average range on standardized achievement tests.
3. Younger children in a grade are more likely to fail at least one grade.
4. Younger children in a grade are more likely to have be referred for academic or behavioral problems.
5. Younger children who were developmentally unready when they started school often have problems that last throughout their school careers.

Developmental lags

A child's age is a significant factor in determining whether she is ready for school. But age is not the determining factor.

Many young children with late birthdays show developmental lags in many areas defined as maturity. If a child shows developmental lags in one or more areas of maturity, it may be wise to have her spend another year in prekindergarten than to have her enter kindergarten. At this early age, a year of physical growth often results in many positive, significant changes. Some lags may improve with the passage of time. Others (dependency, self-discipline) may have to be worked on and don't dramatically improve with another year of growth. However, another year gives you time to develop her responsibility or independent behavior.

If your child shows some marginal immaturity and/or he has already entered kindergarten and has difficulty in the school setting, have him repeat the grade. Most children attend school for 12 or more years. If your child has academic difficulty and it continues through his early schooling, a negative attitude is certain to develop. When in doubt, have your young child repeat a grade. Consult a professional for advice.

75

Learning Disabilities, Dyslexia & Other Learning Problems

Many studies have been done on reasons children have difficulty learning. The more comprehensive the study, the greater the number of causes that have been found. Although this chapter focuses on learning disabilities, I have presented general areas of learning difficulties. Some areas overlap or may interact with one another to produce problems.

Causes of Learning Difficulties

Intelligence

About half of all children in the United States have average intelligence. About 25% are above average, and 25% are below average. Some learning problems result from a depressed level of intelligence. A child's abilities may be in the slow-learner range of intelligence, and he has difficulty competing in an average school setting. Children whose intellectual abilities fall below average often have difficulty competing academically.

Physical (includes neurological)

Sometimes physical problems or disabilities interfere in learning. These may be obvious, such as in a child with cerebral palsy who has motor problems and has difficulty writing. Or they can involve problems with vision or hearing. Health-related problems can also interfere with a child's ability to acquire information in the academic setting.

Genetic

A person who has reading problems is more apt to have a child with reading problems. Skills are often inherited. Learning difficulties can also be inherited.

Developmental lags

Thousands of skills and abilities develop in children. Skills don't develop at the same rate. You might have a 5-year-old who can ride a bike like his 8-year-old brother, but he can't color like a 3-year-old. If there is a lag in a skill a child needs for school (memory, hand-eye coordination, ability to follow directions, attention span), he may experience difficulty. This is discussed in more detail later.

Emotional

Children who experience emotional problems sometimes have difficulty in school. These problems can be a result of environmental conditions (divorce, death of a parent, separation) or they can center around the child's emotionality (depression, anxiety, worry).

Environmental

This can include lack of physical care of a child (malnutrition), a lack of language experience or exposure to educational materials and cultural deprivation.

Education

Inappropriate or ineffective teaching may contribute to a child's learning problems. Difficulties may arise when children change schools and move to a school that is at a higher level than the previous one.

Behavioral

This usually centers around behavioral problems, such as irresponsibility, lack of independent behavior and disinterest in school.

Biochemical

Recently chemical structure of foods, artificial ingredients in foods, drugs, nutrition and their effects on the human body have been studied. Although research is limited and results suggest only a slight connection between food and learning problems, some professionals believe there is a connection between these areas.

Learning Disability

Many children who experience learning problems are given the catch-all label of *learning disability* as the cause of difficulties. Many professionals do not agree on what learning disability means, so it's easy to see why most parents don't know what the term means. Most professionals feel for a child to be classified as learning-disabled he must have average or above-average intelligence or have the potential to function at this level. A child may have average intelligence or superior intelligence but is unable to read.

The term *learning disability* covers a wide range of learning disorders. It usually relates to lags in the development of skills or abilities necessary for learning. This learning problem may occur in several areas.

Learning disabilities are more common in boys than girls and cover a wide range of learning problems. Sometimes they affect reading, handwriting, memory, mathematics or other learning processes. A child may be able to spell cat, but when he sees it written, he can't read it. He can't remember how to pronounce the c or can't blend the sounds together.

Many skills and abilities (memory, coordination, language) develop in children. These skills do not develop at the same rate. Your 7-year-old can hit a baseball like a 10-year-old, but he can't color like a 5-year-old. Your 5-year-old may have an excellent concept of math, but his phonics skills are poor.

All children have strengths and weaknesses in developmental skills, and they do not grow at the same rate. If your child has lags in gross motor coordination and cannot hit a baseball or shoot a basketball, it isn't a big deal. However, if he has lags in auditory memory or similar processing skills, he may not be able to follow verbal directions. He will probably have trouble in school—this *is* a problem. Lags in development of skills needed to acquire academic abilities prevent the child from learning by methods that are successful with most children.

Let's assume an 8-year-old needs 5 basic skills to read. (The actual number of skills needed to read may be 20, 30 or

100.) The child who can read has all the skills developed at the same level, as represented by the diagram below.

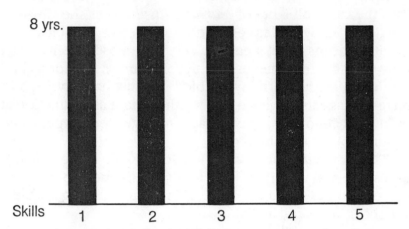

A learning-disabled child shows uneven development of the skills necessary to read, as indicated by this diagram.

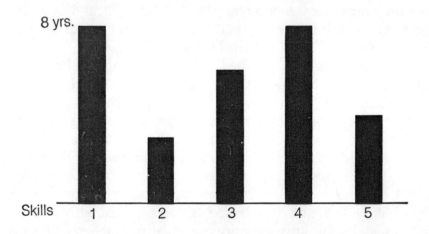

This child can perform some parts (skills 1 and 4) of the reading process excellently, but he has difficulty in other areas (skills 2, 3 and 5). When it becomes necessary to use all the skills together, he can't read. Although skills 1 and 4 are adequate, skill 2 may be 4 years below where it should be.

You can observe this child and see he can learn in many other areas and is not stupid (he can take his bike apart or put together complicated models). He may be classified as lazy or not caring about school. In addition, his performance at school is often inconsistent. One day he gets an A, the next day an F. This may lead you to feel he isn't trying.

But when the inconsistent performance is more closely analyzed, it is directly related to the skill being used. Schoolwork done on Monday required skill 1, and the child did well. On Tuesday, the work was similar but required skill 5. The child did poorly. When this is considered, his inconsistent performance is more understandable. He may have difficulties grasping some concepts (phonics, blending sounds) but does extremely well in other areas (math).

Signs of Learning Disabilities

The signs or symptoms of learning problems related to developmental lags are many and complicated. They usually occur in clusters. I discuss the most frequently occurring, common areas below.

Visual processing or visual perceptual-motor problems

Children have difficulty perceiving things visually. Their eyesight is usually excellent, but they may have trouble in visual discrimination, copying from the board or a book, reverse letters or numbers, confuse b and d or p and q, read "on" for "no" or "saw" for "was." See Chapter 77, Perceptual-Motor Deficits.

Auditory-processing or auditory perceptual problems

The child has nothing wrong with his hearing but has trouble processing or making sense out of information he hears. The child may have trouble discriminating between two words of similar but not identical sound such as "book" and "brook." Lags in language development may be present.

When a word is broken down into its phonic elements, the child may have difficulty putting parts together to form a word he knows. He may have trouble remembering what is read to him, but he remembers what he reads or vice versa. He may have difficulty remembering a series of directions or numbers. See Chapter 69, Following Directions & Auditory-Processing Problems, for more information.

Memory problems

He may remember things he sees but not what he hears or vice versa. He may show excellent memory at times and very poor skills in this area at other times. He may be able to remember things that happened months or years ago (long-term memory) but can't remember what he studied last night or what he ate for lunch (short-term memory).

Coordination problems

This could be in gross- and/or fine-motor coordination. He may have trouble riding a bike, throwing a ball, copying from the board, poor handwriting and using eating utensils. These problems as related to school performance are discussed in Chapter 77, Perceptual-Motor Deficits.

Problems forming concepts and abstracting

The child may have trouble applying information or problem-solving skills that he learns. It is as if he has to relearn the entire process. He has trouble making generalizations or inferences. He may not "catch on" to jokes most of his age mates enjoy. He has trouble in math and can't understand the rules of some games.

Overactivity, attention deficit and impulsivity

Some children with deficits in attention, impulse control and concentration problems may have difficulty in acquiring information or in performance. See Chapter 52, Overactivity, Attention-Deficit Disorder & Hyperactivity.

Labels for Learning Problems

Although classifications help identify or label the problem, they don't provide specific information needed for dealing with or developing educational plans. Recent trends emphasize terms, labels and classifications that relate to the *cause* of the difficulty. One stresses perceptual-motor functioning, and the other stresses language functioning. See Chapter 69, Following Directions & Auditory Processing and Chapter 77, Perceptual-Motor Deficits.

Aphasia—Without the capacity to interpret and express language.

Alexia—Without the capacity to read or interpret letters or words.

Acalculia—Without the capacity to understand and interpret numbers and engage in problem solving dealing with numbers.

Apraxia—Without the capacity to make movement.

Agraphia—Without the capacity to make fine-motor movements, especially writing.

Dyslexia—Disturbed function in the process of reading or interpreting letters or words.

Dyscalculia—Disturbed function in the process of understanding and interpreting numbers.

Dyspraxia—Disturbed function in the process of making fine-motor movements, such as writing or drawing.

Dysgraphia—Disturbed function in the process of making a fine-motor movement, such as writing and drawing.

Dyslexia

When the primary problem is reading, the child may be *dyslexic*. Though dyslexia means a disturbance in the ability to deal with words, it has become a catch-all word describing anything from a mild reading problem to a severe handicap. In some situations, the word *dyslexic* is used to describe any child who shows one or more of the symptoms described in the above section. I discuss *dyslexia* because it is becoming a very popular term. It is used to describe many types of learning problems or children who have difficulty competing with other students in school.

Many children with learning problems usually show a cluster of symptoms or signs. When this cluster involves specific characteristics, the child is *dyslexic*. The major symptom of this condition is an inability to read. I have seen children in fifth grade who were reading on a seventh-grade level and the parents were told the child had dyslexia. This is inconsistent with the definition.

Authorities on dyslexia have proposed many different factors to explain the origin of the disorder. In spite of this disagreement, all the experts agree dyslexia is nothing more than a specific language problem. It describes only one part of the comprehensive field of learning disorders.

Some specific symptoms of dyslexia include:
1. Inability to read.
2. Tendency to read words backward, such as "was" for "saw." Even in high school, what we call "nuclear" may be "unclear" to the dyslexic.
3. Words come out wrong, "basgetti and cheese," or in the wrong order, "please up hurry."
4. Lack of dexterity and problems in fine-motor coordination.
5. Memory problems (immediate recall or short-term memory).
6. Auditory difficulties, inability to sound back words or sounds that are heard.
7. Visual-memory problems, inability to visualize objects, words or letters, difficulty with copying materials from a book or off of a blackboard.
8. Inability to convert visual symbols into their auditory equivalent to pronounce words correctly when reading out loud.
9. Difficulty with mental arithmetic or math concepts may accompany the inability to read.
10. Organizing and managing life are difficult. Possessions, homework instructions, sense of direction or time may often get mixed up.

Additional information about dyslexia is available from: **The Orton Dyslexia Society, 724 York Road, Baltimore, MD 21204, phone 800-ABCD-123.**

Why Does My Child Have a Learning Disability?

When I'm asked this question, my response usually is, "I do not know." It's difficult to determine why a particular child has a learning disability. Through interviews and collecting background data, the best a professional can do is make an educated guess about the cause of the learning disability. There are several theories that explain the origin of the type of learning disability.

Brain damage or brain injury

Damage to the brain can occur before birth, at birth or after birth. This damage or injury is identified as a destruction of nerve tissue. Inadequate prenatal care, inadequate nutrition on the mother's part, use of drugs by the mother and other similar factors may influence healthy development of the fetus. When this occurs, there is a probability of inadequate development.

Complications at birth may also result in brain damage. Childhood illnesses (high fever) or accidents can result in brain damage.

Developmental lags

This is slowed growth and slowed process of physiological development. Certain skills do not mature as they should. The child develops more slowly than his peers in some areas.

Genetic factors

Learning disabilities can be inherited. Most of our children's traits and characteristics are inherited from us and our parents. Just as the parent who is a talented artist is more likely to have a child who is artistically inclined, the parent who has or had reading difficulties is more apt to have a child with similar problems.

There also is the possibility of chance variation in genetics. Two tall people are more likely to have a child who is tall, but sometimes two tall people have a short child. Through chance variation, it may be possible that families that do not have histories of learning difficulties may have a child who shows these problems.

Dealing with the Problem

It's very difficult to determine the cause of the learning problem. But the cause is not as important as the treatment. No matter what the cause, methods to deal with the problem are very similar.

There are various methods to help children with learning disabilities who experience academic problems. Attempts to deal with the problem result in significant improvement, slight improvement or no improvement.

Let's go back to the example I used earlier about the child who can't hit a baseball. Your child can't hit a baseball with a bat when it is pitched to him. You could tell the child, "Every day after work when I come home from work, we're going to practice baseball." Every afternoon after work you practice throwing to him so he can learn to hit the ball.

For some children, a short period of practice results in significant improvement. Others, even with a very long amount of practice, show only slight improvement. Some children, after a short or long period of practice, show almost no improvement.

Children whose skills will improve show it over a relatively short period of time—a month or so. For the child who doesn't show any major improvement over the same period of time, two other conditions may occur. You may need to put the ball and bat in the closet and wait a few months until some physical maturation occurs. With time and some practice, this child can begin to hit the ball. For another child, time and practice will not enable him to hit a baseball. A very similar process occurs when attempts are made to deal with learning problems.

Dealing with Developmental Lags

There are three ways to deal with children with developmental lags or learning disabilities.

Strengthen skills needed for learning

If a child has a reading problem, sometimes it's recommended that emphasis *not* be placed on reading skills but on the development of the abilities the child needs to read. Rather than working on reading, the child may be involved in language therapy to help strengthen auditory memory or processing skills. This is similar to a child experiencing perceptual-motor difficulties. Rather than directly working on academics (tutoring), attempts are made to strengthen the child's weak skills. See Chapter 69, Following Directions & Auditory-Processing Problems and Chapter 77, Perceptual-Motor Deficits. Treatment usually involves having the child in therapy with a developmental optometrist, occupational therapist or speech-and-language therapist.

Strengthen academic skills

This is tutoring. If a child has problems in reading, get him a tutor to help develop his reading skills. If English or math is a weak area, have someone work directly with the child to strengthen these skills.

Fit school to the child

The child who has learning difficulties may need individual consideration in the classroom. The child who has visual perceptual-motor difficulties and trouble writing may need to do his tests verbally.

A child who has trouble following verbal directions given in a series may need to receive them one at a time. The child with the learning disability needs work presented at a level, rate and in a manner that recognizes his strengths and weaknesses.

Many times these children need a smaller classroom or a school environment with a small pupil-teacher ratio. In a smaller setting, work can be individualized. Some schools can and are willing to do this; others are not. If the school is unable to work around the child's difficulty, find another school. Special education is an attempt to place the child in a smaller classroom setting so he can receive more individual attention.

See Chapter 82 on Special Education and Chapter 67, Children Who Need a Smaller Classroom Setting or Pupil-Teacher Ratio.

Learning Disabilities—Things to Consider

Learning styles

All children have *learning styles*. Children have strengths and weaknesses. Some learn better if they utilize one skill more than another. If a child is a visual learner, he acquires information better if he sees it than if he hears it. He won't benefit from lectures or similar methods of presenting information. It is better to provide him with visual aids to capitalize on his learning style.

Try to identify your child's strengths, weaknesses and particular learning style. Try to place him in a school environment that can work around and with his individual strengths and weaknesses.

Continuous assessment

If your child is in therapy (perceptual-motor training or language therapy) or a particular learning program is designed to strengthen skills necessary for learning, there must be continuous assessment. This determines whether treatment results in improvement. If treatment will benefit the child, you should see some results.

Some children do not significantly improve skills through training. Only time helps. Some children have been in this training for 2 years and have improved. But they didn't improve because of the training. Improvement occurred because of physical development.

Fad treatments

Be cautious of fad treatments. Many programs are expensive and make claims of success that are not supported by scientific research.

Ask professionals in your area and your child's pediatrician about particular programs. Gather as much information as possible. Be very hesitant about programs that do a lot of advertising, require up-front money and guarantee success.

Tutoring

For a child who has academic problems, try tutoring. If your child has trouble reading, have him tutored. Try to find someone who specializes in your child's area of difficulty. Individual tutoring is best. The smaller the group of students being tutored, the better.

Individualized instruction

The most effective method of dealing with a child with a learning disability is to get him in a school or classroom setting where some individualization of instruction and consideration can be given to him. This may involve special education. It could also involve a school with a small pupil-teacher ratio.

Putting it all together

All children have strengths and weaknesses. Many children show the characteristics of a learning-disabled child. Many research studies tested children having trouble in school and children not having trouble in school in basic skill areas (perceptual-motor skills, language skills, memory skills). Without the child's report-card grades or achievement level, it was often difficult to identify the children who had problems and those who did not.

If your child shows some of the characteristics mentioned above, it doesn't mean he has a learning disability. All of us compensate for our weak points. Some children are able to do it much better than others. Some do not have problems in school, even though they have some weaknesses in the skills necessary for learning. The major criteria is if he's doing poorly in school.

76

Monitoring School Behavior & Performance—Home-School Communication Systems

For a child having behavior and/or performance problems in school, communication between the parent and teacher or administration is a necessity to deal with the problems effectively. The first step is to establish an open line of communication between you and school personnel. By doing this, you can stay informed about the problem and deal with it before it gets out of hand.

Many schools have built-in communication systems, such as report cards, progress reports, behavioral reports and incomplete homework slips. Many teachers phone parents to inform them of their child's behavior or progress. You may need to receive more frequent communication from the school. Try to establish some kind of formal communication between you and the school.

Most of the techniques I use to obtain information from the school are designed to require very little of the teacher's time each day or week. Asking a teacher to write a note or call you may involve a lot of time, especially if they have to do this for other students. But if you keep the communication system simple and have it require little of their time, the task becomes easier.

Three-part communication system

The communication system involves three parts—you, the teacher and the child. You are responsible for designing and making the communication system, providing the materials and giving it to the child each day or week. You are also required to administer consequences for appropriate and/or inappropriate behavior.

The child is responsible for getting it to and from school and seeing that the teacher signs it.

The teacher observes the child and checks the appropriate information on the communication system. The teacher is *not* responsible for seeing that the child brings it to her to be signed. This is the *child's* responsibility.

When teachers are made responsible, children learn if they blend into the woodwork at the end of the period or day, teachers are busy with other things and forget to call them up to have the chart checked. The only excuse you take for not having the chart signed is if the teacher died! If the teacher's name isn't in the obituary column the following day, the child gets the consequence for not getting it signed.

If the child has a substitute teacher who doesn't know about the communication system, the child should ask that person to write, "I'm a substitute teacher. I don't know anything about this chart" and have that person initial it.

Be sure communication is set up so the child can't mark the chart himself or change what the teacher writes on it. Have the teacher initial the chart and make her comments in ink or by some other method so they can't be altered.

The reason for establishing good communication between you and the teacher is to be aware of and deal with school problems early, before they get out of hand. Some children respond better if progress is monitored on a daily or weekly basis rather than every 4-, 6- or 9-week period. The sooner difficulties can be identified, the easier they are to treat and the more unlikely they will get out of hand or future problems will develop.

Setting Up a Communication System

Make an appointment to meet with your child's teacher or appropriate school person. Discuss your child's behavior in great detail: how often, when, under what circumstances, in what situations and exactly what occurs. Avoid general terms.

Behavior must be analyzed to determine what corrective system will be used. After the behavior is described and discussed, you can start designing the procedure to be used. Discuss what you will use with the teacher(s). See if they will agree to observe, record or check your child's behavior.

Once this is done, at separate times you and the teacher should meet with your child to explain the system. Explain how he will earn points or how good and bad behavior will be indicated and what the consequences of his behavior will be. Explain exactly what he has to do to get good marks or indications of appropriate behavior. Avoid including too many behaviors. A child may be doing many things in the classroom, such as talking, getting out of his desk, disrupting the class, fidgeting, not doing his work.

Try to analyze the behaviors and target *one*. Although the child may be doing many inappropriate things in school, target one, such as not completing work. If this particular child was doing his work, he'd have less time to disrupt, talk, fidget. Try to target one or two—*no more than three*—behaviors to be worked on.

When starting a communication system, use it on a daily basis. After the child responds well on a daily basis, move it to every other day. Then move it to a week, 2 weeks and longer.

How frequently behavior occurs determines how to set up the chart and break up the daily or weekly period. If a child gets out of his desk 47 times a day, it's ridiculous to say, "If you stay in your desk all day, we'll give you a sticker." It might even be difficult for this child if you break the day into a morning and afternoon period.

His behavior is so severe that the odds of him successfully performing for a 3-hour block of time is impossible. You may want to break the day into 7 to 10 parts. For every period of time he remains in his desk, he is given a good mark. This is explained in detail in the discussion of the types of communication systems. For middle- and especially high-school students, a weekly system is usually more appropriate.

Individualize the system for your child to accommodate his particular area of difficulty or the behavior(s) of concern. Many schools have weekly progress reports they issue if requested by the parents. Many times I prefer not to use the school's system because it involves general comments on the child's behaviors.

I normally try to identify the child's particular problems and design the communication system based on those. Below I give some examples of various types of systems. Use these as examples. Like behavior charts, the number, type and style of communication systems is limited only by your imagination.

Communication systems can be divided into two general areas. One is when the target behavior can occur more than once a day, and the other is when the behavior occurs only once a day.

When Target Behavior Can Occur
More than Once a Day

This type of communication system can be set up on a daily or weekly basis. Behaviors include staying in your seat, getting permission before you speak, completing classwork, fighting, talking in class, homework, participation in class, getting along with other children and similar behaviors.

Time

Decide on a logical way to break the school day into time periods. Talk with your child's teacher and find out how many activities or subjects are normally covered in a school day.

Some teachers divide the day according to subjects (math, reading, spelling) or type of activity (story time, coloring, work sheets). Others use time to split the day into sections (8:30 to 10:30, 10:30 to lunch).

For smaller children who perform more activities in the morning, the first half of the school may be broken into five periods; after lunch may involve only two periods.

Once the division is established, construct a chart.

When using time as a way to break up the day into periods, how frequently the behavior is seen may determine how the day is broken up. A child who does no seatwork in class should not have a communication chart that involves the whole day. You don't want to tell him, "If you do *all* your work today, you'll get a good mark." This is too much for him to handle at one time. Break the day into several periods of time. For each period of time he completes his work, he gets a good mark. The same is true for a child who has trouble staying in his desk. If his communication chart is broken into morning and afternoon, the odds of him being successful are pretty low. It is better to break up the day into hours.

If this system works successfully, increase the time periods. If you break the day into hourly sections and the child responds well, break the day into 2- or 3-hour blocks of time. Under this system he has to be good for 2 or 3 hours to obtain the appropriate mark. Then you can have him respond appropriately for a half a day, then a whole day to get the good mark.

Once the child responds well to a daily system, move it to an every-other-day system, then to a weekly system, then to a every-other-week system.

Let's take an example of a child who continually talks in class. The first thing is to talk with the teacher to get an idea of how frequently the behavior occurs. This will help determine how the chart is divided or how frequently you want to monitor the behavior. If it's very frequent, divide the day into smaller sections of time. The less frequent the behavior, the larger the periods of time the day can be divided into.

Jason's Quiet Chart

	Mon.	Tues.	Wed.	Thurs.	Fri.
Math					
Science					
Spelling					
English					
Social Studies					

Tell your child he is responsible for bringing the chart to and from school and for seeing that the teacher marks it. You and the teacher explain the system to your child. "You have been talking too much in class, so we have set up a chart to help you be quiet. When you don't talk out of turn during a subject (or period of time), Mrs. Jones will put a star on that block. If you talk, you'll get an X in the block."

At the end of the day, your child brings the chart home, and you administer the consequence that was determined. Each star that your child earns during the day may represent 5 minutes past his bedtime. Or he may be working for a reward at the end of the week. The teacher keeps the chart and marks it after each period or the child keeps it and gives it to the teacher at the appropriate time. Your child is responsible for it.

When setting up this system, use positive consequences (reward) whenever possible. When punishment is used, your child will forget to get the chart marked or will lose it to avoid the negative consequence.

If your child's behavior occurs more frequently and the day needs to be divided into smaller sections, use a chart similar to the one below.

Alan's "Be Good" Chart

	Mon.	Tues.	Wed.	Thurs.	Fri.
9:00-9:30					
9:30-10:00					
10:00-10:30					
10:30-11:00					
11:00-11:30					
LUNCH	//////	//////	//////	//////	//////
12:30-1:00					
1:00-1:30					
1:30-2:00					

If you work with your child using a chart similar to the preceding one and his behavior improves, you may want to break up the day into larger sections of time. The behavior is monitored less frequently.

Jason's Quiet Chart

	Mon.	Tues.	Wed.	Thurs.	Fri.
Early Morning					
Late Morning					
Early Afternoon					
Late Afternoon					

Jason's Quiet Chart

	Mon.	Tues.	Wed.	Thur.	Fri.
Morning					
Afternoon					

If your child does well after you start breaking the days into larger segments of time, you may want to work toward a weekly monitoring of his behavior. This can be done with a chart similar to the one on the next page.

Jason's Quiet Chart

	Being Quiet	Teacher initials or comments
Math	Good Fair Poor	
Science	Good Fair Poor	
Spelling	Good Fair Poor	
English	Good Fair Poor	
Social Studies	Good Fair Poor	

If you work with your child using a chart similar to the ones above and his behavior improves, you may want to break the day into larger sections. The behavior is monitored less frequently.

When you monitor your child's behavior less frequently (on a weekly basis), he will bring the chart to the teacher on Friday to be marked. The teacher circles Good, Fair or Poor, depending on the child's behavior during the entire week. Points can be assigned to the adjectives describing behavior. "Good" receives 2 points, "Fair" 1 point and "Poor" nothing.

Your child must earn a certain number of points to receive some type of privilege on the weekend. To have a friend sleep over, the child might have to earn 8 points during the week. The number of points he has to earn during the week is based on how the teacher feels he performed the week before you started the weekly chart. You can meet with the teacher, describe the above chart and ask her, "Jason can earn a total of 10 points if he is quiet all week. If he had had the chart last week, how many points would he have received?" If she says "2," make the goal 5 points to receive the reward. If she says "6," make the goal 7 or 8 points.

You can also use a chart similar to the one below, in which your child receives points. He can earn 0 to 5 points for each class. A 0 shows he had inappropriate behavior all week. A 5 means he was good all week. Three points means he had a fair week and was appropriate 3 of the 5 days.

Jason's Quiet Chart

	Being Quiet	Initials and Comments
Math	4	keep up the good work. B. Smith
Science	5	Great week!!
Spelling	3	Doing Better mary James
English	0	Could Not keep Quiet Mrs Smooth
Social Studies	2	Try Harder. m. Collins

For the child who has problems outside the classroom or in unstructured settings rather than in the classroom, use a chart similar to the one below. This is for a child who fights or doesn't get along with other children.

Chad's Getting Along With Others Chart

	Getting Along	Speaking Nicely	Teacher's Intials
Before School			
Recess			
Lunch Times			
PE			
Waiting for Bus			

If your child cooperates with other children, doesn't get in fights and shares, the section under *getting along* would be checked. If the problems with other kids involve arguing and name calling, a category such as *talking nicely* could be included.

The chart can also be divided according to teachers. For a child having trouble completing homework and classwork, a chart similar to the one below could be used on a daily or weekly basis.

	Homework	Classwork	Teacher's Initials
Mrs. Smith	Complete Incomplete	Complete Incomplete	
Mrs. Dean	Complete Incomplete	Complete Incomplete	
Mrs. Jones	Complete Incomplete	Complete Incomplete	

Many times with older children (middle-school, junior-high and high-school students), you may not want to monitor the behavior on a daily basis. Using a weekly system, your child could take the chart to school on Friday and get all his teachers to initial it. Sometimes with older children you can provide the school counselor with several charts and several self-addressed, stamped envelopes. If the chart is to be mailed to you, run the chart from Thursday to Wednesday. On Wednesday, a counselor goes to the child's teachers to see how he is performing. The counselor puts it in the mail and sends it to you. By doing this, your child avoids the embarrassment of having to take it to the teacher. You can receive it by Friday so you can administer the consequences for the weekend.

Let's take an example of a child who does poorly in school. Charts similar to the ones below could be used.

	Homework	Classwork	Talking in Class	Attention in Class	Initial
Math	Complete Incomplete	Good Fair Poor	Good Fair Poor	Good Fair Poor	
English	Complete Incomplete	Good Fair Poor	Good Fair Poor	Good Fair Poor	
Science	Complete Incomplete	Good Fair Poor	Good Fair Poor	Good Fair Poor	
History	Complete Incomplete	Good Fair Poor	Good Fair Poor	Good Fair Poor	
Reading	Complete Incomplete	Good Fair Poor	Good Fair Poor	Good Fair Poor	

Student _____ **Week Ending** _____

Teacher's Signature	Subject	Classwork: Working or Not Working	Conduct: Good, Bad or Passable	Homework: Complete or Incomplete
	Biology			
	Civics			
	Geometry			
	Typing 1			
	English			

The two charts above are designed to help a child who does poorly in school for reasons other than ability. As you can see, there are no indications of grades on the charts. You are specifically looking at your child's *effort* in classwork and homework and his ability to pay attention in class.

For older children, tell them their job at this point in their life is to attend school and do what they're supposed to do. Everything they do on the weekend is a *privilege*. If they complete their job during the week, they'll have their privileges during the weekend. If they only do 20% of what they are supposed to do during the week, they only get 20% of their privileges. If they do 50%, they get 50% of their privileges.

Break the weekend into five parts (Sunday afternoon, Sunday morning, Saturday afternoon, Saturday morning, Friday after school). For the older child, this may involve weekend nights instead of mornings. The amount of work your child does during the week also determines how much phone time or driving privileges he will have next week.

Frequency

When behavior occurs more than once a day, a chart can be set up based on the number of times a day it occurs. A chart similar to the one below is used.

Tony's Finishing Work Chart

Monday		Tuesday		Wednesday		Thursday		Friday	
O	O	O	O	O	O	O	O	O	O
O	O	O	O	O	O	O	O	O	O
O	O	O	O	O	O	O	O	O	O
	O		O		O		O		O

Let's say the target behavior is completing seatwork. You analyzed the behavior and found seven things your child has to do during the school day—he seldom completes one. You say, "I have put seven circles on this chart. For each assignment that you complete, the teacher will put a star over the circle. When you don't finish, you'll get an X. At the end of the day when you bring the chart home, you can trade your stars for extra play time" or whatever consequence has been determined as valuable to the child.

Another child may be disturbing the class. You analyze the behavior and find out this occurs 10 times a day. Create a chart similar to the one below and have it placed on the teacher's desk. Tell your child that every time there is a disturbance in class (define what you mean by "disturbance" and try to narrow it to as few a behaviors as possible), the teacher will color in one of the circles. You can then set up some type of consequence for the number of circles that weren't colored in.

Alan's "Be Good" Chart

Mon.		Tues.		Wed.		Thurs.		Fri.	
O	O	O	O	O	O	O	O	O	O
O	O	O	O	O	O	O	O	O	O
O	O	O	O	O	O	O	O	O	O
O	O	O	O	O	O	O	O	O	O
O	O	O	O	O	O	O	O	O	O

Target Behavior That Can Occur Only Once a Day

Sometimes the target behavior occurs or can occur only once a day (refusing to do math). When this happens, two systems can be set up.

Several behaviors

A target behavior may occur only once a day, but the child exhibits several different problem behaviors. Eddie rushes through his math seatwork and usually gets it wrong, talks during reading period and runs to the cafeteria for lunch. To deal with these different problems, set up a chart similar to the first one on the next page.

	Mon.	Tues.	Wed.	Thurs.	Fri.
Takes time with Math					
Quiet during Reading					
Walks to Lunch					

Another child has trouble with other specific behaviors in the classroom.

	Mon.	Tues.	Wed.	Thurs.	Fri.
Has all supplies					
Stays seated during Story Time					
Completes phonics worksheet					
Cooperates during free time					
Packs books quietly					

The same procedures as described above would be used with these charts.

One behavior

When there is only one target behavior, use a chart like this.

	Mon.	Tues.	Wed.	Thurs.	Fri.
Turning in Homework					

For a child having trouble concentrating in class, set up something similar to this.

	Paying Attention in Class	Comments
Spelling	Good Fair Poor	
Reading	Good Fair Poor	
Math	Good Fair Poor	
Science	Good Fair Poor	
Social Studies	Good Fair Poor	

If your child is having trouble cooperating with others, use a chart like this. Her teacher can circle the appropriate face and make comments.

	Cooperating with others	Comments
Monday	☺ ☹ ☹	
Tuesday	☺ ☹ ☹	
Wednesday	☺ ☹ ☹	
Thursday	☺ ☹ ☹	
Friday	☺ ☹ ☹	

When incomplete classwork is a problem, a chart similar to this can be used.

	Classwork	Initials or Comments
Mrs. Smith	Complete Incomplete	
Mrs. West	Complete Incomplete	
Mrs. Collins	Complete Incomplete	

Similar procedures as described above can be used with these charts. They can be used on a weekly or daily basis.

Using tokens

Tokens can be used instead of charts to communicate information from the school to the parent. A token can be anything the child can transport from school to home. It could be a sticker, a happy face stamped on the child's hand, a poker chip, a piece of a puzzle, a bean.

One parent was having trouble with her daughter completing her work in the classroom. The little girl wanted a new doll. The mother bought a bag of marbles and gave it to the teacher. Both the teacher and parent told the girl that every time she completed a sequence of her work, she'd get a marble to bring home. At home, the mother got a jar and put a sign on it that read "Laurie's New Doll." Laurie was told, "Each day when you come home from school, put the marbles you have earned in this jar. When it's filled, we will get your doll." Laurie got the doll in a few weeks.

Another parent used tokens to get her son to participate

in class. Darren was shy, timid and didn't say anything in class. He wouldn't respond, even when asked a direct question. Darren's desire to see a professional basketball game was identified as a reward. The mother bought a puzzle (about 25 pieces) and gave the pieces to the teacher. Darren's mother told him and his teacher that each time he spoke in class, he'd be given a piece of the puzzle to bring home. When the puzzle was completed, his father would take him to the game. In about 7 school days, the puzzle was finished and Darren got to go to the basketball game.

Any type of token can be used to get a daily or weekly report on the child's progress. A consequence is identified, and the child is able to trade the tokens for the reward.

Using established lines of communication

Many times children bring things home daily from school. This may be an assignment pad, a particular notebook, folder or workbook. Sometimes children bring home materials on a weekly basis. Every Friday a stack of seatwork comes home or tests are returned every Wednesday. If your child has something that comes from school on a regular basis, it can be used as a communication system.

If your child's assignment book comes home every day, set up a system with the teacher where the day is broken into 5 parts. On the top right of the assignment, the teacher writes a number from 0 to 5 and initials it. If the target behavior was completing work, a 0 means he did nothing, a 5 all of the work, a 3 half of it. The teacher can also write good, fair or poor on something that comes home on a regular basis to indicate your child's behavior in the class setting. Different types of stickers or stamps can also be put on material coming home.

Communication Systems—Things to Remember

1. If your child has problems in school and/or has previously experienced difficulties, don't assume no news is good news. Initiate school contacts.

2. Schedule a meeting with the appropriate school person (teacher, counselor, principal). Discuss the child's problems in detail. Try to identify exactly what is happening, when and under what conditions. Analyze the behavior.

3. Try to establish how frequently behavior occurs. This is very important because it determines how frequently the behavior needs to be monitored and how the communication system is to be established. It also helps establish how much improvement the child has to show to receive the reward. Break up the day into small periods of time so your child can have some success.

4. Be sure you and the teacher have the same understanding of what behaviors are to be monitored and how the system is to be checked.

5. Don't include too many behaviors. One is best. Three or four is the maximum.

6. You and the teacher, at separate times, should explain to your child exactly what he has to do or what he has to avoid to achieve good marks.

7. Provide all the materials for the communication system and construct it. You are also responsible for administering the consequences of the behavior and for giving your child the system to bring to school.

8. Your child is responsible for getting the communication system to and from school and seeing the teacher initials and checks his chart.

9. The teacher should not assume any responsibility for the communication system. She shouldn't ask the child for the system. All the teacher has to do is observe and check the child when he brings the communication system to her.

10. Once a daily communication system is working effectively, increase the length of time being monitored. The child who is monitored on a hourly basis may be moved to a 2-hour basis, then a half-day basis. Extend the time the behavior is monitored when it seems the child is successful. The daily communication system may be moved to biweekly, then weekly and eventually every other week.

11. Keep the system simple so it requires little of the teacher's time.

12. Use positive consequences (reward) as much as possible.

13. Look for gradual improvement. The child who isn't doing any classwork is doing very well if he completes 25% of the work. Once he begins to experience success at this level,

gradually increase the amount of work he has to do to receive the reward. Don't look for significant change overnight. Try to lock the child into the system by having him experience success by achieving goals. Look for movement toward the end goal. Don't try to change the behavior all at once.

14. Be sure you have a place for the teacher to initial the communication system or check it in some manner so you know for sure it's *her* response on the chart *not* your child's. Don't provide the child with an opportunity to forge the chart.

Chapter 10, Using Charts to Change Behavior; Chapter 68, Classwork; Chapter 72, Homework; Chapter 65, Academic & Behavior Problems, and Chapter 66, Bringing Home Assignments, Books, Tests & Notes, also provide information regarding communication systems.

77

Perceptual-Motor Deficits

Some children experience fine-motor and/or gross-motor coordination problems. Deficits in fine-motor coordination are also called *perceptual-motor* or *visual-motor* problems. These difficulties occur much more frequently than deficits in gross-motor functioning. They interfere with school performance more. For these reasons, I've devoted the majority of this chapter to perceptual-motor deficits.

Gross-Motor Problems

Gross-motor coordination refers to skills and abilities we normally think about when we discuss coordination (riding a bike, jumping a rope, playing sports). When a child has problems in this area, he is usually described as poorly coordinated, having "two left feet" or clumsy. While this deficit doesn't interfere with the child's ability to perform in the academic setting, it often produces social problems, especially for boys. These children have difficulty with sports and are usually picked last when sides are formed for a game. They are usually seen as poor athletes, cannot ride a bike as fast as the other children, come in last in races and are often criticized. Problems in this area sometimes produce socialization difficulties or negative attention from the child's peers.

Fine-Motor Problems

Perceptual-motor or visual-motor deficits refer to problems in fine-motor or hand-eye coordination. This pertains to how well the child's eyes and hands work together or how well he can reproduce with his hands what he sees. Children who have difficulties in these areas have trouble with paper-and-pencil tasks. Schoolwork involves a significant amount of handwriting. These children usually have problems in the academic setting as a result of this coordination problem.

As youngsters, children with visual-motor problems often stay away from paper-and-pencil tasks. They don't like to color, draw, cut and paste or practice their ABC's. Handwriting is a difficult task, and it requires a great deal of energy and effort for them. In their early school years, they have difficulty completing seatwork. Penmanship or coloring is poor and work is sloppy and disorganized. They take a long time to complete their written homework. These children often reverse or invert letters and numbers. Sometimes they write words or their names backward.

They have trouble copying from the board because they lose their place, leave out letters, words or whole phrases. It often is a monumental task for you to read what the child has written for his homework assignment. Sometimes they confuse letters, "d's" are called "b's" and "w's" are pronounced "m's." They may confuse or read words backward, such as "saw" is read as "was" or "felt" is pronounced "left."

This is an appropriate time to make a couple of important points. First, the majority of kindergarten children reverse letters and numbers or write them backward. If this is seen in kindergarten, don't be concerned. About 50% of beginning first graders show reversals, but this should be phasing out toward the end of first grade. Only about 10% of beginning second graders have problems in this area. If the characteristics of perceptual-motor deficits are seen at this grade level, there is a strong probability the child has a problem.

Second, the child with perceptual-motor problems doesn't necessarily have eye trouble or poor vision. He could have 20/20 vision and still have difficulty. The trouble is not in his eyes or his hands, but in processing what his eyes see. He sees something, then his brain processes the information and tells his hand what to do. The problem lies in translating or transferring the information from his eyes to his hands. Although these children usually don't have vision problems, it's good to get a vision exam.

Perceptual-motor deficits seen in some children usually result from a developmental deviation or lag. In Chapter 52, Overactivity, and Chapter 75, Learning Disabilities, I explained what was meant by a developmental lag or deviation. You may want to review this. Perceptual-motor deficits from developmental lags or deviations mean the child's hand-eye coordination is slow in developing. He may be 7 years old but shows the visual-motor development of a 5-year-old. The lag in these skills is the result of a development deviation. These deficits usually improve with age. Around puberty (11 to 16) when all skills level out, visual-motor problems improve and often diminish.

In some children, perceptual-motor deficits are related to brain or organic damage. These are usually children who have had some type of head injury or have a relatively low level of intellectual functioning. Hand-eye coordination difficulties don't improve with age in these children, as do those in children with lags resulting from a developmental deviation. These children may show some improvement but generally their visual-motor deficits remain, and they don't show significant improvement with practice. Parents of these children may have to accept the child's difficulties and attempt to work around them.

Perceptual-Motor Training

For some children, perceptual-motor training or therapy is recommended. To better understand the effects of this training and how to assess its effectiveness, let's take an example. We have two 5-year-olds. We put each on a 2-wheeled bike. One rides the bike very well. The other can't ride the bike. For the boy who can't ride, we'd say the skills he needs to ride the bike are not developing as fast as the other child's skills. There is a lag in development. You decide to help the boy learn to ride the bike by practicing with him every evening when you come home from work. For one child, practice helps, and he is riding the bike in a very short period of time. For the other child, the practice doesn't result in significant improvement. Put the bike in the garage, and try again in a few months.

Sometimes practice improves developmental lags. In other cases, practice doesn't result in significant improvement. Time, not practice, is the important factor. Growth may have to occur before practice is beneficial or physical development may be the only thing that brings improvement. In children whose perceptual-motor deficits are related to organic damage, improvement usually doesn't occur.

The same situation exists for perceptual-motor training. Usually improvement is seen in a relatively short period of time if it is to occur. Most reputable trainers or therapists work with a child for several weeks (4 to 6) then make an assessment. If improvement doesn't occur, they discontinue the therapy. I've had parents tell me their child was in perceptual-motor training for 2 years, and he's finally benefitting from it. This child hasn't benefitted from the training. The improvement has occurred because he is 2 years older.

Research does not extensively support the fact that improvement in perceptual-motor skills by therapy results in improvement in academic skills or generalizes to the school setting. Many physicians and scientists don't look favorably on this method to improve school performance. It is recommended that money be spent for tutoring in academic skills. However, this method coud be considered if the therapist is reputable. If your child is receiving therapy, continuously assess the effectiveness of the treatment, especially as it relates to your child's school performance.

Perceptual-motor deficits that result from lags in development may be improved with training. If you pursue this avenue, determine if the person's methods have been effective with others and whether he uses a reputable approach to this form of therapy. Some agencies (medical centers, universities, hospitals) in your community may have perceptual-motor-training programs. Sometimes this training can be obtained privately. Developmental optometrists, physical therapists and occupational therapists usually provide these services. Children enrolled in these programs usually go for 1/2 to 1 hour, 2 or 3 times a week. They engage in activities to build perceptual-motor skills. Usually parents are also given activities to do with the child at home.

At our center, we usually give parents of children with deficits in this area a list of activities to help improve these skills. Generally, parents can try to gear the child's play toward games and activities that strengthen these skills. Toys that require hand-eye coordination skills can be bought. A store that has educational supplies for teachers usually has many games and activities to enhance perceptual-motor abilities. The list below gives you some general ideas of things you can do with children who have visual-motor problems.

Fine-Motor Activities
1. Tracing, coloring, cutting, pasting
2. Dot-to-dot, puzzles, fingerpainting
3. Building models, lacing boards, weaving games, clay
4. Jacks, pick-up sticks, puppets
5. Building blocks, Lincoln Logs, Tinker Toys, Erector sets, Legos
6. Buttoning, unbuttoning, tying, zipping
7. Electronic games (baseball, Atari)

If a child has poor penmanship, it's better to have him practice paper-and-pencil tasks he enjoys (coloring, tracing) than to have him practice his penmanship excessively. While most children who show perceptual-motor deficits don't necessarily have gross-motor coordination problems, practice in this area seems to improve fine-motor skills. Below are some activities that are beneficial for children experiencing gross-motor and/or fine-motor coordination difficulties.

Gross-Motor Activities
It's important for you to understand a child with motor impairment appears clumsy and awkward. He may also appear disoriented. This is usually because he hasn't developed left-right perception. He must learn to move his body in an organized way. To accomplish this, try the following activities.

Activities included in this list are done easily and require no specialized materials. You shouldn't have difficulty doing these with your child.

Walking activities—Have the child walk in various ways (forward, backward, sideways). The child can also imitate various animals (elephant, duck, crab).

Crawling activities—The child can crawl in various ways (move like a snake, worm, soldier).

Walking hockey—Have the child move an object across the floor with his feet to a goal. Use points, and play with teams.

Obstacle course—Arrange an obstacle course using chairs, tables, boxes. Have the child move through the course in different ways.

Balance beam—Put a 2x4 board on the floor. Have the child move on it in different directions.

Exercises—Any exercise is good. Jumping Jacks, hopping, bending are all good.

Other activities—Try dodge ball, leapfrog, Simon says, hokey pokey, bike riding, roller skating, skateboarding , hopscotch.

Ball games—Engage in throwing, catching and kicking activities. This does not necessarily include organized sports. Don't force a child with motor problems into participation in organized sports until he wants to participate.

This list was prepared by Mallary Collins, M.Ed.

School Interventions

Whether or not a child receives perceptual-motor training, major improvement in his school performance will result primarily from a teacher or school system willing to give the child some individual consideration and work around his deficits. Some children with perceptual-motor problems have learning disabilities that significantly interfere with their ability to learn. They have difficulty learning material. They don't learn from the methods that work with most children. Information doesn't get in, and they may require special education or specialized instruction.

Most children with perceptual-motor deficits do not have trouble learning. Their major problem is writing. They have difficulty with handwriting activities. Ask them to write the answer to a question, such as, "What is lightning?" and they'll give you 4 words. Ask them to answer verbally, and they'll give you 4 minutes worth!

Much work in elementary grades involves paper-and-pencil tasks. This child's performance is frequently inadequate. Handwriting is difficult, penmanship is poor, he may not finish his seatwork. Children with this difficulty need less emphasis on written skills and more emphasis on verbal abilities.

You'd never think of putting a child with sight problems in the back of a classroom or expect him to see the board from there if he had difficulty. You'd put him in the front of the room to minimize his difficulties in seeing. You would modify the environment to accommodate his deficits. Many modifications can occur in the classroom and with homework to help a child with perceptual-motor deficits.

Minimize handwriting

The general approach is to minimize the handwriting or perceptual-motor skills and maximize using verbal skills. In most cases, this can be done in an average-size classroom. It may have to be done in a classroom with a smaller pupil-teacher ratio. With fewer students, a teacher has more time to give each child some special consideration. The child with perceptual-motor difficulty may have difficulties copying material, be slow in handwriting tasks and show poor penmanship.

Many children reverse numbers and letters and may add 10 + 31 = instead of 10 + 13 =, spell cat cta or dog as bog. Instead of marking the math problem or spelling word wrong when it's obvious the child has reversed some part of it, the teacher could ask him how to spell the word orally. Or watch him do the math problem.

Give him credit if the problem is correct—but he reversed the numbers. Or use some other method to see whether the child knows the correct information or the correct method.

Penmanship is usually poor. Sometimes it's easier for them to print than to write in cursive (longhand). Don't compare the child's penmanship to others, but to his own previous efforts. If the child is trying his best, he should be graded accordingly.

The child may write slowly and may require extra time to do seatwork. He may need to be graded on what he has completed. A teacher gives the class 10 questions, and students have to write the answers. The child with perceptual-motor difficulties only finishes 6, although he tried hard, didn't fool around and put forth 100% effort. He should be graded on the 6 completed and not receive a failing grade. Or he could be given extra time to complete the task.

A reading teacher gives the class 10 vocabulary words to find in the dictionary, write the definitions and make a sentence using each word. The main purpose of the assignment is for the child to learn how to use the dictionary, learn word meanings and how to use the words appropriately. Copying the definition and writing in a notebook have nothing to do with the learning experience. The exercise may take 1-1/2 hours for a child with perceptual-motor deficits. Minimize the writing or have someone else write the information that the child dictates.

Writing spelling words 10 times each is designed to help the child learn the words. With cooperative parents, the teacher could eliminate the writing and ask you to be sure the child knows the words.

Copying math problems out of the text book or from the board or copying an entire sentence from an English book (to select the correct verb *is* or *are*) will take him a long time. Someone else could copy the math problems or the child could write the correct verb instead of the entire sentence. Parents may be able to purchase textbooks or workbooks so the child can underline words or use other techniques to minimize writing.

Copying from the board and taking notes may also present difficulties. Using a photocopy machine to copy another student's notes may eliminate the problem. These children usually do poorly on some tests. Essay tests and matching questions are particularly difficult for them to complete. Some test questions could be given and answered orally.

Manipulative children

If your child is a con artist or does minimum amount of work to keep his head out of water, be careful when using the above techniques. Some children may use their problem as a crutch. It is difficult for teachers to use the above techniques if the child fools around 80% of the time and only works 20%.

Try to have the child put forth effort 100% of the time to assess if the trouble is with perceptual-motor skills or motivation, irresponsibility or lack of independent behavior. Use positive consequences and methods described in other sections of the book.

78

Preschool & Prekindergarten

Several years ago, many children's first schooling experience was kindergarten. Before that, first grade was initially the first academic experience. Today, many parents work, and many children get their first school experience before kindergarten. A nursery or preschool experience may be necessary when a child is very young. In some cases, children who have not been in preschool are at a disadvantage when they enter kindergarten.

I don't believe it is necessary for young children to receive high-powered academic training before entering kindergarten. However, I think preschool can be beneficial because of other reasons.

One of the major things most children and adults have to do throughout life is deal with other people. Without socialization skills, certain problems develop. Being with other children provides a child an opportunity to interact with or relate to other children and develop skills to deal with other children.

Following rules, completing undesired activities and doing things you have to do because you have to is an important part in successful school performance. The prekindergarten setting involves rules, procedures, do's and don'ts the child must follow. Involvement in this setting helps his adjustment to an academic setting.

For dependent children, a period of separation from parents may be beneficial to help the child develop more independent behaviors. For parents who are with their children 24 hours a day, having the child in preschool for 2 or 3 days a week may give the parent a break.

Children with certain developmental delays (speech) benefit from exposure to other children. Most public-school settings have preschool special-educational programs for children identified as having a specific exceptionality. Contact your local public-school system to see if there are appropriate programs for your child.

The type of preschool that is appropriate for a child must be considered on an individual basis. Some children benefit from a more-structured environment. Others may need less structure. Generally it is better to have the child involved in preschool that is similar to the school environment where she will begin her education. If you plan to send her to a traditional, highly structured school, it is better for her to have a similar type of preschool environment.

Although many preschool environments involve academic-skill development, many are designed to help a child socialize, accept responsibility, adjust to the routines of school and develop other skills that benefit learning and a successful school experience.

Visit several preschools, and talk with administrators. Talk with other parents who have children involved in the program. The more information you have about a program, the higher the probability your choice will be appropriate for your child.

79

Refusal to Attend School

Some children aren't too thrilled about going to school. Others *refuse* to go. They show reactions ranging from stubbornness, defiance and outright refusal to crying, fears, panic, physical complaints and nervousness. Some children show this behavior when they start school, but it may appear at any grade level. School avoidance or phobia is most common during elementary school years.

In most situations, the reason the child refuses to go to school has nothing to do with school! This becomes obvious to parents with a child who acts like this when they try to solve the problem by making modifications in the school setting.

Your child complains, "The child sitting next to me hates me. The teacher is mean and screams too much. The school is too big or hard. The kids do not like me." You talk with the principal and changes are made in the child's school environment (he is assigned a new seat in the classroom, changes teachers, moved to a lower-level class, given less work). Or the parent decides to take the child out of the school and place him in a new school.

Usually shifts in the school environment result in very temporary improvement (a week or so). Most of the time, very slight to no improvement is seen because the problem is usually *not* based in school but is part of the child. He starts a new school or changes teachers and is fine for a couple of days. Then the same behavior surfaces, sometimes even more intense than before.

Most of the time these children don't know what's wrong

or why they feel the way they do. They are often worried, fearful, scared, confused and nervous. If you ask them a hundred questions ("Is it the teacher? Are the kids being mean to you?") you'll probably get "Yes" to most of them. For every problem you solve by changing the situation at school, two more may develop. If the child volunteers a complaint about school and it is corrected, another one is apt to emerge in a few days.

The primary basis of this behavior is a lack of confidence and/or a lack of independent behavior, which may result from several situations.

Separation Anxiety

Separation anxiety is present in many cases of school avoidance and refusal to attend. The child becomes nervous, tense, fearful or upset when he has to function independently or apart from his parents. Fear is not of school but of separation. The object of the child's excessive dependency is usually the mother. She is around more frequently, has been consistently available to him or has been the parent on whom he depends. However, excessive dependency could be directed toward the father or another significant person in his life (grandparent).

He may not let his mother go out of the house without him. Going to the store or to a meeting may become a chore. In other cases, the child doesn't let his parent out of his sight and must be physically in the same room, even the bathroom, most of the time. He may fear sleeping alone and needs to be in the same room with his mother to fall asleep. He may feel his mother is going to disappear or leave him if he goes to school or allows her out of his sight.

But if the child decides to separate from the mother, he can do it. A child comes over to play and they go outside. The child does not seem to miss his mother.

This child will usually promise you anything to get out of going to school or to get you off his back about going to school.

"If I let you stay home today, do you promise to go to school tomorrow?"

"If I buy you those tennis shoes you wanted, will you go to school tomorrow?"

The answer is almost always "Yes" or "I'll try."

The longer the time until the child has to go to school, the more confident he appears and the more promises he will make. On Friday night the child assures you he'll go to school Monday. But as Sunday night approaches, the apprehension, worry and concern increase. On Monday morning, it is full blown and the behavior seen the week before is back.

"What if ?"

Many of these children are filled with thousands of "what if . . ." questions. Although his mother has never been late picking him up for school, every morning she hears, "What if you're not there when school's over? What if you get in a wreck? What if I get sick?" The child seems totally unsure of himself and needs constant reassurance.

These children also show more difficulty when it is time to go to school if they have been home for a while (after weekends, holidays, illness). Mondays are typically the most difficult, and Fridays are the easiest.

Most children are described by their parents and teachers as "good kids" who give very little trouble and don't exhibit behavioral problems at home or school. They tend to be cooperative in many other areas of their life. They usually do well academically and are good students. If you get the classwork and homework from the teacher, they usually do it without a hassle.

By not attending school, they create other worries, concerns and apprehensions that interfere with them returning to school.

"What am I going to tell friends when they ask, 'Where have you been?' 'What happened?' 'Why did you miss school?'"

"I'm going to be lost in class. I won't know what's going on."

"How am I going to catch up on all the notes, classwork, homework?"

Because the dependency is on the mother and the problem is separation from her, this child will usually give less trouble to the father or some other relative. With the mother, he may get dressed without objection and not give trouble getting ready or leaving for school. When she drives him to school, the closer they get to school, the stronger the fear becomes. It is most intense when the child has to get out of the car, leave his mother and go to class. If the father takes him to school, he may show more trouble leaving the house than getting out of the car. If his mother is not home and his father is in charge of the morning routine, he may give little or no trouble.

The problem mainly centers around separation. The child may cry intensely or show extreme reactions when it approaches time for the separation or when you leave. But the behavior usually diminishes rapidly once you've gone. Only in the minority of cases will the child cry or show the extreme reaction for an extended period of time. When you get home from leaving your child at school and call to see how he's doing, you may hear, "He calmed down as soon as you left. He's doing his work, and everything is fine." Believe them! They're not telling you this to make you feel good and not worry.

Keep in mind when dealing with school phobia or fear that the source of the fear is often *not* school. Anxiety and fearfulness result from separation, lack of independent behavior and/or confidence problems.

Why Do Children Refuse to Go to School?

Most reasons children refuse to attend school focus on issues outside the school setting.

Trouble in school

With most children who refuse to attend school, problems lie outside the school situation not with the school. However, sometimes problems may exist at school.

These problems may center around the adults involved with the child in the school situation, the other children and academic or behavioral problems.

I wish I had a dollar for every time a parent told me, "There's a personality conflict between the teacher and my child. The teacher doesn't know what she's doing. The principal's rules are stupid."

There are "squirrels" in every profession, and the teaching profession is no exception. Sometimes conflicts with the adults the child deals with in the school setting may produce problems. Hopefully the professionals involved with the child will realize this and recommend shifting the child to another teacher.

Children who have socialization problems, get teased or picked on and don't have any friends sometimes refuse to go to school. The child may have a reputation and find it difficult to establish a relationship or break into peer groups. Because of these factors, school is not a pleasant situation and becomes something he may want to avoid. Socialization problems are also common with children who experience separation anxiety.

Other children refuse to attend school because they experience problems in the academic setting. They may have academic or behavioral difficulties, and school becomes a negative experience. They tend to avoid it. Although these children may show some behaviors described above, they usually develop physical complaints to stay home, skip school and flatly refuse to go. Or they have excuses for why they can't go to school (the teacher talks too fast, the child next to me keeps bothering me).

For children who have trouble with schoolwork, it's best to get an evaluation to identify the source of the problem. I often see children who show school avoidance and an evaluation sometimes determines that they have a learning problem. Once the problem is identified and steps are taken to remedy the learning deficiency, the reluctance to attend school may diminish.

Socialization problems

Some children who experience difficulty with other children may show school refusal. Children who show dependency and separation anxiety also experience some socialization problems. But these are more a lack of appropriate skills. They aren't picked on by the other children or aggravated by them. The problems revolve around the fact that the child doesn't have many friends, doesn't interact well with other children and may be characterized as a loner. See Chapter 45, Getting Along with Other Children, for a more-detailed description of problems a child might have interacting with his peers.

Child is in control

The child is more in control than his parents. He can do what he wants when he wants for as long as he wants. He develops a disinterest in school and doesn't want to go. So he doesn't.

This may be the child who won't take "no" for an answer and does the opposite of what you tell him. He has a smart answer for everything you say. He's never happy, and nothing you do seems to please him.

The child is very manipulative. If you allow him to control the situation, he may decide not to go to school. The stubborn, strong-willed child and other personality types (pampered, spoiled, babied) are sometimes more in control than their parents. See Chapter 31, Who's In Control? for more information.

Dependency

Children who lack independent behavior often need assistance in problem solving and decision making. They may have difficulty when they're required to deal with situations on their own or are separated from the person on whom they depend. Dependent children often show many of the characteristics of separation anxiety described in the preceding section. See Chapter 39, Dependent Behavior, for a description of causes of dependency and how to promote more-independent behavior in your child.

Environmental changes

Some children who experience changes in their environment show a decrease in confidence. They may be somewhat confused, insecure and uncertain. They may also become very dependent. They usually show the characteristics of the child with separation anxiety.

Changes could be major things, such as a divorce, separation, death of a parent or grandparent, birth of a sibling, moving to a new house, starting or changing schools, illness in the family. It could also be something that seems minor, such as the loss of a pet, different working hours of the parent, death of a distant relative, a friend moving out of the neighborhood, parental conflict, a shift in the daily or weekly routine.

Changes don't even have to be bad or traumatic. It could be a good or positive change, such as a mother quitting work, a father having more time to spend with the child, a move to a new house where a child has his own room.

Something has changed in the child's environment and routine. With some children, this is unsettling and may produce school avoidance. See Chapter 19, Effects of Divorce, Separation, Parental Conflict & Other Environmental Changes on Behavior, for more information.

Dealing with Refusal to Attend School

Most problems require more than only manipulating the school setting. Modifications usually must be made in several areas of the child's life.

Try to identify problem

Talk with the child's teacher, principal, counselor or other administrative person about the problems your child has. See if you can identify a source. Look at your child's personality, your patterns of interaction with him, the way you deal with him and other environmental factors.

If the child is struggling in school or it appears he is having academic problems, an evaluation might be appropriate to see if he has learning difficulties. Even if you don't suspect a learning problem, it may be wise to contact a mental-health professional. The longer the behavior persists, the more difficult it is to deal with. I have found it much easier to deal with a school-avoidance problem when you catch it early.

Talk with school personnel

If you feel a problem exists at school, talk with the appropriate person. If you feel the teacher is the problem, talk with her. If you don't get any satisfaction, talk with the counselor, vice principal, principal or the next appropriate person. If the problem involves other children, talk with school personnel to see what can be done about it.

Treat behavior in matter-of-fact way

Don't use excessive punishment. Avoid criticism, embarrassment, yelling, guilt or similar methods. Don't use fear techniques to try to control this behavior.

"You're going to fail if you don't go to school."

"You're going to be 35 years old before you are out of high school."

"All your other friends are going to advance to the next grade, and you're going to repeat."

Work on behaviors at home

This is *extremely* important. If you can identify dependency in your child, work on developing independent behaviors. Don't pamper, spoil or cater to the child. Establish rules and spell out consequences ahead of time.

If confidence is a problem, use techniques to build it and reduce uncertainty and insecurity.

If there have been any changes in the child's life, try to stabilize the environment by being consistent, establishing routines and becoming predictable. Establish control. You must be in charge not the child. Review the chapters that discuss the behavioral characteristics you are seeing in your child.

Increase socialization

Many children who show school avoidance have difficulty relating to their age mates. Provide opportunities for the child to establish friendships and to interact with his peers. See Chapter 45, Getting Along with Other Children, for additional suggestions.

Use natural consequences

If your child refuses to attend school because he doesn't feel well, tell him, "The doctor said you can't watch TV, read or listen to the stereo because that will stimulate your brain and make you worse. All you can do is lie in bed in a quiet room."

Don't punish the child for not going to school. But don't make it fun when he stays home. Restrict TV and other pleasurable activities.

Tell the child his job at this stage of his life is to go to school and do what he's supposed to do. Play time, movies and having friends sleep over are privileges. If he doesn't fulfill his responsibilities, he won't have privileges. If he doesn't attend school, he won't be allowed privileges.

Get the classwork and homework the child is supposed to complete that day and night. Have him complete it.

Avoid using force or tying the child up and dragging him to school. This may be necessary at a later time. But initially set up consequences so you can get the child to choose to attend school.

Get child to school

Try to get the child to school, even if he doesn't attend any classes. It's better if he's in school sitting in the principal's office or in the cafeteria than at home. The longer he stays at home, the more intense the fears and dependency become. Try to get him to school, even if it's for short periods.

Leave as soon as possible—If you take him to school, don't hang around or linger. The longer you stay, the more difficult the separation. Most teachers are aware of this problem and various methods of dealing with it. Speak with the teacher and develop a plan of attack. Leave as soon as possible—even if the child shows intense reactions.

Try to get father involved—If the mother is primarily dealing with this situation, I often suggest the father get involved and take the child to school or deal with the separation at the home. Many times dependency is specifically related to the mother. The child often gives the father less difficulty.

Work on gradual change

The child's anxiety, worry, fear or lack of independent behavior may be too intense for him to handle a whole day of school. Many times we try to set up a situation where the child identifies the most preferred subject and have him attend school for that subject. In other situations, we might have him attend only the homeroom or first period. After he attends that period, he can call the parent to come get him. If he wants to stay, he can stay for another period.

School avoidance doesn't usually change overnight. Gradual change is what is sought. The first 50% of any behavior is the hardest to change. Concentrate your effort here.

If your child refuses to stay in school all day, every day, work on him staying for one period. When he is successful and feels comfortable with one class, make it two (usually in about a week or 2). Then require three periods. Getting him to stay half the day is hardest. If you can get him to stay until lunch, the second half of the day is fairly easy.

Concentrate on small improvements and change rather than totally eliminating the school avoidance. See Chapter 44, Fears, for a more-detailed discussion of gradually eliminating this type of behavior.

Use positive consequences, incentives and rewards

In the example used above, you may set up a reward system based on the child's school attendance. For every period he attends school during the week, he earns points. If he gets so many points, he may be able to go skating or have a friend sleep over.

Identify things that are important to your child, and use those as incentives. You may also want to use normal activities. If he and his father go fishing every Saturday, he might have to attend a certain amount of school to earn this privilege. If what you ask the child to do is very small (attend school for one period) and the incentive is important, you may get the child going to school. Once this process is started and the child is in school, even for short periods of time, the fear and worry start to diminish and need for dependency is decreased.

Many chapters in this book are indirectly related to the treatment of school avoidance. Review the chapters that pertain to your child's personality characteristics and behaviors for suggestions on how to deal with behaviors and situations that might contribute to a refusal to attend school.

80

Should My Child Change Schools?

I don't often recommend a change of schools, especially as the first step in alleviating a child's difficulty. I feel changing schools should be the *last* thing considered after other attempts have been made to alleviate a child's difficulties.

Often I see children who have been in 3 to 5 schools in 6 years. The parents report difficulty with each school (ineffective teaching, stupid rules, too much homework, not enough homework, too many field trips). Sometimes the child changes because he has had ineffective teachers in all the schools.

My response is, "There are 'squirrels' in every profession, and the teaching profession is no exception. Your child has been extremely unlucky because he's experienced this in all the schools he has attended. If you look at the situation a little closer, the only thing common in all of the schools your child has attended is *him*. Perhaps the problem is more with your child than the school setting."

Many parents are quick to find fault with the school or teaching effectiveness and defend their child or minimize their difficulty by projecting fault elsewhere. If your child has difficulty in the academic setting, look first at what is happening. Try to assess the situation objectively.

Considering a Change of Schools

If you or your child have difficulty with a school and many attempts have been made to change the situation to no avail, a change may be appropriate. Consider a change *only* after attempts to deal with the problem have failed.

Dissatisfaction with school policies, rules, procedures

Parents often spend 20 to 30 minutes telling me everything that is wrong with the school their child currently attends.

"The rules are stupid."

"There's no cafeteria."

"The kids don't have an opportunity to play."

"The teacher is very negative."

After hearing this, my usual question is, "If the school is so bad, why is your child attending that school?"

My children attended a school once where they had a rule that students had to wear dress shoes to school. My children are probably like yours and have four pairs of tennis shoes and one pair of dress shoes. It makes more sense to me to allow the children to wear tennis shoes to school. However, the school's rule was no tennis shoes. Either I had to try to get this rule changed or shut up and abide by the rules.

If my feeling toward the policy was extreme, I should take my children out of the school. You should not directly communicate your feelings to the child that the teacher is ineffective, the principal is crazy and most of the school rules are ridiculous. But if your feelings are so intense, the child will pick up on them through non-verbal behavior or your general attitude. If this is the case, it is probably better to enroll your child in another school.

School suggests it

All schools are not appropriate for all children. Some schools may be what your daughter needs but may be inappropriate for your son. If a school suggests your child not return, I hear them saying they probably feel your child won't benefit from placement in their setting—or they can't provide him with what he needs.

Whatever the reason—behavioral or academic—when this happens, have the school identify the type of setting they feel will be more appropriate. Ask for recommendations.

School level is above child's ability

If you have a child of average intellectual capacity and he is placed in a school geared toward children significantly above average, he may experience difficulty. The same is true of a child in the low-average or slower-learner range in an average academic setting. If the child has to spend a lot of time on his work and is struggling to keep his head above water, then it's best to find a school more in line with his skills.

Some children can't function in large classrooms. This might be true of an overactive child or one who has attention problems. These children need a classroom with a smaller pupil-teacher ratio than the school the child currently attends. If this is the case, a change in schools is warranted.

Smaller classes are also appropriate for children with academic difficulties or those requiring special attention. In a small class, work can be individualized and presented at a rate that fits the child's ability. If the school your child attends doesn't have this classroom setting or he needs a special-education setting, a change in schools will probably be beneficial.

Repeating a grade

If your child has to repeat a grade it may be wise to change schools.

Child has reputation he can't change

Some children—because of their behavior, attitude or patterns of interaction—develop a detrimental reputation in the school. This could involve two areas, one with the adults interacting with the child and the other with his peers.

The administration and staff may see the child as disruptive, slow or having behavioral problems. Even though he makes changes in his behavior, they aren't sufficient to shake this reputation. This is seen in overactive children who have been disruptive, distracting or seen as significant behavior problems for 3 or 4 years. When placed on medication, his behavior changes dramatically. But his reputation doesn't.

The other situation occurs with the child's peers. Some children with socialization problems have been rejected, teased or ostracized by their peers. They may have difficulty breaking into a peer group. They can't make friends and fail to develop appropriate patterns of interaction. This is especially true if the child has been in the school for several years and is in the upper elementary grades.

The child with general socialization problems may not be

able to change or do anything to change his reputation with his peers. In these situations, it may be necessary for the child to change schools to get a new start and shake the reputation.

School can't meet child's needs

A child may have certain needs or behaviors that require modifications of the school's approach to the child. The child with perceptual-motor deficits may require more verbal learning experiences than written work. The child with an attention deficit may need his work periods broken up more frequently than another child with an adequate ability to concentrate.

If the school can't meet the child's needs, it's appropriate to find one that can. In some situations, it is better to fit the school around the child's needs than to try to fit the child into the school.

Refusal to attend school

This is difficult to deal with because in most cases, the causes or reasons the child refuses to attend school have nothing to do with the school itself. This is especially true in the case of school phobias when a child shows extreme anxiety, fear, worry and uncontrolled behavior when it's time to go to school. In these situations, other modifications must be made. See Chapter 79, Refusal to Attend School.

In other situations, children want to change schools because they have academic trouble. In these situations, a change of school may be appropriate because of some of the reasons listed above. Some children refuse to attend school because they don't like the school or would prefer to attend another academic setting. If this is the case, listen to the child. Consider his needs and wishes. This is especially true in older elementary-age children or high-school students.

Change in schools alone usually doesn't help

In most situations where children have academic or behavioral problems, a change in the school setting doesn't usually alleviate the problems. Other modifications or interventions must be part of the solution.

In most of the situations discussed above, this is the case. It's the exception rather than the rule that a change in the child's school setting alone totally alleviates the problems.

81

Should My Child Repeat the Grade?

Trying to decide whether a child should repeat a grade or move to the next grade is similar to voting in a political election. You don't vote for the best choice but the lesser of the evils. In trying to make this choice, you try to assess the advantage and disadvantage of each option. You avoid the choice that involves more disadvantages.

Repeating the grade might involve some initial frustration and disappointment for the child, but after this reaction he might experience 9 months of positive attention from his school involvement. The same child moved to the next grade when he isn't ready to handle the situation may experience 9 months of frustration, failure and struggle.

Below is a list of some indications of possible school problems and reasons for considering retention. In some situations, repeating the grade is beneficial. In other cases, repeating won't help, and other things must be done. Other situations may require repeating the grade, plus additional interventions.

Indications of School Problems

The child's life, and possibly yours, revolves around school and schoolwork. It may seem he is going to school 24 hours a day. He wakes up, goes to school, comes home, does homework and goes to bed. This cycle is repeated daily. He doesn't seem to have much time to play because of schoolwork. He is unable to become involved in extracurricular activities (baseball, scouts, dancing) because he wouldn't have time to do his schoolwork.

At breakfast or on the way to school, you may hear his spelling words or go over questions for the science test. In this situation, the child, as well as you, will probably burn out by fourth or fifth grade.

You can only run so fast, so far and for so long then you give up. Although the teacher says the child should only spend 30 to 45 minutes a night on homework, your child averages 3 to 5 hours. Most of your interaction with your child may center around school and academically related material.

There is more to life than school. If this situation exists early in your child's education, it's almost certain that he, as well as you, won't be able to maintain this intensity very long. This definitely indicates a problem.

Homework is a hassle

Although most children aren't thrilled about doing homework, most complete it without significant problems. If it's a total battle, screaming match or fight every night to get the child to do the homework, it may indicate school problems.

If it seems like you have to tie your child in a chair every night to get the homework completed, it's probably not a good thing to continue to do. Although you're getting the homework done, the child isn't developing independent or responsible behavior. See Chapter 72, Homework.

Trouble keeping up or maintaining passing grades

You may have to review spelling words over and over again before it sinks in. Long hours must be spent studying for a test just to make an average or low-average grade. When comparing notes with other parents, your child's study time is significantly greater than most other children.

Frequent complaints from school or teacher

This may involve concerns regarding performance (he has difficulty doing the work, incomplete classwork, poor test grades, inability to grasp material). Or it may involve more behavioral concerns, such as difficulty with other children, daydreaming, overactivity or discipline problems.

Physical complaints

The child may start developing physical concerns; these may revolve around schoolwork or attending school. It may also involve a refusal to go to school in the morning. Or your child may frequently call you from school with various physical complaints and requests to come home. Complaints don't seem to have any physical basis and are primarily designed to avoid school or school-related work.

Mood changes

Children having difficulty in school often experience a lowering of their frustration tolerance. They appear to become easily upset, agitated and frustrated. Their mood may change from very pleasant to extremely upset and fretful. The normally relaxed, happy child may become quarrelsome and cranky. The child may seem unhappy, depressed or look like something is bothering him.

School tires child

The child frequently comes home from school tired or exhausted after an average day. Homework or school-related work tires him.

Summer and school holidays are wonderful!

Your child's behavior and your interaction with him significantly improves during the summertime or over long holiday periods. He is a different child during these times when school and schoolwork aren't a concern. The child may not dislike school—the work is the problem. If you could find a school that only involved play, interacting with other children and pleasurable activities—not schoolwork—your child's attitude and behavior would be similar to that shown on holidays.

Why Children Are Retained

Repeating a grade is usually considered when a child is immature or has not acquired the skills necessary for promotion to the next grade level. There are several areas where children may be behind their classmates. See Chapter 47, Immaturity, for a detailed discussion of various lags in skill development.

Physical difficulties

These revolve around lags in physical-skill development. The child is unable to perform physical activities at the level of his classmates. He may have difficulty coloring, writing, tying shoes or catching a baseball.

Academic difficulties

This involves the acquisition of school-related information. The child may have trouble keeping up with his classmates and may be behind in his skills. This could be due to several reasons including a poor foundation, specific learning disabilities, placement in a school setting too academically advanced for the child, depressed level of intelligence and not completing required classwork or assigned homework.

Social difficulties

This is an inability to relate to other children in an appropriate manner. It may involve a lack of age-appropriate skills or the development of inappropriate kinds of interaction. The child may be 7 but relates, plays and presents himself socially as a 4- or 5-year-old.

Emotional difficulties

These involve children who don't show the same emotional development as their peers. This may involve whining, baby talk and similar reactions.

Behavioral difficulties

This child may show problems in attention, concentration, self-discipline, ability to sit still and responsibility.

When Will Repeating Help?

In some situations, repeating the grade alone is beneficial to a child. In other cases, it won't help significantly. Whether a child repeats a grade or moves on to the next grade, several other things must be done to improve the child's academic behavior and/or performance.

Repeating the grade by itself is generally beneficial when another year of physical development will improve the child's performance or there is a lack of foundation in academic skills. Children who are young for their grade or have late birthdays sometimes show immaturity in several areas. A child with a late birthday may be 6 months to a year younger than most children in his class. Age difference is significant in lower grades where 6 months of physical growth results in considerable changes.

For children in this category, repeating a grade or starting school a year later is very beneficial. Many times this alone will produce the desired changes. See Chapter 74, Is My Child Ready for Kindergarten? for details.

Achievement deficits

Some children are intellectually capable of functioning in the present school setting but show a lag in the development of academic skills. This can be due to a poor foundation. This child will generally benefit from repeating the grade. A child may be at the end of third grade in his placement, but his academic skills are only at the end of second grade or beginning-third-grade level. This academic deficit may be due to numerous factors, such as poor school attendance, not doing the required homework or seatwork, ineffective teaching, a change of schools.

If the child advances to the next grade level, he will have academic difficulties because of the discrepancy between his acquired skills and the expected skills. Repeating the grade places him at a level consummate with his abilities. Some children who have specific learning disabilities or other behavioral concerns also show this poor foundation. But in these situations, repetition alone won't help the child.

Development lags

Some children who show lags in the development of physical skills also benefit from a year of growth and maturation. This is similar to the child with a late birthday. In other situations, lags in physical development improve with time but don't improve significantly in 1 year (perceptual-motor difficulties, auditory processing).

Immaturity

When other areas of immaturity are the cause for the child's difficulty, repetition of the grade alone will *not* result in significant improvement. This is usually the case with a child who has the academic skills necessary for successful performance at his grade level, but other factors contribute to his poor performance. This is also the case with a child who has a specific learning disability; repetition will not be beneficial.

Lack of responsibility

Let's say your child is at the end of third grade and his academic skills are at the end of third grade or above. However, he is failing school because he isn't preparing for tests, has missed a significant amount of homework, is inattentive in class and doesn't complete the required work. He receives poor grades because of a general lack of responsibility rather than inadequate skills.

Repetition of the grade alone won't benefit him. Some type of intervention must be made to help improve the areas of difficulty.

Performance problems

Another child at the end of fifth grade shows academic skills equal to his grade placement but has extreme difficulty writing or expressing himself with paper and pencil. Handwriting is difficult, and he is slow doing his work. He receives failing grades because he doesn't complete tests or classwork. He may only finish 10 problems on the math test when he's supposed to do 20, but the 10 problems that he has finishes are correct.

This child's academic difficulties are primarily related to his performance not his ability. Asking him to repeat a grade and show knowledge through a similar fashion (handwriting) won't result in significant improvement in his performance.

Learning disabilities

The child with a specific learning disability or lag in a skill that prevents him from learning by methods that are beneficial to most children won't significantly improve his performance by just repeating a grade.

Suppose you had difficulty seeing. I give you a book and ask you to read a particular chapter. After you finish reading the book, I give you a test on the chapter, and you fail the test. The reason you have difficulty performing is because you didn't acquire the information. Asking you to reread the chapter and giving you the test again is ridiculous because you would fail again.

Children who don't acquire information the way most children do won't significantly benefit from repeating a grade and being taught in the same way.

Rather than repeating the same procedure, a better way to deal with the problem would be to get you a pair of glasses so you could see the information on the page or provide you with the written information in verbal form. I'd put it on a tape recorder, and you could listen to it. By readjusting the methods of teaching, you'd be able to acquire the information.

Children have particular learning styles and learn through a variety of methods. If a child's learning style is different from most children, he won't acquire information if taught in a certain way. He must be taught differently. Placement in a special-education class or a smaller classroom where work can be individualized or presented in a way equal to his strengths and weaknesses is more beneficial. Whether we say a fifth-grade child is in eighth grade, fifth grade or third grade isn't as important as presenting the information in a way he can learn.

Repetition of a grade for these children won't result in significant benefit. Sometimes when a child repeats the grade, he does well the second time. But the next year when he starts the new grade, he has difficulty. Repetition may be needed. If repeating the grade is used as the solution for this child, it will take him 24 years to get out of school!

What are some solutions?

For most children with school-related problems, many things can be done. Whether a child repeats the grade or moves to the higher grade, other interventions can and must be made to improve school performance.

The child who is irresponsible, shows a lack of interest in schoolwork and has academic skills but fails will have difficulty next year if nothing is done. For this child, attempts must be made to develop a more-responsible approach to schoolwork and other areas of his life that reflect similar behaviors and attitudes.

The child who has academic skills but his performance is inadequate because of poor fine-motor coordination may need modifications in the school environment. More emphasis needs to be placed on verbal communication of information and less on paper-and-pencil tasks.

The child who shows emotional, social or behavioral

immaturity will benefit from becoming a year older. Techniques must be used to develop maturity. By doing this, schoolwork will improve. Sometimes the child with adequate academic skills who receives borderline grades because of a lack of responsibility, dependent behavior or attention deficits may need to repeat the grade. It will take some time to develop the independent or responsible behavior or work on improving his attention span.

Review Chapter 47, Immaturity, Chapter 40, Developing Responsible Behavior, and other chapters pertaining to the school problem your child has under the section School Concerns.

Repeating a Grade?—Things to Consider

1. If your child has difficulty in school, meet with the teacher, principal or counselor to find out exactly where the problems lie. Have them define exactly why the child has problems. Avoid vague concepts. Have them define *exactly* what they mean by "immature." Does "behind in his work" mean he is lacking in phonics skills or basic math facts? Is he doing poorly because he doesn't turn in required homework or complete the assigned classwork?

Define the child's specific areas of difficulty. This must be known before any attempts to deal with difficulties can occur.

2. Find out exactly what the school has done to correct the situation and what else can be done (reading lab, peer tutoring, different consequences for inappropriate behavior, reward for appropriate behavior, giving tests orally).

3. Try to make interventions to correct the child's difficulty as early as possible in the school year. Many people wait until the last report card to deal with difficulties. This is too late and a very ineffective method of resolving the problem.

4. If the child's problem is purely academic, consider working with the child and giving him some additional instruction besides homework. Check with the teacher. She may be able to give you some activities or direction to help strengthen the child's weak areas. Consider tutoring or moving to a lower level of the same grade. Be sure the child does the necessary homework to prepare for class.

5. If the problem is behavioral, you need to identify situations in the child's total environment (home and neighborhood) where similar behavior is seen. At first, focus on changing the behavior at home and in the neighborhood rather than at school. If some changes are seen at home, but the improvement has not extended to the school situation, focus on school behavior. You may want to set up some type of home-school communication system to monitor the child's behavior.

6. If the problems are academic *and* behavioral, try to identify the one that seems most important. This may be difficult because it is similar to the question "What came first, the chicken or the egg?"

If it seems like the child's behavioral difficulties are resulting in poor academic performance, focus on the behavioral difficulties. On the other hand, the child may seem to have behavioral difficulties because of academic deficits, and he doesn't understand the work. Attempts should be made to alleviate these weak areas and to build academic skills. At times it may be appropriate to try to obtain improvement *both* behaviorally and academically.

7. If these suggestions don't result in significant improvement and repeating the grade is considered, don't take it personally or let pride or emotions influence your objectivity. When a teacher or school suggests your child repeat a grade, they are usually implying what they see in your child may not result in successful performance in the next grade at their school.

The suggestion is made to minimize frustration, failure and difficulty for the child. This suggestion doesn't automatically imply you're an inadequate parent or the teacher is out to "get" your child. It is not a direct reflection of your competency as a human being. Don't try to defend the child or become defensive. Listen to what school personnel say so you can *objectively* evaluate and deal with the situation.

8. The next best step is to have the child evaluated to rule out a specific learning disability, behavioral or emotional problems or physical, speech, vision or hearing difficulties.

9. Implement the suggestions that result from the evaluation (tutoring, speech or language therapy, counseling, family therapy, glasses).

10. If repeating the grade doesn't seem like it will help, work on what will (develop more responsible or independent behaviors, improve homework or study skills, do things that may improve the child's attention span or decrease his level of activity).

Does he need a special-education class?

Will a less academically advanced school be more appropriate?

Is a school with smaller classes the answer?

If the school says your child needs to repeat the grade because he won't be able to function adequately in the next grade level at the school, it may not always mean the child can't function adequately in the next grade level at another school.

11. Will work over the summer help? Sometimes when summer school is recommended for a child it is more beneficial to have him receive individual tutoring to strengthen academic weaknesses. Sometimes arrangements can be made with the school so individual tutoring takes the place of a formal summer school. The decision to repeat may be made at the end of the summer, in some cases.

12. It's usually better to have a child repeat a grade in lower grades than in upper grades. It's often believed the earlier a child repeats the grade the more beneficial and the less detrimental it is. In the lower grades, it is sometimes better to have a child repeat. Attending summer school to pass may just mean fighting and struggling next year in the following grade.

For older children, summer school or a change of schools may be a better option. For older children, repetition is more of an option when and if they are changing schools.

13. If a child will repeat a grade before the end of school, don't tell him. Wait until the last report card to inform the child of the decision. I often see children who shut down completely and stop doing work in school in January when they find out that they'll repeat the grade. This is a normal reaction.

If you knew you were going to be fired from your job in 9 weeks, your effort, motivation and performance would suffer. If a child knows at the end of the third reporting period he will repeat, he's not apt to want to do the required work for the remainder of school. He probably won't.

14. Explain to the child why it is necessary for him to repeat the grade. I usually discuss this in terms of a lack of foundation. I tell the child, "Suppose someone came into the office and asked us to go outside and change the carburetor on his car. Would you be able to do it?"

Usually the answer is "No."

I then explain, "The reason neither of us could change the carburetor isn't because we're stupid or have problems. It's because we don't have experience or foundation in changing carburetors. If we went across the street and spent a couple of weeks at Tony's Auto Repair watching him change carburetors and working on it, we'd gain more knowledge. Three weeks later the same person comes in and asks us to change the carburetor, and we could. The reason for the improvement is because we have obtained the foundation that was missing."

15. If a child repeats a grade at the same school, it's best if he has a new teacher.

16. When a child repeats a grade, it's more appropriate to have him attend a different school.

17. For the child who has difficulty in school, whether he repeats the grade or not, establish an open line of communication with the school the following year. Don't assume no news is good news. The teacher might have from 30 to 150 students in his classes, and your child may be overlooked. Put an "X" on your calendar every 2 or 3 weeks to remind yourself to talk with the teacher.

82

Special Education

Most parents have the wrong idea about special education. They equate special education with mental retardation. If someone says, "My child is receiving special-educational services in his school," most listeners think the child is retarded.

I tell parents, "I think your child will benefit from a resource room or special-education class."

They often respond, "I thought you just said he was average intelligence. Why does he need special education?"

To view special education as *only* providing services to mentally retarded children is like saying, "The only type of car anyone needs is a station wagon." Special education provides a wide range of services for children who have physical, behavioral or academic problems or who will benefit from a smaller, more individualized learning environment. Although mentally retarded children are included, they represent only a small portion of the children served. The belief most people hold regarding special education is very inaccurate.

Special-education classes are designed to meet the educational needs of many students who have difficulty with or do not benefit from a regular classroom setting. These students will not learn by the same methods used to teach the majority of the student population.

There are two types of special-education classes: self-contained classes and resource rooms. In a self-contained special-education class, the child usually remains in the same classroom and receives specialized services the entire day.

A resource-room provides children with part-time services

in special areas. The child attends regular classes for part of the day. The other part, he receives individual attention in his weak subjects in a special-education class. Resource rooms are more common in public schools. They are used to avoid labeling and to keep the child in as many regular classes as he can handle.

Special-education classes offer two advantages: First, they place the child in a classroom with a smaller pupil-teacher ratio than regular classes. With fewer students, the teacher can give more individual attention to each child. Work can be presented in a manner and at a rate commensurate with the child's strengths and weaknesses. The special education teacher can use the child's abilities to teach and train him in weak areas.

Secondly, special-education classes make learning and school a pleasant, positive experience to keep the child motivated. Many children who require special education have had months, if not years, of failure, frustration and negative attention in school.

These children can't compete in a regular classroom. Because their weaknesses have been continually emphasized, they turn off to school and show a lack of interest in academic work. They may avoid sitting down with a book or doing anything that resembles schoolwork.

Special-education classes are designed to present work to ensure success and achievement. Learning becomes a positive experience. Combined with teacher emphasis on the child's accomplishments and strong points, it maintains a child's interest and motivation in academic endeavors.

There are many types of special-education classes or resource rooms.

Gifted and talented

These classes are for children with significantly above-average levels of intelligence. Work designed for average students may be below their level. Some regular classes are boring for these children. The special-education classes individualize the work for the child and present it at a stimulating level.

Learning disabled

This type of special-education class is designed for students who are average or above average intelligence who are prevented from learning in a regular class setting. See Chapter 75, Learning Disabilities, for a more detailed discussion.

These children can learn but have difficulty learning by methods used in a regular classroom. They must be taught in a specialized way. The teacher in the special-education class or resource room prescribes work in a manner that will help learning. Children with learning disabilities just need to be taught differently to learn.

Emotional or adjustment difficulties

This special-education service is for children who have the ability to learn, but emotional and behavior problems interfere with their ability to perform in a regular classroom setting. A small class that focuses on behavioral and emotional difficulties is necessary to give the child an opportunity to learn.

Educationally handicapped or slow learner

These classes are designed for children who fall within the gray area between average and mild mental retardation. See Chapter 73, Intelligence. *Slow learner* means exactly what it says. These children can learn, but at a pace slower than the child of average intelligence. You're an average student, and I am a slow learner. The teacher gives us 10 math problems and 15 minutes to complete them. You finish all 10, but I complete only 6. Give me another 10 minutes, and I'll finish all of them.

Special-education classes for slow learners are designed to present work at a rate that fits their learning style.

Physical problems

A variety of special-education services are available for children with physical difficulties that would interfere with their ability to perform in a regular class setting. These may include children who are handicapped, visual or hearing impaired or children with speech difficulties. These classes are designed to meet the physical needs of the child and provide the necessary therapy and learning materials designed to compensate for the child's physical impairment.

Mental retardation

This special-education service is for children whose level

of intelligence falls below the slow-learner range of intelligence. Classes for the mildly mentally retarded are designed for children who can learn, but only to a certain level. Classes for the moderately mentally retarded are designed to teach children personal self-sufficiency and daily living skills necessary for living in society.

Multiple handicapped

There are special-education classes designed to provide services for children who suffer a combination of several of the difficulties described above.

How big is the problem?

It is conservatively estimated that 10% of all students have difficulty in school. Some children experience monumental difficulties if they don't receive assistance.

Special education not always helpful

In the 1960s and early '70s, special education was seen as a solution for all problems of children experiencing difficulties in school. As a result, many children were placed in special-educational settings. In the late 1970s and early 1980s, research data indicated special education was not beneficial for all children with academic problems. In fact, a large group of children received little, if any, benefit from special-class placement.

Trends

The trend of the '80s was away from special-educational as the first step in solving a child's academic difficulties. Placement in a special class, for some children, is now seen as the *last* step to take after other attempts have failed. The emphasis is to try other things to keep the child in regular classes or to avoid labeling and unnecessary placement.

If a child has learning or behavioral problems, modifications may be made in the classroom or teaching methods. Other things may be tried before a child is considered a candidate for special-educational placement.

Each state has different procedures and guidelines to determine eligibility for special-educational services. Your local school system has information regarding the services available and criteria for eligibility.

83

Sports, Dancing, Clubs & Other Activities

It's important for a child to develop interests and hobbies. There are several benefits from this. I have included this chapter in the section on School Concerns because a child having difficulty in school needs to develop other areas of his life where he can experience positive feedback. Everyone has strengths and weaknesses.

There are many things we can do as well or better than other people. There are many things we can't do as well or things other people do better than we can.

If a child's life revolves around school and he has difficulty, it's hard for him to see other positive qualities because school is the only thing he can use to compare himself to other children . . . and this is one of his weak points.

You want your children to look at their overall positive and negative qualities and not place a great deal of emphasis on their weaknesses. A child struggling in school might think, "Johnny is making better grades than I am, but I can play baseball better than he does." Or "Mary is on the honor roll, but I'm a better dancer than she is." If the only thing the child has to compare to Mary and Johnny is school performance, feelings of inferiority and inadequacy are apt to develop.

Some children I see go to school 24 hours a day. They go to school, come home and study, take their bath and go to bed. This is repeated 4 or 5 nights a week. Parents tell me they can't get involved in any other activities because of schoolwork. Most of the time these kids have difficulty in school.

If this is the case and outside activities can't be considered, perhaps a change in schools is appropriate. Something needs to be done to allow the child to have some free time to engage in other activities. Children who start their schooling experience this way rapidly lose interest in school.

Another reason children do not become involved in outside activities is because it's an inconvenience to parents to take them to practice, meetings or activities. Realistic problems exist with working parents when they can't transport the child to activities because of their work schedule. If this is the case, get the child involved in the activity then work out some arrangement with other parents who have children in the same activity.

The hobbies, activities and interests can be a variety of things, such as, hunting, fishing, scouts, dancing, gymnastics, drama club, French club, karate, baseball, football, basketball, racing remote-control cars, drill squad, soccer, involvement with a church youth group, computer club, art classes and music. Having the child involved in these activities produces several positive results.

Interests are developed

Probably the only common element in children who are involved with the law is a lack of interest in activities or hobbies. They live day to day. Unhappy, depressed children usually aren't involved in activities. I'm not saying that if your child isn't a cheerleader or doesn't play football that he or she will become a juvenile delinquent or depressed. I am saying many children who experience problems aren't involved in outside activities.

Children who have interests are able to set goals and work toward them. They often have things to look forward to. Many times I see children who are not involved in activities and don't do well in school. One reason is because they say life is boring and they have nothing to look forward to.

If I have a fishing trip planned on the weekend or some other enjoyable activity it seems to make my week pass faster. If the child has things to look forward to, the unpleasant parts of his life (school) tend to not look as big. Life in general is a process where goals are set and you work toward them. Sports, scouts and other activities usually involve a similar process.

Sometimes the child's interests and the activities can be used as incentives or rewards to help other areas of difficulty. A child who is extremely involved in karate and is having trouble doing his homework may be told, "You will only be able to go to karate class if you finish your homework before 6:30."

When using activities as rewards or incentives, avoid taking the child totally out of the activity because you lose the leverage. A young girl who is thoroughly involved in dancing is doing poorly in school. She isn't paying attention or completing her classwork. Don't say "If your schoolwork doesn't improve, I'm taking you out of dancing."

It would be better to say, "I'm going to get a report from your teacher every day on your attention in class and completion of the work. On the days you pay attention and do your work, you can go to dancing. On the days you don't complete the work, you can't go to dancing."

Once you completely remove the child from an enjoyable activity, you lose a source of motivation.

May help with self-discipline

Many activities have rules, regulations, do's and don'ts and procedures that must be followed. Outside activities help children set goals and usually involve certain behaviors that must be followed to attain the goals.

Provides socialization experience

The way you learn to deal with people is to be with other people. Outside activities provide opportunities for a child to interact with children his own age. This is extremely beneficial for children who lack socialization experiences or don't have many children in their neighborhood to play with.

By becoming involved at the local playground, the child comes in contact with many children who may not live in your immediate neighborhood but live close to your home. Involvement in these activities gives the child other opportunities to learn to relate to people and to develop friendships.

Builds confidence

A person who is confident in himself knows his strengths and weaknesses. The confident person, when asked a question he doesn't know the answer to, can readily say, "I don't know." If you ask the same person to perform some kind of activity he is incapable of doing, he'll tell you.

For a person to have confidence in himself, he has to see areas in his life that are positive and successful. The child must be able to see skills he has that are better than other children.

If the only thing the child is involved with is schoolwork and he has trouble, it's extremely difficult for him to develop overall confidence.

Outside activities give the child a skill, activity or knowledge that may be unique for him. "I may not be able to get the same grades as Jeff, but I know more about karate than he does."

I'm not saying you have to get your child involved in 37 different activities. Some children go to soccer practice on Tuesday and Thursday, a scout meeting on Friday and take music lessons on Monday and Wednesday. Saturday and Sunday usually involve games or scouting activities. A lot of times these children tell me, "I wish I had some free time just to play."

Involve the child in outside activities but not to an extent his entire life is structured around them. Kids need time just to be kids and to play.

Some parents have their children involved in sports or music because they want them involved in it. The child could care less. The other day a child told me he didn't like taking piano lessons. When I asked him why he was taking them, he said, "My mother said I have to take it because I have a talent in music."

Don't live your life through your child's activities. Don't pressure him to continue in things in which he has no interest.

Give the child an opportunity to experience the sport or activity. Then listen to what he says after he has been involved in it for a period of time.

Here's the general procedure I normally use for children who are hesitant to become involved in any activities. Let's say you have a young girl who likes to dance and constantly dances around the house and loves music. She expresses an interest in going to dancing school. When the time comes to register, she doesn't want to participate.

Many times a child is hesitant to get involved because of the newness of the situation, she doesn't know what to expect or she may lack a little confidence in this area. Identify an incentive (sleeping out), and tell the child, "You've been wanting to go spend a weekend at your aunt's house. Go to dancing for five times. At the end of the fifth time, I'll ask you if you want to continue taking lessons. If you still want to be involved, you can continue dancing. If you want to quit, that's OK. You can quit. Regardless of your decision, if you go to dancing five times, you can spend the weekend at your aunt's house."

Dealing with situations like this allows you to avoid two mistakes—not getting the child involved in something she will enjoy or forcing her to continue participating in something that isn't a positive experience.

84

Summer School & Tutoring

Most children view summer school and tutoring like adults view income tax, house payments and utility bills. It isn't something you look forward to. It is something you dread and want to avoid. However, some children need additional services or are required to attend summer school. "Extra" schoolwork is a necessary evil to be dealt with.

Summer School

Summer school is usually a result of the child not performing during the 9 months of the regular school year. It is considered because the school suggests or requires it. Or you feel additional work in a particular subject is necessary. Summer school is considered, recommended or required in three general situations.

To pass a subject or earn credits

The fifth-grade student fails reading and must attend summer school to advance to the sixth grade. The high-school freshman fails English and must attend summer school because he needs four credits in English to graduate from high school. This is probably the major benefit of summer school.

Perhaps your elementary-school child is struggling in school and is barely passing. Summer school is a frequent activity for the child. It might be wise to get an evaluation to determine the reason for the child's difficulty in school. For the child who has to attend summer school frequently, consider something different. It may be more appropriate to have him repeat a grade. Or a change of schools may be necessary. See the appropriate chapters in this section on School Concerns for additional information.

To strengthen academic skills

Summer school may be required or recommended for the child who barely passes or fails a particular subject to help develop weak academic skills. Summer school is designed to strengthen the child's foundation and to strengthen academic weakness.

When this is the reason for summer-school attendance, we try to substitute tutoring for the formal classroom summer-school setting. In general, individual or very small group tutoring strengthen skills better and faster than traditional summer school.

Some schools allow you to substitute a certain amount of individual tutoring in place of summer school. This individual or small-group work is seen by the school as equivalent to the formal summer-school setting.

Consequence of not performing in school

In this situation, summer school is usually seen as punishment for not performing during the regular school year. This usually occurs when a child has the academic skills necessary for adequate achievement in school but doesn't perform. This is usually the case of the irresponsible child who does not do what he is supposed to do (homework, classwork, studying for a test) and performs poorly. It's almost as if summer school is designed to get the child's attention, make him realize the wrong he has done during the school year and change his attitude toward school for the next year.

Big, severe or harsh punishments don't work well with some children. For some, going to summer school won't offset the fact they got away with not doing homework 483 times, paid attention in class 30% of the time and only completed 40% of the classwork. This one big punishment won't change some children's attitudes.

If this is the primary reason for summer school, it won't be beneficial. It's better to do many small things during the school year as a consequence for his poor performance than to do one big thing at the end of the school year. Monitor the child's school performance on a weekly basis. His privileges for each weekend can be based on his performance. If he completed the required schoolwork and did what he was supposed to do during the week, he earns privileges for the weekend.

Another situation is the child who is told if he doesn't perform in school during the regular school year and has to go to summer school he won't be able to go with the family on summer vacation. This also is a big punishment that occurs over a long period of time. With some children, this is a very ineffective method to change school behavior.

If summer vacation or any big reward is used, it's better to break the performance period into small segments. After Easter, monitor the child's weekly school performance. He can earn points for completing work or doing what he's supposed to. If he receives a certain number of points by the time summer occurs, he can go on the summer vacation. If he doesn't receive the points, he won't go.

Tutoring

Tutoring is usually recommended or considered for the child who demonstrates academic weaknesses. The primary purpose of tutoring is to develop academic skills and strengthen the child's foundation. Tutoring can occur during the school year, over summer vacation or as a substitute for summer school. This attempt at dealing with academic weaknesses can be done individually or in small groups. Tutoring can be beneficial in several situations.

To strengthen academic weaknesses

The fifth-grade child may be reading on a third-grade level. He has difficulty with fifth-grade work. In this situation, tutoring is designed to build the child's reading skills. This particular type of tutoring usually involves working with the child at his current level. The tutor works with the child in reading on a third-grade level. This type of tutoring doesn't involve any work with the child's current subjects, homework or classwork. It is primarily designed to strengthen weak skills and usually continues until the child's skills have significantly developed or he is on grade level.

To clarify information or give child better understanding of material

Your child has just started learning about fractions, and you have difficulty helping him with the work and getting him to understand the concepts. A brief amount of tutoring may be beneficial. For the high-school student having trouble in chemistry or geometry, working with a teacher in this area may clarify some of the concepts and allow him to understand the material.

This type of tutoring is usually brief, infrequent and designed to get the child over a difficult period of time or a stumbling block he encounters in a certain subject.

To help child with homework

If you work, have difficulty doing homework with your child or don't understand the material enough to help the child with his homework, a tutor may be employed to do this. This type of tutoring involves a person helping the child with his homework, studying for a test or helping him prepare for the next day of school.

Some after-school programs provide this service. For this type of tutoring, it may not be necessary to have a teacher work with the child. A high-school or college student could perform these services.

Things to Consider

1. Summer school and/or tutoring alone don't usually develop responsibility, self-discipline or motivation. If you have a child who has performance problems at school—not because of his ability—but because of other factors, these services alone will not be beneficial. Try to develop an overall level of responsibility or self-discipline. That involves working on behavior in the home and in the neighborhood that is similar to those that were interfering with the child's school performance. Try to change the habit and develop a responsible child in many areas of his life.

2. Tutoring is more likely to build academic skills and strengthen weaknesses than is summer school.

3. Summer school is most beneficial when it occurs infrequently and is used to allow the child to pass to the next grade

or to earn credits toward graduation.

4. If you have a child who frequently has to attend summer school or receive tutoring, it is wise to have an evaluation to determine what the problems are and how to solve them. A child in this situation may need to repeat the grade or change schools.

5. The smaller the pupil-teacher ratio, class size or tutoring group, the more beneficial it is.

6. If tutoring is recommended to strengthen academic skills, be sure you get a qualified person who specializes in the area in which your child has difficulty. Get a reading specialist to tutor your child in reading.

7. If the tutoring doesn't seem to benefit the child, ask questions. Are we working on the right problem? What else should be done? What can I do to help at home? Is the problem correctly identified?

8. If the child sees a tutor once or twice a week, be sure you get material and suggestions from the tutor so you can work on similar areas at home during the rest of the week.

9. If the tutor says the child is improving or shows results that indicate it, but the child's performance in school has not significantly improved, start asking questions. Maybe the child doesn't need tutoring as much as he needs motivation or responsibility. Has the problem been correctly identified? What else needs to be done? How can you get this improvement to occur in school so the child's performance will improve?

85

Conclusion

If you have read the material in this book, understood the concepts and techniques and have applied them consistently and faithfully, you'll still experience problems with your children. Being an effective parent means you cope with problems as they occur—not that you eliminate problems. If you don't want to experience problems with children, don't have children! If you have children, you'll usually have problems raising them. Little children—little problems. Big children—big problems.

I haven't provided all the answers to reduce all the difficulty you will have with your children. But I hope the information presented in this book will increase the techniques you have available to deal with your child's behavior. Hopefully, this book will make it easier for you to understand, live with, relate to and interact with your children on a daily basis. The approach presented should reduce the antagonism between you and your children and create a calmer, happier home environment. If you use the techniques in this book, you'll get a more relaxed home environment and increase the probability your children will be happy and become well-adjusted adults who can cope effectively with their environment and adulthood.

If you feel you have used the techniques successfully and improvement hasn't occurred, consult someone (your child's pediatrician, a mental-health professional who specializes in children) who knows more about child behavior and development than you.

Index

4645